Florin Oprescu
Power and Literature

Mimesis

Romanische Literaturen der Welt

Herausgegeben von
Ottmar Ette

Band 71

Florin Oprescu

Power and Literature

Strategies of Subversiveness in the Romanian Novel

Translated by
Monica Oprescu and Bianca Popescu

DE GRUYTER

Printed with founding from Rosita Schjerve-Rindler-Memory Fund/
Gedruckt mit Förderung des Rosita Schjerve-Rindler-Gedächtnisfonds

ISBN 978-3-11-070977-3
e-ISBN (PDF) 978-3-11-060537-2
e-ISBN (EPUB) 978-3-11-060305-7
ISSN 0178-7489

Library of Congress Cataloging in Publication Control Number: 2018026143

Bibliographic information published by the Deutsche Nationalbibliothek
The Deutsche Nationalbibliothek lists this publication in the Deutsche Nationalbibliografie;
detailed bibliographic data are available on the Internet at http://dnb.dnb.de.

© 2020 Walter de Gruyter GmbH, Berlin/Boston
This volume is text- and page-identical with the hardback published in 2018.
Typesetting: Integra Software Services Pvt. Ltd.
Printing and Binding: CPI books GmbH, Leck

www.degruyter.com

Contents

Argument —— 1

1	**The Criticism of Ideas on Power —— 8**
1.1	Theories on Power. From the Social and Philosophical Analysis to the Aporias of Literature —— 8
1.1.1	*The will to power* and its Ideological Foundation within the Republic of Letters —— 8
1.1.2	The Sociological Perspective on Power —— 18
1.2	The Literature and its Battles on the Field of Power —— 26
1.2.1	The Canon Battlefield —— 26
1.2.2	The Novel Battlefield —— 37
1.2.3	Subject-Voice-Diathesis. The Pragmatical Power Taxonomy in Literature —— 49
1.2.4	Subject-Voice. A(n) nearly (Im)Possible Epic Equation —— 53
2	**The Active Power of the Subject —— 58**
2.1	The Fanariot Power in XIXth Century. At the Doorway of Sunrise —— 58
2.2	The Writer at the Doorway of Sunset —— 75
2.3	The Old Parvenu at the Doorway of the Novel —— 82
2.4	Scenes from the Socio-political Life and the Hierarchization of Power —— 89
2.5	The Physiognomy of the Activist-Arriviste and the Gradual Instruments of Power —— 100
3	**The Reflexive Power of the Subject —— 108**
3.1	In Search of Power Authenticity —— 108
3.2	The *Power* of the Interwar Novelistic Canon —— 120
3.3	From the *Literaturisation* of the Autobiographical Trauma to the Reflexive Power —— 130
3.3.1	The Surrealist Dare. The Autobiography of "[…] a man cut in half by a window" —— 131
3.3.2	The Occurrence of the Subject in the Immediate Reflexivity —— 137
3.4	The Cinetic Anamorphosis of the Reflexive Power —— 146

4	**The Passivity of the Subject faced with the Power of History —— 162**
4.1	The Teratology of Totalitarian Power. The Romanian Case —— 162
4.1.1	The 'Cultural Revolutions' and the Illusions of Mass Power —— 162
4.1.2	Victims and Heroes of the Socialist Battle —— 166
4.2	*The Most Beloved Man on Earth* and the Passivization of the Subject, Faced with Excessive Power —— 176
4.2.1	The Preda Case. *The Raving* of the Most Contested Prose-Writer —— 176
4.2.2	The Most Passive Man on Earth. Illusions, Isolation and Passivity —— 185
5	**The Impersonalization of Power in Contemporary Novel —— 198**
5.1	The Memory of Power, the Power of Memory and the Narrative Typology of the Postcommunist Novel —— 198
5.1.1	Memory, History, Novel-a Variable Balance —— 198
5.1.2	Contemporary Novel as a Novel of Failed or Reclaimed Memory —— 211
5.1.3	The Transitional Novel. A Modular Typology —— 217
5.2	The Impersonalization of Power and the Stigma of Historical Memory —— 226
5.2.1	The Novel without Memory and History in the Ecuation of Impersonalization. From Apud to Vienna and back —— 226
5.2.2	The Transgressive Method of Impersonalization —— 235

Conclusions —— 245

Bibliography —— 252

Index —— 264

Argument

The Study of Power in Literature. 'The Rupert Constant'

"La prose demande, pour se développer, une certaine rigueur, un état social différencié; et une tradition: elle est délibérée, construite; créer une littérature c'est créer une prose."[1]

In 1957, during his British exile, Chaplin released a film, reflective of the political context of the '50s and especially of the manner in which he understood the utility and usefulness of film in explaining the ideological slips of the middle of the century. It is the film *A King in New York* in which the director uses a satire to poke fun at *McCarthyism*, using it as instrument for exposing communist hunting excess, denouncing the inquisitorial practices of unmasking the communist 'subversives' and 'traitors' in the American society of the '50s.

The hunt for 'the reds under the beds' presumed an ideological excess of the '50s, in a world affected by the trauma of the war. That had known the horrors of mass killings, the feeling of extinction, the immanency of nuclear entropy, all these accentuating the paralyzing fear and total suspicion amongst the constitutive states of the Cold War. The medium of transmitting these controlled fears was in Chaplin's case the film and the determining character, who denounces the pseudo-pacifist rhetoric of the '50s, is the child Rupert Macabee, interpreted in the film by Chaplin's own son. Young Rupert is the editor at a school paper, playing the adult role of a historian who gives an anarchist discourse to the exiled king. He is reading Marx during the Kings' visit to the school when in the school's publishing press Shadov demands to know: "Are you a communist?", to which Rupert replies: "Cannot one read Marx without being a communist?" He perorates with a mechanical voice and delivers a stereotypical, ideological discourse about the terror and the atrocity of life in Western society. This image from *A King in New York* is one of the strongest critiques of the '50s against 'rhinocerisation' through seductive ideologies, giving a perspective over mass manipulation through the power of fear. The young Rupert is a propaganda machine, having lost his childhood, becoming an adult against his will. Through his un-natural discourse he shows the effect of continuous ideology pressure against man.

In fact, Roland Barthes observed the myth of the "Poor and the Proletariat" in Chaplin's films, confirming: "His anarchy, politically open to discussion, perhaps

---

[1] Emil Cioran: *Oeuvres*. Paris: Gallimard 1955, p. 855.

represents the most efficient form of revolution in the realm of art."[2] It is certain that the media was one of the most expressive way of denouncing all forms of political excess through his new expressive power of images in the tradition proved by Orson Welles, with his radio reading from the novel of H. G. Wells, *The War of the Worlds* or by his own *Citizen Kane*. Nevertheless, the tradition of literature cannot be ignored, even if there is an artistic discourse which permanently explored the territory of revolt against the officialising of excess, this was literary discourse, in its diverse forms and formulas. The great texts of our literary tradition, whether we are talking about Dante, Cervantes, Goethe or Shakespeare, denounced imbalance, social inequities, forms of excess.

The critique of excess is therefore one of the supreme stakes of modern art and especially of literature, even when literature does not render the world it is born indirectly, reflecting within the interiority, reflexivity of its characters the negative effects of a dysfunctional, exclusivist world, integrative through uniformity.

The self-reflexive compensation of the modern novel proves exactly this fact. The Proustian centering on memory or the continuous flux of Joycean narrativity for example, are not direct discourses of unmasking social excesses, but effects of a social modernity predisposed to excess and the alienation of the Subject. From this point of view we notice that the modern novel proposes a social symptomatology of excess as a representative form of modern collectivity, which goes beyond traditional aesthetical formulas of the novel. In the second half of the last century, of the Herderian *Zeitgeist*, in the discussion about the utility of art in society instruments of sociological or political philosophy were used in the discussion. Because the exclusively hermeneutical arguments could not cope with the expansion of the social sciences and the aesthetical autonomy, or with the cult for art demonstrated its 'uselessness' in the process of social autonomy of the subject, the public figures of the '60s brought literature out of Sainte-Beuve's 'tour d'ivoire'. The instrumentalization of literature in the social battle has reactivated the interest of its study as a social fact or phenomenon, understood as "toute manière de faire, fixée ou non, susceptible d'exercer sur l'individu une contrainte extérieure."[3] This constraint of literature was seldom approached with methods coming from the sphere of sociological critique, from the theories of literary sociology promoted by Robert Escarpit, to the theory of 'social field' of art by Pierre Bourdieu.

As a follow-up of the writing zero degree, theorized in 1953 by Barthes, Escarpit spoke about a certain type of 'sursignification', meaning "un au-delà

---

[2] Roland Barthes: *Mythologies*. Selected and translated from the French by Annete Lavers. New York: The Noonday Press 1972, p. 39.
[3] Émile Durkheim: *Les règles de la méthode sociologique*. Paris: PUF 2005, p. 14.

du langage"⁴ in the spirit of an anticipative kind of post-structuralism, a fact which made the debate take place outside the limits of the text, as well. The literary sociologist observed, after a long period of hermeneutical interest of a comparative type, that the literary phenomenon results from a balance between 'adéquation', as form of adjustment of the discourse to the historical background and 'affrontement', an opposition, subversive formula. The situation of literature "entre les contraintes de la situation historique et la liberté de l'écrivain en tant que significateur"⁵ reconfirms the interest of literary sociology for the constraint and determinism of the medium and a certain type of social existentialism of literature.

Anticipating Goldmann, with his book which has made history among the disciples of the discipline, *Pour une sociologie du roman* (1965), Escarpit declared himself, implicitly, through the study *Sociologie de la littérature* (1958), against French historical comparatism. He proposed a change of perspective, from the high, isolating and purist meta-literary discourse, to the statement that literature, especially the novel, function according to an actantial model of human relationship exchange. So the novel functions not only as autonomous 'literary fact', meaning a fact that makes sense only in a given community gear. "Le nouvel équilibre"⁶ searched by the critic leads to the definition of the specificity of literature as 'dialogic' reality, meaning taken over later by Bakhtin.⁷ The objective of the theorists who understand the socio-literary dynamics in such a manner would be that of recomposing "l'histoire des hommes en société selon ce dialogue des créateurs de mots, de mythes et d'idées, avec leur contemporains et leur postérité que nous appelons maintenant littérature."⁸

The most famous theory of referring art to a 'social field' belongs to Pierre Bourdieu. Literature was not seen exclusively "as a socially symbolic act",⁹ but as a cultural product of a certain society, therefore determined historically. Referring to the utilitarianism of the sociological theory in the 'field of literature', Pierre Bourdieu describes the 'rules of literary art' by asking himself:

> Does the claim for the autonomy of literature, which found its exemplary expression in Proust's *Contre Sainte-Beuve*, imply that the reading of literary texts should be exclusively

---

4 Robert Escarpit: *Le littéraire et le social. Eléments pour une sociologie de la littérature.* (Avec Charles Bouazis, Jacques Dubois, Robert Estivals). Paris: Flammarion 1970, p. 13.
5 Escarpit: *Le littéraire et le social*, p. 13–14.
6 Robert Escarpit: *Sociologie de la littérature*. Paris: Presses universitaires de France 1958, p. 127.
7 Mikhaïl Bakhtine: *La poétique de Dostoïevki*. Paris: Seuil 1970.
8 Escarpit: *Sociologie de la littérature*, p. 127.
9 See Fredric Jameson: *The Political Unconscious. Narrative as a socially symbolic act*. London and New York: Routledge 1983.

literary? Is it true that scientific analysis is doomed to destroy that which makes for the specificity of the literary work and of reading, beginning with aesthetic pleasure?[10]

Out of the desire to find instruments in order to deconstruct the myth of aesthetical exceptionalism of literature and its ineffable nature, which intrigues and displeases the French sociologist, he looks for the answer of the utility of art in the sphere of sociology. Bourdieu demonstrates the dependency of literature on a determined 'social field' which sets certain specificity. He explains "the literary field in the field of power"[11] and extrapolates the criticism levelled at by the adepts of a literary, multiculturalist canon, by those who lamented the aesthetic exclusivism of canonical literature. For Bourdieu the emergence, the sustenance and perpetuation of literature is the result of a relational social mechanism, functional in a specific power context:

> The field of power is the space of relations of force between agents or between institutions having in common the possession of the capital necessary to occupy the dominant positions in different fields (notably economic or cultural).[12]

Here the concept of power reflects the relational character between the two 'fields'. Bourdieu analyses the manner of hierarchical positioning of literature, as a symbolic good at the interference between the powers aggregated within the social field. We understand its endeavour as an analysis of the position of literature as an artefact, referring especially to an exterior mechanism and not an interior one, of representation of the social power in a given history. The force of literature comes from here and it is what Gadamer, cited by Bourdieu, was interested in. Literature manifesting a "resistance to whoever would translate it into the identity of a concept, has been precisely for me the point of departure for my hermeneutic theory."[13]

Whether referring to the external premises of literary sociology (Escarpit, Goldmann, Bourdieu) or the internal ones, of structural narratology fashionable in the '60s–'70s, (Greimas, Souriau, Bremond), we observe the interest in explaining literature's functioning models by reference to a model or a context. This fact leads to the interests of the neo-historicists (Greenblatt, Montrose) who convincingly debate the formalist void of literary analyses, placing history in a privileged position this time.

---

10 Pierre Bourdieu: *The Rules of Art. Genesis and Structure of the Literary Field*. Translated by Susan Emanuel. Stanford: Stanford University Press 1995, p. XVI.
11 Bourdieu: *The Rules of Art*, p. 215.
12 Bourdieu: *The Rules of Art*, p. 215.
13 See Gadamer. In: Bourdieu: *The Rules of Art*, p. XXI.

Therefore, from the integrationist model of literary sociology, to the exclusivist one, centred on structuralism's actantial model, a change of paradigm in the second half of last century can be observed. The change comes from the interest in giving a utility, a functional explanation of the literary discourse by linking it to a group and according to the relations which are being established between its members. But the social relational pattern to which literature refers, imposes a concept, which translates a certain social hierarchy in this case a decisional substantial hierarchy of a group, this being included in the concept of power in the '50s. The representative function of literature places this concept at the basis of actantial relations that are established in a narration which produces such a mechanism, a social pattern, deconstructing it, denouncing it or functioning as a symptomatology of the excess or alienation provoked by this. The excess itself is a product of power disequilibrium.

One of the pioneers of the structuralist concept of power, Robert Dahl, started from the observation that interest in a normative concept, which is relational and substitutive for any human interaction has existed since ancient times, mentioned by the most important analysts of the social, such as Plato, Aristotel, Machiavelli, Hobbes, Pareto or Weber.

> Doubtless, it would be easy to show, too, how the word and its synonyms are everywhere embedded in the language of civilized people, often in subtly different ways: power, influence, control, pouvoir, puissance, Macht, Herrschaft, Gewalt, imperium, potestas, auctoritas, potentia, etc.[14]

Therefore, we start from the assumption that literature is also a discourse about power or, better said, a critique of the wrong use and excess of power in a given society. This *hard* premise has an evident assumed risk, if we think that literary schools of the last century, seen as a century of the hard theories on literature, have tried the legitimation of the idea of its aesthetic 'autonomy', therefore they arguing the idea of literature as a parallel discourse, or at least indirect one on society. Furthermore, the conclusion that literature in general and the novel in particular, as a type of the narrative representation of the world, is an authentic discourse analyzing this consubstantial level of the society, the relations of power carrying another risk: of placement within *medias res*, sometimes exaggerated of reality. But the manner in which we have chosen in the present research to come closer to a reality which brings nearer the perspective of the creators of literature and then its theoreticians. For example, 'the reality' represented by the novel is that from Italo Calvino's volume *The Uses*

---

14 Robert A. Dahl: The Concept of Power. In *Behavioral Science*, 2:3, 1957: July, p. 201.

of Literature.[15] In the essay entitled 'Levels of Reality in Literature', in which, a year before the publication of the ingenious narrative experiment *Se una notte d'inverno un viaggiatore* (1979), Calvino questions the manners in which literature relates to literature and implicitly the contextual resorts which form the basis of the literary story. For Calvino, narration presupposes, before the labyrinth of reception, in which the reader plays a determining part, a true 'reality' stratification, triggering the configuration of the meaning of the work. These levels of reality with which the novel operates are meant to code the reality of the 'social field' and to get us closer to the idea of a 'sursignification' which Escarpit discussed.

To search for the *morphology of power* in a novel presupposes, therefore, to identify its juxtaposed levels of discourse and reality, the manner in which the novel decomposes the reality in which it was born and the manner it discusses it, therefore demonstrating implicitly its anistoric character. 'The logic of the literary field', to continue with Bourdieu's concept, is that the novel juxtaposes 'worlds':

> [...] paradoxical worlds capable of inspiring or of imposing the most disinterested 'interests'-the principle of the work of art's existence in what makes it historic, but also transhistoric, is to treat this work as an intentional sign haunted and regulated by something else, of which it is also a symptom.[16]

Referring to Maurice Mandelbaum's thesis, from *The Anatomy of Historical Knowledge*, Paul Ricoeur endorses a similarity between history and narration, a recovery and recomposition of the anthropological structural model. "My thesis is that historical events do not differ radically from the events framed by a plot."[17] Nevertheless, seldom has the novel operated a process of history *anamorphosis*, meaning an intentional deformation of it, in order to restore the balance lost in our excess culture. Stigmatized by power, which sometimes even instrumentalised the novel in favour of legitimating its excess, literature in totalitarian times being a good example, the novel has built a level of reality through which to reflect, denounce and rebuild a perverted social balance. The subject of the novel, following a known social model, is a mimetic or anamorphotic reflection of a social hierarchy, of some relations of power. The present study follows four types of categories, four typologies of the reflected power (active, reflexive, passive and impersonal) in four novels from different periods, novels that demonstrate the

---

[15] Italo Calvino: *The Uses of Literature*. Translated by Patrick Creagh. Harcourt Brace Jovanovich 1987.
[16] Bourdieu: *The Rules of Art*, p. XX.
[17] Paul Ricoeur: *Time and Narrative*. Volume 1. Translated by Kathleen McLaughlin and David Pellauer. Chicago: Univeristy of Chicago Press 1984, p. 208.

link between the historical reality and a given historical reality. But the novels analysed here do not confine themselves to a precise, accurate representation of a certain historical reality reflected within literature, a gesture sufficient for a social fresque, but insufficient for a literary discourse. The discussed novels describe a transhistorical reality, are placed in realities which decompose histories, of the Time and Subject, even antagonising them.

'The interest' of the morphological analyses of power in narratives from different periods is therefore determined by the conviction that the novel represents the predilect formula of some superior artistic conscience which betrayed history and therefore power, always placing themselves in a samizdat-like position. The substantial belief of their narrative endeavour is that literature is a discourse inevitably subversive when facing a culture of the excess of power.

1 The Criticism of Ideas on Power

1.1 Theories on Power. From the Social and Philosophical Analysis to the Aporias of Literature

1.1.1 *The will to power* and its Ideological Foundation within the Republic of Letters

> Why, I, in this weak piping time of peace,
> Have no delight to pass away the time,
> Unless to spy my shadow in the sun
> And descant on mine own deformity:
> And therefore, since I cannot prove a lover,
> To entertain these fair well-spoken days,
> I am determined to prove a villain
> And hate the idle pleasures of these days.
> Plots have I laid, inductions dangerous,
> By drunken prophecies, libels and dreams,
> To set my brother Clarence and the king.[1]

In this excerpt from the historical drama, *Richard III* (1592), Shakespeare describes a covert and mysterious inner tendency of Richard, the future King. Namely, a temptation that amplifies an inner call to acquire power. The powerful Richard, the pretender, dreams of a compensatory force, since, unable of being loved for what he is, he sets out to make himself loved by any means. The tragic nature of the character is emphasized by the frustration brought about by his physical deformities, by anticipating his marginal destiny, but also by challenging his Divine Right and his belief in free will.

Predestined for loneliness, unloved and suffering from a complex due to the marginal role he plays within the politics of the kingdom, Richard is dominated by this inner force to gain power, to change his destiny, even by means of Machiavellian acts of unimaginable cruelty. The desire to acquire power and, implicitly, to gain a position of power and, therefore, overcome his physical distortions and the Divine Right, is generated and fuelled by an inner authority that cancels out any of his affects. In other words, Richard as a tragic character, as a representation of human physical and psychological deformities, only changes

---

[1] William Shakespeare: *King Richard III*. The Project Gutemberg. Posting Date: March 7, 2015 [EBook #1103], Release Date: November 1997, p. 12–13. Consulted at the web adress: http://www.gutenberg.org/ebooks/1103 [26.04.2018].

https://doi.org/10.1515/9783110605372-002

his condition within a social and political context that amplifies his tragic nature. Even this implicit Shakespearian criticism places him within the context of an increased supremacy of Elizabethan Calvinism and of religious fatalism, when divine determinism was grounded in the fact that God punishes evil by evil.[2] His image is Machiavellian, a representation of evil that often triggers homicidal instincts in man.

Through Richard, Shakespeare is testing the evolution of the need for power, which Elias Canetti called "the specific passion for power, the passion for survival".[3] But the power of individual evil, in Richard's case, intentional and calculated, therefore rational, is not complete in the absence of a perspective on the historical context that offers a historical representation "as political power".[4] Literary history is full of numerous such examples of a representation which Nietzsche rightfully called *The Will to Power*.[5] These representations describe the amplification and transformation of the individual will to power, as seen in the case of this Shakespearian character, to a will to power of dominant groups that, throughout human history, have imposed their own rules on the majority of people through authoritarianism.

As a continuation of this idea, again in *The Will to Power*, Nietzsche speaks of the concept of *perspectivism*, meaning the extensive potential of power, for "every centre of force-and not only man-construes all the rest of the world from its own view-point, i.e. measures, feels, forms, according to its own force".[6] This is ultimately the meaning of the Nietzschean statement:

> My idea is that every specific body strives to become master over all space and to extend its force (-its will to power:) and to thrust back all that resists its extension. But it continually encounters similar efforts on the part of other bodies and ends by coming to an arrangement ('union') with those of them that are sufficiently related to it: thus they then conspire together for power. And the process goes on.[7]

This Nietzschean finding is meant to remind us of the relation between individual power and group power. Essentially, individual power is the one that 'negotiates' its dominant position within a certain group that often manifests its role of

---

[2] See Janis Lull. In: William Shakespeare: *King Richard III*. Janis Lull (ed.). Cambridge: Cambridge University Press 1999, p. 8.
[3] Elias Canetti: *Crowds and Power*. Translated from German by Carol Stewart. New-York: Continuum 1978, p. 246.
[4] See Lull. In: Shakespeare: *King Richard III*, p. 8
[5] Friedrich Nietzsche: *The Will to Power*. Translation by Walter Kaufmann and R. J. Hollingdale. Edited, with Commentary by Walter Kaufmann. New York: Vintage Books 1968.
[6] Nietzsche: *The Will to Power*, p. 339.
[7] Nietzsche: *The Will to Power*, p. 340.

force through a common ideology, in turn negotiated or imposed. According to Nietzsche, individual power is the one that fuelled the theories of certain famous psychologists, such as Freud and his theory on the power and the domination of pleasure, Adler and his individual psychology based on the sensation of power or Frankl and his will of an existential meaning. Therefore, *the subjective, individual, behaviourist power* anchored in the subconscious becomes, according to the Nietzschean theory, *political and social power* justified or not on behalf of an ideology, which is an immutable historical process. As a matter of fact, in *The Will to Power*, Nietzsche also presents his structural vision of Machiavellian power:

> *On the 'Machiavellianism' of Power*
> The will to power appears
> a. among the oppressed, among slaves of all kinds, as will to *'freedom'*: merely getting free seems to be the goal (religio-morally: "responsible to one's own conscience alone"; "evangelical freedom," etc.);
> b. among a stronger kind of man, getting ready for power, as will to overpower; if it is at first unsuccessful, then it limits itself to the will to *'justice'* i.e., to the *same measure of rights* as the ruling type possesses;
> c. among the strongest, richest, most independent, most courageous, as "love of mankind" of 'the people', of the gospel, of truth, God; as sympathy; 'self-sacrifice', etc.; as overpowering, bearing away with oneself, taking into one's service, as instinctive self-involvement with a great quantum of power to which one is able to give direction: the hero, the prophet, the Caesar, the savior, the shepherd; (-sexual love, too, belongs here: it desires to overpower, to take possession, and it *appears* as self-surrender. Fundamentally it is only love of one's 'instrument', of one's 'steed'-the conviction that this or that belongs to one because one is in a position to use it). *'Freedom'*, *'justice'*, and *'love'* !!![8]

Therefore, the Nietzschean conception of power is associated with a Machiavellian meaning, even when connected with a 'will for freedom', being attributed to a selfish impulse, to a preservation instinct, in favour of the individual and not of the collectivity. But this manner of Nietzsche approaching power with a Machiavellian meaning must also be attributed to the general framework of his book, *The Will to Power*, where he is interested in and meditates on the idea of the *nihilism* of modern society, which also makes him a role model for many philosophers of the 20th century.

But the feeling of power, in the sense of authority and autonomy over oneself and others, is the essence of ideas on power. Even when establishing a literary canon, in terms of standardisation, selection and imposition,[9] as will become

---

[8] Nietzsche: *The Will to Power*, p. 407.
[9] See Virgil Nemoianu; Robert Royal (eds.): *The Hospitable Canon. Essays on Literary Play, Scholarly Choice and Popular Pressure.* Philadelphia and Amesterdam: John Benjamins Publishing Company 1991; Harold Bloom: *The Western Canon. The Books and School of the Ages.* New York:

apparent from this chapter, as a result of the "strong thought"[10] of the authoritarian aesthetical modernity, it is still a result of exerting power as a recognised authority of literary criticism. Particularly eloquent in this regard is the status of the Romanian literary canon and which could be described as cyclically relevant to the exercise of power in the battle between politics and aesthetics. Throughout approximately 150 years, decisive for the modernity of the Romanian estate and culture, from 1859, when the *Union of the Romanian Principalities* took place, under the reign of Alexandru Ioan Cuza and until after the fall of the Communist regime in 1989, as part of the canonical battle for the 'autonomy of the aesthetic', once every 50 years, Romanian literature was under the authority of certain dominant figures. We refer here to Titu Maiorescu at the end of the 19th century, Eugen Lovinescu during the inter-war period and Nicolae Manolescu in the '80s of the last century. It is relevant that, within this battle of literature trying to gain its autonomy from political power, the ideology of the aesthetics has been used as a form of art freedom by all these literary critics. But this battle for a literary canon has a specific meaning in the discussion on forms and the formulas of the literary authorities establishing the 'compulsory' hierarchies of Romanian literature. The illustration of this literary 'battle' will constitute a special topic within this first chapter.

Nevertheless, the forms of power moving past the relative and speculative scopes of psychology, this being one of the major debate directions of the concept in the 20th century (Freud, Adler, Frankl, Foucault, Deleuze etc.), cannot be dissociated from the structuring force of the concept: *ideology*. Four of the ideas mentioned by Terry Eagleton in the attempt to define another theoretically unstable concept, *Ideology*, helps us in the attempt to establish the operating framework for *Power* and, later on, the manner of its literary representation. Ideology is analysed by the leftist literary theoretician as being:

> [...] (b) a body of ideas characteristic of a particular social group or class;
> (c) ideas which help to legitimate a dominant political power;
> (d) false ideas which help to legitimate a dominant political power; [...]
> (j) the conjuncture of discourse and power;[11]

Structured according to ideology, power becomes a concept that operates in the context of the *dominant groups* that thus *legitimate* their authoritarian decisions,

---

Harcourt Brace & Company 1994; Virgil Nemoianu: *A Theory of the Secondary. Literature, Progress and Reaction*. Baltimore: John Hopkins University Press 1989.
10 Gianni Vattimo: *The End of Modernity. Nihilism and Hermeneutics in Post-modern Culture*. Translated and with an Introduction by Jon R. Snyder. Cambridge: Polity Press 1988.
11 Terry Eagleton: *Ideology. An Introduction*. London and New York: Verso 1991, p. 1–2.

starting from utopian ideas, such as the common good, absolute freedom, or a perfect society. Thus, the ideology of power entails a form of legitimating actions.

> A dominant power - states Eagleton - may legitimate itself by *promoting* beliefs and values congenial to it; *naturalizing* and *universalizing* such beliefs so as to render them self-evident and apparently inevitable; *denigrating* ideas which might challenge it; *excluding* rival forms of thought, perhaps by some unspoken but systematic logic; and *obscuring* social reality in ways convenient to itself.[12]

Such an operating formula is especially characteristic, at least through its visibility, of societies subject to totalitarianism. The discursive deformation of reality in favour of the exercise of power by a single person or by a group of persons has been a generalized phenomenon, for example during the fifty years of Romanian Communism. Literature, and art in general, has been a perfect ideological instrument for representing the perfect world and the new man. Totalitarian power may be defined by transferring Max Weber's concept of 'economic domination'[13] and adapting it to a broader concept of 'social domination'.

In the same direction, that of the results of exerting power, speaking of "Forms of power", Bertrand Russell aphoristically argued that "Power may be defined as the production of intended effects."[14] In other words, the concept of *power* has a *quantitative* meaning, as Russell also remarks. But Russell's theory reveals a unidimensional perspective, analysing exclusively pressures and actions in terms of influence exerted on the individual. According to the British philosopher, the individual is influenced:

> a. by direct physical power over his body, e.g. when he is imprisoned or killed;
> b. by rewards and punishments as inducements, e. g. in giving or withholding employment;
> c. by influence on opinion, i. e. propaganda in its broadest sense.[15]

This theory has only quantitative or unidimensional aspects, as mentioned before, but is also purely descriptive, instrumenting the individual and reducing them to a set of automatisms that can be induced, for instance, by persevering education. In this regard, Russel offers a relevant example, namely to the way in which trained animals experience the power of education.

---

12 Eagleton: *Ideology*, p. 5–6.
13 See Max Weber: *The Theory of Social and Economic Organization*. Translated by A. M. Henderson and Talcott Parsons. Edited with an introduction by Talcott Parsons. New York: Free Press 1947; and Max Weber: *Economy and Society: An Outline of Interpretive Sociology*. Edited by Guenther Roth and Claus Wittich. Berkeley: University of California Press 1978.
14 See Bertrand Russel. In: Steven Lukes (ed.): *Power (Readings in Social & Political Theory)*. New York: New York University Press 1986, p. 9.
15 See Russel. In: Lukes (ed.): *Power (Readings in Social & Political Theory)*, p. 19.

But the meaning of power over people is based on a certain poetics of the influences that generate, in the words of Harold Bloom, an 'anxiety of influences'. The effects of influence on people, the intentional effects mentioned by Bertrand Russell or Talcott Parsons[16] can most easily be observed through the mediation of the mediation of the work of art, which is represented by the literary text, even if most of the times indirectly, as 'metanarratives'[17] of the relationships the creator of the text has had with various social and historical ideologies that directly or indirectly determined their education. Therefore, the counterexample offered by literature is that power is also a more complex phenomenon of passive influence and sedimentation. Metanarratives and their literary recurrence are merely ideological formulas and strategies of exercising direct or indirect political power. On the other hand, what Lyotard calls postmodern 'disbelief' in metanarratives is not an absolute empowerment of aesthetics but rather its restructuring according to a paradigm of deconstruction and reconstruction.

Historical and legitimating metanarratives of modernity rooted in the mentality of the Enlightenment, mentioning historicized ideas, such as the advancing of history, good and absolute freedom and the power of science have been replaced in the second part of the last century with other ideologies that legitimated power as a natural part of organised society. Poststructuralist ideologies, such as ethnicity, race, class, gender, religion, which have gradually become metanarratives as well, played a determinant and strategic role in the process of selection and 'liberation' of art from the 'tyranny' of aesthetics that is no longer regarded as the only criterion of canonical selection. Gradually, this has determined genuine clashes of ideologies, between the defenders of stability and stabilization of the aesthetic hierarchy and the leftist neo-historicists who understood and labelled canon as an echo of a conservative, retrograde thinking. The difference between the canonizing right that tries to preserve the literary canon, whose stability it attributes to the specialists, and the challenging and critical left that suggests the 'liberalization' or the liberation of the canon from the dominance of the aesthetic, is similar to the historical 'battles' between the high-end, elitist art and the low-end/popular art. On the one hand we ascertain that 'nothing goes', on the other hand, we are obliged to ascertain that 'anything goes'. Nevertheless, is this not an ideological battle for power, similar in discourse to the "Quarrel between the Ancients

---

[16] Talcott Parsons: On the Concept of Political Power. In: *Proceedings of the American Philosophical Society*, vol. 107, no. 3, 1963, p. 232–262.

[17] Jean-François Lyotard: *La Condition postmoderne: Rapport sur le savoir*. Paris: Éditions de Minuit 1979 and for the English translation see: Jean-François Lyotard: *The Postmodern Condition: A Report on Knowledge*. Translation from the French by Geoff Bennington and Brian Massumi. Foreword by Fredric Jameson. Manchester: Manchester University Press 1984.

and the Moderns" (*Querelle des Anciens et des Modernes*)? Do these clashes of forces in the 20th century not use the arsenal of opposite ideologies that aim to take over the manner of establishing a canonical hierarchy? In the end, if we are to go back to Eagleton, this entire belligerent rhetoric certainly proves the manner in which a canon is replaced by another, according to a propitious context or propitious circumstances favourable to power. From this point of view, literature proves to be the exponential field for observing the morphology of power and for practicing the semiotics of power, where divergent ideologies, aroused by the critical propensity of literature, have constantly caused a canon to be replaced by another. This is what the biography of literary ideas proves par excellence.

Paradoxically, the most authentic forms of such typologies of power are precisely represented by literature. It is paradoxical because literature is simultaneously a series of micronarratives reflecting reality, and the discourse most distant from it. This paradox can be explained as follows: first of all literature 'despises' the world both it and its creator come from, in the sense that literature has always had a *critical discourse* on the time/society it was born in, being the main anti-establishment, reactionary discourse denouncing the world and, secondly, it is ALSO the result of a reaction that takes place in the consciousness of its creator, which is a result of the time/society in which they live. For example, *Richard III*, in which Shakespeare, through Richard, delivers a critical discourse on the Elizabethan Era and the values imposed through its ecclesiastical power and therefore political power. Richard's monstrosity is thus an implicit criticism of and contempt for the monstrosity of medieval obscurity. However, the Shakespearian drama, as the majority of Shakespeare's works, is born in a context that favours such criticism and therefore the text is a representation of the forms of power during that period. In the end, this paradox is also one of the reading keys of literature. It is understood as a form of reflection according to the discourse it adopts regarding its world and its author, as reflecting, most of the times in an allegorical manner, and either accepting or denouncing this world. And, in this context of representing forms of power, ideologies of power, literature, through its discourse, also has the role of reflecting on the condition of a given society at a given time, on the functions and especially the dysfunctions of its world. Its critical discourse must have a curative function, as long as the Author-Context-Text-Reader formula is accepted.

A diachronic look at the literary texts that also suggest representations of power also reveals a secondary function, additional to the critical discourse, of its positioning in relation to a certain society. The functioning manner of the text within the society it was written in, but especially within the society it imposes itself on, reflects the way literature is seen from one context to another, meaning it can also function as a barometer for the artistic conscientiousness of a society at a given moment in time. For example, in Romanian literature, the texts of the chroniclers from the 15th century are often analysed as being the first literary writings, although written in Slavonic, and are especially seen as having Slavonic and, especially, as having a predominantly historical, descriptive 'function'. The partial and dispersed elements of a descriptive artistic language, constantly dominated by the obsession of the 'truth', can only constitute the beginnings of the Romanian literary language at most.

Given this context, it is therefore necessary to ask how the late emergence of Romanian literature can be explained? Is the contextual, socializing approach based on the late formation of the Romanian state complete? The Romanian principalities have always been regarded as being 'on the move and unsettled', as the chronicler defines them, meaning in a permanent state of instability, dependent on the administrative power of dominant nations, in a broader historical and geo-political context. The political power of an important Romanian group which has had a quantifiable impact on Romanian culture has actually only been a reality during the second half of the 19th century, through the ideological militancy of the 'Junimea' group led by Titu Maiorescu. The result of Maiorescu's theories, amongst which the most important would be that of the 'autonomy of the aesthetic', has led to the occurrence of literature, in the form of the canon of the 'Great Classics' (Eminescu, Caragiale, Creangă, Slavici). Following the steps of the previous movement of the '1848 generation', Titu Maiorescu challenges the 'imitations', the literature of translations and the 'forms without content'.[18] The literature representative for a community, also subject to a process of ideological selection performed by a dominant group at a given moment in time,[19] is the result of a complex process of positioning according to the context and the status of knowledge. It is not merely a 'noble uselessness'. But literature certainly entails more than self-referential language, meaning it speaks not only of itself, but it is also a discourse regarding the world in which it speaks, suggesting the invisible image of the said world to the competent reader, thus revealing apparent mundane forms.

The time schedule of literature is laid out both horizontally, meaning that it cannot disregard the context of its world, as well as vertically, so that it is a test of

---

18 See Titu Maiorescu: *Critice* (Critiques). București: Minerva 1973. In Romanian language, the expresion 'forme fără fond' contains an implicit criticism towards the imitations of forms from other literatures, without content relevance for Romanian culture at the moment.

19 The unfortunate destiny of the first and only genuine epopee of Romanian literature, *Țiganiada sau tabăra țiganilor* (Țiganiada or the Gypsies' Camp), by Ion Budai-Deleanu, which was written in 1800 (1st ed.) and in 1812 (2nd ed.) and published only in 1875, is relevant for setting up a late Romanian literary canon. The criticism of the Habsburg administrative power, in an allegorical manner, but also the social and political framework in Transylvania, caused this epic to be known quite late.

its human nature, regardless of the historical time it describes. That is to say, Shakespeare's drama can be read and has been read by specialists both in the context of the Elizabethan Era, in the absence of which, for example, ascension to the throne or the Divine Right of regents would have no meaning for Richard, but also according to an extra-contextual message of an eternal battle for power, for controlling devastating passions, that has been waged inside of men just forever. Approaching Goethe's *Faust* according to the classical themes analysed by literary criticism, such as philosophy, religion, culture and politics, would not be possible without bringing into discussion the rationalist spirit of the Enlightenment, without the dispute between science and spirituality that animated that period of time. From this point of view, Faust is a character searching for the power of knowledge, which belongs to the irrational Mephistopheles. But the pact made with him is a pact against the religious, political and scientific obscurantism that preceded the century of the Enlightenment. Moreover, *Walpurgis Night* is regarded as a Goethean criticism against the French Revolution and the damaging idealism of the modern spirit generated by this movement. However, Faust is a prototype, an image of the spirit that sacrifices itself for knowledge. As a matter of fact, this reading also offers us a sense of the 'contemporaneousness' of a literary text. Literature thus offers us a representation of the *political power* with historical value and explains social phenomena in a given context and a representation of the inner *subjective power* that dominates the human being like an 'archigenre', therefore a constant of it.

But the tradition of 'selecting' the power of literature that serves the interests of a collectivity is much older, dating back to Greek antiquity. Repudiating poets that *imitate* and deform the meaning of things according to their verse-writing abilities through which they embellish nature is a direct consequence of the praxis promoted by Plato's *Republic*, of his moral doctrine and his philosophy with a pedagogical and canonical stake. The 'divine' aestheticism of poets could not and would not function in a *Republic* regulated by precise laws:

> Now, as it seems, if a man who is able by wisdom to become every sort of thing and to imitate all things should come to our city, wishing to make a display of himself and his poems, we would fall on our knees before him as a man sacred, wonderful, and pleasing; but we would say that there is no such man among us in the city, nor is it lawful for such a man to be born there. We would send him to an other city, with myrrh poured over his head and crowned with wool, while we ourselves would use a more austere and less pleasing poet and teller of tales for the sake of benefit, one who would imitate the style of the decent man and would say what he says in those models that we set down as laws at the beginning, when we undertook to educate the soldiers.[20]

---

[20] Plato: *The Republic of Plato*. Second Edition. Translated with notes and an interpretive essay by Allan Bloom. New York: Basic Books, p. 76.

The laws that govern the Republic must be generally valid for Plato, therefore it was inappropriate for the poets to stray from it. In other words, the role of literature in the ideal Platonian Republic would have been to imitate solely the moral, legitimated, therefore *canonized* beauty, unanimously accepted as an invariable marker for a just society. This had to be observed precisely in order to preserve the political power. The poets of 'aesthetic beauty' would have 'corrupted' the Platonian ideals of a beauty which was moral, transcendent etc. Educating soldiers, the young men guarding the fortress, is the essence of a society's organization in the Platonian Republic. From this point of view, political power, the power of strict rules, of utilitarian ethics, is meant to impose literature as a practical discourse. Thus, Plato's discourse is implicitly a discourse on political power and literature's role within a society governed by ethical laws, therefore transferable to aesthetic laws as well.

The dependency of the literary text on a precise context could be proved throughout the history of literature and theoreticians have attempted numerous times to analyse literature as a representative discourse of its time. The relationship between literature and its historical context that determines its existence is one of a 'principal'-'secondary' type, to borrow the well-known distinction which Virgil Nemoianu introduced in 1989 in his book, *A Theory of the Secondary. Literature, Progress and Reaction*.[21] In other words, literature would be a secondary discourse of history/context, if one is to relate to the main human interests.[22] Starting from here, it could be tempting to believe in the 'ivory tower' of the writer who boasts freedom of imagination and creates according to values that establish his literature in the field of a unanimously recognized literary canon. But this autarchy of literature is contradicted later on by the reputed American professor of Romanian origin, when problematizing the formula for the *popular success* of literature within the process of canonization, in the volume edited together with Robert Royal, *The Hospitable Canon. Essays on Literary Play, Scholarly Choice and Popular Pressure*, or when stating that a canonical literary text is "a bestseller of the historical majority".[23]

In other words, even if it is a secondary discourse, literary discourse is deeply related to the context that both generates its occurrence and postulates its historicity. Moreover, literature has sometimes been considered a main kind of discourse, precisely because of its pragmatic function of being used as an instrument and vehicle of ideologies from the field of power. Even when not obliged to function according to the norms or the restrictive and closed canons of the dominant social power, as is the case of the Romanian proletarian culture, literature

---

[21] Nemoianu: *A Theory of the Secondary*, 1989.
[22] Nemoianu: *A Theory of the Secondary*, 1989, p. 6.
[23] Nemoianu; Robert Royal (eds.): *The Hospitable Canon*, p. 232.

has functioned as a critical mirror for a dehumanised society, and the examples of the naturalistic novel are relevant to this end.

The conflict between history and literature has concerned several generations of theoreticians who wanted to explain these pragmatic elements of the literary discourse, in the attempt to assign a main public function to it. For example, the neo-historicist Louis Montrose[24] claimed, through the theory of "the historicity of texts" and "the textuality of history" that a given text is incorporated into a social and cultural context and that understanding and even preserving the past can only be done through the "surviving textual traces of the society in question".[25] This interdependence, this fundamental coexistence between text and history through a subtle and almost ineffable process, up to their identification, is an exaggeration, probably born of the neo-historicists' desire to break away from Marxist theories regarding the relationship between the dominant classes and literature. While Marxist criticism sees a relationship of domination over literature on behalf of a social class that uses and instruments literature in this process of perpetuating and expanding control, the neo-historians are recuperating the stories of the oppressed for a precise reason: to discover and to demonstrate the efficiency of the oppressive apparatus.[26]

For the neo-historicist critics, the relationship between literature and society is nevertheless absolutized, the literary texts having specific functions inside a precise social network operating with power structures.[27] Unlike for Marxists, literature being able to function as social rhetoric, a special use of social imagination in/through a critical language.

1.1.2 The Sociological Perspective on Power

As seen before, the debate on the concept of power, often regarded as a key concept in the Western tradition,[28] and the search for its functioning norms, precisely to avoid an excess of power, have existed since antiquity. Since Aristotle's reflections on the power and authority of the law, to Machiavelli, Nietzsche or Hobbes, the concept of power has been placed at the core of philosophical, political, moral or sociological preoccupations. However, the American political

---

24 See Louis Montrose. In: Harold A. Veeser (ed.): *The New Historicism*. New York: Routledge 1989.
25 See Montrose. In: Veeser (ed.): *The New Historicism*, p. 20.
26 See John Brannigan. In: Julian Wolfreys (ed.): *Literary Theories: A Reader and Guide*. Edinburgh: Edinburgh University Press 1999, p. 419.
27 See Brannigan. In: Wolfreys (ed.): *Literary Theories*, p. 420.
28 Talcott Parsons: On the Concept of Political Power. In: *Proceedings of the American Philosophical Society*, vol. 107, no. 3, 1963, p. 232.

scientist Robert Dahl claims that from Aristotle to Machiavelli or even Thomas Hobbes, the analysts of the concept of power have not conducted complex, axiological research on it, due to the fact that the meaning of concepts associated with power, such as *influence, authority* or *rule* always seemed "clear to men of common sense."[29]

The power terms used by Aristotle, such as *power, influence, authority* and *rule* or those used by Machiavelli, such as *empire, force, potency* and *authority,* seem to be too general and insufficient for explaining the operating mechanism of power. As a matter of fact, Talcott Parsons also criticized Hobbes' tradition and the general and "conceptual diffuseness"[30] brought about by the tendency to treat the concept of power through the capacity to attain ends or goals. At the same time, Parsons rightfully criticizes the Weberian thesis on power as well, precisely as being excessively selective. However, he places himself in the same direction as Foucault when understanding the complexity of the scope of power and the institutionalization of authority. Remaining however on the level of political sciences, although he aims to start solely from the economic theories and to explain the functioning of power within the logical system of society in general, Parsons also reduces power to a social system and to the manner of 'legitimizing' power actions. Starting, however, from the question Hugh V. McLachalan asks,[31] "Is *power* an evaluative concept?", we must note that the debate on this concept has been more descriptive than evaluative or, even less, interpretative. Even when the argumentation tends to explain the particular and arbitrary nature of an individual's options, as MacLachalan attempts to do in the article cited here, as a result of the criticism against the sociological perspective, the analysis cannot separate itself from exposing certain social patterns and canons, which are quite mechanical and functionalist. These are often amended by the literary discourse, which demonstrates the inefficiency of schemes in general and that of the sociological ones in particular. The sociological tradition tracks the manner of society functioning from the perspective of power terminology, while modern sociology instruments the concept, demonstrating the manner in which our society is dependent on a certain hierarchy, determined by the gain of certain interests, especially as a dominant group that exercises its authority to that end.

But the term 'authority' entails that a certain group or person can both argue for and prove the need for a specific position which is acquired within the public space and has not always been valid. Often, authority has been acquired

---

29 See Robert Dahl. In: Lukes (ed.): *Power (Readings in Social & Political Theory)*, p. 39.
30 Parsons: On the Concept of Political Power, p. 232.
31 See Hugh V. McLachalan. In: John Scott (ed.), *Power: critical concepts*. London: Routledge 1996, p. 308–324.

by exerting certain manipulations or through a chain of hierarchical influences. The distorted manner of obtaining authority and implicitly a certain form of power is denounced, for example, by literature that displays images of groups or persons that exert their power over the others, without having acquired justified meritorious and therefore recognized authority. One of the best-known dystopic allegories of power excess from the previous century was the one suggested by George Orwell, in *Animal Farm* (1945). The Russian revolution in 1917 and the totalitarian system enforced in Russia once Stalin came to power are the two historical moments that constitute the historical scope of the novel. But here we see a transgression of history and through the allegorical strategy a denunciation of the grotesque universe of dehumanization and absurd arbitrariness of excessive power of all times. Violent authoritarianism and the downthrow of humanistic values are criticized in a world with intentionally diffused values.

In the same way, i.e. the analysis of the concept of 'authority' and not of 'authoritarianism', the image of the intellectual, is for instance that of a person enjoying a certain public authority, conferred by their knowledge, but especially by their actions in the public space, therefore by their commitment. Starting from a syllogism in the *Prison Notebooks* of the Italian political philosopher Antonio Gramsci, we could admit that in any society, especially the modern one, "All men are intellectuals, one could therefore say: but not all men have in society the function of intellectuals."[32]

He distinguishes between 'traditional intellectuals', such as professors, priests etc., who perpetuate a certain tradition/authority/spiritual memory, and 'organic intellectuals', those who are directly connected to the social classes and who exert a direct and constant influence over the relationships between such classes. These intellectuals are the ones controlling, deciding and manipulating in favour of certain groups of people who want to control the masses. This is how intellectuals with precise responsibilities emerged in our industrial/corporate society, and the examples given by Gramsci are relevant: the technician in industry, the expert in political economy, the attorney etc. Following Gramsci's typology of intellectuals, the 'Orientalist' Edward Said also discussed the representations of the intellectual in our society by relating them to their relationships with power.[33] Today, Said continues, taking the same Gramscian direction and speaking about the specialist in publicity or in public relations that

---

[32] Antonio Gramsci: *Selections from the Prison Notebooks*. Edited and translated by Quintin Hoare and Geoffrey Nowell Smith. New York: International Publishers 1992, p. 9.
[33] Edward Said: *Des intellectuels et du pouvoir*. Traduit de l'Anglais par Paul Chemala et revu par Dominique Edde. Alger: Marinoor 2001, p. 16.

establishes the new social culture and that has an important role in setting up cultural hierarchies in media.

But, when referring to culture, this time the artistic one, we ask ourselves what is the function of literature, as an intellectual discourse, in this divided, hybridized social mechanism? Starting here, if the field of literary research from the second half of the previous century is considered, it is apparent that, first of all, a diversification of literary and cultural studies, characterizing the continental movements, in particular the French ones. Along with the post-structuralist debates in the '70s regarding the heteroclite and relativistic nature of humanistic sciences, as a response to or criticism of the inflexible theoretical models of structuralism, literature was an instrument of argumentation. From the indetermination of meaning and the open work,[34] to Emmanuel Levinas'[35] restructuring of meaning and significance, to searching for a metalanguage adequate for semiotics in the vision of Rolland Barthes or to Derrida's deconstruction and the technique of dissemination, a true repositioning of literature in the field of humanistic sciences is dealt with. It had to respond to a major challenge, being used as an arsenal in arguing for the specificity and the role or the utility of postmodern humanism in the context of the social and historical remappings of the '60s–'70s. The autarchy of structuralism was becoming insufficient for demonstrating the need for literature, for example, within an applied society that was incrementally searching for answers outside the laboratory.

In regards to this post-structuralist repositioning of literature, which began in the '60s, the major role is definitely held by Michel Foucault, who was directly interested in the manner and model of functioning of the 'world' of the literary text in analogy with society. Many of his texts between 1954 and 1988, reunited in the *Dits et écrits*[36] volumes, use precisely the principles of literary texts as definitive arguments for restructuring society's manner of functioning. For example, in 1964, he actively participated in debates on the novel or poetry[37] and in 1969 he suggested the famous model of analysis of the discursive authority within a novel, starting from the question "Qu'est-ce qu'un auteur?"[38] Concluding that "l'écriture est maintenant liée au sacrifice, au sacrifice même de la vie", he recognized a change of perspective for, if throughout history literature had the mission

---

34 Umberto Eco: *Opera aperta*. Roma: Bompiani 1962.
35 Emmanuel Levinas: La signification et le sens. In: *Revue de Metaphisyque et de Morale*, 69 (2), 1964, p. 125–164.
36 Michael Foucault: *Dits et écrits*. Vol. I–IV. Edition établie sous la direction de Daniel Defert et Francois Ewald, avec la collaboration de Jacques Lagrange. Paris: Gallimard 1994.
37 Foucault: *Dits et écrits*, p. 338–390.
38 Foucault: *Dits et écrits*, p. 789–809.

to ensure immortality to the writer, then at the twilight of modernity our world "a reçu maintenant le droit de tuer, d'être meurtrière de son auteur."[39] For Foucault, 'la fonction-auteur' is linked:

> [...] au système juridique et institutionnel qui enserre, détermine l'univers du discours; elle ne s'exerce pas uniformément et de la même façon sur tous les discours, à toutes les époques et dans toutes les formes de civilisation; elle n'est pas définie par l'attribution spontanée d'un discours à son producteur, mais par une série d'opérations spécifiques et complexes; elle ne renvoie pas purement et simplement à un individu réel, elle peut donner lieu simultanément à plusieurs ego, à plusieurs positions-sujets que de classes différentes d'individus peuvent venir occuper [...].[40]

It is a vision of 'the author function' within the literary discourse, admitting that it is indeed about an 'ideological function' of proliferation of meaning.[41] In the spirit of the dominant idea animating the Foucaultian research, i.e. the social analysis of the concept of power, this debate on the author's function is implicitly related to establishing or searching for the position, role and function of the author within the hierarchy of the literary discourse. In other words, this analysis is rather an analysis of the social function of the author in terms of the social and historical and philosophical framework of their time.

In a debate published under the title of "Les intelectuels et les pouvoirs"[42] Foucault argued in what regards his own research could be seen as autobiographical extrapolations because, as he said, "Mes livres ont toujours été mes problèmes personnels avec la folie, la prison, la sexualité."[43] It can therefore be understood that the author does not have a solely discursive function, not even in the case of a non-literary text, which completes the prior answer to the question "What is an author?" In the end, the interest in the auctorial instance translates a much broader vision on literature than a simple transfer from sociology. The projections of the author's world into the world of the text are essential in analysing the literary discourse, a fact recurrently proven by Foucault. Since his texts seem like "autobiographical fragments" to him, the author-image and the text-world cannot be dissociated.

In this article, we notice that Michel Foucault is also a continuator of the Gramscian ideas regarding the organicity of the intellectual in the public space,

---

39 Foucault: *Dits et écrits*, p. 793.
40 Foucault: *Dits et écrits*, p. 803–804.
41 Foucault: *Dits et écrits*, p. 811.
42 Foucault: *Dits et écrits*, p. 747.
43 Foucault: *Dits et écrits*, p. 748.

nuancing his convictions on the social framework of power, i.e. what he calls 'power relations'. He admits that power entails:

> [...] des relations, c'est-à-dire ce qui fait que les individus, les êtres humains sont en relation les uns avec les autres, non pas simplement sous la forme du désir, mais également sous une certaine forme qui leur permet d'agir les uns sur les autres et, si vous voulez, en donnant un sens très large à ce mot, de se 'gouverner' les uns les autres.[44]

This is a form of legitimizing the discourse of power from the perspective of social analysis. Even though this transfer to the literary discourse lacks functionality most of the time, the impact of Foucault's research on humanistic studies and on their generalization to cultural studies has been considerable. However, I would say it is rather about searching for a new language in order to justify and support the paradigmatic changes that took place during the second half of the previous century. The ideological framework types of this discourse often go unnoticed and the applicability of such theories becomes almost impossible. His research is located on the border between sociology, philosophical speculation and the essay of a moralist substance. In regards to the field of sociology from the second half of the previous century, Stephen Lukes' theory on the concept of power is well known. In fact, this theory is one of the most debated upon[45] regarding the functionality of the concept in the public field, defining the active mechanisms of power as being constitutive to any hierarchically stratified society. Moreover, what makes Lukes' research on the typology and functionality of 'powers' noteworthy is the subtle opposition to Foucault's ideas on the impossibility of freedom in the context that we depend on the framework and actions of power. In his well-known essay, *Power: A Radical View*,[46] the American sociologist tries to prove, contrary to the Foucauldian tendency to close down the debate on power, concepts such as *freedom* or *autonomy* by looking at the patterns of existing power.[47]

Starting therefore from the social framework of power, Stephen Lukes is the one who describes the three dimensions of *Power* in the context of the debate in the North-American political and sociological sciences of the '70s, starting from a methodological dilemma, such as "How to think about power theoretically and

---

44 Foucault: *Dits et écrits*, p. 750–751.
45 See Keith Dowding: *Power*. Buckingham: Open University Press/Minnesota University Press 1996 and Keith Dowding: Three-Dimensional Power: A Discussion of Steven Lukes' *Power: A Radical View*. In: *Political Studies Review*, Volume 4, Issue 2, May 2006, p. 136–145.
46 Steven Lukes: *Power. A Radical View*. Second edition. London: Palgrave Macmillan 2005.
47 Dowding: Three-Dimensional Power, p. 136.

how to study it empirically."[48] In order to prove the empiricism of the theory, he distinguishes between "three dimensional perspectives" of power, as follows:

a. **The Unidimensional Perspective**: "the intuitive idea of power".[49] A has power over B up to the point in which they can determine B to do everything that B would not normally do;
b. **The Bidimensional Perspective**: "to the extent that a person or group-consciously or unconsciously-creates or reinforces barriers to the public airing of policy conflicts, that the person or group has power";
c. **The Tridimensional Perspective**: A can exert power over B, determining them to do what B does not want to do, but also practices their power over B by influencing them, shaping them or determining their wishes.[50]

The unidimensional perspective on power is associated with individual wishes of control in order to gain power and is reflected in the relationships between people, while bidimensional power entails an extrapolation of the desire for power in the public space, determined subjacently by other interests as well. Tridimensional power claims that desires are also the result of a social construct, meaning they are determined by social restraints, therefore subject to control. Through this category we can speak of manipulating desires according to the interests of the dominant group and this perspective would be complete precisely because of the systemic easiness to explain, justify, argue for or legitimate domination or authority.

The first two forms of power displayed are criticized by Lukes who underlines their incapacity to notice the 'systemic' aspects of power. The first is criticized as being excessively tributary to behaviourism, and the second as being a continuation of Max Weber's idea, "for whom power was the probability of individuals realizing their wills despite the resistance of others" and "to whom power was the probability of individuals fulfilling their desires despite the others' resistance."[51] This is also the reason why in his book, *Economy and society* (1978), Max Weber adopts the concept of 'domination', which he defines in the article entitled "Domination by Economic Power and by Authority", as "one of the most important elements of social action."[52] Seen as a form of power, or as a special case of power, domination is identified by Weber within the ensemble of society, as playing "the decisive role particularly most important social structures of the

---

[48] Lukes: *Power. A Radical View*, p. 1.
[49] Robert A. Dahl: The Concept of Power. In: *Behavioral Science*, 2:3 (1957: July), p. 201–215.
[50] Lukes: *Power. A Radical View*, p. 27.
[51] Lukes: *Power. A Radical View*, p. 26.
[52] See Max Weber. In: Lukes (ed.): *Power (Readings in Social & Political Theory)*, p. 28.

past and present."⁵³ Connecting domination strictly with the social mechanisms determined by the manufacturing of economic goods, Weber probably remains a point of reference for the exertion of socio-economic power in visible, public and conscious terms in society and less for understanding the individual principle of action, defence or counter-reaction mechanisms of the Subject while exerting domination. The role of sociology in describing this form of power also demonstrates the limits of discipline, i.e. its unidimensional, descriptive nature, without being able to understand more than a factological network of power. In fact, Max Weber states that:

> [...] the sociologist is guided exclusively by the factual existence of such a power of command, in contrast to the lawyer's interest in the theoretical content of a legal norm. As far as sociology is concerned, power of command does not exist unless the authority which is claimed by somebody is actually heeded to socially relevant degree. Yet, the sociologist will normally start from the observation that 'factual' powers of command usually claim to exist 'by virtue of law'. It is exactly for this reason that the sociologist cannot help operating with the conceptual apparatus of the law.⁵⁴

In this finding, one notices the limits of discipline and the inapplicability of sociological theories to the literary discourse, especially when such theories cannot exceed the level of descriptiveness, therefore of the factological. Opposition comes precisely from the fact that we are witnessing a clash between the factological, descriptive discourse of sociology and the evaluative and critical discourse of literature. Nevertheless, one must notice the intermediary positioning adopted again by Michel Foucault who tries to look for and describe precisely the architecture of the Subject in this relationship of forces. The Foucauldian analysis is certainly situated at the crossroads between sociology, political philosophy and literature. Hence, its speculative nature. In a study entitled *Disciplinary Power and Subjection*,⁵⁵ Foucault admits, contradicting the unidimensional perspective in Hobbes'*Leviathan*, that:

> [...] rather than ask ourselves how the sovereign appears to us in his lofty isolation, we should try to discover how it is that subjects are gradually, progressively, really and materially constituted through a multiplicity of organisms, forces, energies, materials, desire, thoughts etc. [...] Well, rather than worry about the problem of the central spirit, I believe that we must attempt to study the myriad of bodies which are constituted as peripheral subjects as a result of the effects of power.⁵⁶

---

53 Weber. In: Lukes (ed.): *Power (Readings in Social & Political Theory)*, p. 28.
54 See Weber. In: Lukes (ed.): *Power (Readings in Social & Political Theory)*, p. 35.
55 See Foucault. In: Lukes (ed.): *Power (Readings in Social & Political Theory)*, p. 229–242.
56 See Foucault. In: Lukes (ed.): *Power (Readings in Social & Political Theory)*, p. 233.

What Foucault brings to the discussion on the concept of power is the fact that he tries to question the role of the Subject and the effects of power on the subjects, in the sense of marginalizing one or the other. Thrown away to the outskirts, the Subject is the primordial interest of literature as a secondary discourse, in Nemoianu's view. The novel discovers the Subject isolated by the ignorance of the others, hidden behind complexes discovered and exploited by psychoanalysis at the beginning of the 20th century and pulverized to disappearance. The effort to recover and recompose the Subject has often been the stake of the modern novel, from Kafka to Proust, Woolf, to contemporary prose writers, such as Philip Roth or Salman Rushdie. However, this reclusion, alienation and insulation is rendered magisterially through the character of Grigor Samsa, from the Kafkian *Metamorphosis* which, when transformed "into a frightening bug" and anticipating the consequences, asks himself: "How about if I sleep a little bit longer and forget all this nonsense?"[57] and this flight is precisely the encounter between the Subject and the world and the marginalization by the power of the majority.

1.2 The Literature and its Battles on the Field of Power

1.2.1 The Canon Battlefield

The indirect debates on the implications of power within the 'literary field', if we are to take over Pierre Bourdieu's[58] consecrated formula, were centred on the problematic of standardizing the literary canon.[59] From establishing the 'mandatory canonical lists', to the obsession with literary hierarchies, the stake of the canonical 'battle' was to free literature from the authorial pressure of the dogmatic criticism imposed by the legitimised iconic figures of the literary history.

The literary canon was defined as a set of general standards, rules, originating from the field of power, which suggested a distinction between value and non-value, by defining a corpus of representative and dominant literary texts that have marked the history of literature and which deserve to be remembered as

---

57 Franz Kafka: *Metamorphosis*. Translated by David Wyllie. Release Date: August 16, 2005 [EBook #5200]. Consulted at the web adress: http://www.gutenberg.org/ebooks/5200 [26.04.2018].
58 See Bourdieu: *The Rules of Art*.
59 A partial argumentation regarding the theoretical debate on the canon and its variations within the Romanian territory can be found in Florin Oprescu: Literatură și canon istoric (Literature and historical canon). In: *Philologica Jassyensia*, Year VII, Issue 2 (14) 2011, p. 343–351.

being the value and hierarchical emblem of a period and of a national culture. To this end, an American critic such as John Guillory[60] resumes the 'cultural capital' concept from Pierre Bourdieu's project on the sociology of art, explaining that a literary canon is not merely a matter of representativeness of a social group, but also a process of preservation of the 'cultural capital' and an exercise of 'literacy' in school. This could confer students the power "to realise their own interests within an alien and manipulative social order."[61] Continuing the same theory of Bourdieu, he admits that the distribution of the cultural capital follows a pattern or a structure of social relationships.[62] The American critic uses a 'political' argument when revising the canon, i.e. "the argument that the works thus revalued are important and valuable cultural works".[63] The debate on the necessity or uselessness of a literary canon starts from the necessity to overthrow and redefine values according to their own criteria of value, of denying tradition, of redefining the present from the perspective of novelty, i.e. precisely what Nemoianu said would represent the secondary category of literature, as compared to its historical primordiality.

Recurrent in the field of religious ethics,[64] the term 'canon' applied to literature, has thus meant an 'officialising' of a uniform literary corpus, starting from the aesthetic evaluation of literature, 'strong thought'[65] of a modern type, applied to literature, meant to radically separate literary texts by means of an aesthetic discernment. In fact, if we are to remain within the field of Gianni Vattimo's dichotomies, we should admit that the 'canonical battle' was born as a result of a 'weak' disguised 'revolution' suggested by postmodern reasoning. In other words, modern 'strong thought' is the one that has configured the canonical chain in what regards the aesthetic evaluation, while postmodern 'weak thought' (*pensiero debole*) has tried to dislodge the too blunt and univocal view on literature. The modern dwarfs standing on the shoulders of the ancient giants, in a peculiar historical circularity, have proven to be postmodern in the century of the modern. As a matter of fact, even Harold Bloom, the unconditional defender of

---

60 See John Guillory: *Cultural Capital. The Problem of Literary Canon Formation*. Chicago: The University of Chicago Press 1993.
61 Charles Altieri: *Canons and Consequences: Reflections on the Ethical Force of Imaginative Ideals*. Evanston: Northwestern University Press 1990, p. 4.
62 Guillory: *Cultural Capital*, p. 6.
63 Guillory: *Cultural Capital*, p. XIV.
64 See the expression of 'religious canon' originating from the canonical understanding of the ecclesiastic rule. As a matter of fact, the main difference between the two types of 'canons' would be that the religious one postulates a 'closure', while the literary canon is permissive in what regards its rereading and reinterpretation.
65 See Vattimo: *The End of Modernity*.

the 'autonomy of aestheticism', therefore of the literary canon in its 'strong', powerful variant, both in his 1973 book, *The Anxiety of Influence. A Theory of Poetry*[66] but especially in his famous and explicit essay, *The Western Canon. The Books and School of the Ages*,[67] seems to also originate from the ideological revolutionary context of 1968, be it French or American.

Mircea Martin, in the foreword to the second Romanian edition of *The Western Canon*,[68] admits that a correct understanding of the context that prepared and made this book possible would entail a turn of view to the '60s–'70s, "when authors like Foucault or Derrida translated the objective animus of the objective Parisian youth as a new historical and literary epistemology. The oppressive nature of any scientific and cultural authority and the discriminating prejudices of the current intellectual activity were being passionately and brilliantly underlined."[69] This context has allowed for the unconstrained development, especially within the young generations in the Anglo-Saxon territory, of new revolutionary ideologies such as deconstructivism, feminism, Marxism, multiculturalism, postcolonialism etc. It gradually led to a genuine confrontation of ideologies between the defenders of a literary value stability and the leftist neo-historicists who understood canon as an echo of a debilitated, revolute thinking. The difference between the canonical-radical right which tries to preserve literature in favour of the specialists and the Marxist left that aims to liberalize literature is similar to the one between the 'nothing goes' vs. 'anything goes' type of 'trenchant' discourses.

Harold Bloom's *Elegy for the canon*, in spite of managing to polarise even more acutely the sides involved in the battle for the canon, has at least succeeded in stabilising the 'traditionalist' position of the historicist-aesthetic evaluation of the literary phenomenon. Bloom's radicality and intransigency, visible in his selection of genetic poles of the Western canon, together with the provisionality of his 'Appendix', starts from a romantic nostalgia of selection and from a stable ideology of the literary field. Placing Shakespeare at the 'centre of the canon' and continuing with Dante, Chaucer, Cervantes, Montaigne, Moliere, Milton, Goethe, Wordsworth, Austen, Whitman, Dickinson, Dickens, Eliot, Tolstoy, Ibsen, Freud, Proust, Joyce, Woolf, Kafka, Borges, Neruda, Pessoa, Beckett, the American critic

---

66 Harold Bloom: *The Anxiety of Influence. A Theory of Poetry*. Second Edition. New York and Oxford: Oxford University Press 1997.
67 Harold Bloom: *The Western Canon*.
68 Mircea Martin. In: Harold Bloom: *Canonul occidental: cărțile și școala epocilor*. Ediția a 2-a. Translated by Delia Ungureanu, Preface by Mircea Martin. București: Art 2007.
69 Martin. In: Harold Bloom: *Canonul occidental*, p. 5.

1.2 The Literature and its Battles on the Field of Power — 29

from Yale only operates with an exclusivist, individualist selection of major canonical points of reference. Bloom's immovable principle is that:

> [...] ideology plays a considerable role in literary canon-formation if you want to insist that aesthetic stance is itself an ideology, an insistence that is common to all six branches of the School of Resentment: Feminists, Marxists, Lacanians, New Historicists, Deconstructionists, Semioticians.[70]

Nevertheless, in spite of a significant difference between Bloom's closed list, substantiated by the principles of aesthetic validation and the infinitely open list of this 'School of Resentment', we invariably notice the same ontological tendency of an anthropological nature to standardize, even if from the perspective of dynamiting the norms. "When the School of Resentment, Bloom wonders ironically, becomes as dominant among historians and critics as it is among literary academics, will Matisse go unattended while we all flock to view the daubings of the Guerrilla Girls?"[71] But the standardizing obsession, if we were to comparatively observe the evolution of canonical classifications, we would find out that the difference between the West and Romania is eloquent in what regards the ampleness of the debate and of the structuring of the discourses.

Therefore, in 1998, the list required by *Modern Library* from the Anglo-Saxon literate 'specialists' contains neither more nor less than 100 books of English, while within the Romanian territory *Academia Cațavencu* has asked the current cultural public figures for a top ten of their personal saving options on the eternal and illusive deserted island. The harsh debate brought about by the Anglo-Saxon list has started from the acknowledgement that there are obvious shortcomings generated by the excessive subjectivity of selections and by discrimination based on class, gender, ethnicity etc. The conclusive finding was that "Eurocentrism has prevailed over ethnocentrism in terms of the literary norm."[72] But in this analysis, it was not the contextual point of reference that prevailed, but a certain value analysis of an aesthetic nature, which created indeed a certain separation generated by the analytical criteria of the 'primacy of the text'.

However, the Romanian ranking had a personal value to begin with, the subjective criteria being implicit, so that the selection of the public figures questioned was, naturally, more eloquent about the selector than the selected authors and texts, due to the specificity of the inquire. One of the most insightful analyses

---

[70] Bloom: *The Western Canon*, p. 527.
[71] Bloom: *The Western Canon*, p. 527.
[72] Cosana Nicolae: *Canon, canonic. Mutații valorice în literatura americană contemporană* (Canon, Canonical. Value Mutations in the Contemporary American Literature). București: Univers enciclopedic 2006, p. 6–7.

of the cleavages of the debate within the American territory belongs to Cosana Nicolae, who, in the volume entitled *Canon, canonic. Mutații valorice în literatura americană contemporană* (Canon, Canonical. Value Mutation in the Contemporary American Literature), rightfully admits that:

> [...] the left wing is made up of the Marxist relativists who undermine the ideals of the American nation through their lack of value discrimination, and the right wing seems to be made up from patriarchal capitalists who want to maintain their status by keeping literature outside the social space and outside certain canonical parameters set according to *universalistic* judgments.[73]

As a matter of fact, in what regards the observation of the evolution of the canonical or anti-canonical approaches to literature, Cosana Nicolae offers for the first time a careful and scholar synthesis of the American phenomenon. She ascertains a classicised symptom of the literary debate overseas, leaving open the public debate on the relativization of the conflict within the European territory and of the de facto inexistence of a Romanian debate. Cosana Nicolae's observation regarding the liberalisation of the American literary field is conclusive: "The public controversies in what regards the canon of the American literature have currently crossed the climax, and the literary field has fitted in writings of women, American minorities, non-Europeans or representatives of sexual minorities.[74] We are, therefore, witnessing a mutation of the literary judgment from the aesthetic to politics and identity, therefore a change in the private nature (private and rationalistic) of the literary analysis, towards contextualisation, i.e. towards the communitarian-public space. The individualistic and subjective policy of the 'powerful' aesthetic modernity has been replaced by the policy of the 'weak' diversity.

On the other hand, starting from Cosana Nicolae's analysis, which successfully observed the canonical 'contradictions' within the American territory, we can only ascertain the absence of active debates with significant results in what regards the (in)stability of the Romanian literary canon. We can nevertheless identify moments that have generated a significant jamming of the distinct understanding of value resettlement following the political change in 1989. Beyond the infertile[75] positions of the debate launched by the *Dilema* magazine

---

[73] Nicolae: *Canon, canonic*, p. 100.
[74] Nicolae: *Canon, canonic*, p. 248.
[75] The inefficiency of the debate is clear from the fact that the weapons of the game have not been dictated by analytical reasoning based on stable revisionist ideologies, with efficient results that would bring about valid distinctions in what regards the (in)validity of the Eminescian canon, but rather as we often see in the background of the Romanian society, only *resentful* and humourful tendencies against the Eminescian 'traditionalist'.

(issue 265/1998) regarding the 'Eminescian canon', preceded by issue 245/1997 that heralded the 'canonical battle', by the special edition of the *Euresis* magazine (1997–1998), by the eclectic volume coordinated by Marin Mincu, entitled *Canon și canonizare* (Canon and Canonization)[76] or by authors who in their essays resume the idea of the debate on the Romanian literary canon,[77] the Romanian 'canonical battle' has not had any noticeable results that would demonstrate the liberalisation of the literary discourse. We cannot state with precision a distinct moment in the post-Decembrist canonical 'revolution', for the education reform has been and still is slow in occurring, and since we cannot speak of a unitary existence of a coherent movement of affirmation of certain ideologies such as the American anticanonical ones: Feminists, Marxists, Lacanians, Neohistoricists, Deconstructivists, Semioticians. The ideological void of Romanian poststructuralism comes from the non-existence of a coherent critical discourse of the paternalist 'Eurocentrism' of the Romanian culture, permanently located within the area of influence of the great empires, in distinct waves: Byzantine, Turkish, Russian, German, French and American. The 1848 revolution, the 'Junimist' canonical model imposed by Titu Maiorescu, the post-war 'Lovinescian' modernism or the 'Călinescian' literary historism, but also the aggressive instauration of the radical protochronist 'canon' after World War II only prove the cultural dependence on exterior paternalistic models. The relative ideological meltdown of the '60s generation, culminating with the illusion of the undermining of the Russian communist ideological canon with Nicolae Ceușescu speech in 1968, generated by the invasion of Czechoslovakia by the Soviet troops, the weak postmodern convulsions of the '80s generation and especially the illusive democratisation of the free debate as a result of the changes after 1989, were not the premises for the objective debate and for a valid canonical re-evaluation, as seen from the analysis of the precarious status of the Romanian society and implicitly of literature.

The distinct moments of the theoretical debate of the 'canonical battle' within the Romanian 'post-Decembrist' territory are dominated, as I said, by a chronic eclecticism that has translated an eternal impossibility to methodically and ideologically deconstruct from within the subject. Critical revisionism has meant the re-reading of the 'classics', the canonical re-reading using the same instruments. Paradoxically, the most prolific critical re-evaluation throughout the literary history has been again that of Eminescu's, who has generated genuine canonical

---

76 Marin Mincu (ed.): *Canon și canonizare* (Canon and Canonization). Constanța: Pontica 2003.
77 See for example Sorin Alexandrescu: *Privind înapoi, modernitatea* (Looking back at Modernity). București: Univers 1999 and Virgil Nemoianu: *Tradiție și libertate* (Tradition and freedom). București: Curtea-Veche 2001.

revisions, from the renewing critique of Titu Maiorescu, to the rhetorical challenge of Alexandru Macedonski, from the thematic and historiographical exploitation of George Călinescu, to Ion Negoițescu or Ioana Em. Petrescu's critique of a phenomenological ancestry, to list just a few of the most important axiological evaluations of the *professional* Eminescian aesthetic canonical critique, if we were to recover Adrian Marino's classification. Without having anything to say regarding the process of Eminescian updating, the supporters of 'anticanonization', due to a lack of analytic instruments, could only criticize the festive dogmatisation and to stigmatise the 'Eminescian' canon in terms of an excessive accumulation related to the *historical* nature of the canon, if we were to maintain Marino's taxonomy.

> Beyond the awareness of its marginality and its *complexes*, the Romanian literature seems to be a framework propitious for decanonisations and recanonisations. In Romania, at the end of the '90s, people were talking about a *case* for Eminescu, a game of pros and cons of receiving the *national poet* that displays at least the fatigue of the exclusively encomiastic approach to this author, upon which the dominant discourse of each era built, for various reasons, motivations for the coherence of our national spirit.[78]

Therefore, we speak of an Eminescu of the national Junimist reanimation, of failed symbolist ideals, of Călinescu's discourse on identity, of repeated and nationalistic proletarian seizures, when the poet became the image of ultimate nationalism. To all this one added the image of the minor Romanticism prompted by the school during the Communist period, through its curricula and manuals loaded with poems selected ideologically or from within the field of adolescent grandiloquence.[79] This reading proves precisely the historical destiny within the public space of the approach to the stages of reception of the 'Eminescian' canon.[80] For certain, in this regard, we can notice 'an Eminescu' of Titu Maiorescu, another one of George Călinescu, a different one belonging to the reclaims of the '60s generation, 'an Eminescu' of the Communist national ideal and definitely an Eminescu of transition and 'post-Decembrist' relativisations.

Adrian Marino, one of the most competent voices of the 'idea of literature' within the Romanian cultural space during the last half a millennium, admits in 1997, in his *Biografia ideii de literatură* (The Biography of the Idea of Literature), that:

---

[78] Nicolae: *Canon, canonic*, p. 16.
[79] For example, the textbook of *Limba și literatura română* (Romanian Language and Literature), 9th grade, A. Gh. Olteanu, Maria Pavnotescu, București: Editura Didactică și Pedagogică, 1984, contains texts such as: *Împărat și proletar* (King and Proletarian), *Scrisoarea I*, (Letter I), *Floare albastră*, (Blue Flower), *Sara pe deal* (An Eve on the Hill) and *Luceafărul* (The Morning Star).
[80] In this direction, we can also see Iulian Costache's study, entitled *Eminescu. Negocierea unei imagini-construcția unui canon, emergența unui mit* (Eminescu. Negotiating an Image-the construction of a canon, the emergence of a myth). București: Cartea Românească 2008.

Strictly preferential lists belong to a closed, normative, restrictive and officialised ideological system, through the authoritarian enforcement by the religious, didactic or academic institution of each era. The *official canon* and *culture* become essentially synonymous. Through the books proclaimed as *canonical*, a community defines its spiritual image and respectively its system of spiritual values.[81]

Marino is also the first Romanian theoretician attempting to classify the canonical typologies, thus trying to clarify the variables of this taxonomic category. An image of the spiritual values of a society, the canon can be analysed according to at least four large distinct categories:

a. *professional*-of research, education or general cultural;
b. *ideological*-of Anglo-Saxon influence, centred on the relationship between literature and race, class and gender;
c. *geographical*-Western, Eastern, Asian etc.;
d. *historical*-those standardised throughout time "by means of successive accumulation and historical verification", these being imposed by the *institutions of the literary canon* (school, through curricula and textbooks, specialized literary criticism, but also due to the public impact).

In this context, one of the most important manners of configuring and stabilising the Romanian spiritual image proves to be the one related to the historical category of the literary canon, meaning that it is fundamentally connected with the way in which the 'canonical authors' have been defined throughout history predominantly due to the educational system, to the "institutions of the literary canon", through curricula and textbooks.[82] John Guillory's synthesis highlights the fact that, both the formation of the canon, but especially the debate regarding the necessity of the existence of a canon are matters of power, based on contradictory ideologies. Canonical 'revision' comes "without question from the political discourse-liberal pluralism-to which we owe the most successful progressive agendas of the last three decades."[83] While within the American space, the climax of the "pedagogical debate"[84] was reached through discussions regarding the "composition of the course on Western culture in 1987–1988" at Stanford University and, in particular, through the curriculum for world literature, entitled *The*

---

81 Adrian Marino: *Biografia ideii de literatură* (The Biography of the Idea of Literature). Vol. IV. Cluj-Napoca: Dacia 1997, p. 225.
82 See the argument and the debate in the first chapter of John Guillory: *Cultural Capital*, entitled "Canonical and Noncanonical: The Current Debate".
83 Guillory: *Cultural Capital*, p. 3.
84 Nicolae: *Canon, canonic*, p. 7.

Great Books, within the Romanian territory, a genuine debate on the evolution of undergraduate and graduate curricula has never taken place, which generated either a formal restructuring of the wording and apparent 'deterritorialization' of the historical corpus of the texts studied, either an acute and dramatic misappropriation of the undergraduate curriculum from literary analysis towards formal communication matters.

The only opening towards an analysis of the historical category, meaning of the role played by curricula and textbooks in the stability of the canonical memory was seen in the special edition of *Euresis* (1997–1998), which dedicated an entire chapter to such analysis, although Mircea Martin also offers a challenging perspective in his opening article entitled "Du canon à une époque post-canonique".[85] He ascertains, using solid arguments, that accepting a new work within the curricular canon is so difficult precisely because there are two different 'canonical practices', sometimes convergent, but never concurrent. We speak here of the 'aesthetic and/or critical canon' and the 'curriculary literary canon'. In the end, this debate on the 'lists of canonical authors' has amplified the discrepancy between the aesthetic practice of literature and the curricular one, becoming an ideological and political, editorial etc. debate with major implications. Virgil Nemoianu discusses the formula for achieving *success with the public* in the volume edited together with Robert Royal, entitled *The Hospitable Canon. Essays on Literary Play, Scholarly Choice and Popular Pressure*,[86] the critic resuming the anticanonical hypothesis of literature seen in terms of receiving and building a public memory that imposes the 'bestseller' and implicitly the canon. Nemoianu also establishes the criteria for the anticanonical discourse:

a. the lack of axiological literary value;
b. the intelligentsia's duty to analyse the present and deconstruct the past;
c. traditional anti-elitist;
d. freedom from the domination of masculinity;
e. the expansion of popular culture and the cancellation of intransigent borders between 'low' and 'high' in what regards art;
f. the denunciation of the exclusivity of the Western masculine and 'white' canon, in favour of globalization and diversity.

The theories regarding the diversification of the canon or even the dynamitation of the historical canon, by diluting the criteria for its standardization are

---

[85] Mircea Martin: Du canon à une époque post-canonique. In: *Euresis*, issue 1997–1998, București: Univers, p. 3–25.
[86] Nemoianu; Royal (ed.): *The Hospitable Canon*.

resumed in the volume entitled *Tradiție și libertate* (Tradition and freedom), since this refractory attitude against the *canonical tradition* seems to have been born from the desire to denounce 'Eurocentrism' and even 'textocentrism', in favour of the 'multiculturalist' discourse, that is in favour of pushing the literary discourse towards the social and political area. Thus, a formula such as "Culture is our business *and* business is our culture"[87] legitimates the expansion of culture in general and implicitly of literature within the overly generous context of the public, social, political and even economic space, because the public success of literature seems more than ever umbilically tied to the economic mechanism of production, promotion and editorial marketing.

Sorin Alexandrescu, one of the first objectors to the Romanian 'aesthetic canon' during the post-Decembrist period, trenchantly suggested "a speedier end to the aesthetic canon",[88] although he admits the beneficial existence of the 'canonizing' critical instances throughout the history of modern Romanian literature. Speaking of the four critical points of reference of the canonical formation, Titu Maiorescu, George Călinescu, Eugen Lovinescu and Nicolae Manolescu, the essayist confirms that:

> The formation of the canon or that of the self-awareness of modernity is due to them, in terms of the following great dimensions: the autonomy of the aesthetic from the political and the ethical ones, a definitive scale of literary values, aesthetic points of reference (particularly French), centre/periphery hierarchy, historical series, recurrent themes, national homogeneity, literary strategies in relation to power, be it democratic or totalitarian and especially the models for textual interpretation.[89]

Although the voices advocating the abandoning of the 'supremacy of the aesthetic canon' have been numerous in our case since 1989, justifying its historical necessity before the year in question and its usefulness and caducity after it, we are forced to ascertain that, looking around us and observing the latent modernization of Romania and even the mental traditionalism of our society, the *end of the aesthetic canon* cannot occur. In fact, those advocating the negation of 'aesthetocentrism' within the Romanian territory fail to speak of another form or formula for validating *literarity* within the public space, and only ascertain the incumbency to renounce the canonical form of "aesthetic conservatism",[90] and only ascertain deconstruction. Moreover, in the Romanian public space there

---

[87] Robert E. Babe: *Cultural Studies and Political Economy: Toward a New Integration*. Toronto: Lexington Books 2009, p. 4.
[88] Alexandrescu: *Privind înapoi, modernitatea*, p. 149–154.
[89] Alexandrescu: *Privind înapoi, modernitatea*, p. 150.
[90] Alexandrescu: *Privind înapoi, modernitatea*, p. 154.

is no 'multiculturalist' *tradition*, since it lacks a feminist, neo-historist, Marxist, gender or ethno-egalitarian discourse, therefore lacking the other counterweight of the balance to grant us the middle vision. The *weak* ethical and aesthetic voice of the 'postmodern' Romanian society is rather traditionalist, generated by the historical inertia, possibly explainable, a recurrence of our *media res*, our recent totalitarian past. The school, the representative cultural institutions, but also the political and administrative ones assigned for promoting culture, the cultural printed media, the book production and promotion systems, the visible cultural public figures are only, most of them nevertheless, subservient to a dominating mindset. The reformation of the Romanian society is reflected invariably in the reformation of culture, literature, education etc.

With good reason, Harold Bloom's *list* is maybe overly *canonical* or we could say that, in turn, he is a different sort of 'resentful' due to an overly intransigent method of aesthetic dissection, but the aesthetic function of literature is a *sine qua non* condition of its *literarity*. However, expanding the literary boundaries is compulsory and this is not necessarily performed by replacing a canon with another of class, race, gender or national, but by encouraging the revision of literary history according to its specific contexts as well, but especially through a methodological foundation of the discourse on literature. Only by doing so can we understand that we must discuss a text such as Ion Budai-Deleanu's *Țiganiada* from an aesthetic point of view, speaking also of the national majority-minority relationship and of the necessity to change the permanent need of the heroic-national assumption of our historical destiny, or that we must analyse without any interdiction the context of political engagement through several texts of a poet such as Nichita Stănescu, however, without overlooking and even forgetting to counterbalance it by arguing that, from an aesthetic point of view, the poet of the *11 Elegii* (11 Elegies) risks being ignored because we take the ideological 'play' of the poet in the '60s too seriously.

In the conclusions to her essay, *Canon, canonic* (Canon, Canonical), Cosana Nicolae starts from Gilles Deleuze and Felix Guattari's taxonomy in *Capitalism and Schizophrenia*[91] that is the *territorialisation*[92] and *deterritorialization*.[93] The borders of the Anglo-Saxon canon, constantly undergoing renegotiation, have stopped Eurocentrism from being a reality of literature during the second half of the 20th century.

---

91 Gilles Deleuze; Felix Guattari: *Anti-Oedipus. Capitalism and Schizophrenia*. Translated from the French by Robert Hurley, Mark Seem, and Helen R. Lane. Preface by Michel Foucault. Minneapolis: University of Minnesota Press 1983.
92 Seen as a solidification of identity, a stratifying gesture within a territorial framework.
93 As a movement of identity change targeting power, with the purpose to elude the games of power.

To open the canon is to renounce the exclusivist policies and to expose the exceptional, Adamic myth of the American. The consequences of this transformation were felt the strongest within universities, where the battle against any exclusivist borders between male and female, high and popular, Western or non-Western, Northern or Southern was legitimated.[94]

We are therefore witnessing the context of the 1980s that was heading for a change in the direction of the aesthetic evaluation of literature towards the political and identity one. The effects of such a paradigm shift are to be observed. But what goes on in the Romanian territory? Starting with the first forms of *literarity*, the founders of the literary canon found themselves compelled to defend literature from history's aggressions. Ever since the birth of the first forms of the literary discourse, our canonical authors have found themselves in the paradoxical situation of creating in a 'moving and unsettled country', within a continuous identity crisis at the interference of influences, too many times undigested. Thus, the canonical standardization of the important critics over the last 150 years have also been identity shields against the aggression of history and the political seizures, as Sorin Alexandrescu rightly noticed in favour of the necessity of the canonical debate: Maiorescu-promoter of the autonomy of the aesthetic to the detriment of the political and of demagogy, Lovinescu-reactionary against two traditional, conservative literary schools of Russian influence ('Poporanismul' and 'Sămănătorismul') and Călinescu-open-minded and rejecting nationalism and anti-Semitism during the Antonescian period.

Consequently, the analysis of the manners of configuring the literary canon reveals the necessity of debating over its situation within the Romanian territory, precisely in order to objectively analyse its identification criteria, not necessarily of its deterritorialisation, but of a global re-analysis of the texts representative to our cultural identity and not that of the 'canonical authors', too many times exhausted by the nostalgic power of the postmodern dwarves on their shoulders.

1.2.2 The Novel Battlefield

"Novels, novels, it's time for novels..."[95]

In a text from 1890, entitled "De ce nu avem roman" (Why we don't have a novel), Nicolae Iorga connected the absence of the novelistic genre in our case to general causes of a social nature that determine primarily an ill-suited condition for the

---

94 Nicolae: *Canon, canonic*, p. 249.
95 Cicerone Teodorescu. In: Aurel Sasu and Mariana Vartic (ed.): *Bătălia pentru roman* (The battle for the novel). București: Atos 1997, p. 163.

"life of the artist in our case." He admits that the existence of the novel would have required "a highly modern social category, people of literature as a profession",[96] assertion apparently surprising for the future ideologist of the Romanian 'Sămănătorism'. This professional determinism entails, from the author's perspective, a direct connection between the modern profession of the novelist and thus the significantly long period of time allotted to the occupation of 'novelist', time required by this genre.

If initially it was tempting to believe that, as a continuation of the Maiorescian ideas, the theoretician understands the relation between social modernity (as modernization), mentalities and aesthetic modernity, it can now be seen that he refers to a certain favourable social framework. In fact, the preoccupation with literary social determinism, that is the connection with the social environment would culminate in Iorga's case with the takeover in 1903 of the control over the *Sămănătorul* magazine (1901–1910), and him being the main person responsible for the anti-Junimist ideology of the magazine, for the conservatism, the idyllic turn-over, and, in general, the rejection of literary 'modernisms', in favour of traditionalism.

However, this is not to say that the beginning of the 20th century was not relevant to the debate regarding 'social frameworks' of the Romanian novel and Emanoil Bucuța's assertion remains definitive. In an article in 1933, published in *România literară*, he estimated that over the precious fifteen years, Romanian literature had evolved "under the sign of the novel", and the eye of a careful beholder could ascertain that the explosion of the genre during the interwar period was as if "the Romanians had gone to war as lyricists and came out of it as epicists."[97] At the same time, Garabet Ibrăileanu supported the birth of the "big, social, complicated" novel[98]; Pompiliu Constantinescu admitted that the "Romanian novel is, par excellence, social"[99]; Dan Petrașincu spoke, in 1934, of the "trend of the social novel."[100] On the contrary, Mircea Eliade, among the first writers to speak within the Romanian territory of Proust, Svevo, Joyce or Woolf, recommended, again in 1934, the reinvention of the novelistic character in favour of a new type of realism, for the reality of the modern, he says, "is its abstractness, its polymorphy and amorphy",[101] recommending that the novelists about

---

96 See Nicolae Iorga. In: Sasu and Vartic (ed.): *Bătălia pentru roman*, p. 27.
97 See Sasu and Vartic (ed.): *Bătălia pentru roman*, p. 152.
98 Garabet Ibrăileanu: *Campanii*, (Campaigns). București: Minerva 1971, p. 206.
99 Pompiliu Constantinescu: *Conceptul de realism în literatura română* (The Concept of Realism in Romanian Literature). București: Eminescu 1974, p. 183.
100 Dan Petrașincu. In: Sasu and Vartic (ed.): *Bătălia pentru roman*, p. 166.
101 Mircea Eliade. In: Sasu and Vartic (ed.): *Bătălia pentru roman*, p. 177.

to forget about Stendhal and Proust. Others, such as I. Valerian or Cezar Petrescu mourned the lack of readers, which exposed the Romanian novel, be it social or subjective, to extinction.

Admitting the novelty of this epic genre, especially in the Romanian literature, Cezar Petrescu[102] claimed in 1923 an incompatibility between the 'modern' Romanian writer and society. Starting from Paul Bourget's theses in *Réflexions sur l'art du roman*, and implicitly from his conflict with Albert Thibaudet, which also demonstrates that the Romanian debate regarding the novel is imported, Cezar Petrescu speaks of the novel of manners and the necessity of the novel of character. This can be achieved by the direct connection between the writer and the social environment and by a thorough analysis of the psychological effects on the typical characters, which allows him to believe the thesis novel rather in than in the novel of manners, as with Bourget whose explanation included verbs such as 'inquiring' and 'painting' reality in detail. Although Bourget rejected the label of naturalism, it is indeed a form of naturalism which, as Ion Negoițescu claimed in his unfinished and too little known and appreciated *Istoria literaturii române* (History of Romanian Literature), dominates the Romanian novel at the beginning of the past century.

Starting from these observations, Cezar Petrescu would also support an incompatibility between the artist and the modern society:

> The Romanian writer has been especially separated from society. He has been uprooted. Most of the times the son of a peasant or of a little provincial bourgeois, leaving behind the environment of his first youth, he was left outside of the social establishments. He lived in a special world. The coffee-shop or the literary or the literary circles have more than once isolated him from life. He looked at society from the outside, as a man glimpsing at life's gesticulation through a window, without entering the intimate and spiritual mechanism of an inner side. Without being a direct partaker to the problems of a certain class of society. Without being a partaker of the spasms of ascension of individualities struggling to climb, through what was once called a phenomenon of social capillarity, as high as possible from one class to another, the writer was not attracted by the problems of the society outside of which he lived, because he did not know them profoundly, and did not have where to know them either.[103]

Cezar Petrescu's assertion is relevant, but not for explaining the absence of the genre in our case, but rather for the lack of understanding modernity at the beginning of the 20th century and for the break between the traditionalist spirit and the aesthetic modernity. Like Nicolae Iorga, Cezar Petrescu draws the distinctive lines of the modern artist, but understands his being in anacrony with the times. The relevance of the fragment is that the description of the physiognomy of

---

102 Cezar Petrescu. In: Sasu and Vartic (ed.): *Bătălia pentru roman*, p. 51.
103 Cezar Petrescu. In: Sasu and Vartic (ed.): *Bătălia pentru roman*, p. 51.

modernity as introspective, aggressed and uninterested in the social landscape and its mechanisms is accurate, but the presumption of its non-contemporaneousness or inefficacity is false. This leads to an opposition to the principles of the Maiorescian 'autonomy of the aesthetic' and two interdependent conditions that made the battle for the novel so fiery within the Romanian territory at the beginning of the last century:

a. the break between traditionalists, conservatives who saw the novel as a determination of the social environment, and the modernists who understood the autonomy of the genre and the modern spirit through its isolation from the social and its exploration of the subjective chiaroscuro;
b. a kind of incompatibility or a loss of synchronism between social modernity and aesthetic modernity, that is between the traditionalist mentality within the Romanian territory and the modern spirit, a fact recurrent during the last century, which also generated the recurrence of a type of realism.

When a critic spirit as subtle as Perpessicius becomes exasperated by the redundancy of the debate over the novel, in an article published in 1925, entitled "Înflorirea romanului" (The Blossom of the Novel),[104] he only issues a warning that more important than the sterile theoretical battle between traditionalists and modernists is the emergence of certain new novels in Romanian literature and, implicitly, their maturing and *synchronization*. Even if he concludes that "[...] not even today are we spared the lament prior to the war that we have no novel. In our literary life, the novel has always been a nightmare, or better said, the uncle from America everyone speaks of, waits for and who must never come."[105] In this context, he speaks of the new novels of observation and analysis, such as, *Pădurea spânzuraților* (The Forest of the Hanged) and *Adam și Eva* (Adam and Eve) of Liviu Rebreanu, or *Venea o moară pe Siret* (A Mill Came Down the Siret River) by Mihail Sadoveanu or *Domnișoara din strada Neptun* (The Damsel on Neptun Street) by Felix Aderca.

It is therefore apparent that prior to World War I the Romanian novel was poorly featured, both numerically and qualitatively, by *Ciocoii vechi și noi* (The Old and New Parvenus) (1863) by Nicolae Filimon, *Viața la țară* (Life in the Countryside) (1894) by Duiliu Zamfirescu, *Dan* (1894) by Alexandru Vlahuță, *Mara* (1906) by Ioan Slavici, the historical novels of Mihail Sadoveanu, *Bordeeni* (1912) and *Neamul Șoimăreștilor* (The Șoimărești Kin) (1915), or, in Anton Cosma's view, at least in the preparation of the novelistic genre,[106] a travel journey such

---

104 Perpessicius: *Opere* (Works) II. București: Editura pentru Literatură 1967, p. 26–29.
105 Perpessicius: *Opere* (Works) II, p. 26.
106 Anton Cosma: *Geneza romanului românesc* (The Genesis of the Romanian Novel). București: Editura Eminescu 1985, p. 81.

as *Peregrinul transilvan* (The Transylvanian Pilgrim) (1863–1864), by Ion Codru Drăgușanu. A critic such as Mihail Ralea dedicated an ample study on the causes of the inefficacity of the genre within the Romanian territory, starting from the debate and the question "Why do we not have a novel?",[107] published in *Flacăra* magazine, in 1927. Referring to the method established by Ferdinand Brunetière in *L'évolution des genres*, Mihai Ralea adopts the strategy of evolutionism and literary transformations of the genres according to the historical parameters of a given moment, such as "the type of psychology of a certain moment in time, its ethnic nature, its social structure."[108]

This transformationalist thesis is based on the idea of tradition, i.e. of 'a' tradition in the history of the genre, not necessarily novelistic, but epic, such as 'epopeea', i.e. of an epic practice. Ralea ascertains that in our literature, the epic genre was practised until lately rather through the epic poem, such as *Toma Alimoș, Mihu Copilul, Miorița* (The Ewe) or *Dumbrava Roșie* (The Red Grove), while in other literatures with a novelistic tradition, the epic was gradually replaced concomitantly with the formation of a new taste for literature, i.e. the birth of a new type of reader. 'The bourgeois public' is in Ralea's opinion responsible for this metamorphosis and for the emergence of a new sensitivity, anchored in its contemporaneity and not in a distant and idealized history. For example, when analyzing the epic poem *Dumbrava Roșie* (The Red Grove) by Vasile Alecsandri and the impact of its reading within the Maiorescian 'Junimea', as compared to the effect of the short story *Sărmanul Dionis* (Poor Dionysus), by Mihai Eminescu, conservatorism and a lack of modern aesthetic taste among the readers of the circle are found.

George Panu, in *Amintiri de la Junimea din Iași* (Memories from 'Junimea' from Iași), is overly enthusiastic, suddenly taken over by a "feeling of admiration"[109] for this heroic poem, whose chapter entitled '*Țara în picioare* generated huge enthusiasm with *Junimea*',[110] reminiscent of the "classical heroic life".[111] By comparison with Alecsandri's poem, Eminescu's short story *Sărmanul Dionis* (Poor Dionysus) generates rather negative reactions, being understood by the artisans

---

107 This article of Mihail Ralea sparked the critical reaction of Camil Petrescu who in 1927 published in *Viața literară* an article in which he acidly responded to the hypotheses listed by Ralea; another reaction belongs to Eugeniu Sperantia who, in turn, attempted to debunk Ralea's principles in an article published also in 1927, in the *Cele trei Crișuri* magazine. See the articles in the anthology published by Sasu and Vartic (ed.): *Bătălia pentru roman*, p. 74–82.
108 Mihail Ralea. In: Sasu and Vartic (ed.): *Bătălia pentru roman*, p. 75.
109 George Panu: *Amintiri de la Junimea din Iași* (Memories from *Junimea* in Iași). Iași: Polirom 2013, p. 91.
110 Panu: *Amintiri de la Junimea din Iași*, p. 89.
111 Panu: *Amintiri de la Junimea din Iași*, p. 90.

of the *Junimea*, except for Maiorescu, as a 'philosophical phantasmagoria',[112] being apparently 'rescued' solely by the genius of Eminescu's artistic language, therefore from an aesthetic point of view. From George Panu's comments it can be concluded that Eminescu's lack of interest in 'historical truths', in exact descriptions of settings or in the coherent epic plot displeases the listeners of the circle. "As a short story, i.e. in terms of description, details, underlining characters and vivid life, it is rather weak. It is clear from afar that Eminescu had not consumed his readings well and had failed to grant *Sărmanul Dionis* (Poor Dionysus) at least the nature of a fantastic short story."[113]

We therefore understand one of the reasons why we did not have a novel during the 19th century, the specialized reader of the epic genre having more of an anachronic taste for this genre, appreciating the dynamics, the logic and the balance of the epic plot, the grandeur of the descriptions and the representation of mundane characters, to the detriment of the renunciation regarding a referential nature, of the amalgamation of narrative plans, of the character duplication and of the definitive rejection of the nationalist-moralizing themes, specific to the modernity of the Eminescian prose. It is therefore understandable why Eminescu "seemed to be out of his element precisely at Junimea, being sorry not to have been born during the time of the old Alexander the Good."[114]

Eminescu's short story could have been, during mid-19th century, an admirable example of the changes undergone by modern prose and of the alienation of the Subject and his escape from the immediate, therefore from the rejection of the anachronisms of referential historicism, dominating over the Romanian epic genre up to the 20th century. Indeed, the Dan-Dionysus game is not related to the disguises of the fantastic prose, but to the Romantic isolation of the modern Subject and the drama of knowledge. From the point of view of modern aesthetics as well, although tributary to the Eminescian lyrical romanticism, *Sărmanul Dionis* (Poor Dionysus) represents within the pauper epic panorama of the period a spectacular evolution, with spectacular semantic misappropriations, with self-reflexive metaphors and with ample and complex phrases, attesting to the fact that aestheticism was becoming a stake in itself. But this prose only had a future, notwithstanding its anticipatory power, much later on, perhaps during the interwar period through Mircea Eliade's prose and through a critical reassessment of George Călinescu and its lack of success as seen today demonstrates the lack of modern taste precisely amidst the 'Junimea' circle as well as the recurrence of promoting an epic

---

112 Panu: *Amintiri de la Junimea din Iași*, p. 94.
113 Panu: *Amintiri de la Junimea din Iași*, p. 99.
114 Panu: *Amintiri de la Junimea din Iași*, p. 99.

conservatism. On the one hand, Ralea's critique is confirmed, for in the absence of an epic, the taste for such a genre, exhausted within other literatures, went unconsumed within the Romanian territory and was a genuine obsession during the 19th century. Together with a lack of bourgeoisie within the Romanian territory, when analysing such cases, one notices a lack of modern aesthetic taste as well.

Aside from Titu Maiorescu, a promoter of the values of the modern spirit, even the specialists in literature did not understand the need to synchronize with a certain kind of modern sensitivity, starting from the change in theme register, up to the aesthetic stake of literature. In other words, this was a crunch moment in the birth of the novel, through the formation of a public consciousness of actuality. The lack of bourgeoisie up to the end of the 19th century and the anachronism of literature creators and critics, the absence of a public due to the preponderance of the agrarian structure of the society and implicitly the overwhelming degree of illiteracy are the effects of historical processes that played a determinant role in the late emergence of literature.

Illiteracy,[115] for example, was a concrete, social reality in the Romanian countries during the 19th century and was a determinant factor in the late emergence of writing in Romanian and, implicitly, of national literature, which was observed by an ample series of researchers, from Titu Maiorescu in the 19th century, to Mihail Ralea, Sorin Alexandrescu, Nicolae Manolescu in the 20th century or Eugen Negrici in our century. The last one rightfully admits in his *Iluziile literaturii române* (The Illusions of Romanian Literature), that:

> The researchers of the first three centuries of *literature* written within the territory inhabited by Romanian overlook, embarrassed, the matter of literate people. The few squires schooled in Poland, in Italy or at Istanbul, willingly or unwillingly becoming, sometimes precisely due to their intellectual authority, political characters, have lost the chance of deepening and fully exploiting their science.[116]

This assertion is as true as it can be, but it is just as true that the primordial interest of these squires, of our first bourgeoisie, was not of a literary nature, but of a historical and political one, of settling the 'moving and unsettled' country, of unity, independence and formation of a national consciousness.

The Union of the Romanian Principalities in 1859, under the reign of Alexandru Ioan Cuza, the son of the Moldavian chief of administration, Ioan Cuza, and Sultana, coming from the Cozadiny family, who were Phanariots, is one such essential historical moment that contributed to the formation of the Romanian

---

[115] See also Sorin Alexandrescu: *Paradoxul român* (The Romanian Paradox). București: Univers 1998.
[116] Eugen Negrici: *Iluziile literaturii române*. București: Cartea Românească 2008, p. 120.

state during the 19th century. Cuza's contribution is essential for the resolution of the illiteracy problem as well, due to the reforms imposed by the government led by Mihail Kogălniceanu, such as the educational reform of 1864. Thus, primary school became obligatory and the first Romanian universities were founded in Iași (1860) and Bucharest (1864). Cuza and Kogălniceanu's contribution was thus essential in the formation of the modern state and, implicitly, in the creation of a favourable context for Romanian modernity. Their political implication was a historical necessity at the end of the 19th century.

But the fact that Romanian literature during the 19th century is the result of a number of educated and warm-hearted 'squires', eager for culture, such as the poets Văcărești, Conachi, Alecsandri, Ghica, Kogălniceanu, Negruzzi, Heliade, Asachi, Bolintineanu etc. is admitted also by the artisan of the Romanian modernism, Eugen Lovinescu.[117] In the context of the battle for the novel, Eugen Lovinescu undoubtedly plays a determining part, counterbalancing the conservative discourse of the promoters of traditionalist values. He understands, obviously following Maiorescu's ancestry, that tools were needed for the formation of the modern Romanian civilization and literature was one of them. At the same time, it is not the predominance of the reader and their education that are the objectives of Lovinescu's critical discourse, but that of the writer who will gradually shape the modern 'taste' for the novel and for literature in general. Lovinescu updates and particularizes Maiorescu's ideas precisely in *Istoria civilizației române moderne* (The History of Modern Romanian Civilization) (1924–1925) where, starting once more from sociology, that is from Gabriel Tarde's theses of the imitation of cultures, he argues that imitation has functioned as a protean mechanism within Romanian culture and has gradually moved from the forms criticized by Maiorescu to creating its own content, in fact a modernist one. It is the first time in the battle of ideas on the modernization of Romanian society that, along with the theses of renunciation of the 'harmful imitations' or authenticity of the rural idillysm, of the past-centred conservatism, imitation has been valued, by understanding the need for *synchronization* of Romanian society. One must note that Eugen Lovinescu's ideas are in accordance with the time and depth of the reforms envisaged at the dawn of the birth of the 'România dodoloață' (Bulgingly chubby Romania), as Blaga would put it in a playful way. His role in this process of synchronising literature with the spirit of the time is similar to that of those responsible for the first genuine reforms, A. I. Cuza and M. Kogălniceanu, which can be proved by his two major works, *Istoria civilizației române moderne* (The History

---

[117] Eugen Lovinescu: *Opere* (Works). București: Minerva, p. 174–182.

of the Modern Romanian Civilization) (1924–1925) and *Istoria literaturii române contemporane* (The History of Contemporary Romanian Literature) (1926–1929).

In regards to art, Lovinescu proposed the principle of 'mutation of the aesthetic values', to which he attributes a fertile role in the creation of the late Maiorescu-like 'content', which implicitly supports the idea that the 'shortcoming' of Romanian literature and implicitly the absence of the novelistic genre during the 19th century were a historical circumstantial phenomenon. In Lovinescu's opinion, the resistance to appropriations was rather damaging to the pursuit of autochthonous contents. In other words, without the practice of Romanian language, without the exercise of the complex novelistic genre, with the frustration generated by the lack of national unity including, in terms of language, constantly searching for the local, differentiating values, the Romanian writer of the 19th century failed to create authentic literature, most of the time with admirable energy, effort and will for literature. Lovinescu proposes a new optic, i.e. to exercise genres already established in the West, to promote the literature of young writers who had already studied in France or Germany, and to practice new aesthetic formulas that might contribute, and did so at that time, to forming a reader. The proof of the results brought about by these methods are the writers promoted during the *Sburătorul* literary circle, such as Camil Petrescu, Hortensia Papadat-Bengescu, Ion Barbu, Anton Holban, Gib Mihăescu, i.e. some of the canonical writers of reference for Romanian literature. Through Lovinescu, the role and utility of erudite public figures in creating an authentic kind of literature can be seen. This, therefore, brings to mind Negoițescu's assertion regarding the role of the critic in catalysing Romanian modernism and implicitly the modern Romanian novel: "Bourgeois and therefore urban, aesthete and therefore cosmopolite, Lovinescu has become the theoretician of Romanian liberalism, due to a high need to explain himself."[118]

Thus, aestheticism was becoming the defining formula for the canonical selection during the interwar period, and the critic did not hesitate to become enthusiastic, not even in 1920, when the novel *Ion* by Liviu Rebreanu came out, in which he admired the epic force, the surpassing of the descriptive frontier and the probing of human contradictions. Through aestheticism, the Romanian novel seemed to endure the conservative ideological assaults at the beginning of the century or the extremist ones during the interwar period.

Nevertheless, the case of the Romanian novel is more complex than that, this resistance manifesting itself during the period of Romanian modernity,

---

[118] Ion Negoițescu: *Istoria literaturii române* (The History of the Romanian Literature). Cluj-Napoca: Dacia 2002, p. 213.

especially during the post-communist period, as a formula of late ostentatious and neoavant-gardist riot, and the specific case refer to the '60s generation and implicitly to the prose writers of this generation, such as Ștefan Bănulescu, Nicolae Velea, Nicolae Breban, George Bălăiță, Dumitru Radu Popescu, Sorin Titel, Augustin Buzura. The history of Romanian literature is marked by genuine 'survivals' through the aesthetic[119] in front of the ideological aggressions from the 19th and the 20th century. We can identify an inverted image throughout Romanian literature: through the aesthetic, literature has endured its contact with history. The representative case in this sense is that of the Romanian novel that has evolved in a contrasting manner. On the one hand we have the direct narratives of the confrontation between the individual and history and its aggressions, and there are numerous examples here, from *Ciocoii vechi și noi* (The Old and New Parvenus) by Nicolae Filimon, to *Gorila* (The Gorilla) by Liviu Rebreanu, to *Cel mai iubit dintre pământeni* (The Most Beloved Man on Earth) by Marin Preda. This is the direct novel that reflected and marked history in people's memory. On the other hand, we identify the indirect novel, i.e. a novel that takes refuge in the aesthetic in order to overcome the blockage of history and here we can read novels such as *Craii de Curtea-Veche* (Gallants of the Old Court) by Mateiu Caragiale, *Groapa* (The Hole) by Eugen Barbu, *Zenobia* by Gellu Naum, *Cronică de familie* (A Family Chronicle) by Petru Dumitriu, *Cartea Milionarului* (The Book of the Millionaire), by Ștefan Bănulescu, up to the textualist experimentalism of the '80's prose. In regards to some of these novels, the refuge in aestheticism seems like a disguised reaction to the abuses of history, and this is what Monica Spiridon also referred to when speaking of the "subversive antitotalitarian nature"[120] of the experimental literature during the second half of the 20th century. They succeeded in avoiding the memory of the ideological pressures, by escaping history and isolating themselves in the labyrinth of imaginary levels of reality.[121]

The battles for the Romanian novel continued throughout the 20th century, not only during the interwar period. Following the dramatic purges of the 'Obsessive decade' and the victory of the proletarian novel during this period, which will be observed in a special chapter of this work, came the "era of a relative ideological meltdown" in the '60s–'70s. As previously stated, it is the time of a

---

[119] See Alexandrescu: *Privind înapoi, modernitatea* and Nicolae Manolescu: *Istoria critică a literaturii române. 5 secole de literatură* (The Critical History of the Romanian Literature. 5 Centuries of Literature). Pitești: Paralela 45 2008.
[120] Monica Spiridon, Ion Bogdan Lefter, Gheorghe Crăciun (eds.): *Experimentul literar românesc postbelic* (The Post-War Romanian Literary Experiment). Pitești: Paralela 45 1998, p. 16.
[121] Calvino: *The Uses of Literature*.

relative liberalization, and the Romanian novel seems to profit from this new historical fact. Although part of the generation of young prose writers during this period succumb to the ideological pressures[122] in order to get published, by comparison to the previous decade, thirty years later, the generation from the '60s rediscovered the interwar modernism and this latent force is be visible in novels such as *Vânătoarea regală* (The Royal Hunt) by D.R. Popescu, *Cartea Milionarului* (The Book of the Millionaire) by Ștefan Bănulescu, *În absența stăpânilor* (In the Absence of the Masters) and *Animale bolnave* (Sick Animals), by Nicolae Breban, *Absenții* (The Absentees), by Augustin Buzura etc. When discussing the '60s generation novel, Nicolae Manolescu is right to suggest a conversion of it "from the socialist realism to a so-called modernity. Writers such as Preda or Barbu, subservient to the backward formula of literature from the previous decade, become the pioneers of the new novel, especially in terms of the theme."[123] Is this a victory of the 'doric' novel,[124] if we are to abide by the classification of Nicolae Manolescu?

For certain, following a period in which the novel had been sacrificed and defeated by the Marxist-Leninist ideology of the '50s, it succeeded in imposing itself, both within poetry, as well as history, through specific strategies, aestheticism being one of them. The young prose writers would overcome the complex of marginality and would live, at least for a period of time, with the conviction that the novel can explain and rebalance the world after the flood, precisely because through the novel the effects of the excess of power, the animalic irrationalism of extremisms are visible and denounced, and this is a 'therapeutic' prose formula. This is probably the most victorious period for the novel that discovers its critical ambition, and the novelistic discourse becomes radical, as it can be observed, for example, in Nicolae Breban's novels, but especially in those of Augustin Buzura. This also confers the novel a privileged place, gradually becoming a main discourse, which would also determine its ill-fated destiny in the '80s. The novel's popularity came, as Nicolae Manolescu says, from its liberalization, surpassing

---

122 In an article published in the 13th issue of 2008 *România literară*, entitled "Generația mea în anii 60" (My Generation during the '60s), Gabriel Dimisianu explains the adherence of young people to the ideology of those times: "Psychologically, this is explained by their eagerness to become published and by the conviction they had been inculcated with, or which they had reached on their own, that they would fail to assert themselves from a literary point of view unless they made some compromises. Nothing going on at that particular moment in time led them to believe that things would be different in the near future. On the contrary." Consulted at the web adress: http://www.romlit.ro/generaia_mea_n_anii_60 [26.04.2018].
123 Manolescu: *Istoria critică a literaturii române*, p. 1097.
124 Nicolae Manolescu: *Arca lui Noe. Eseu despre romanul românesc* (Noah's Ark. Essay on the Romanian Novel). București: Minerva 1980–1983.

the "field of literature, becoming a cultural and social phenomenon."[125] In terms of prolixity, it is a victory resembling that of the '30s.

However, this victory of the novel was a short-lived one, because after the 'Theses from July 1971', art became once more, a seemingly even stronger instrument of propaganda and ideological control. Probably aware of the risks of this artistic liberalization, Nicolae Ceaușescu would enforce a set of measures meant to counterbalance the forces involved in the fight, and the censorship institution thus became essential in the publishing of novels.

> Following 1971, the battle became overt. The new adversary was more perfidious than the previous one, ultimately defeated without a fight. Socialist realism no longer represented a concrete literary reality following the sudden ideological and political desovietization in 1964. Due to the July theses, the criticism had to face not so much the party Censorship (which abated as an institution in 1977), but rather the revival, under the name of protochronism, of certain paranoid and, ultimately, irrational isolationist tendencies, supported aggressively by the writers and critics won over by national-communism.[126]

The Romanian novel thus entered a new survival battle, this time against the forceful comeback of the personality cult and the protochronist tendencies. Radu G. Țeposu is the critic who intercepted the time schedule of this postmodern battle of the '80s generation, following *Istoria tragică și grotescă a întunecatului deceniu literar nouă* (The Tragic and Grotesque History of the Dark Literary Decade of the 1980s) (1993). Prose writers such as Mircea Nedelciu, Gheorghe Crăciun, Ioan Groșan, Bedros Horasangian, Cristian Teodorescu or Petru Cimpoeșu use the weapons of postmodernism, such as playfulness, bookishness, intertextuality, parody or pastiche in order to alienate themselves from the grotesque neorealism of the last decade of communism. The ideological pressures, the authoritarianism of censorship, but also the adherence to the postmodern poetics of the fragment turned the short prose into the preferred genre of these prose writers, to the detriment of the novel. The latter seemed to have definitively lost the battle, becoming an anachronic and forbidden genre, and the Romanian decline of the genre seemed to be in accord with that undergone by other literatures, except that within the Romanian territory there was also the pressure of power. It is only during post-communism that we see a rediscovery of the genre, which seems to also apply in the case of the writers during the 1980's that reconvert themselves into novel authors, such as Gheorghe Crăciun, Cristian Teodorescu or Petru Cimpoeșu.

During the contemporary period we have thus seen a rediscovery of the epic genre and of the novelists. This is a time of fight between two generations, the

---

[125] Manolescu: *Istoria critică a literaturii române*, p. 1097.
[126] Manolescu: *Istoria critică a literaturii române*, p. 1202.

representatives of two interlacing histories. On the one hand, the comeback of certain 1980s prose writers, such as Cristian Teodorescu, Gheorghe Crăciun, Petru Cimpoeșu or even Horia Ursu, or the reconversion of others, such as Mircea Cărtărescu from poetry to novel and the rediscovery of lost prose writers, such as Gabriela Adameșteanu, Dumitru Țepeneag, Norman Manea or Herta Müller can all be noticed. Moreover, the novel of the new generations has emerged, which is not a novel of current understanding of the past, as is the case of previous writers, but rather one of understanding the present and its thorough destructuring. We may refer to it as neorealism which returned powerfully due to authors such as Radu Aldulescu, Dan Lungu, Filip Florian, Florina Ilis. The second perspective is that of magical surrealism of certain authors such as Răzvan Rădulescu, Petru Cimpoeșu or Bogdan Popescu. Even this representation of the genre according to generations is able to prove that the Romanian novel has been rediscovered during the post-communist period. Is this a victory of the novel against the anxieties of transition? The next struggle of the novel will probably answer this question.

It is possible to assess a simultaneously fluctuant and circular evolution of the Romanian novel, from its defeats to its victories, in the fight against history and its authoritarian pressures. Whether speaking of the interwar period as one belonging to the novel; of the 'Obsessive decade' and of the aggression of the proletarian novel; of the novelistic reanimation during the '60s; of the dissolution of the 1980s novel or the contemporary neorealism, the Romanian novel is an indisputable proof of the battle between art and history. The two antagonistic discourses, that of the authoritarian and exclusivist history and that of the critical and universalistic art have permanently clashed. The novel has been and still is a preferred genre for transgressing history, i.e. its manipulative and ideologizing discourse. From this point of view, Romanian literature proves the generic vitality of literature, precisely because it has been exposed to the extremes of power of history, but has nevertheless managed to survive, whether canonically or non-canonical.

1.2.3 Subject-Voice-Diathesis. The Pragmatical Power Taxonomy in Literature

Returning to the main Nietzschean concepts from the *Will to Power* the destruction of the category of the *Subject* can be noticed. This figure of the "fractured subject",[127] that Luc Ferry observed in his analysis of *The Will to Power* starts

---

[127] Luc Ferry: *Homo Aestheticus. The Invention of Taste in the Democratic Age.* Translated from French by Robert de Loaiza. Chicago & London: University of Chicago Press 1993, p. 31.

from ascertaining that this dynamiting of the subject/Cartesian substance does not bring a certain unity. Ferry's finding is that through the philosophy proposed by Nietzsche we witness a postmodern anticipatory perspectivism, a gain of a metaphysical kind of individualism that transgresses the limits of the subject. This may be the main aspect of our culture.

Nevertheless, an important category of modern narrativity has searched with considerable recrimination to reconstitute the subject annihilated by previous poetics. In fact, the subjective novel places any search for the ultimate truths in the subject, reconsidering its power to survive the aggressions of modern mundaneness. Seemingly in contradiction with the Nietzschean philosophy explained by Ferry, the modern novel reconsiders the subject and places it in a central position in this process of narrative dissection.

Even contemporary prose writers, such as Milan Kundera, when theorizing on the novelistic genre, try to define the stake of narrativity. Although insistently underlining the idea of not having "la moindre ambition théorique",[128] Milan Kundera, in his dialogue with Christian Salomon, on the *Art of the Novel*, published in a volume edited by Gallimard, in 1986, asserted categorially that "tous les romans de tous les temps se penchent sur l'énigme du moi."[129] To this end, he invoked and retrieved an entire epic tradition, from Boccaccio, Dante to Cervantes, of the author in search of the Self increasingly obscured into the depths of the inner life, insufficiently described and incompletely captured by the action. Joyce's lesson, which Kundera learns in what regards this constant and desperate search for the self, is paradoxical, and regards the entire modern subjective novel that surprises us with the following fact: "plus grande est l'optique du microscope qui observe le moi, plus le moi et son unicité nous échappent."[130] In the case of the modern novel, the optics of the microscope is amplified ad infinitum, precisely in order to reflect on the incommensurability of the Self and even its dissolution.

This atomizing of the Self in the modern novel entailed a new poetics, generated by the change in the modern paradigm, in accord with another dissolution, that of the bourgeoisie and implicitly of the bourgeois taste for the narrative. This change, in the meaning of an evolution, is also noted by Nicolae Manolescu,[131] who resorts to Ortega y Gasset's categories from *The First Meditation on Don*

---

[128] Milan Kundera: *L'Art du roman*. Paris: Gallimard 1986, p. 9.
[129] Kundera: *L'Art du roman*, p. 39.
[130] Kundera: *L'Art du roman*, p. 41.
[131] Nicolae Manolescu: *Metamorfozele poeziei. Metamorfozele romanului*, (The Metamorphoses of Poetry. The Metamorphoses of the Novel). Edition supervised by Mircea Mihăieș. Iași: Polirom 2003, p. 112.

Quixote and from *Thoughts on the Novel*. Starting from the acceptation of the first modern artists about the novel, i.e. that the novel is "an aesthetic affirmation of the quotidian",[132] Manolescu accepts the idea of a transposition of the action from the exterior towards the interior, as a result of the fact established by Gasset that the novel evolves from narration to representation or "from the epic subject to analysis: it pays attention to figures, characters, in their internal nature, rather than to the plot."[133] The self-exile of the Subject from the mechanics of the plot has also meant a backlash generated by the aggressions, i.e. the power of the capitalist society, which caused an incompatibility between the sensitive nature of the artist and the merchandising of society.

The hunt for the mysterious Self that governs modern prose has functioned according to varied strategies, often contradictory, sometimes with apparent renunciations. The subjectivity and self-reflexivity of some of modern texts, from Proust to Woolf or Camil Petrescu in fact, in Romanian literature, is replaced by an aesthetocentric transitivity generated by the 'death of the author' or its intentional invisibility from the narrative picture. In fact, a genuine cult of the art in the absence of the Self is created, and the Avant-gardist experiments or the textualism of the 1980's writers are eloquent in this sense. However, the result is once more disappointing, the modern author finding out that obscuring the Self behind the cult of the art is not sufficient. To this end, Thomas Pavel asserts the following, when speaking of the modern novel, referring to *Doctor Faustus* by Thomas Mann: "The worship of art for its own sake, the novel concludes, is more likely to lead to damnation than to redemption."[134] Is this a certain 'resistance', a defence to the excess of aestheticism of the realistic and naturalistic novel?

However, being strongly dependent on a certain favourable social and cultural context, the Romanian novel has had an evolution profoundly determined by the stages of social modernization and modernity, which often in the history of the genre made it seem like the Romanian novelist was more interested in representing history instead of explaining and criticizing it, and the definitive proof is that of the recurrence and power of the realistic novel, from Filimon to Rebreanu, Preda, Buzura, with echoes up to the current neorealism, visible in novels such as those of Petre Cimpoeșu, Dan Lungu or Radu Aldulescu. Excessively exposed to history and too often aggressed by it, the Romanian novel first tried to explain the relations between the Subject and the world in which it exists. This positioning

---

[132] See Ortega y Gasset. In: Manolescu: *Metamorfozele poeziei. Metamorfozele romanului*, p. 112.
[133] Manolescu: *Metamorfozele poeziei. Metamorfozele romanului*, p. 112.
[134] Thomas Pavel: *The Lives of the Novel. A History*. Princeton/ Oxford: Princeton University Press 2013, p. 283.

has resulted in observing and describing certain relations of power and the manner in which they modify the behavioural structure and the existence of the Subject. The Self has hidden away or has completely vanished behind appearances that assured the Subject of its survival through adaptation.

In the end, the panopticism of which Michel Foucault spoke in his book from 1975, entitled *Surveiller et punir. Naissance de la prison*,[135] seen as a manner of observation and control within the society dominated by power, is a metaphor that can be applied to the literary discourse as well. The Romanian writer has constantly felt surveyed by an authoritarian eye, and their reactions have been either to hide the Self to dissipation, or to adopt an impersonal discourse that would directly or indirectly represent either the anxieties of the excess of power which was exerted over them, or the traumas caused by history. Thus, in what regards to the modern novel, we can state directly that it is not only a ceaseless search, a Proustian hunt for the Self, but also a post-Proustian novel in which we witness a polarization of the Self and from here on, an identity dilemma as well.[136]

This crisis of the Self basically translates an identity crisis of the Subject, and Kundera explained the change in the paradigm produced within the modern novel through Kafka's novel, in which K's dilemmas are the Subject's dilemmas, as part of a profound identity dilemma, being expelled by history. Evidently, this is a particular pattern of self-reflexivity, although the Subject seems rather aggressed by a certain 'predisposition' to inadaptation, finding himself in a personal dilemma. His actions, or rather his inactions, are amplifiers of these dilemmas, because, as Kundera also admits, starting truly from the Heideggerian 'in-der-Welt-sein', the Subject and the World have created an interdeterminable character and, therefore, the Subject will never be able to relate solely to its own arbitrary choices and without any agreement or disagreement with the World. The relation with the Subject or his actions will constantly be related to History or the favourable context for extrapolating its dilemmas. The novel will thus function as a mirror of the analysis of the Subject's manner of acting (as a predication) and relating to the actors of History. We implicitly admit that only in this way "Non seulement la circonstance historique doit créer une situation existentielle nouvelle pour un personnage de roman, mais l'Histoire doit en elle-même être comprise et analysée comme situation existentielle."[137] The example of the equation explained by Kundera is from his novel entitled

---

[135] Michel Foucault: *Surveiller et punir. Naissance de la prison*. Paris: Gallimard 1975.
[136] Kundera: *L'Art du roman*, p. 45.
[137] Kundera: *L'Art du roman*, p. 56.

The Unbearable Lightness of Being (1984) and focuses on Alexandre Dubcek and the *weakness* he shows when he has to speak on the radio, following the pressures of the Russians and his meeting with Brejnev. Kundera reads Dubcek's weakness as a weakness in the face of a larger force, in other words his meeting with History, which creates such a memorable existential situation for its character. History is but a favourable context for the extrapolation of a cutoff situation, of a disagreement between the Subject and the World, a representation of an action of domination and inhibition of the Subject, taking into account that the novelist, "Le romancier n'est ni historien ni prophète: il est explorateur de l'existence."[138]

But following the pragmatics of a novelistic discourse by referring to the position of the Subject in the discourse and its actantial relations with the historical framework from which the Subject is extracted, we should understand its position of *force* or *power* and that of *weakness* in relation to this determining context and its representative Actors. This is what we would call an *analysis of the novelistic actantial hierarchy* that explains the manner in which the Subject relates itself to a certain event and to the agents holding an active and, therefore, determining role in the action, i.e. the manner in which it succeeds in acting in this *equation of power*.

1.2.4 Subject-Voice. A(n) nearly (Im)Possible Epic Equation

Criticising the theoretical model of *the intellectualist philosophy* "which treats language as an object of contemplation rather than an instrument of action on power",[139] Pierre Bourdieu offers a turning point in understanding the pragmatics and the uses of our language. Having the idea that the act of speaking functions as an action of "a conjuncture, an encounter between independent casual series", the French sociologist evaluates the boundaries of grammar, of linguistics as a subject matter describing the mechanism of language, in defining meaning. In the end, his theory on the functioning of language, meant as a criticism against the Saussurian linguistics model and against the theory of Chomskian linguistic competences, is set within the wider context of a linguistic 'market', in other words of a situation, a common environment of communicational exchange. However, the warning of the sociologist in the chapter entitled 'The Economy of

---

138 Kundera: *L'Art du roman*, p. 63.
139 Pierre Bourdieu: *Language and Symbolic Power*. Edited and introduced by John B. Thompson. Translated by Gino Raymond and Matthew Adamson. Cambridge: Polity Press 1991, p. 37.

Linguistic Exchanges' is evidently set in the context of the social symbolism of language, for he says:

> One should never forget that language, by virtue of the infinite generative but also originative capacity - in the Kantian sense - which it derives from its power to produce existence by producing the collectively recognized, and thus, realized, representation of existence, is no doubt the principal support of the dream of absolute power.[140]

However, if in the language-world equation we were to replace language, as a production of referential meaning in a precise context, with artistic language, the equation, as was demonstrated at the end of the previous chapter, raises a few questions. The artistic language that literature operates with then creates the connexion with the world as well, with the communicational context, but especially the disruption from it. In this context, to say that literature functions as a simple representation of the world is no longer sufficient, and to say that language is a support or an instrument of power is no longer valid. Moreover, the exceptions of the literary language as a support for power confirms the rule that literature is a secondary discourse, that often circulates in parallel with the world it starts from and its language is also a manner of putting it between brackets or undermining it. In fact, the utility of sociology stops where literature begins to become self-referential, where it loses the connexion with the social 'field' in which it is produced. Perhaps the means of describing the manner of functioning of literature must be sought precisely within the science of language. This preoccupation could capture not only the manner in which the artistic language of literature is structured starting from the pragmatic usage of language, but especially the manner in which it operates semantically, that is the manner in which literature speaks to us and the position it has in relation to the world of its birth.

In *Gramatica limbii române* (The Grammar of the Romanian Language)[141] from 2008, Gabriela Pană Dindelegan asserted that "voice is a *syntactic* and *pragmatic* category, which interests both the verb, as well as the ensemble of the sentence, since it engages the verb and its actors (with the syntactic roles and functions attributed to them): the Subject-Agent and the Object-Patient."[142] While from a syntactic point of view, voice expresses a classical relation between the Verb-Subject and the Direct Object, or the Verb-Subject, from a modal point of

---

140 Bourdieu: *Language and Symbolic Power*, p. 42.
141 See Pană Dindelegan. In: Valeria Guțu Romalo (ed.): *Gramatica limbii române* (The Grammar of the Romanian Language). București: Editura Academiei Române, 2008.
142 See Pană Dindelegan. In: *Gramatica limbii române*, p. 480.

view,[143] from a pragmatic point of view, voice "shifts the communicative interest from the Agent-Subject (active voice) to the Patient-Subject (passive voice), to the process itself, without referring to the actors/arguments (impersonal voice)."[144] In this sense, the author discusses "a reorganization of the syntactic structure (as a syntactic hierarchy, respectively as a thematic hierarchy of the components)", and the result of this restructuring is that of directing the receiver towards the components of the sentence: subject, verb, direct object, according to the 'communicative interest'. This hierarchy suggests a positioning according to who performs the action and who holds a certain control over it and over the discourse.

In French, the term diathesis is of a Greek provenance and indicates a semantic orientation rather than a syntactic one, circulating in the past century in parallel with the 'voice' one, that probably expressed an exclusivist reduction to the discursive level, and therefore syntactic, of the analysis of the relations between the Subject and the actors. Even the fact that in Greek, the term of a medical origin, expressed a hereditary or constitutional 'disposition', or rather 'predisposition' to a certain malady indicates a certain pragmatic orientation of the action towards a particular context that would determine the establishing of the actantial hierarchy. It is about a precise relation between the condition (disposition or predisposition), understood as an action expressed by the verb, and the participant or participants to this action. "Le terme de *diathèse* désigne aussi l'orientation du verbe vers un actant particulier, alors que la notion de *voix* des grammairiens de l'époque classique désigne plutôt une forme de conjugaison du verbe."[145] In other words, the difference presented previously between the semantic and pragmatic level of the discourse and the syntactic one. Starting from this finding, Muller confirms that the signification of voice is more clearly oriented towards the pragmatic nature, which in fact allows it to define diathesis as "la hiérarchie effective des rôles actantiels associés aux fonctions grammaticales dans un énoncé en prenant pour forme de base la construction usuelle du verbe."[146] This hierarchy, according to Muller, is in fact established starting primarily from the syntactic subject, but taking into account the secondary actors as well. In other words, it is about a certain "actantial hierarchy" determined by "des choix communicatifs du locuteur."[147]

---

143 Michael Metzeltin: *Semiologia puterii* (The Semiology of Power). Traducere de Oana Balaș. București: Editura Universității din București 2016, p. 28.
144 Dindelegan. In: *Gramatica limbii române*, p. 480.
145 Claude Muller: Diathèse et voix en français. In: *Interaction entre sémantique et pragmatique, Actes du XI Séminaire de Didactique Universitaire*. București: ASE 2005, p. 73–95.
146 Muller: Diathèse et voix en français, p. 77.
147 Muller: Diathèse et voix en français, p. 93.

Hierarchical arrangement, seen as a "A system in which members of an organization or society are ranked according to relative status or authority",[148] entails the analysis of a certain pragmatics of the discourse, in other words its classification according to the position of the speaker or that of the subject in action towards the other actors. In order to determine this position and the role of the subject, we are required to analyse the relations of subordination between the actors and their respective functions and, especially, the position of the subject. This analysis entails the identification of certain relations of power clearly reflected in the discursive system in which:

a. The Subject has control over the action, being active and determining including the existence of the actors;
b. The Subject has control over his own actions, self-determining his existence;
c. The actor/actors has/have control over and determine the actions of the passive Subject;
d. The holder or holders of control over the action are uncertain, undefined, the action being of an impersonal nature.

Starting from this discursive level, we in turn identify four manners of relating literature to society by relating it to the operational mechanisms of power. In the field of Romanian literature, the morphological functioning relations of the equation of power would be displayed as follows:

a. **The active power of the Subject as is the case in Nicolae Filimon's novel, *Ciocoii vechi și noi* (The Old and New Parvenus)**
   In this novel from the 19th century, the Subject acts according to his own person, in an individual interest and in order to gain power which here means accumulating wealth by any means. The hierarchization of power through its active instrumenting entails a path of decline, the moralist dimension of this genre of novel being often a distinctive feature. The novel of active power shows forth and sets out arguments for the harmful effects of passive power reduced to the Subject's interest.

b. **The reflexive power of the Subject, as is the case in Max Blecher's novel, *Întâmplări din irealitatea imediată* (Occurrences in the Immediate Reality)**
   Here the Subject is disguised by the Self, placing itself in a centripetal search of reflexivity, specific to the modern subjective novel. The illusive reality is

---

[148] See the definition of 'Hierarchy'. Consulted at the web adress: https://en.oxforddictionaries.com/definition/hierarchy [26.05.2018].

replaced by a sensitive "unreality", profoundly anchored in a subjective place and time, often recovered through a subjective, Proustian memory. The Subject of Blecher's occurrence, suspended between the distanced reality and the oppressive biography, searches for his power in order to survive such tragic suspension, and its inexhaustible source is his own reflexivity.

c. **The passivization of the Subject in the face of Power, in Marin Preda's novel, *Cel mai iubit dintre pământeni* (The Most Beloved Man on Earth)**
Facing the oppressive system, the Subject is dominated by the political power, defeated by the 'gorilla' of his time. Power is exerted from the outside, and he switches from an active stage to a passive one. The power of the communist ideologies, denounced in *Delirul* (The Raving), becomes suffocating in *Cel mai iubit dintre pământeni* (The Most Beloved Man on Earth). Here, Victor Petrini is a victim of an oppressive system in which his freedom is annihilated and power becomes the appanage of an absurd world. The action starts from the Subject and returns to the Subject and the final relation takes place only in connection to his own lack of power, with his passivity or, ultimately, his resistance in the face of power.

d. **The impersonalization of the Subject when facing power, in Horia Ursu's novel, *Asediul Vienei* (The Siege of Vienna)**
Within contemporary prose we witness an apparent discontinuity in the relation between the Subject and the action. The Subject lives in a world in which everything 'is said', 'is done', 'is told', as an echo of the dissipation of individuality. The Subject gradually becomes 'anonymous' in this dislocation. He is part of an anonymous group, until he intermingles with it. His character is at best representative. Horia Ursu's Subjects no longer hold any power, and the polarization and impersonalization of power is a characteristic of a devalued and confusing world.

All these relations of power exposed here prove more than the normative or descriptive nature of power, as analysed in social sciences. These relations prove the 'utility' of literature in general and that of the novel in particular when we try to 'read' the manner in which literature denounces the excessive nature of reality. The novel itself proves to be a discourse about its world, having a therapeutic or, at least, a *transgressive* function as well. In other words it offers the reader a solution for excess, a realistic mirror or an introspection instrument capable of correcting an excessive proximity of the reader with the world in which he lives. Searching for the ideal reader, this novel also comprises, as literature always has, a complex parable of the relations established at a certain point between a society and the revelatory functions of art. This way literature itself becomes a form of power.

2 The Active Power of the Subject

2.1 The Fanariot Power in XIXth Century. At the Doorway of Sunrise

> "No matter how poor the country is,
> It's so sweet when one can say:
> This is my country, I'm from here!"[1]

In 1784, Immanuel Kant offered "An Answer to the Question *What is Enlightenment?*"[2] The Kantian understanding of *Aufklärung* is for the first time, as Michel Foucault[3] noticed in his response to the *Enlightenment* in 1984, a *negative* one, being regarded exclusively as *Ausgang*, in the meaning of 'exit', 'escape' from the state of 'minority', or 'immaturity' that would characterize the world at the end of the 18th century:

> *Enlightenment is mankind's exit from its self-incurred immaturiy. Immaturity* is the inability to make use of one's own understanding without the guidance of another. Self-incurred is this inability if its cause lies not in the lack of understanding but rather in the lack of the resolution and the courage to use it without the guidance of another. *Sapere aude!*[4]

Foucault also admits that Kant's *Aufklärung* is a rational process in the history of ideas. This is a cultural progress: "sans doute tres singulier qui a pris conscience de lui-même en se nommant, en se situant par rapport à son passé et par rapport à son avenir et en désignant les opérations qu'il doit effectuer à l'interieur de son propre present."[5]

The examples given by the philosopher from Königsberg and resumed by Foucault are eloquent for the manner in which human 'minority' can be explained as a state of absolute obedience, as an accepted and comfortable passivity in the face of a recognized authority: such as when a book replaces understanding,

---

1 Ion Budai-Deleanu: *Țiganiada sau Tabăra țiganilor (Țiganiada or The Gypsies' Camp)*. Edition and glossary by J. Byck. București: Editura pentru Literatură 1964, p. 24. Fragments from this subchapter, regarding the meaning of 'Enlightenment' in Ion Budai Deleanu's *Țiganiada*, could be also finded in: Florin Oprescu: *Țiganiada*, un canon littéraire manqué. In: *Perspectives contemporaines sur le monde médiéval*. Pitești: Tiparg, p. 89–92.
2 See Immanuel Kant. In: James Schmidt (ed.): *What is Enlightenment? Eighteen-Century Answers and Twentieth-Century Questions*. Berkley; Los Angeles: University of California Press 1996.
3 Foucault: *Dits et écrits*, p. 679–688.
4 Kant. In: Schmidt (ed.): *What is Enlightenment?*, p. 58.
5 Foucault: *Dits et écrits*, p. 681.

when the priest replaces conscience and when the doctor prescribes the diet we should follow.

Human 'majority' will come to be not by a lack of obedience to the unanimously accepted authority that has the eternal tendency to operate according to the motto: 'Obey, don't think!', but by free submission situated under the dome of reason, according to the Kantian formula for Enlightenment: "Argue as much as you will and about whatever you will; *but obey*!" Kant's examples are again eloquent: the officer must obey the orders of his superior, but nothing can stop him from arguing *publicly*[6] on the opportunity or utility of that order; the citizen must pay his taxes, but as a scholar, he has the duty to express in a public manner his thoughts on their injustice; the priest is obliged to conform to the credo of the Church, "But as a scholar he has the complete freedom, indeed it is his calling, to communicate to the public all his care-fully tested and well-intentioned thoughts on the imperfections of that symbol and his proposals for a better arrangement of religious and ecclesiastical affairs."[7]

Therefore, only by relating this 'Ausgang' to what Foucault calls *the ethos of modernity*, which is an attitude toward history rather than a certain period of it and a manner of relating to the world, i.e., a critique, a way of making public use of reason, can we understand the complexity of our modernity.

In other words, ever since 1784, at the dawn of the French Rrevolution, visible in the Kantian response to the necessity to clarify the 'high' message of the *Aufklärung*, a re-problematization of the manner in which we relate to the consensual authority had been needed. This would be the human manner of overcoming its minority, generated in Kant's opinion by laziness and cowardice, which ensured a minor comfort for one. The Kantian stake was predominantly to understand the *minority* of human conditions, deprived of reason, in order to outwit them. In the century of the discovery of the East and its exaggerated exoticism, the philosopher from Königsberg certainly did not mean the Eastern reasoning, but rather having a critical position against the *minor* prejudices of the West. The power of reason that Kant speaks of is certainly from the category that was debated upon and continued during the past century by sociologists or politologists, such as Keith Downing, with a distinction between 'the power to' and 'the power over', found under the sway of the decision of the rational. It can

---

6 See Kant. In: Schmidt (ed.): *What is Enlightenment?*, p. 60. The essence of the Kantian distinction is between "the public use" of reason, the key to humanity's *freedom and majority*, meaning that use that anyone makes "*as a scholar [Gelehrter]* before the entire public of the *reading world*" and "the private use" of reason "which one makes of his reason in a certain *civil post* or office which is entrusted to him."

7 See Kant. In: Schmidt (ed.): *What is Enlightenment?*, p. 60.

be said that the distinction between power to and power over is a kantian one, showing the continuity of this understanding of *Aufklärung* as a never-ending process. For Dowding "*power over* refers to an asymmetrical relation between two or more actors, while *power to* consists in the ability of the actors themselves to carry out certain specific outcomes."[8]

During the same century of 'reason', 63 years prior, in 1721, in his *Persian Letters*, Montesquieu subtly critiqued the Western pre-settings regarding the Eastern world, whilst simultaneously adopting, through his characters Usbek and Rica, a falsely admiratory attitude towards Western values. Montesquieu's naïve travellers discover and describe in an epistolary form for the Persians who remained at home the cultural differences between the Eastern and the Western worlds. They naively discover the manners, laws and conditions of life in the 18th century West, but without making any acid comments on one culture or the other other as Montesquieu's epistolary novel contains an implicit criticism of the Western self-sufficiency, but also of the excessive Eastern patriarchate.

Of the 161 letters published under the circumspection and protection of anonymity, which nevertheless suggests that the Enlightenment was an unfinished project,[9] following Habermas' point of view on the 'negative' theory of the Enlightenment offered by Immanuel Kant, relevant to this analysis seems to be 'Letter XXX'. In it, Rica speaks of the strange 'curiosity' of the Parisians who, when he turns out in his Persian clothing, stare at him and wonder at his natural 'quality' of being Persian. Below is the ironic story of the Persian on the extravagant curiosity of the inhabitants of Paris:

> Je souriais quelquefois d'entendre des gens qui n'étaient presque jamais sortis de leur chambre, qui disaient entre eux : "Il faut avouer qu'il a l'air bien Persan." Chose admirable ! Je trouvais de mes portraits partout ; je me voyais multiplié dans toutes les boutiques, sur toutes les cheminées, tant on craignait de ne m'avoir pas assez vu. Tant d'honneurs ne laissent pas d'être à charge : je ne me croyais pas un homme si curieux et si rare ; et, quoique j'aie très-bonne opinion de moi, je ne me serais jamais imaginé que je dusse troubler le repos d'une grande ville, où je n'étais point connu.[10]

---

8 See Pamela Pansardi. In: Keith Dowding (ed.): *Encyclopedia of Power*. Los Angeles: Sage Publications 2011, p. 521.
9 It is important to mention here the answer given by Immanuel Kant to the question: *Qu'est ce que les lumières ?*, from *Critique de la faculté de juger suivi de Idée d'une histoire universelle au point de vue cosmopolitique et de Réponse a la question : Qu'est ce que les lumières ?* Published under the supervision of Ferdinand Alquié. Translated from German by: Alexandre J. L. Delamarre, Jean-René Ladmiral, Marc B. de Launay, Gallimard, Paris 1985.
10 Charles-Louis de Secondat, Baron de La Brède et de Montesquieu: *Lettres persanes*. Édition revue et annotée d'après les manuscrits du chateau de la Brède avec un avant-propos et un index par Henri Barckhausen. Paris: Hachette 1913, p. 61.

His ironic smiling to these people, who have "barely come out of their room", turns into perplexity in the face of an absurd situation and question, critically suggested by the abrupt ending of the letter:

> Je demeurais quelquefois une heure dans une compagnie, sans qu'on m'eût regardé, et qu'on m'eût mis en occasion d'ouvrir la bouche: mais, si quelqu'un, par hasard, apprenait à la compagnie que j'étais Persan, j'entendais aussitôt autour de moi un bourdonnement : "Ah ! ah ! monsieur est Persan ? C'est une chose bien extraordinaire ! Comment peut-on être Persan ?"[11]

But such candours are recurrent, especially when witnessing the encounter between two very different cultures such as the Western and the Eastern ones. For example, in Romanian travel literature from the 19th century we find both naivetés and hyperboles concerning the West, as well as critiques of the social 'insufficiency' of the Principalities, brought about by cultural prejudices, but also by the awareness of their dependence upon a socio-political context. The notations made by educated travellers, such as Dinicu Golescu, *Însemnare a călătoriei mele* (An Annotation of my Journey) (1826), Nicolae Filimon, *Escursiuni în Germania Meridională* (Excursions to Meridional Germany) (1860), Ion Codru-Drăgușanu, *Peregrinul transilvan* (The Transylvanian Pilgrim) (1865) or later on Mihail Kogălniceanu, in his *Scrisori. Note de călătorie* (Letters. Travel notes) proves that these seekers of a unitary national conscience have become aware of the differences between the Enlightened West and the exotic East.

On the other hand, the foreign travellers to the Romanian Principalities during the 18th and 19th centuries, research scholars, diplomats or intellectuals,[12] on their way to the East, build a genuine image, a colourful picture of these territories located at the interference of powers, cultures and times. In the absence of a national literature, of a national state, these accounts often set up a relevant profile of a Romanian border identity, between Western realities and Eastern customs and Western ideals. In addition to the unique image of the Romanian society at the dawn of its modernization, the same foreign travellers are also responsible for configuring a Western image of the Orientalism of the Romanian world. In other words, the Romanian world's image during mid-19th century is sometimes also a creation of the Western pre-settings regarding the East. Regarded as border territories between the West and the East, as a result

---

11 Montesquieu: *Lettres persanes*, p. 62.
12 See Simona Vărzaru (ed.): *Prin Țările Române. Călători străini din secolul al XIX-lea* (Across the Romanian Principalities. Foreign Travellers from the 19th Century). Anthology, translation, introductory study and notes by Simona Vărzaru. București: Sport-Turism 1984, p. 17.

of the Ottoman presence, the Principalities have been the centre of interest for Western diplomats, but also for their imagological victims.

The well-known researcher of postcolonial worlds, Edward Said asserted in his book, *Orientalism* (1978), a relational theory on the Western representations of the East. He said that, since the knowledge of the East by the West was generated from the position of power of the West, the West generated the East, the oriental and its world. In other words, Said supports the theory that the East, or at least its image, is Western.

> There were of course innumerable voyages of discovery; there were contacts through trade and war. But more than this, since the middle of the eighteenth century there had been two principal elements in the relation between East and West. One was a growing systematic knowledge in Europe about the Orient, knowledge rein-forced by the colonial encounter as well as by the widespread interest in the alien and unusual, exploited by the developing sciences of ethnology, comparative anatomy, philology, and history; further-more, to this systematic knowledge was added a sizable body of literature produced by novelists, poets, translators, and gifted travelers.[13]

However, he goes on to say the determining role in this 'creation' of the Eastern imaginary is played by the second element, meaning that:

> Europe was always in a position of strength, not to say domination. There is no way of putting this euphemistically. True, the relation-ship of strong to weak could be disguised or mitigated, [...]. But the essential relationship, on political, cultural, and even religious grounds, was seen—in the West, which is what concerns us here—to be one between a strong and a weak partner.[14]

The differences between the two worlds, at least on an imaginary level, seem to be the result of the West's positions of power. Often, Western culture understood the Eastern world as being irrational, depraved, simplistic and instinctual, 'different' from the Western rational, virtuous, moral and civilized 'values'. However, the observations made by foreign travellers to the Principalities are not merely a barometer of Eastern conservatism, but also of the cultural Western prejudices, as seen in Montesquieu, of the exclusivist and authoritarian manner of understanding other cultures. In the end, the 'minority' Kant spoke of when describing the ethic of the Aufklärung is subject to the idea of Eurocentric exclusivism, as has often been the case with the legitimation of the power of Western ideals.

Such an observer tracking the transformation tendencies within the Principalities is the French writer and politician Saint-Marc Girardin who in 1836

---

[13] Edward Said: *Orientalism*. New York: Pantheon 2003, p. 39–40.
[14] Said: *Orientalism*, p. 40.

published his *Travelling and Study Memories* (Amintirile de călătorie și de studii).¹⁵ He admits that:

> The Principalities are now facing a special crisis situation: they live under Turkish oppression, but are thriving, without knowing what their political destiny will be (...); a society struggling between the old Western customs and the new European ones, who took from the Western civilization rather its exterior aspects and its elegance, than its specific spirit and substance; a general transformation of the houses, of the manner of acting, the laws and even the language: this is the show offered by the two principalities today.¹⁶

In 1835, the young officer from the Prussian army and its future marshal, Helmuth von Moltke, passes on his way to Stambul through Bucharest, and in his travel notes he describes some of the distinctive features of the capital undergoing modernization in the second part of the 19th century and at the dawn of 20th century modernity:

> It surprises you to find in this wasteland [author's note - of Wallachia] a city like Bucharest with almost 100.000 inhabitants. Bucharest has palaces, societies and visits, theatres, milliners, newspapers and luxury carriages; but once you step foot outside the town, you are thrown once more into barbarism.¹⁷

When characterizing Bucharest, von Moltke perceives the strong contrast reigning over this cultural border city: "In Bucharest you can see the most sinful shacks alongside of palaces built in the most modern style and Byzantine churches; the most grievous misery and the most extravagant luxury reign side by side; Asia and Europe seem to meet in this town."¹⁸

The traveller is thus surprised by the striking contrast between the old and the new, between the Western influences and the Eastern customs converging here. The Bucharest world in 1835 seems to this foreign traveller, educated in the spirit, harmony and balance of the Western values, a strange association and overlapping of worlds that seemed incompatible to him. Here, the disparity between 'civilization' and 'barbarism' does not seem to exist. The two live side by side. At least this is the opinion of the Westerner searching for the Eastern exoticism.

However, the explanations to this eclectic coexistence are determined by the history of this world, exposed to powers from all cardinal points. The 'barbarism'

---

15 In Vărzaru (ed.): *Prin Țările Române*, p. 59–62.
16 In Vărzaru (ed.): *Prin Țările Române*, p. 62.
17 Apud George Potra: *Bucureștii văzuți de călători străini. Secolele XVI–XIX* (Bucharest through the Eyes of Foreign Travellers. XVI–XIX Centuryes). București: Editura Academiei 1992, p. 157.
18 Apud Potra: *Bucureștii văzuți de călători străini*, p. 157.

seen by Moltke and other travellers seems to be attributed to the Ottoman domination lasting for over a century in Moldavia and Wallachia. On the one hand, it is about the precarious material conditions of the people, kept at the limit of survival because of excessive duties and, on the other hand, by the influence of certain Western customs related to public life. In this context, the majority of the observers associate the deplorable economic state of the Principalities with the Phanariots' 'evil'. The role of the Phanariots was indeed decisive in perpetuating certain customs with negative effects on the ordinary people who found themselves obliged to contribute both to covering the excessive expenses of the Porte, through the tributes paid, with the wellbeing of the rulers sent by Stambul to govern them, but also to maintaining the status of the native masters mediating the relationships between the Ruler and the population. On the other hand, the effects of the Phanariots' rule (1711–1821) on Moldavia and Wallachia were also evident with regards to the birth of a national Romanian awareness, by relating it to the administrative power imposed by the Porte and in underlining the crystallization of a native Romanian conscience of power and the ways of gaining it.

Ever since the 17th century, in the context in which the Ottoman administration began to feel the need to negotiate new treaties with the neighbouring states in order to preserve their regional influence, the phanariots had started to hold important functions in mediating diplomatic parleys. This was due to their knowledge of Western languages and cultures. The Phanariots were thus the dragomans who had prospered commercially and who had gained considerable economic, political and religious power, as a result of knowing the cultures they traded with. In the 18th century, the power of the phanariots, the Greek merchandisers and the aristocratic Byzantine clerics grew to such an extent that their decisions had political and religious consequences.

Moreover, the Greek historian Svoronos[19] supports the idea that we are witnessing, in this process of ascension of the Phanariots, the birth of a new type of national identity, reduced to the dimensions of their social class, the identity created by the dominant class by virtue of preserving the hereditary right of succession and individual prosperity. The consequences of this fact would be self-destructive for the Phanariots and this self-erosive power can be proved by looking at the history of the Phanariots in the Romanian Principalities and the effects on the subsequent native rule. In addition to the historical documents that prove this fact, significant arguments can be found in the travel literature of foreign travellers or in the fictional one, such as Nicolae Filimon's novel, *Ciocoii vechi și noi* (The Old and New Parvenus). From this point of view, Filimon's novel is a fresco of the

---

[19] Nikos Svoronos: *The Greek Nation*. Athens: Polis 2004, p. 91.

process of accumulating power by preserving and increasing personal wealth and implicitly the administrative power from one generation to the other, but also a moralizing fable that starts with and returns to the proverb: 'Like father, like son!'.

Regarding the situation of the Romanian Principalities and their being directly influenced by the East through the Ottoman Empire, Keith Hitchins mentions that "Ottoman suzeranity was the overwhelming fact of political and economic life for the Romanian principalities during the period bounded by the Treaty of Kuchuk Kainardji 1774 and the beginning of the Greek War for Independence in 1821."[20] This fact has not only a historical value as such, but also an evaluative and even interpretative one, for the American historian underlines the 'dynamism' of this half a century for the Romanian Principalities. He admits that "vassalage, however onerous, could neither stop the evolution of institutions nor stifle the spread of ideas."[21] He refers with certainty to the promotion of the ideas of Enlightenment that were making history in the Western Europe and were migrating towards the Principalities as well. Paradoxically and contrary to the interpretation of certain autochthonous historians, Hitchins claims that:

> The rationalisation of government, the concentration of powers in the hands of the prince and the expansion of the bureaucracy, the codification of laws, and the secularisation of public life, all hallmarks of modern society, moved forward inexorably.[22]

The globalizing view on the dynamism of modernization is also valuable, for the administrative restructuring of the Principalities eventually led, in the 19th century, to the formation of the unitary Romanian state. We are speaking of the Kantian *Ausgang* which, with a unanimously recognized historical gap, occurs in the Principalities during the century of independence, as a result of a favourable context, but especially as recognition of a common, authentic, individual and independent identity. Both the Ottoman suzerainty, manifested through the Phanariots' rule, as well as the increased Russian and Western interest resulted in the national Romanian identity being a product of the cultural syncretism exerted as multiple influences on the Principalities. This can be deduced from, amongst other sources, the multitude of travel observations made by foreigners in the Principalities throughout the 19th century.

Regarding the history of the Phanariots' presence in Moldavia and Wallachia, a key moment is considered to be the restoration of the patriarchate of Constantinople inside the town in 1601, in the neighbourhood called *fanal* (old beacon-tower),

---

20 Keith Hitchins: *The Romanians. 1774–1886*. Oxford: Clarendon Press 1996, p. 5.
21 Hitchins: *The Romanians*, p. 5.
22 Hitchins: *The Romanians*, p. 5.

which also granted it significant political power. In order to maintain and especially in order to extend this influence within the empire, an administrative net would be woven around the patriarchate, in which the Greek merchandisers would play a significant role. They profit from their education and their Western knowledge, since, as observed by researchers of the history of the Ottoman Empire, the Turkish culture was reserved to merchantry under any conditions and foreign languages were despised, since they appreciated Arabic and Persian.

As Djuvara says, by referring also to Toynbee's references in *A Study of History*, Alexandru Mavrocordat should be seen as "the great predecessor of the Phanariots",[23] former great dragoman[24] of the Porte during 1673 and 1699. Because of him, the status of the dragomans became important, and they no longer held merely an administrative, interpretative role, but also gain the function of rulers or even of representing diplomats of the Porte. "Under his long *ministry* the fate of the Greeks in Constantinople improves significantly and a genuine tradition is initiated: the Phanariots will no longer be solely merchandisers, exchangers, medics, but also administrators, intermediaries, informants."[25] The functioning of the empire was tied to their abilities in the 18th century, which granted them significant power, be it unstable but decisive, when it came to the fall of the Empire and influencing the customs within the areas managed. We witnessed a gradual transfer of power in favour of its preservation, which would paradoxically mark precisely the end of the Ottoman power, but not of its effects on the Principalities.

"In the 19th century, the foreign observers claim that a third of the reserves of Constantinople came from the Principalities."[26] This economic domination led to a harsh counterbalance of the relationships between the squires, owners of large agrarian estates, and the peasants burdened by tributes and increasingly indebted, as the Ottoman domination required more agrarian resources in order to maintain an empire undergoing an economic crisis and decline. This adverse crisis of the Ottoman Empire created the favourable context for the emergence of the Phanariots, who were efficient administrators, with good knowledge of the neighbouring cultures and of the languages of the people they traded with and skilful negotiators with the local powers.

---

23 Neagu Djuvara: *Între Orient şi Occident. Ţările Române la începutul epocii moderne 1800–1848* (Between the East and the West. The Romanian Principalities at the Beginning of the 1800–1848 Modern Age). Translation by Maria Carpov. Bucureşti: Humanitas 2002, p. 28.
24 The term 'dragoman' initially meant 'the interpreter' of the foreign embassies and legations, used by the Turks as well in their political and commercial relationships with the West.
25 Djuvara: *Între Orient şi Occident*, p. 30.
26 Djuvara: *Între Orient şi Occident*, p. 25.

Therefore, in 1711 (Moldavia) and 1716 (Wallachia), the Ottomans introduced the Phanariots' families, as a result of the socio-political transformations taking place at the beginning of the 19th century, to the increased political influence of the magistrates of Greek origin and of the need to ensure an efficient administration in terms of collecting the tributes. In this context, thirty-one Phanariots (from 1711 to 1821) ruled on the thrones in Moldavia and Wallachia seventy-five times.

The Phanariot's rule emerges in the context of disorganization and weakening of the local squire power, of the native elective monarchy. Many Greeks considered that obtaining an administrative function within the Principalities was an opportunity for them to increase their personal wealth and/or political influence regardless of any compromises that had to be made, far away from the Sublime Porte and without the mercantile difficulties from the Ottoman Empire. Sometimes, even the matrimonial alliances with native squires were also conducted in order to preserve their power.

The custom of appointing Phanariots' rulers was pretty simple and efficient and it included the use by the chief dragoman of the Sublime Porte by any means in order to obtain the princely title, including significant 'gifts' for which they even borrowed money. Therefore, once they got to the Principalities, with a considerable entourage made of their family members, but also of their creditors, during their mandate they aimed to recover their initial 'investment', and the means used apparently disregarded any laws, morality, local customs etc. The economic results of appointing Phanariots were the harshening of the tax policies and implicitly the depletion of the population and the enhancement of social contrasts. Often, the reforming initiatives of certain rulers such as Constantin Mavrocordat or Alexandru Ipsilanti in terms of bondage or of the red tape legislation would encounter the resistance of the native squires from the Divan who, in turn, attempted to preserve their local power, having the same objective as the Phanariots: to preserve their wealth and their traditional rights, and implicitly their power. These clashes resulted in petitions to change the rulers, submitted in 1820 both with the Porte and with the Habsburg Empire or Russia, i.e. the powers gravitating around the Romanian territories.

In a text from 1741, entitled "Capuchehaiele lui Constantin Mavrocordat despre necesitatea mituirii diverșilor dregători otomani" (The Diplomatic Representatives of Constantin Mavrocordat on the Necessity of Bribing the Various Ottoman Rulers)[27] evidence of the complaint lodged against the gradual degradation of the power relationship in Moldavia and the description of the excesses

---

27 Apud Bogdan Murgescu (ed.): *Istoria României în texte* (The History of Romania in Texts). București: Corint 2001, p. 173.

attributed to the throne of the country can be found. Below is the content of Mavrocordat's report regarding the bribing of the rulers:

> Your Highness chides us for the gifts we give, but otherwise we could not have done anything; however it is not a good thing to give either, for these times are of such a nature that the Porte of the Grand Vizier and those around him are immeasurably greedy and all of them, including the smallest employee, are like wild beasts. When they ask for something, first they do it gently, then they use abominations, force, threats and you cannot fight them anymore.[28]

Gentleness, abominations, force, threats are the instruments of power enforcement used by the rulers to obtain a bribe.

For this analysis, it is necessary to observe both the relations of power established through the Phanariots' rulers, as well as the results of such lordships and, especially, their impact on the native lordships and the local customs. Evidently, the interest of the Phanariots in accumulating economic capital and political and religious influence prevailed, despite all the more or less successful attempts at reformation. Also obvious is the gap created and maintained by such lordships, between the population and the administration, by abusively enforcing taxations and a discretionary law. In order to describe the process of modernization of Romanian society, it is important to question what the role played by the native lordships that followed the 1821 movement led by Tudor Vladimirescu was. This analysis is necessary precisely because it is already common knowledge that the period of one hundred years of Phanariot rule had a notable impact on the transformation of the ethos and of the power relations within the Principalities.

Neagu Djuvara, in order to depict an objective picture of the social transformations brought about by these lordships, quotes in his book, *Între Orient și Occident. Țările române la începutul epocii moderne* (Between the East and the West. The Romanian Principalities at the Beginning of the Modern Age), the opinions of foreign travellers regarding the striking contrast between the Phanariots' administration and the native squires on the one hand and the rest of the population, impoverished, exploited and humiliated on the other hand. In fact, the portrait of the Phanariots depicted in his campaign log by the French general Langeron is relevant for their status of moral degradation, but also for the exertion of active power over the population:

> They are the ones mediating, the ones scheming, instigating and often completing all the iniquities conducted daily at Constantinople by a bloody governance, where no law

---

28 Apud Murgescu (ed.): *Istoria României în texte*, p. 173.

or belief abating the savagery of their employees who, all of them (including the highest ranking rulers), are of a bad ancestry and can only make it through this cursory life by pushing their enemies to perdition or by killing them. The only purpose of these Phanariots, aimed at since their earliest childhood, is to become a ruler in Wallachia or Moldavia. In order to fulfil their purpose, no inequity seems too great to them, no lowness too humiliating. Should a brother, uncle, cousin or even parent stand in the way of their aspiration, poison or the headsman's axe gets rid of them; for when you cannot annihilate those who might be damaging to you yourself, you denounce them, and there is only one step from denunciation, of whatever nature, to death, in Constantinople. The well-known greediness of this contemptible governance leads to the places coveted. In order to get there, you become dog-poor, and then you steal and rob to rebuild your wealth. A newly appointed ruler leaves Constantinople with debts of two-three million piasters. After four, five or six years of ruling, he returns with a wealth of five-six million, when given the time to gather it: but, in general, he is banished, exiled or beheaded after a few years of good living or if people find out that he has gathered a fortune large enough to be taken away from him.[29]

Ioan-Aurel Pop and Sorin Șipoș, in the radiography of the "qualities and flaws of Romanians", analyse Antoine François Le Clerc's notations. He, as did other travellers through the Romanian Principalities, observes the humiliating condition of the people there for, he says:

[...] the inhabitants of Moldavia and Wallachia [...] are possibly more oppressed than any other people within the Turkish Empire and it would undoubtedly be impossible for them to bear the effects of the financial requests of the tyrants should the wonderful fertility of their soil fail to provide the means to do so.[30]

In regards to the power relations within the Principalities, governance, the same Le Clerc writes:

[...] is never given to the worthiest. It is always the most generous [towards the sultan] and the one making the most promises that gets it. Also, the weakness of these princes who come to power because of money, and who are also deposed because of money, is a constant adversity for the nation they govern. The people are always at the mercy of a tyrannical and miser ruler, which the Turks change as they will [...]. By means of an astute politics, the Turks have left the rulers with some prerogatives to flatter their vanity. They allowed them to keep their titles of princes and to have a numerous court and entourage that would maintain the illusion of their former greatness.[31]

---

29 Apud Djuvara: *Între Orient și Occident*, p. 23.
30 Apud Ioan-Aurel Pop; Sorin Șipoș: Despre calitățile și defectele românilor într-un manuscris redactat de Antoine François Le Clerc (On the Qualities and Defects of Romanians in a Manuscript edited by Antoine François Le Clerc). In: *Familia*, issue 11–12, (469–470), November-December 2004, p. 261.
31 Apud Ioan-Aurel Pop; Sorin Șipoș: Despre calitățile și defectele românilor, p. 261–262.

The enforcement of a status of force was done through the right of appointment by the Porte, sufficient to exert control over the territory governed and including through the customs perpetuated, from the rite of audiences, to the oriental vestiary glamour, that entailed significant financial efforts, or by means of the entourage and the details of public presences. We find out that, dominated by the model of power exertion of the Phanariot ruler, the native squires:

> [...] spend entire fortunes on clothing and sumptuous harnesses, brought from overseas and if any of the rank and fashion, such as the logothete Costache Conachi, strays from the luxury rule by living more modestly and with a less glamorous representation, they are ridiculed and given various nicknames, accused of avarice, while others, such as the cupbearer from Iași, Lazu, are addressed satiric verses that barrack their worn outfits deemed inadequate for certain Moldavian squires.[32]

The bewilderment of the foreign travellers, observers of the luxury spectacle enacted by the squires, is well matched. Caragea's secretary, the Swiss Recordon asserted the following with regards to their vestiary luxury: "First, you should know that the outfit of a squire in Wallachia, without counting the jewels, costs in fact up to three-four thousand francs",[33] while Laurençon claimed that "Vienna sells a lot of its most elegant carriages to Wallachia. I believe that, if we take into account the population, there are only a few cities in Europe where one can find so many teams as in Bucharest. Each merchandiser has his own carriage, and the squires change theirs every year."[34]

Robert Ker Porter, after crossing the Principalities, speaks of the exuberant lifestyle of the squires, which "can hardly be bested in any of Europe's capitals. The balls and parties they throw, with the dresses and jewels their wives wear, surpass any imagination."[35] The oriental influence is evident even in their outfits.[36] The social status and the power of the ruler is noticed in the abundance of expensive oriental elements that are part of their outfit: *bashlik*,[37] *surplice*,[38]

---

[32] Alexandru Alexianu: *Mode și veșminte din trecut: Cinci secole de istorie costumară românească* (Fashions and Clothes of the Past: Five Centuries of Romanian Dressing Fashion). București: Meridiane 1987, p. 139.
[33] Apud Djuvara: *Între Orient și Occident*, p. 110.
[34] Apud Djuvara: *Între Orient și Occident*, p. 111.
[35] Apud Djuvara: *Între Orient și Occident*, p. 111.
[36] Djuvara: *Între Orient și Occident*, p. 54.
[37] 'işlik': Expensive fur hat or cloth, cylindrical worn by princes, boyars and sometimes by their wives, and lateron by merchants (tc. başlik);
[38] 'surplic': Long coat wore in the past by Romanian boyars and musicians;

fermenea,[39] *biniş*,[40] *slippers, shalwars, ciacşîrii*[41] or part of the women's outfit: *shalwars, surplice, vest, purdah, biniş*. As a counterpoise, when travelling through Europe, a local squire this time, Dinicu Golescu, observes a contrast between the apparel of the Vienese women and those from Bucharest at the beginning of the 19th century, their fashion evidently influenced by orientalism and the luxury that reflected social status, therefore the position of hierarchy and social power. The Romanian squire travelling at the gates of the West ascertains the oriental influence on the vestiary preferences of Romanian women and the excess that generates, in his view, bad taste and snobbery:

> The stupid jade-wearing a cloth of ten florins, made of clean cotton and beautifully tailored; and the noble rich lady-wearing a dress made of Maltese silk, or *croază*,[42] or *percale*,[43] clean and body tailored, beautiful [...]. Whoever sees the high ranked ladies in Vienna and ours, [...] will consider the Vienese as poor and ours governed by luxury, millionaires.[44]

It is a game of appearances that maintains a type of power determined by material ostentation and flashiness for:

> [...] the truth is entirely the opposite: the former have enough, but do not like luxury and speckled clothing. And ours are pretty poor, because all the merchandise is tally bought, until they start bidding their estates, but they are terribly governed by luxury. They would rather leave their children starving at home than go out for a walk without hundreds of other little pieces sewn in various ways, which they call accents, and which double the expense.[45]

But the surprising contrast is not only between the Principalities and the Western world, but within them as well. Romanian travellers such as Ion Codru Drăguşanu, Dinicu Golescu or Nicolae Filimon, from the second half of the 19th century, are interested firstly in the contrasting image with the other countries, with the purpose of implicitly expressing their disappointment and regret for the precarious social conditions at home, where people live under a political and economic domination. The foreign travellers notice the poverty of the inhabitants with the same compassion, but also look for the explanations for this given state, seemingly expressing less moral judgment in their considerations.

---

[39] 'fermenea': Short coat made of cloth embroidered with silk and fur worn by the boyars (tc. fermene);
[40] 'biniş': Boyar long ceremonial robe with wide sleeves (tc. biniş);
[41] 'ciacşîrii': Turkish wide trousers (tc. çaksır);
[42] 'croază': Material woven in four threads (fr. croisée);
[43] 'percale': Cotton clothed thin and smooth (germ. Perk);
[44] Dinicu Golescu: *Însemnare a călătoriii mele* (An Annotation of my Journey). Foreword by Marin Bucur. Bucureşti: Minerva 1971, p. 69.
[45] Golescu: *Însemnare a călătoriii mele*, p. 69.

In this sense, Leonardo Panzini, the former preceptor of Alexandru Ipsilanti's children, notes that:

> Such a beautiful country elicits the mercy of the foreigner and that of the European who thinks about its state of poverty and abasement... After being for so long at the Turkish government's beck and call, actually sold by it, always falling prey to the greediness of the rulers sent to it, not to govern it, but to rob and impoverish it, it is indeed a miracle that the people here have not already lost everything and that the land is not merely a dwelling for wolves and bears.[46]

The observations of Louis Parrant, the vice consul of France in Moldavia, in the report he sent to Talleyrand on June 11th 1789, also reveal the estate of this principality under the Ottoman domination. On the one hand, he is enthusiastic in regards to the fortunate 'location' of the Principality, due to its geographic variety and its fertile potential. However, he opposed to the principle of nature, in the full spirit of the French Enlightenment, reason, or the effects produced by human 'sins' on nature. The two major 'sins' contributing to the decline of Moldavia are 'governance', on the one hand, and 'depopulation' on the other, seen as the effect of the first sin.

> This province, *Parrant says*, also has a master, but a foreign master who robs it, who is forced to rob it and to do it with incredible haste. The ministers in his proximity know how to do exactly what he does. All the employees are careful to follow their example, so that the entire governance is merely a robbery; all its members are leeches willing to suck even the last drop of blood of the emaciated crowds. Here, goods never return where they left from: perhaps a piaster has never left the court to be put back into circulation. The new needs of the ruler must be met with new incomes. Not even the most unusual occurrences would untie the strings of a bag once it has been filled. Everything is kept carefully and sent to Constantinople, to pay the friends and protectors of the ruler, who thus prepares his own victories.[47]

Such characterizations of the effects of the Phanariots' rule repeat themselves and receive a stereotypical nature. The general consul of England, W. Wilkinson, also speaks of the destruction of the "public spirit of the Moldavians and the Wallachians" through the political system introduced by the Phanariots leading them. 'Dishonesty', 'servile obedience', 'pretence' and 'lie' are categories which the English consul uses to analyse the decadence of these Greeks. Moreover, the consul of Austria, Raicevich, considers the 'tricks' and 'injustices of the Greeks in Phanar' to be renowned. He believes it is sufficient to remind people that: "many

---

46 Apud Djuvara: *Între Orient și Occident*, p. 34.
47 Apud Djuvara: *Între Orient și Occident*, p. 35–36.

of them have ended with a noose around their neck, that no Greek has made a fortune and that the two provinces have been ruined and almost deserted."[48]

There is a double hierarchical type of power relations held by the ruler in the two countries. Often mentioned is the obedience relation to the Porte that appointed the ruler and regarded him as an administrator, out of an economic interest, while the ruler had absolute power over the subjects from the domains administered. In other words, by the end of the 18th century slave-like relationships in the two Principalities had developed. Neagu Djuvara confirms it:

> Although the Porte tended, as of the 18th century, to consider the rulers of Moldavia and Wallachia as simple province governors, it has not touched the laws and customs of the place, it has not dented the absolute power of the ruler, power that included the right to life and death over its subjects. In fact, although the Turk burdened the country from an economic point of view, and eventually appointed the rulers, he left them all the attributes of sovereignty, in addition to those of declaring war and minting coins.[49]

Therefore, in addition to the external and monetary politics, the ruler had absolute and unaltered power, on a local level, except for when failing to observe the requests of the Porte.

A useful and consistent work for witnessing the excess of power of the rulers from the Principalities is *Osservazioni storiche, naturali e politiche* (Napoli, 1788), belonging to Ignaz Stephan Raicevich, the interpreter of ruler Alexandru Ipsilanti and the future Austrian consul in the Principalities between 1782 and 1787. It was a very successful book, being translated into three editions: 1789 (Vienna), 1790 (Strasbourg) and 1810 (Vienna), and republished in 1822 in Milan and Paris.[50]

Raicevich says that, despite the uncertainty of the 'oppressor', constantly being threatened by the scheming for power and the susceptibility of the Porte, his actions are arrogant and aggressive towards the inhabitants of the Principalities. Apparently taking the advice of the Machiavellian 'Prince' to target at any cost the abuse of power in order to preserve it, the consul considers that "there is no governance more tyrannous than the one exerted by the rulers of Wallachia and Moldavia". In regards the manner of selecting these oppressors, it can be seen that the only criteria which counts for their 'elevation' to the rank of rulers of these countries are the financial ones and the plots, and the methods used to acquire their absolute power will also destroy them. In other words, the matter of tyrannical authority through terror and not as a natural

---

48 Apud Djuvara: *Între Orient și Occident*, p. 36–37.
49 Djuvara: *Între Orient și Occident*, p. 57.
50 See Potra: *Bucureștii văzuți de călătorii străini*, p. 65.

right or a right earned through the will of the society, but through the mediation of forces exterior to it, is seen as an excess of power that will eventually turn against the tyrant.

Raicevich also considers that the "tyrant is in a precarious situation and is often, a common person without any talents, elevated by Greek scheming, money and the favour of the Ottoman Porte and who is destroyed or returned to his vainness by yet another plot.[51] The ostentatious custom of power show-off is intentionally exaggerated, the tyrant wanting to impose respect on the local subjects through fear, because:

> The tyrant is so severe with his subjects who are unlucky enough to moan under such a yoke that a squire who has the misfortune of approaching the ruler comes to them shaking and with a much more servile attitude. I have seen many who, when lifting the door and going into the audience they wanted, they make the sign of the cross, asking for the help of their patron saint. The chosen ones are permitted by the ruler to kiss his hand, for squires usually kiss his feet or the bottom of his coat.[52]

In fact, the Austrian consul describes the entire ritual of maintaining the existent power relations when appointing these rulers, from the pompous public appearances, to the allotting of governance-related responsibilities, to completely assuming the role of an 'enlightened' sovereign, by appropriating "the entire apparatus of grandeur and glamour of a sovereign".

The consul also notices the contrasting nature of Bucharest during that period of time. On the one hand, he appreciates the order and the guarantee of the decisions taken by the authority of the rulers, noting that in Bucharest "at night, there are stationary guards in various slums, in addition to those patrolling the streets for protection against fire and thieves. There are also announcers letting the inhabitants know when to sweep up their streets and to clean their chimneys and who make known the new commands and legislations. At night, everyone is forced to carry a torch and the alehouses must be closed."[53] On the other hand, his observations also refer to the transmission of certain diseases among the squires of the Court, for the squires, whether busy or not, spend their day "in a circle, talking", this custom being attributed to "idleness and vanity".[54] This is a process of contaminating the native lords with the habits of the Phanariots, development that has enhanced the decadence of this social class and the decreasing of the state modernisation.

---

51 Apud Potra: *Bucureștii văzuți de călătorii străini*, p. 65.
52 Apud Potra: *Bucureștii văzuți de călătorii străini*, p. 65–66.
53 Apud Potra: *Bucureștii văzuți de călătorii străini*, p. 68.
54 Apud Potra: *Bucureștii văzuți de călătorii străini*, p. 67.

2.2 The Writer at the Doorway of Sunset

The image of the Romanian writer from the 19th century seems, in general, marked by a search for forms (literary currents, genres and species) and for autochthonous formulas of expression (literary language) within the Romanian territories that would gradually form during the interwar period. This search has meant a series of successive practices with the Western literary schools, from the critical spirit of the French Enlightenment, as is the case with Ion Budai Deleanu, to the exoticism of the French Romanticism, as is the case with the Văcărești poets, or the Faustian effervescence of the German Romanticism, as is the case with Mihai Eminescu, and the critique of social manners, if considering of Ion Luca Caragiale.

The European travels of the Romanian writers of the 19th century are dominated by contradictory feelings, from the ecstasy of the Wallachian traveller, Dinicu Golescu, in the face of the European civilization in *Însemnări ale călătoriei mele* (Notes from my Journey) (1826), up to the realism and sobriety of the 'reportage' loaded with moral meditations and revealing parables of Nicolae Filimon, from *Excursiuni în Germania meridională* (Excursions to Meridional Germany) (1858). Gradually, the educated traveller/observer becomes aware of the importance of what will later be analysed by Boas as 'cultural relativism', which entails the understanding of the differences between and the different historical rhythms of each culture, in a more complex analysis, of convergent historical and cultural factors of each culture, at a certain moment in time. Therefore, a gradual birth of an identity conscience and of the autonomous cultural identity is being witnessed. Literature is the mirror of this gradual metamorphosis.

Maiorescu's *autonomization of aestheticism*, probably the most important and defining formula for the end of the century, is a central stake of the critical spirit of Romanian culture during the age of 'colonizations'. Standing in front of the 19th century mirror, the Romanian writer finds forms that do not belong to them, a lack of authenticity, the serious expression of a West that does not represent as above but towards which they aspire and which they crave for, a language undergoing formation, where the regional register and that of copied neologisms coexist, often times in a disharmonic manner, themes that are foreign to them and which they do not understand, an entire world in which 'Romanianness' is not recognized. Writers such as V. Alecsandri and I. L. Caragiale have managed in the 19th century to ironically capture the 'unfinished' nature of the structuring of an authentic identity, at the border between national and various influences. Alecsandri in his comedies, especially in *Chirița în provinție* (Chirița in the province) (1855), ironizes the educated and nobiliary pretences of the rural squires, characterised in the end by lack of culture and snobbism. The classic dialogue between 'madam' Chirița and the French professor Șarl has made a career in the analysis of the representation of the superficiality of the influences later on criticized by Titu Maiorescu. Chirița smokes 'cigarres de Halvanne', while Șarl is exasperated by her free translations, which seem brutal French adaptations in the new Romanian literary languge. When she wants to know if the teacher is content with her son Guliță results in learning French, the dialogue becomes hilarious. The famous imitations, aberrant linguistic calques such as 'furculision' (fr.'fourchette'), 'fripturision' (rom. 'friptură'; engl. 'steak'), 'învârtision' (rom.'a învârti', engl. 'to turn arround'), determine the exasperation of 'Monsieu Șarl', the French teacher of the young squire:

> CHIRIȚA: C'est qu'il est très… zburdatic… mais avec le temps je sui sure qu'il deviendra un tambour d' instruction.
> ȘARL (cu mirare): Tambour?…
> CHIRIȚA: Oui… adică, dobă de carte… tambour… nous disons comme ça en moldave.
> ȘARL (în parte): Ah bon!… la voilà lancée.
> CHIRIȚA: Et alors nous l'enverrons dedans.
> ȘARL: Où ça, madame?
> CHIRIȚA: Dedans… înăuntru… nous disons comme ça en moldave.
> ȘARL (în parte): Parle donc le moldave alors, malheureuse.
> CHIRIȚA: Et voyez-vous, monsieur Charles, je ne voudrais pas qu'il perde son temps pour des fleurs de coucou.
> ȘARL: Pour des fleurs de coucou?
> CHIRIȚA: C'est-à-dire: de flori de cuc… nous disons comme ça…
> ȘARL: En moldave… (În parte.) Cristi… qu'elle m'agace avec son baragouin!
> CHIRIȚA: Aussi, je vous prie… quand il se paressera… de lui donner de l'argent pour de miel.
> *ȘARL: Comment*?… que je lui donne de l'argent?
> CHIRIȚA (râzând): Non… Să-i dai bani pe miere… de l'argent pour du miel… c'est correct… nous disons comme cela…
> ȘARL: C'est convenu… en moldave… Vous parlez comme un livre.
> CHIRIȚA: Merci… j'ai apprendé toute seulette le français… pre legea mea.
> ȘARL: Est-se possible!… C'est extraordinaire… Hé bien, votre fils vous ressemble… il a une facilité! dans quelques années il parlera aussi bien que vous.
> CHIRIȚA: Quel bonheur! Gugulea nineacăi… Auzi ce spune monsiu Șarlă… zice că ai să vorbești franțuzește ca apa… N'est-ce pas, monsieur Charles, qu'il parlera comme l'eau?
> ȘARL: Comme?… Ah oui, oui… vous dites comme ça en moldave. Oui… oui.[55]

If Alecsandri ironizes the superficial, absurd forms of linguistic deviancy at the interference with the French language and due to the lack of culture of the small Moldavian squires, following Maiorescu's critique, Caragiale has certainly succeeded in capturing this broken mirror of influences. The dialogue between its two characters, Farfuridi and Cațavencu, from the comedy *O scrisoare pierdută*

---

[55] Vasile Alecsandri: *Comedii* (Comedies). Edition by Georgeta Rădulescu-Dulgheru. Antologie by Aurora Slobodeanu. București: Minerva 1984, p. 203–204.

(A Lost Letter) (1884), reflects the superficial understanding of the European influence, as well as the direct critique of the autochthonous conservatism:

> **Farfuridi** (stuffy): Yes! Progress! Progress without conservation, when we well see that Europe...
> **Cațavencu** (interrupting in a barking tone): I don't want to know, my good fellow, to know of your Europe, I want to know of my Romania and my Romania alone... Progress, my good fellow, progress! In vain do you come with gooseberries, with antipatriotic inventions, with Europe, to deceive the public opinion.[56]

In other words, the contradiction of the Romanian spirit during the 19th century, in Maiorescu's sense, is between the progressive, modernizing values of Europe, brought about by the Enlightenment and the conservative, anti-progressive autochthonism. Caragiale's critical spirit, a feature that is the foundation of his comedies, is truly revealed in a famous letter sent to his friend, Alexandru Vlahuță, a letter denoting the inner knowledge of the forms without content that characterized the Romanian society during the 19th century:

> *Moftangioaica română*[57] only speaks Romanian avec les domestiques, otherwise only French- and is now taking classes of English language. Every day, the finical woman overturns entire stores, from the highest shelf to the lowest one, looking for samples and, malheureusement, never finding what she needs. Rich and poor, she often happens, out of distraction, when the merchandiser is looking elsewhere, to drop something in her muff or under her mantle. [...] The finical woman always stops her coupe across the street. She believes that there are only two cities in which one could live: Paris and București![58]

In the fragment above, the overlapping of customs from different geographic territories generates snobbism that is filtered through Caragiale's critical spirit and depicted through his pungent irony. Irony is therefore the predominant register used to illustrate the superficial manner of assuming and affirming the Romanian identity by relating it to the influences that have exerted pressure on its formation. From Alecsandri's Chirița that promised her subjects justice "with whiplashes on their back", to the local progressiveness of Caragiale's finicky, 'choosy' people, the Romanian writer has mirrored the shallowness of the identity beliefs of a 'changing and unsettled' world up to 20th century modernity.

---

56 Ion Luca Caragiale: *Opere. Teatru* (Works. Theater). Ediție de Al. Rosetti, Șerban Cioculescu, Liviu Călin. Preface by Alexandru George. București: Editura Fundației Culturale Române 1997, p. 177.
57 The term used by Caragiale is derived by the Romanian word 'moft', which meens 'trifle' or 'caprice' representative for a snobish person or defining a 'choosy' person.
58 Ion Luca Caragiale: Moftangioaica. In: *Moftul român*, Nr. 5/11 February 1893. Consulted at the web adress: http://www.digibuc.ro/colectii/moftul-roman-1893-c5023 [25.09.2016].

While in the case of Alecsandri and Caragiale, the literary stake of the discourse is a critical one, subjacently suggesting the superficiality of autochthonism, in the case of the Romanian travellers to the West, the situation is somewhat different. The Romanian travellers at the gates of the West, perhaps except for Kogălniceanu, as we have already seen, only criticize a lack of national conscience, a lack of genuine Western values, the relative and superficial civilization dominating only the surface layers of the Romanian society. These travellers adhere almost unconditionally to the values of Western culture, to the moral norms and the civilization that have built the strong, forceful image of Europe which can still be related to today. This, of course, speaks of the unconscious adherence of these half-learned travellers to the exceptionalism-based values of Eurocentrism, i.e. the values of power imposed by the European culture during colonialism, up to the modern period.

As seen in the case of the thesis displayed by Edward Said, through which the East is depicted as an image of the West, therefore, as a form of reductionism of non-Western cultures to the criteria that have defined Western culture throughout time, the critics of Eurocentrism have deemed its enforcement to have been determined by criteria related to power. They refer to economic power, to expansion through colonization, or to the religious power, from the medieval crusades to the Christian missions. Proclaiming the universal dimension of certain concepts such as democracy, scientific and economic progress, Christian ethics and morals etc., the West forcefully imposed itself as an absolute and ideal model, often being criticized as a new form of Ethnocentrism, paradoxically turning against its own humanistic ideals. The current debates on Eurocentrism have often often highlighted the fact that, in the postmodern age, a relativisation of values would not generate force relations that would lead to the weakening of local identities in the favour of generalist and global and relativist ones.

In the landscape of an identity crystallization of the 19th century Romania, literature has often played a relevant role, proving precisely the Eurocentrist mirage of the Romanian writers standing at the Western gates. Prior to Maiorescu's critique of the forms without content assumed by the Romanian culture, there are few examples of authors who succeeded in understanding the necessity to preserve and cultivate local values in this battle with the empires gravitating around and exerting power within the Principalities. Such an example is nevertheless Nicolae Filimon, who in 1858 journeys to Western Europe, and wrote a travel log entitled *Excursiuni în Germania meridională* (Excursions to Meridional Germany). In 'Chapter XV', entitled "Căpitan Vlad Nicoară din Dobriceni sau asedierea Vienei de Kara-Mustafa vizirul" (Captain Vlad Nicoară of Dobriceni or the siege of Vienna by Kara-Mustafa the vizier), a moral history can be found that could also function as an ethno-genetical story of the identity and cultural options that form the ground for the formation of the modern Romanian state.

Nicolae Filimon describes and dramatizes a history from the time of the Vienna siege, when, together with Kara-Mustafa's army there were also ten thousand Romanians led by Prince Șerban Cantacuzino. A Romanian detachment led by Captain Vlad Nicoară of Dobriceni is captured by the Polish led by King Sobieski. The discussion between the King of Poland and Captain Nicoară is a pretext for Filimon to display his principles regarding maintaining one's independence and religious freedom. Surprised that Prince Cantacuzino is on the Turks' side, although being a defender of the cross, the Polish king wants to understand this paradox. The answer given by the Romanian captain explains the situation to the king:

> The peoples have two religions. One of them is called independence and the right to exist as nations. Therefore, Your Majesty, we, Romanians, in order to be able to defend our nationality and our political existence, preferred to obey the Ottomans and to join them in the fight against the Jesuitism of Christian governments.[59]

The captain explains to the king that the Ottoman sultan is not as dangerous to maintaining national and religious identity, since he allows the governance of local rulers and does not attempt to convert the Romanians to Mohammedanism. The association with Christian neighbours, Nicoară goes on to claim, would have led to endless battles "of assimilation or fusion" waged against the "insidious propagandas of Catholicism and Lutheranism". The example given is that of the Romanians in Transylvania, who, "after losing their political rights, are now in danger of losing including their nationality and religion."[60] In other words, Cantacuzino's captain exposes a fear of annihilation to the extent of losing one's identity, which often forced the Romanians from the Principalities to prefer to obey the Porte, which targeted first of all the payment of tributes which, gradually, once the crisis of the Ottoman Empire started, in turn became overwhelming. The moral of Filimon's story is that Poland itself suffered as a result of defending the Austrian monarchy, being dismembered, despite the saving effort of defending Vienna.

Filimon's *Excursions*, in spite of their documentary nature, of a descriptive 'reportage' without any considerable aesthetic claims or with rare compared and relevant comments, provide a reminder of the nationalistic load

---

59 Nicolae Filimon: *Opere* (Works). Edition by Mircea Anghelescu. București: Univers Enciclopedic 2005, p. 531.
60 Filimon: *Opere*, p. 532.

these travellers were armed with. National passion is felt perhaps even when they criticize the 'insufficiency' of the Principalities and the manners of the native squires. They live nevertheless in the age of identity reaffirmation of the nations, of reconsideration of national virtues. Even when the traveller invests Captain Nicoară with diplomatic abilities and moral judgment, creating a connection between autonomy and religion, we see a reduction of identity to the criteria of religious freedom, which is of course a reasoning precedent to Enlightenment.

Recomposing the image of Bucharest during Alexandru Șuțu's period, with the intention of rebuilding the setting for the action of *Ciocoii vechi și noi* (The Old and New Parvenus) novel, Constantin Mateescu, in his biography *Pe urmele lui Nicolae Filimon* (In Pursuit of Nicolae Filimon) (1985), reminds us of the fact that almost all the foreign travellers are surprised by the large number of churches that had been built the last years of the Phanariots' rule.[61] He resumes Wiliam Hunter's observation: "When I tell you that the large number of churches in Bucharest equals 360, you will deduce that all the inhabitants must be priests. Indeed, I believe a high percentage of them are."[62] To counterbalance it, if considering to the fact that the number of other elementary institutions meant for people, such as hospitals, was extremely low, the same Mateescu demonstrating that in Bucharest in 1813, there was only 10 doctors and one chemist's shop,[63] we can infer how preoccupied the Phanariots' administration must have been with the development of the town. The obvious balancing of the local power towards the church reveals the false interest for compensatory spiritual freedom, to the obvious detriment of primary necessities, from infrastructure and sanitation, to the vital ones, such as hospitals, medics, and pharmacies. The Ottoman occupation through the Phanariots functioned rather as an economic colonization, being only implicitly legitimated by military threat, and more so by simulating an absolute religious freedom and therefore by maintaining religious identity. Nicolae Filimon's novel proves the opposite of Captain Nicoară's affirmations, the new parvenus also arguing their right to lead and therefore to continue exploiting and oppressing people through the right of appointment and divine investiture.

The day following the betrayal, capture and murder of Tudor Vladimirescu, Dinu Păturică, the representative 'new parvenu', depicted by Nicolae Filimon, receives as a reward from Ipsilanti the position of sub-prefect of Prahova and Săcuieni, the phanariot lord estimating he is even to receive the future office of

---

61 Constantin Mateescu: *Pe urmele lui Nicolae Filimon* (In Pursuit of Nicolae Filimon). București: Sport, Turism 1985, p. 19.
62 Apud Mateescu: Pe urmele lui Nicolae Filimon, p. 19.
63 Mateescu: *Pe urmele lui Nicolae Filimon*, p. 30.

"caimacam[64] of Craiova".[65] After several days of feasts and cheerfulness to celebrate the obtaining of this office, Păturică starts his administration with an astute rethoric exercise of invoking the divine power in favour of his inalienable right to search for the 'happiness' of the people over whom he gained power by becoming a 'master'. In a time when, the narrator tells us, "faith proclamations and professions were in fashion",[66] the new parvenu reads his own proclamation in front of the people gathered there, the deed in itself representing a political and religious form of legitimating his rule, and therefore his power:

> Brother's *boieri*, merchandisers and peasants,
> The Divine providence, having mercy of this miserable country, has elevated me to the merit of sub-prefect of these two counties. God almighty knows better than all of you the scalding burning in my heart for your happiness. Be then certain, my brothers, that as long as I am with you, nobody will be burdened one brass above what the law decides. Honest people who fear God will fulfill the official taxation of ruling from now on; bribes and frauds will be completely absent. Those abused should come to me and will find justice; for I want the rays of happiness to pierce through to the scummy cottage of the peasant.
> Amen, hear, hear.[67]

Reading such a proclamation, "with a dramatic accent and the rhetorical gestures used by Păturică when pronouncing it", seems to have a strong effect and leave an 'impression' on the auditors not used to such performances. Having come from Bucharest to rule over the two counties, Păturică rhetorically legitimates his power by appealing to guarantee human right and equality. His proclamation, progressive for the two counties, signifies an extension of the strategies used to legitimate power following the model of the capital of Wallachia, but also an inceptive formula of the active power the new parvenu holds, the only guarantor of justice and common good. Dinu Păturică's path, as observed by Nicolae Filimon, is representative of the manner of deployment of the active power, power that gradually evolves towards absolute domination, excess, exploitation and manipulation of others.

The strategies of the Subject on this path of exerting active power are varied and based on his practical abilities and his capacity to adapt his instruments to the changing situations that interfere throughout his path. The Subject, Dinu Păturică in this case, and his active power become representatives of an age when Moldavia and Wallachia held an intermediary position between Western ideals

---

[64] High official rang in the 19 Century Moldavia and Walachia used to replace the vizier and administrate the province (tr. kaymakam).
[65] Filimon: *Opere*, p. 240.
[66] Filimon: *Opere*, p. 41.
[67] Filimon: *Opere*, p. 241.

and Eastern reality. In this environment of identity confusion and political instability, power belongs to the Subject and is of a progressive-active and speculative nature, being argued for by absolute 'rights', such as appointment or divine 'anointment'.

Olsen and Marger[68] have analysed the concept of power as an interactive process, following the capacity of an actor, or actant in this case, to have active or potential social power. The resources of power are essential in this exercise of power and when such resources are converted to actions over or even against the others, this power becomes active. The resources available, if looking at the active power of the actant, when referring to this literary case study, the progressive power of the 'parvenu' on the others, are of a material nature and the forms of exerting power and the despotism of the actant also grow in direct ratio to their amplification. When distinguishing the "Types of authority and imperative coordination", in reference to the socio-economic organization, Max Weber established the "bases for legitimating" power, identifying three pure typologies of legitimating authority, i.e. a. rational knowledge or expertise relevant from a situational point of view; b. equal rights; c. traditional beliefs; d. charisma.[69] However, Marvin Elliot Olsen supplements Weber's theory by speaking of a tacit acceptance of authority as well.

2.3 The Old Parvenu at the Doorway of the Novel

In 1913, Eugen Lovinescu prophetically asserted, intending to draw a scheme of the Romanian epic in its evolution, but also the recurrence of the Romanian realism, that "the future of our novel will thus come from the furrow of N. Filimon's *Parvenus* (Rom. ciocoi). The semi-centenary of this lasting work ought also to remind us of what a novel should be: an image of the life circumstances from a certain age."[70] Let us not forget however that Lovinescu's anticipation occurs in full critical impressionism, meaning the moment of an organic vision on literature and in the search of the narrative genotype.

But the critic charts the physiognomy of the novelistic hero up to then, by asserting that "the predominant hero of the Romanian novel is the *failure*".[71] The rhetoric in the following paragraph is eloquent for the conception of the

---

68 Martin Marger; Marvin Elliot Olsen (eds.): *Power in modern societies*. Boulder: Westview Press, 1993, p. 2–3.
69 Weber: *The Theory of Social and Economic Organization*, p. 324–329.
70 Eugen Lovinescu: *Opere* (Works). Vol. V. București: Minerva 1987, p. 182.
71 Lovinescu: *Opere*, p. 182.

theoretician of modernism on the typology of the new character and his power relation with his world:

> And now the following question arises: is the Romanian society, in general, made of spiritually distinguished people, but unprepared for fighting, incapable of action, defeated beforehand? And if not, then why has our literature turned this failure into some kind of a national hero?[72]

The typology of Lovinescu emerges from the battle of the critic with the protochronist tendencies of Romanian criticism at the beginning of the 20th century, respectively with Constantin Stere and Garabet Ibrăileanu's *poporanism* populism or with Nicolae Iorga's *sămănătorism*. *The Failure*, as a Romanian prototype of the Romanian novel, a genre almost inexistent up to the moment of this socializing Lovinescian generalization, is merely a historically generated typology, lacking an exclusively Romanian literary representation. Literary realism has generated such generalizations, precisely in order to prove its function of social epic, in a period when the novel represented the masses. Thus the general stake is historical and reflects the opposition proposed by the novel of the 18th and 19th centuries against the noble idealism of human destiny in general. In the face of History, man can only be a Failure. Thomas Pavel's arguments regarding the 'social anthropology' proposed by the novel are relevant for the Romanian debate on this species. In fact, the thinker of the novel describes the birth of the pre-modern novel of the 16th and 17th centuries as a confrontation, transferred to the subgenres. He is pointing to the most important feature of the novel and of literature in general: the flexible reference between contextual determinism and autonomy. Pavel states that "while literary and, more generaly, artistic genres are linked to the social and intelectual life of their time, they also enjoy a qualified autonomy."[73]

At the same time, the novel of the following two centuries proposes an association of the "the gradual increase in social mobility and equality and it coincided with a propensity to blend the older narrative subgenres into a single, flexible genre–the modern novel."[74] The novel of the 18th century questions the effect of the moral law and the individual's freedom to decide his actions, while the novel of the 19th century is dominated by the substitution of idealistic moral points of reference with the power to determine the environment that polishes one's character and destiny. Thus, as Thomas Pavel confirms, "when characters cannot gain acces to their own innermost recesses, when their understanding of themselves and of

---

72 Lovinescu: *Opere*, p. 182.
73 Pavel: *The Lives of the Novel*, p. 19.
74 Pavel: *The Lives of the Novel*, p. 19.

moral requirements become blurred, they exemplify the *enigmatic psyche*.[75] This is the background for the emergence of the novel of the Failure, where the typology of the character owes it all to the battle between the individual, but representative, consciousness, the empty idealness of society and this emergent, atopical *psyche*, wich is the soul of the modern novel. The radical change of outlook occurs with the novel of the 20th century, once the individual escapes from the prison of his environment and is transferred to that of his own sensitivity.

The typologies of the modernist novel are subject to the 'man without qualities' as conceived by Musil, in other words without having a direct conflict with the environment, but in conflict with his own *psyche*. This 'foregone failure', as Lovinescu would have labelled him, no longer preserves anything, for example, from the tragic Flaubertian predestination of Emma Bovary or the physiognomy of the rebelling loser, Etienne Lantier, in Zola's *Germinal*.

Under these conditions, it should be implicitly asked if Lovinescu's generalization is valid, in the context in which a typological discussion on the Romanian novel is possible merely when referring to the interwar period, the moment of its genesis and diversification. However, in order to attempt more of an identification of the sources of Nicolae Filimon's novel, Nicolae Manolescu's mentioning, which comes as a continuation of Nicolae Iorga's exegesis,[76] or the Călinescian clarification[77] of Balzac's sources and of the popular novel is opportune. Manolescu understands the convergence of "two stylistic traditions during the middle of the Romantic decade."[78] It is firstly about a memorialising experience specific to the 1848 generation, which Filimon had already experimented in his 'reportages' from *Excursiuni în Germania meridională* (Excursions to Meridional Germany). Secondly, in Manolescu's view, it recovers the tradition of "Balzac's and popular novel (physiognomy, sensational, thesis etc.)."[79]

One fact is nevertheless certain when searching for the sources of this novel: it lacks a Romanian tradition of the genre, although some literary critics place it within the ancestry of Negruzzi, Odobescu or Hasdeu's proses.[80] This fact grants it not only disadvantages caused by the lack of epic and novelistic exercise in

---

75 Pavel: *The Lives of the Novel*, p. 18.
76 Apud Gabriela Danţiş (ed.): *Nicolae Filimon*. Anthology, foreword, chronological table and selective bibliography by Gabrilea Danţiş. Bucureşti: Eminescu 1980, p. 6.
77 George Călinescu: *Istoria literaturii române de la origini până în prezent* (The History of the Romanian Literature from Origins to Present Day). Edition and Preface by Alexandru Piru. Bucureşti: Minerva 1982, p. 361–364.
78 Manolescu: *Istoria critică a literaturii române*, p. 348.
79 Manolescu: *Istoria critică a literaturii române*, p. 348.
80 Henri Zalis: *Nicolae Filimon*. Bucureşti: Tineretului 1958, p. 159.

Romanian, such as an inherent lack of coherence of the account and an eclectic style that have led to the difficulty of classifying the style,[81] but also advantages, such as its innovative and experimental nature,[82] or the practice of a meta-literary conscience, fully proved in the 'Dedication' of the novel, a true ironical strategy of searching for the ideal reader. Our author seems to be familiarized with the tradition of the idealistic European pre-modern novel, be it Hellenistical, chivalric or pastoral and consciously reacts to the role literature should have in compliance with its times. It is thus possible to fathom the observations on Balzac-like aspects of the novel *Ciocoii vechi și noi* (The Old and New Parvenus), by identifying precisely the picaresque resources of Filimon's novel. It is about recovering this epic tradition and anchoring it in the known history of the author, marking through the destiny of his picaro, Dinu Păturică, the climax of the Phanariots' period. The novel's duty to the comical tradition is acknowledged by the author in the very 'Dedication' of the novel, where he converts the ironical register into a specifically picaresque one, dotted with "the cruel humor of amoral picaresque stories, though without an amoral protagonist."[83]

Even the hybridized aesthetic formula that Vianu spoke of is typical for this novelistic historical category. In a world where we witness the chaos of moral norms and where in favour of arguing the absolute power of the hero, Christian moralizing elements or religious identity criteria are invoked, the picaro speculates man's primary need of human standardization. His moral conscience is non-existent and the world moral and ethical norms are lost. In such a context, "social norms are imposed by sheer brutality, and the bonds between people have been degraded beyond all remedy."[84] The subject is only aware of the people fearing Christian morality, a people that is passive when threatened with the punishment of transcendence, and transforms this fear in an energy capital that will serve its active power.

Following this line of conviction that Filimon's novel recovers the tradition of the picaresque novel from the 16th century, one should implicitly wonder if

---

81 Tudor Vianu: *Arta prozatorilor români* (The Art of Romanian Prose Writers). București: Contemporanul 1941. He saw the novel as a combination of genres, from the memorialistic nature, to the social novel, social and documentary study.

82 Ion Negoițescu: *Analize și sinteze* (Analyses and Syntheses). București: Albatros 1976, p. 90–91. He spoke more explicitly of the 'suffering' of the aesthetic in Filimon's case, but, except for its aesthetical imperfections, he appreciated this "model as imperfect and contradicted in terms, as pregnant". George Ivașcu, in *Istoria literaturii române* 1 (The History of Romanian Literature 1). București: Editura Științifică 1969, p. 501, also criticized the schematics of the composition and the imbalance of consistency of certain paintings, some too burdened, others too brief.

83 Pavel: *The Lives of the Novel*, p. 71.

84 Pavel: *The Lives of the Novel*, p. 59.

Filimon's novel is a realistic one of a Balzac-like type, as often remarked upon by its interpreters, from Iorga, to Călinescu and Manolescu. Among the first to doubt the realistic elements of Filimon's prose is Eugen Simion who, in an article from 1969, challenged the realistic and critical dimension of the author, granting him a more romantic one, which is 'temperamentally' and 'stylistically' observable[85] and classifying the novel as a part of the category of 'apocalyptical novels' during that period of time. The same idea is resumed in the *Introduction* to the 2005 edition by Mircea Anghelescu,[86] the critic deeming the prose to be of a different nature than Balzac-like, "due to its taste for the violent contrast, falling rather under Romanticism, and more specifically the crepuscular Romanticism, that of the popular and mystery novel, in which the past becomes the place of battle among certain schematic human typologies, derived from a typological abstraction, with an ethic content: good and bad, squires and parvenus. An exemplary fragment from the chapter 'Până nu faci foc, fum nu iese' (There is no smoke without fire), reveals the typical romantic framework, overly present in Filimon's novel and often in contrast with the urban universe of Bucharest at the beginning of the 19th century:

> It was one of those summer nights when the whole nature opened up the treasures of its amazing beauties, in order to give us a perfect idea of its sublimeness; the celestial canopy was of a delightful blue; the stars scattered upon its endless surface were full of a magical light this time; the moon, whose pale and sweet face fills sensitive hearts with longing and ardour, hanged between the towers of the Cathedral and, unable from that holy place to pursue her ardent amour with the young shepherd Endymion, her lover since pagan times, she seemed to look with rapacious joy upon so many lovers caressing one another fierily under its amorous rays. The warm breaths of the spring wind were so mild, that only the leaves of the popular swung idly.[87]

On the other hand, Șerban Cioculescu asserted that *Ciocoii vechi și noi* (The Old and New Parvenus) is "a novel of the erstwhile Bucharest!",[88] thus a realistic fresco of the town at the interference of times and worlds, as noted by numerous foreign travellers located at the gates of the Sunrise. In other words, the reputed critic shifts the emphasis from our picaresque hero's destiny to the contrasting image of Bucharest, "in its variegated architecture, in its variegated costume, in the multiplicity of social aspects between 1814 and 1825, this is the

---

[85] Eugen Simion: Primul nostru romancier (Our First Novelist). In: *România literară*, 2nd year, issue 36, September 4th, p. 13.
[86] Mircea Anghelescu. In: Filimon: *Opere*, p. XXIII.
[87] Filimon: *Opere*, p. 57.
[88] Șerban Cioculescu: *Prozatori români* (Romanian Prose Writers). București: Eminescu 1977, p. 60.

objective image, appearing to be a fantastic diorama coming off when reading the novel."[89]

When comparing the realistic fresco of the town at the beginning of the 19th century with that of Bucharest at the end of the same century, then a reference to Ion Marin Sadoveanu's novel, *Sfârșit de veac în București* (End of Century in Bucharest) (1944) would be relevant.[90] Bucharest's urban landscape in Sadoveanu's novel is specific to the realistic prose, reconstructing in detail the contrasting topography of the town at the end of the century. Sadoveanu is only partially a descendent of Filimon's, following through the destiny of the arriviste Iancu Următecu, a series of other destinies with which he interlaces, but also creating a picture of the town, from its architecture to its interiors with furniture and household details in an ample thorough descriptive exercise of an evident Balzac-like origin. In the process of describing a world found at the interference between the East and the West, Sadoveanu makes use of the arsenal of descriptive punctiliousness, and Următecu, indeed a descendant of Dinu Păturică, is one of this world's stage props. In Filimon's case however, we do not witness a descriptive abundance, neither the realistic ability of Balzac-like prose writer to control every detail of Păturică's world. The character is central in this description and around him a declining world is being built. The details congeal according to the parvenu's character and diminish once he controls the destinies of the others.

Therefore, *Ciocoii vechi și noi* (The Old and New Parvenus) is only partially a novel of the Phanariots' period, rebuilding this picture in pieces. It is firstly a novel of Dinu Păturică, of the arriviste who gradually comes to hold power, of the picaro that is in fact a representative anti-hero who will live within the limits of his social determinism, failing on his active path towards absolute power. The structure of the novel, with autonomous episodes fragmenting the story, creating the impression of an epic incoherence, contributes to the conviction that the objective set by the author in the 'Dedication', is to draw a portrait of the 'parvenu' and not of Bucharest. On these grounds, Filimon's realism could be placed more within the lineage of the picaresque novel, than within the realistic monolith of Balzac-like origin that would rather characterize a novel such as that of Ion Marin Sadoveanu's. Moreover, the obvious intention of the prose writer is to explicitly and virulently criticize the manners of the central character, to highlight them through intensive focus, often to the detriment of epic cohesion

---

89 Cioculescu: *Prozatori români*, p. 60.
90 Also see Aurel Martin's comparison in the 'Foreword' to the Nicolae Filimon edition: *Ciocoii vechi și noi* (The Old and New Parvenus). București: Editura pentru literatură 1964, p. XXXVIII–XXXIX. He notices the distillation of Sadoveanu's epic and the detachment from the action, filtered through the experience of the interwar Romanian realism, unlike Filimon's founding action.

and aesthetic harmony. The active subject, aware of his actions, patient, hypocritical and perfidious, intransigent and ambitious to the point of destructiveness is the stake of this novel, representative for the first category of power relations in Romanian literature.

Nicolae Filimon eloquently places the beginning of the action of this "original novel" at the border between the 'old', represented by the great *postelnic*[91] Andronache Tuzluc, the favourite of George Caragea, the Phanariot king, and the 'new' represented by Dinu Păturică, who is to become Tuzluc's favourite and will eventually replace him. The novel is circular; however, it is not a Balzac-like circularity, but an intensification of the moralizing intention that in fact dominates the entire novel, "to be a parable to the people". We notice such a circularity during the last meeting of the parvenus, the narrator imagining the two 'funerals', that of Dinu Păturică, who died in prison, and that of 'postelnic' Andronache Tuzluc, blocking each other's way on a narrow street in Bucharest, on which Costea Chiorul was 'pinned' as punishment. Their meeting reminds us of the first one, when Păturică arrives at the courts of 'postelnic' Tuzluc and begins his ascension. The scene is indeed part of the rounded picture of the narrative, but the stake is to underline in a moralizing manner the effects of power excess. Filimon's moral is obvious, closing the picaresque ending with its critical comment: "This is how these three scoundrels end their life career. Chance had willed them to meet once more before appearing in front of God to realize what evil doings they had accomplished on this earth."[92]

But in order to consolidate the idea that the circularity of *Ciocoii vechi și noi* (The Old and New Parvenus) firstly emphasizes moral, more precisely, the fatal effects that the excess of illegitimate power has on the picaro, we notice that when describing the agonic ending of the character, the narrator points once more the divine legitimation and the Weberian legal right, nevertheless, arbitrarily established by the despot and its evil effects on the person being legitimated. The scene in which Filimon re-establishes justice reminds the reader once more of the moment of Păturică's proclamation, when he claims the divine 'providence', but this time, at the end of the novel, closing the circle by summoning divinity bears a different meaning. If in his initial proclamation, Păturică exploits the popular irrational mysticism in order to self-legitimate his active power, in the end, the narrative voice hunting Păturică the prisoner takes the form of his father's voice. The anathema of power excess thus belongs to the

---

[91] 'postelnic' was an historical rank held by boyars in Moldavia and Wallachia, coresponding to the post of chamberlain.
[92] Filimon: *Opere*, p. 257.

father, therefore the paternal power rebuking him in a hallucinatory manner, psychologically torturing him:

> [...] with a ghastly voice: 'You bastard son! Look at the state your viciousness and pride have brought me into! God, whom you have despised for such a long time, announce you, through me, that you should redeem your soul through repentance, for your body will not leave this place alive.[93]

The force of the primary unconsciousness surfaces as a moralizing voice and de-legitimates the active power of the character, asking him to regain his reflexive power, in order to re-establish his personal balance. The narrative voice is the one hiding behind the paternal moral one and the one heralding the degradation and the end of the Subject deluded by the infinite nature of active power. The shadow of the father resembles the hallucinatory shadow of Popa Iancu, the brother of Stavrache the tavern keeper from Ion Luca Caragiale's naturalistic short story *În vreme de război* (In Times of War) (1898). The moral induced in both texts through the naturalistic instrument of madness belongs to the author camouflaged behind the hallucinatory masks of those who have gone who hold a power legitimised in the unconsciousness of the characters, but which surfaces when the Subjects lose control of the world articulated by or through their active power.

2.4 Scenes from the Socio-political Life and the Hierarchization of Power

In the 'Epilogue' to *Ciocoii vechi și noi* (The Old and New Parvenus) the author proposes a sequence of a scene from the social life in Bucharest in 1825, with the marriage of the former court bailiff of *postelnic* Andronache Tuzluc, Gheorghe, to "beautiful Maria, the daughter of *ban*[94] C.". He even receives the "caftan of great sword bearer", becoming "*caimacam*[95] of Craiova".

In fact, the descriptive, panoramic intention imprinted by the author on the narrative *ab initio* also disguises the moralizing temptation, derived from the popular tradition of the Romanian epic to that date to re-establish in the story a moralizing balance, according to which Good conquers Evil. Identifiable within the first phase is the fictionalized image of the town described during a

---
[93] Filimon: *Opere*, p. 253.
[94] 'ban' designates a public oficial rank of governor of a province (Oltenia) during the Phanariots' regime.
[95] 'caimacam', at the beginning of 1761 was an oficial substitute of the Turkish 'vizier'.

time of celebration, "on St. George's Day, the old patron saint of Romania", the scene depicted by including lyrical effect reminiscent of Negruzzi or Russo's prose, to which Filimon the moralist adds his critical touch, with the town being decorated with flowers, grass, willow, fir trees planted in the ground and coloured ribbons which all resemble an "improvised garden". The Bucharest painting of this ceremonial event is firstly a fresco of social hierarchies during the first part of the 19th century, and Filimon follows the example of Negruzzi when describing the society's stratification of Wallachia. However, bellow is the image of the royal cortege showing the hierarchization of power, as outlined by the narrator.

Behind the princely carriages, located at the centre of the procession, other social categories that participate directly in the event that ends the *Ciocoii vechi și noi* (The Old and New Parvenus) are positioned, thus maintaining the idea of a pre-set and stable order standardizing the administration of the principality. Therefore, the guilds constituting "that showiness of greatness known only at the Oriental courts".

From a lexical point of view, Șerban Cioculescu[96] was right in claiming that the author of the *Parvenus* is often not very far away from *Povestea vorbii* (The Story of Speaking), which is also confirmed biographically, through the friendship between Nicolae Filimon and his illustrious predecessor, Anton Pann. The inventory of lexical variations, from popular lexical forms, to the richness of the Turkish or Greek neologistic register, to provincial and even archaic words or other forms of popular vocality by means of yotizations and rhotacisms determines Cioculescu to consider the author a philologist, thus an author educated in the variety of language. "The description of the local features of the Phanariot period, *the literary critic asserts*, is obtained through a large number of Turkish and Greek words, which, just like in Ion Ghica's *Scrisori* (Letters) contribute to the enrichment of the descriptive palette."[97] The listing of the participants to this celebration contains an implicit hierarchization of an Oriental nature, not only through vocabulary, but also by the placement of persons within the cortege in the order of importance, following the social model of the Porte.

The following fragments at the end of the novel are eloquent when it comes to completing a social picture of the administration of the principality that preserves its power by maintaining the public ritual. Ion Ghica spoke of the novel as "a collection of true and vivid paintings of our customs and manners during

---

[96] Cioculescu: *Prozatori români*, p. 59–105.
[97] Cioculescu: *Prozatori români*, p. 100.

the transition period",[98] but from this ample painting, the very "inhabitants of Bucharest" are missing. Or better said, their presence is neutral, being regarded as a unitary unstratified mass of no interest to our narrator, who lacks the interest or the ability to know the psychology of the masses, which emphasizes the passive power of the crowd and the active power of the orientalised administration. Clumsy, the narrator's eye vaguely and lapidary distinguishes that "Mogoșoaiei bridge was full of onlookers of both genres and from all classes of society, well dressed and smiling", or that on both sides of the road flanked by soldiers, "pyramids of meddlers were formed, impatiently waiting for the royal cortege to pass by". This celebration also seems improvised, as was the case with the Bucharest garden on the verge of celebration. A break in Filimon's painting that unconsciously transposes the social gap imposed, maintained and even exacerbated by the customs of the Phanariots' rule.

Perpessicius considered this novel to be "a fresco of manners",[99] but the fresco of manners depicts the Phanariots exclusively and it especially depicts the impact of their manners on the local squires and on the members of the administration of their court. In order to underline the manner of active exertion of power on people, in the chapter entitled 'Scene de viață socială' (Scenes of social life),[100] we encounter such a fresco, rather moral than social. Shifting from the lyric effusions of a Romantic nature at the beginning of the chapter, by changing from the epithet of "the beautiful autumn days of 1817", to the metaphor of the days 'flying by' and continuing with the pastel image of winter that "strips trees and covers fields and towns with the veil of sadness and monotony", the narrator quickly moves to describing the people from the 'middle class'. He ascertains that the people forming the middle class of Romania in 1817 are "long accustomed with the Oriental life full of laziness and poetry", therefore outlining a category of people who seem to have taken over part of the monotony and drowsiness that has come to be expected from from the Romantic descriptions or paintings regarding the East. It is the same Oriental air found, for instance, in Dimitrie Bolintineanu's *Florile Bosforului* (The Flowers of Bosporus), when "the night is beautiful, the Bosporus balmy", thus a romantic temptation of the Oriental exoticism.

However, the ethnographic interest of the author, i.e. to describe the small interests and occupations during the leisure time of the middle class in Bucharest, reveals the contact between the East and the West, or the oriental background of simple pleasures and the occidental temptation of the novelistic culture.

---

98 Apud Danțiș (ed.): *Nicolae Filimon*, p. 34.
99 Perpessicius: *Opere* II, p. 5.
100 Filimon: *Opere*, p. 104–115.

The description of the country dances constitutes such an opportunity of the eclectic culture in the 19th century. Each *"isnaf*,[101] artisan or family head" laid their table on the grass, indulging in cheerfulness, and when they started dancing the "ancestral hora and the merry dances", associated with "the Neapolitan tarantella so beloved by the entire Latin people", even the older ones "pulled out their long *binişe*,[102] rolled up the coat tails of their surplices". But this combination of music and autochthonous dances and the oriental clothing of the parvenus, makes the author discontent with the 'grotesque effect' generated by this mixed world, as we can notice in the chapter entitled 'The Music and the Choreography during Caragea' (Muzica şi coregrafia în timpul lui Caragea). This image creates an instance of disharmony displays Păturică's guests, dancing "with the coat tails of their surplices up to their girdle", or "with red *ceacşiri*,[103] with *meşi*[104] and yellow slippers", either to the "so-called Napoleon's march and other recreation music pieces very fashionable at that time", or to other western dances, such as "the monotonous minuet, the classic dance of the European salons,[...], the French cotilion, the German waltz and the Scottish dance brought from the bottom of Britain."[105]

Tired because of the effort of practising unknown dances, but from taking over the western custom in the Oriental clothing, the parvenus are revitalized only by the autochthonous songs and dances, i.e., the *"pristoleanca, chindia* [...] or *zoralia"*.[106] This is the image of an eclectic society whose 'forms without content' Maiorescu would later criticize. These rapid transformations taking place in Romanian society in the 19th century were a result of the westernization of the Principalities, especially following the Russian-Turkish war of 1768–1774. The contact the squires had with the Russian officers, educated in Europe, marked an important moment in the beginning of the Europeanization of Romanian society at the end of the 18th century and beginning of the 19th century. But the rapid changes also marked the eclecticism of influences that created an image of such of a society.

Is this the Bucharest of a mixture of cultures and influences, between Europeanizing tendencies and Oriental traditions that both fascinated and frightened

---

[101] 'isnaf': a turquish term for *guild*, defined as "A medieval association of craftsmen or merchants, often having considerable power." (see https://en.oxforddictionaries.com/definition/guild).
[102] 'biniş': Boyar long ceremonial robe with wide sleeves, rom tc. *biniş* (see: https://dexonline.ro/definitie/biniş) [27.04.2018].
[103] 'ciacşiri': Turkish large trousers, from tc. çaksır.
[104] 'meşi': Boots without heels.
[105] Filimon: *Opere*, p. 126–130.
[106] Names of popular dances in Wallachia.

2.4 Scenes from the Socio-political Life and the Hierarchization of Power

any foreign traveller in search of the meaning of this world? The striking contrast noticed by the majority of travellers to this world of contact is also generated, rightfully so, by the social difference and the status of the two extremes constituting Romanian society in the 18th and 19th centuries, between luxury, the opulent life of the squires and that of the parvenus in their entourage and the poverty of the peasants forming the rural outskirts of the town. The inexistence of an autochthonous middle class may be the explanation for this contrast.

Pompiliu Eliade, in his Ph.D. Thesis from 1898, delivered in the Sorbonne and entitled *De l'influence française sur l'esprit public en Roumanie. Les origines. Étude sur l'état de la société roumaine à l'époque des règnes phanariotes*, concluded upon elaborating the profile of the Phanariot ruler within the panorama of the society during the Old Regime, precisely on the absence of a middle social category.

> The peasants or the oppressed on the one hand, the squires or the oppressors on the other, a clergy unworthy to be paid attention to, devoid of any influence, almost outside of society, an all-mastering ruler: there seems to be a link missing in this social hierarchy. There is no intermediary class; there is no so-called bourgeoisie.[107]

The literary historian circumscribes the social situation in Romania to a model disputable nowadays, or in any case current at the end of the 19th century, but questioned at the end of the 20th century by some sociological analysts and/or politologists,[108] who consider the Marxist instrument of description of the societal stratification to not be currently out of date. As will be seen we will see in the temporally progressive analysis of the various novels and the way they relate to the paradigm of power,[109] social organization at the beginning of the current century is determined rather by what Turner calls status politics. It refers to the organization of status groups standardized by distinct objectives and not by social classes that are in conflict due to contradictory interests, creating the premises of certain conflicts in the social field.

---

107 Pompiliu Eliade: *Influența franceză asupra spiritului public în România. Originile. Studiu asupra stării societății românești în vremea domniilor fanariote* (The French Influence on the Public Spirit in Romania. The Origins. A Study on the State of the Romanian Society during the Phanariot Rulings). Translated to Romanian by Aurelia Creția. Foreword and notes by Alexandru Duțu. București: Univers 1982, p. 100.
108 See Jonathan H. Turner: *Societal Stratification: A Theoretical Analysis*. New York: Columbia University Press 1984 and Peter Saunders: *Citizenship and Social Theory*. London: Sage Publications 1993.
109 Relevant in this sense is the analysis of a novel such as *Asediul Vienei* (The Siege of Vienna), (2007; 2012) by Horia Ursu, where community is reduced to a common, amorphous and inactive class, engaged in the process of social erosion of transition (see supra).

Should Max Weber's theory again be considered, according to which the social stratification is reducible to the concept of power, ascertaining that this concept of power is relevant to the structuring of the social class as a result of obtaining and managing material commodities, then Pompiliu Eliade's analysis is also somewhat relevant to the 19th century. Weber spoke of power as "the chance of a man or of a number of men to realize their own will in a communal action even against the resistance of others who are participating in the same action."[110] On the other hand, "Economically conditioned", power is determined by "finding inner satisfactions, a probability which derives from the relative control over goods and skills and from their income-producing uses within a given economic order."[111]

Eliade rightfully asks himself who are the merchants, the traders of clothing, the tavern keepers, the grocers mentioned including by the foreign travellers to the Romanian Principalities? This intermediary social class mediating the sale of commodities from producers to squires is made mostly of 'foreigners', Eliade tells us, tributary to the identity mentality during the 20th century, when the Armenians, Greeks, Turks, Jews who, together with Romanians, formed the social landscape of Wallachia. At the same time, the merchandise the travellers wonder at and which emphasizes the contrast between the Oriental social landscape and the mixed items, be they Oriental or Occidental, are imported, as seen previously. When correlating the Weberian thesis of class-goods-power with the picture depicted by Eliade and not only him, but also by all those who describe the disastrous economic and social effects generated by the Phanariots' rule, an understanding of the social gap that led to the end of this rule and motivated the new parvenus to escape the enslavement of poverty can be developed:

> The squires, *says Pompiliu Eliade*, use weird words to designate all those who fail to reach the level of squire, who are not part of the nobility: they call them *rude* or, even more significantly, *stupid*. Therefore, from their point of view, the entire society is divided on the one hand into nobles, and on the other hand, into *rude* and *stupid* people.[112]

In this social painting it is easily understood why the royal cortege is constituted according to the model of stratification of powers within the royal courts, while the 'rude' and the 'stupid' gather to watch the parade of power legitimation. It is also understandable why Filimon focuses on the social life at the squires' court, where the parvenus, those who have rapidly and by using the same corrupt means reached the status of squire, imitate mixed Eastern and Western customs.

---

110 Weber: *Economy and Society*, p. 926.
111 Weber: *Economy and Society*, p. 302.
112 Eliade: *Influența franceză asupra spiritului public în România*, p. 101.

The narrator describes such a scene taking place during winter, on November 30th, on St. Andrew's Day, at the court of 'postelnic' Andronache Tuzluc, when, in order to maintain his leverage of power, he prepares an impressive meal combining the Eastern luxury with the finest local dishes. The manner of spending their leisure time also differs, in the Weberian terms of obtaining a personal satisfaction, for the "squires and the very wealthy people were very different from the people regarding their parties". Following the culinary excess, the author describes the card game and the immorality of vice, for "the scandalous life and depravation taking huge proportions also infected and demoralized to a high degree the entire society", claims the narrator in a generalizing excess. The hierarchization of power is visible even in the serving of coffee, for the servants who carried out this Eastern ritual, "knowing very well the rules of hierarchy, being servants in a big house, they first went to Prince Costache, then, gradually, to all the others and fulfilled their duties with elegance and precision".

The scenes witnessed in the squires' houses are exclusively scenes of social life, reflecting precisely their minor, passive role, according to the Kantian formula, in establishing politics within the Principalities, in imposing authentic national politics. They do not have a political life, but rather on the contrary: they astutely avoid getting involved in the political debates on power, implicitly legitimising the idea that the ruler appointed by the Porte has absolute power. The political discussion on the laws prepared by Caragea for the country is interrupted by Prince Costache who "wanted to break that conversation whose seriousness hid only lies and flattery". The parvenu's politics, Filimon tells us in the 'Prologue' to his novel, shows a strategy, a dodging way in order to preserve his power, his social position:

> The parvenu or the little parvenu, now a statesman, is different from the honest man due to several deeds, and especially due to his demeanour. He does not definitively support any political doctrine, does not become a faithful follower of any party, and not because he has a righteous and unbiased spirit, but also in order to exploit simultaneously all the doctrines and parties to his benefit.
>
> The love for his country, freedom, equality and devotion are the sacramental words of the parvenu, which he utters in public and private gatherings; but these civic virtues, which he shows off, are only the steps of the ladder he wishes to climb to power; and sometimes, when they are not enough, he runs to strangers and receives from them offices in his country.[113]

Conjugating the repeated political avoidance of his characters, with the moralizing omniscience of the author in the 'Dedication', 'Prologue' and 'Epilogue' or in his comments throughout the actions, the distancing from the model of Anton

---

[113] Filimon: *Opere*, p. 8–9.

Pann, mentioned by critics such as Mircea Muthu (1976) or Șerban Cioculescu (1977) is also noticeable. Seemingly returning to Eugen Simion's assertions in 1969, Mircea Muthu also explains this 'retrospective' conscience[114] of Filimon through his romantic attitude, to which one could add the practical sense of the fresco and public moral. Maybe this is implicitly one of the deficiencies of Filimon's prose, which succumbs either in the face of the pictorial risk, descriptive to the extent of prolixity, as seen in 'Scene de viață socială' (Scenes of social life), or in the face of the deeply and inquisitorial moralizing risk, culminating with the drastic and not so credible punishment of the negative characters. A dichotomization circumscribed to the deficiencies of this founding prose. "Details sometimes aggregate in a monstrous manner, flaunting the exterior painting, the forms sinning through the excess of refinement, specific to the Phanariots' Alexandrinism. The Byzantine glamour is copied more to the letter and less in spirit, clothes replacing people in genuine masquerades."[115] This Balkanic carnival, a mirroring of social life under Filimon's quill, is often punctuated by the author with incisive moral comments. In this Balkanic diorama of decadence, the hierarchy of irrevocable power and the implicit rights of those holding it are the only certitude and assurance that active power, the one the Subject holds over the others is the only substance of this world. Such active power is progressive, directly proportional to the public offices held by the Subject, and aiming at absolute power.

Such a hierarchy of the Phanariots' society is captured in chapter twenty-three as well, entitled 'Slugile boierești' (The Manorial Servants). During the time when "the elite of the Bucharest society was entertaining itself in the theatre hall, listening to Rossini's music and watching the magnificent glamour of Caragea and his children", therefore in a different scene of social, not political life, while the squires were spectators, in an adjoining room their servants wait to serve their masters. The servants have the same hierarchy as their masters', which marks the idea that the servants' social life copies that of their masters', with them thus holding within their society the same active power as the squires:

> Among the servants (rom. 'feciori') there is a sort of long established hierarchy, just like that in the squires' homes: the great *ban* is the squire, the baker and the camper as well; but the *ban* and those equal to him sit at the same table with the ruler, while the smallest squireens shiver because of the cold in rooms or light up the chibouks of the important squires. Starting from this rule of distinction, the domestics (rom. 'feciorii') serving the important squires occupied the best places in beds, and the others sat one by one, crowded like sardines in a barrel.[116]

---

[114] Mircea Muthu: *Literatura română și spiritul sud-est European* (Romanian Literature and the South-East European Spirit). București: Minerva 1976, p. 154.
[115] Muthu: *Literatura română și spiritul sud-est European*, p. 155.
[116] Filimon: *Opere*, p. 172.

2.4 Scenes from the Socio-political Life and the Hierarchization of Power

The idea emphasized by the author in this chapter is that including the bottom of society, the stratification of the new parvenus anticipates the climbing up within this hierarchy that will allow them to have servants in their turn, closing the circle of power:

> An honest man, *according to the voice of the narrator at the end of the chapter*, would have been scandalized when seeing these audacious servants hastily taking off the squires' coats and endeavouring to dust them off and smooth them out, so that one could not tell they had been misused during the representation.[117]

The scenes of social life proposed by Filimon in *Ciocoii vechi și noi* (The Old and New Parvenus) are powered by its 'retrospective' conscience that Muthu spoke of, by the Romantic energy, but also by the author's training. The need to train and educate an autochthonous public, be it readers, or theatre or opera spectators, is obvious not only through the novel published in 1862, but also through the activity of opera and concert chroniclers. Thus chapters such as 'Muzica și coregrafia în timpul lui Caragea' (Music and choreography during Caragea), 'Teatrul în Țara Românească' (Theatre in Wallachia) or 'Italiana în Algir' (The Italian language in Algier) are understood as being indissolubly connected to his critical experience as a music chronicler, conjugated with a moral conscience. Even his *Excursiunile în Germania meridională* (Excursions to Meridional Germany) are punctuated with comments on the spirit of the peoples encountered and the type of musicality that characterizes them, sort of anticipating Blaga's theory of an accord between musicality and the unconsciousness.

The Romantic impetus animating Filimon's spirit is indeed similar to that of the culture chronicler who, in addition to being bound to be moralizing in his critique, he must also have to be aware of 'colonization', meaning to be aware of educating a raw public. The novelist knows that his novel is a novelistic 'chronicle' of a period foreshadowing the formation of the modern national identity, and the 'novel', as a fictional writing is a form of representation ensuring the reader's education through distancing. A 'denunciation' of the active power of the 'squireable' Subject is witnessed, meaning he is not born a squire, but becomes a squire, and the practices ensuring his becoming a squire are blameable. Mircea Anghelescu in his 'Introduction' to the 2005 critical edition, noticed that "in Heliade's opinion, the parvenu and the squire are not social categories, but embodied moral principles."[118] We therefore start from the principle that Filimon instantiates, the dramatizasion of the moral formation of the Romanian social state in the

---

117 Filimon: *Opere*, p. 178.
118 Anghelescu. In: Filimon: *Opere*, p. XX.

first part of the 19th century, de-structuring the social category holding the active power, i.e. the squires. "Lordliness has comprised and comprises in itself all the functions of the country, civil functions, judicial functions, public instructions and especially military ones, opened for all the country's sons. Every Romanian was born and is born squireable."[119] To be 'squireable' means the absence of such a social class, but especially the springs determining the birth of the active power of the old or new parvenu, who progressively becomes a squire through the active power he cultivates and which is directly proportional to the office he holds and which ultimately determines the end of the parvenu as well.

Heliade Rădulescu also warns of the danger the 'new parvenu' represents to 'the old parvenu'. The instruments of the active power of the new parvenu have diversified, adapting to the socio-political changes undergone by the Principalities, increasingly drawn to the mirage of the expanding West. Here is how Heliade Rădulescu characterizes the change devoid of content of the instruments of the parvenu's active and progressive power:

> The nowadays parvenu and especially the one since 1848 to date steals in the name of disinterest, devotion and martyrdom and bluffs in a manner that would leave all the old parvenus agape. He wipes public and private gold coins with the most progressive of manners and without fear of any punishment and murders you with his French words, both him and his madame and demoiselles: who is more patriotic and more liberal than him? Because he no longer steals like in Phanar, but like in Paris; he no longer aspires for the Police Station, but for the Prefecture, he no longer wants to be a Sword bearer, but a General, he no longer aspires for Stewardship and being a Logothete, but for the Ministry; he is no longer a copyist, but a secretary.[120]

The reinstrumentalization of the parvenu's progressive power is a normal historical process of orientation and adaptation of the parvenu to the history which he wants to be part of, because his impressive intuition makes him understand that history can be manipulated in favour of his power, as long as it is an active power. In addition to the eclecticism with amusing effects of their loan translations of regional, Turkish and French words, as seen in Alecsandri's *Chirița*, Heliade Rădulescu's fragment also explains the reorientation of the parvenu's interest towards the Western manner of structuring power: Prefecture, General, Minister, secretary etc. However, there is always a constant interest in stealing, and the only thing that changes is the tool used, this time, of a Western nature. In fact, this proces follows the 'Integrational' model of Romanians, and this is also the starting premise of historian Keith Hitchins as well, when analysing the

---

[119] Apud Anghelescu: In Filimon: *Opere*, p. XX.
[120] Apud Anghelescu. In: Filimon: *Opere*, p. XXII.

situation of the Romanians between 1770 and 1860. He starts from the consideration that:

> The course of events between 1770s and the 1860s reveals one central fact about the evolution of the principalities-their steady integration into Europe. Integration, not Westernization, is the proper word, since their reception of European models and experience was an act of adaptation rather then of imitation.[121]

But the general term used by the American historian to characterize Romanian society at the beginning of the 19th century is that of 'non-unitary'. And here, the contribution of the ruler Constantin Mavrocordat ever since the 18th century seems to have been important for clarifying social statuses even within the manorial class. Mavrocordat's interest in organizing this class through hierarchization is of course determined by his desire for a better relation to the kingship in order to increase political and social control. Gradually, the squires' lifestyle begins to change, with the decline of the Ottoman Empire and due to the Western influences accepted and adopted by the Phanariots. The boieri become rulers and within the mechanism of preserving and 'activating' power, "state service established one's place in the boier hierarchy, but the control of land continued to determine membership itself in the boier class."[122]

Both the result and victim of the hierarchization of power and of the weakening of its legitimation, therefore of the progressive activism in order to reach the pyramid of power, 'the new parvenu', Dinu Păturică is the representation of this corrupt, schematic and predictable world in which gaining power is the only genuine purpose. By virtue of exposing the strategies of accumulating power capital, the image of Dinu Păturică is dramatized, a narrative strategy in fact specific to the entire text that oscillates between the novelized fresco of the period and the dramatization of the central character, with the intention to intensify his exponential destiny. In a world where the unanimously legitimated official instruments of power are missing or are weakened intentionally, the parvenu develops his own instruments for acquiring and self-legitimising power, and from this point of view, his power is of an active type. The Subject turns his action to the chaotic, imprecise and 'shifting' public space, progressively controlling and dominating it, exploiting its weaknesses brought about by its 'lack of settlement', as the chronicler would say. His figure is emblematic to the paradigm of active power in the 19th century.

---

[121] Hitchins: *The Romanians*, p. 2.
[122] Hitchins: *The Romanians*, p. 61.

2.5 The Physiognomy of the Activist-Arriviste and the Gradual Instruments of Power

While through the programmatic, expository fragments of the novel, the author strategically searches for the "the brilliant Evening Stars of vices" ("stăluciți luceferi ai vicielor") (*Dedication*) to whom to dedicate the novel and, later on, creates the historical portrait of the universal parvenu, "from the parvenu with a surplice and ink bottles on his waist belt from the Phanariot times, to the parvenu dressed in tailcoats and white gloves of our times" (*Prologues*), the first chapter of this "original novel" opens with one of the most vivid portraits in Romanian literature, that of Dinu Păturică. His portrait, which barely hints at the signs of ambition and cunning, instruments that will turn him into the perfect representative of the parvenu, will indirectly be completed by his progressive immoral actions throughout the action. However, it is not solely a portrait of Dinu Păturică, but also an individualized social fresco, relevant through the physical traits of the arriviste and through the suggestive usage of an archaic vocabulary, with lost sonorities, which Tudor Vianu also mentioned in *Arta prozatorilor români* (The Art of Romanian Prose Writers).[123] Such a complementary portrait, both physiognomic and vestiary, also marks the slow, progressive and active transition from the simplicity of the servant to his later official status, when he wears "a suplice and *giubea*[124]".

As we have already seen, the oscillation between the moral portrait and the physical one (physiognomic and vestimentary), is an auctorial gadget used to describe the manner in which the social image of power is set up:

> On an October morning, in 1814, a young man of 22, short, having dark skin, black eyes full of craftiness, a straight nose with a rather cocked tip, a sign of ambition and coarse pride, dressed in a damask surplice torn at the back; with *caravani*[125] from house cloth, dyed brown; belted with a piece of clothing with its edges sawn on a sewing frame; with bare feet thrust in some saffian *iminei*,[126] which used to be red once, but had lost their colour because of their old age; with colossal brass ink bottles on his girdle; wearing a *cauc*[127] on his head, whose colour was not easily identified because of the patches of various matters used to botch it, and wearing as principal attire a *fermenă*[128] de *pambriu*[129] the colour of

---

123 Tudor Vianu: *Arta prozatorilor români* (The Art of Romanian Prose Writers). București: Contemporanul 1941, p. 60.
124 'giubea': Long and large coat often lined with fur worn in the past by the boyars (tc. cüppe).
125 'caravani': Large trousers and tight from the knee down (bg. Karavan).
126 'iminei': Turkish pointed shoes (tc. yemeni).
127 'cauc': Tall and round cover for the head, wored in the past by boieri (tc. kavuk.).
128 'fermenea': Short coat made of silk, lined with fur, which was wored by boyars (tc. fermene).
129 'pambriu': Merino wool fabric.

wheat, lined with red *bogasiu*;[130] this is the young man standing on the stairs of the house of the great *postelnic* Andronache Tuzluc, leaning on the poles of the entrance and lost in meditations which, reflected in his features, clearly showed that he was only preoccupied with the ambitious plans laid in front of him by his vivid imagination and the obstacles encountered in fulfilling them.[131]

A careful observer of details and experienced as an opera chronicler, where elocution plays a primordial role, Nicolae Filimon creates the first complex portrait in Romanian literature, by describing Dinu Păturică. It is not solely about the portrait of the aspiring parvenu in the first chapter, dedicated to him and which the entire literary critic emphasizes, but about a portrait in evolution and in accord with its progress within the hierarchy of power. Moreover, the author's contribution to Romanian portraiture is essential because of the psychological touches attributed to the parvenu. Like an echo of the classicist theatre, where the details of the physiognomy betray typological automatisms, Filimon's portraits play an essential role in outlining their psychic features.

From the very beginning, literary criticism has placed Filimon's portraiture under the sign of influences and correspondences. George Călinescu appreciates his Stendhalian typology of his hero, Dinu Păturică, "a Wallachian Julien Sorel",[132] or the "Balzacian technique",[133] Tudor Vianu identifies similar procedures with Costache Negruzzi (*Arta prozatorilor*), while Șerban Cioculescu reminds us of the founder of the 'pseudoscience' of physiognomy, the Swiss Lavater, a model for Balzac, but also of the same Balzac's Rastignac and Stendhal's Julien Sorel, for Păturică is dominated by ambition, by will. Either way, he is a forerunner of Romanian characters such as Tănase Scatiu, Lică Trubadurul, Gore Pirgu, Iancu Urmatecu or Stănică Rațiu.

Omniscient, the author of *Ciocoilor vechi și noi* (The Old and New Parvenus) builds an active character, constantly fighting for power, which is shown in every detail of his actions. Feeling it was his duty to denounce the parvenu's tricks to gain power and "to assert the means he used in order to fulfil such aspirations", the author looks upon the success of Dinu Păturică in conjunction. In addition to his innate features, he also depicts the effects of his 'parvenu' education, as reflected in the chapter entitled 'Educațiunea ciocoiului' (The education of the parvenu). Thus, the author is aware that, in order to master "hypocrisy and intrigue", the parvenu, with his native intelligence, quickly understands that, in addition to "wine tithes", "taxes on sheep breeding" and "tolls on chimneys",

---

130 'bogasiu': Soft material, oriental cloth used mainly for linings (tc. bogasɪ).
131 Filimon: *Opere*, p. 11.
132 Călinescu: *Istoria literaturii române de la origini până în prezent*, p. 361.
133 Călinescu: *Istoria literaturii române de la origini până în prezent*, p. 362.

meaning the ability to collect fees or taxes that are due to the state, he must ensure himself an education that would facilitate his progress within the social hierarchy. The dialogue between *postelnic* Andronache Tuzluc and Dinu Păturică opens the road to power for the latter and marks the beginning of the end for the former. The aspiring young man began by "rubbing the feet" of Tuzluc, aiding him to get dressed and wash, bringing comfiture, coffee and chibouks and continuing with education, the first step in acquiring the abilities to gain power.

When learning the Greek language and literature, as the bases of a humanistic culture and as an exercise of tolerant power, the parvenu asks himself:

> Of what use was to him to know a dead language and its literature so repugnant to his character and intentions? "Homer, Pindar, Sophocles, Euripides, Anacreon, Sappho etc. are good for women and womanisers, said the parvenu to himself, contemptuously. I need books that would sharpen my mind, which would teach me how to rise to greatness. Plutarch comes to mind, Caesar's *Comments*, *The History of Mankind*, the lives of the great men from the past and current centuries, these are books which, by reading them, one may say with one's heart at rest that one has not wasted time reading them in vain.[134]

However, in his master's library, Păturică finds, among other books, "a treatise on physiology and the works of Machiavelli, which he read and studied very carefully; in short, he did all he could to perfect himself in the art of hypocrisy and perfidy." Loyal reader of Machiavelli, Dinu Păturică fails to understand the meaning of the balance of ruling, as Machiavelli understands it in *The Prince* for instance, for he is merely self-educated in ancient literature. He fails to understand the moral and profoundly humane sense of this literature and his hermeneutic sense is drastically reduced to projecting these characters in distant history, which denotes a deformed understanding, a 'misreading' of the model offered by Machiavelli. Dinu Păturică's Machiavellian nature is reduced to using Machiavelli's stratagems for his own interests and transforming them into instruments used to exert excessive power. As stated by Șerban Cioculescu, "The chibouk handler of the *postelnic* is a disciple of Machiavelli, but before reaching the highest step of social hierarchy he breaks his neck because of greed."[135] But the Machiavellian nature assumed by Păturică in the *postelnic's* library is merely of surface, since he only assumes the instruments of gaining power, the active sense of power of the new parvenu now articulating around his own person and the progression within the hierarchy of power. He only partially applies the Machiavellian strategy of applying evil, the Prince functioning according to the formula:

---

[134] Filimon: *Opere*, p. 39.
[135] Cioculescu: *Prozatori români*, p. 78.

Whence it is to be noted, that in taking a state the conqueror must arrange to commit all his cruelties at once, so as not to have to recur to them every day, and so as to be able, by not making fresh changes, to reassure people and win them over by benefiting them.[136]

Dinu Păturică acts progressively and according to the situation he exploits to the maximum in favour of his interest to rise. While the violent actions of the Machiavellian Prince are quick, immediate and cumulative, in his favour but also that of his subjects, the actions of Filimon's new parvenu are slow, progressive and circumstantial, and this turns him into a maleficent Subject, precisely because of the active and constant nature of his excess of power. A relevant example in this case is the one in which, by gaining trust in his servant Păturică, who appears before the squire "with a face more humble than that of a monk", the *postelnic* Andronache Tuzluc assigns him a first mission to supervise, to follow his mistress, *Chera*[137] Duduca. It is the first time the parvenu becomes aware of his master's weakness, i.e. his love and jealousy. While Tuzluc suddenly becomes irrational, the maleficent intelligence of Păturică becomes active. Păturică's inner monologue, after the Phanariot entrusts him with the mission that will initiate his decline and Păturică's ascension, is relevant for the parvenu's power strategy:

> I've got in my hands the Greek's concubine, his chief passion; I finally have the key to that bright future I've been dreaming of for so long. Happiness, priceless happiness!... This is a key to the very gates of Heaven... And why not?... Eve took Adam out of Heaven, to create the opportunity for another woman to open it to him later on. A woman made the Greeks, as the books say, fight for years. The harem favourites hold in their hands the fate of the Turkish kingdom; even here, we see the lady turning the court and the whole country as she pleases and, if she changed my master from a *ciohodar*[138] into a great *postelnic* and *cămăraș*[139] why shouldn't Duduca make me a powerful, happy man too?... There are many such examples. How many were like me, or even worse than me, for, thank God, I'm not a gipsy, and yet, through jades and other parvenu tricks, even gipsies are now part of the nobility, for there's no room to swing a cat from *postelnics*, logothetes and treasurers. Take heart, my dear Păturică! Tomorrow you will put your *işlic* on and, should God be on your side, it won't be long before you own innumerable estates, gipsies and wealth and then who will dare come and bring you to book for the means used to acquire it all? Let them come, if they can![140]

---

136 Niccolo Machiavelli: *The Prince*. Translated into English by Luigi Ricci. London: Oxford University Press 1921, p. 36.
137 'Chera': Lady (ngr. kérá).
138 'ciohodar': position at the boiar court in Wallahia and Moldavia, having the obligation to take care of the shoes of the boiar; lackey (tc. çuhadar).
139 'cămăraș': position at the boiar court responsable with the administration of the boiars pantry or store rooms for goods.
140 Filimon: *Opere*, p. 44.

In fact, Chera Duduca is the feminine counterpart of Dinu Păturică, or, as the same Șerban Cioculescu asserted: the "moral doublet" of the new parvenu, the feminine character he regards as an instrument for obtaining power and as a partner in crimes. Their asociation is a powerful one, "so they realise with double powers the convergent aims"[141] The woman is a 'means' or a "conquered social commodity",[142] an agent that will contribute decisively to the ruining of Andronache Tuzluc and the increase in the Subject's active power. The portrait of Chera Duduca and the explanation for the magnetism she exerts on men is also relevant when describing the path Păturică followed in his ascension to power:

> This oriental Venus, coming from the scattered remnants of the Greek population in Phanar, just like erstwhile her god-like ancestor had come from the wind-blown sea foam, was of a perfect beauty, a vivid intelligence and a fine and skilful spirit. The life full of parental indulgence she had spent since her first childhood years and the lack of education unveiled in her numerous wishes discordant with her social status. She especially loved luxury; she loved the noisy life; in short, all her happiness consisted in immediately fulfilling her smallest and most extravagant caprices.[143]

Filimon the portrayer succeeds here, and not only, to create the image of the modern lady, challenging because of the paradoxes of her existence, between the physical diaphanousness and the decadence of her tastes, customs and caprices. In this portrait, in addition to an indication of the sources of her decadence, an admiring tone in the face if this crepuscular beauty can also be identified. While Dinu Păturică foreshadows, as has been mentioned previously a series of characters in Romanian literature, such as Tănase Scatiu, Lică Trubadurul, Gore Pirgu, Iancu Urmatecu or Stănică Rațiu, Chera Duduca can be placed in the ancestry of Rașelica Nashmansohn, Masinca Drângeanu, Ela Gheorghidiu, Emilia Răchitaru or Ada Razu.

The chapter entitled 'Femeia a scos pe om din Rai' (The woman pulled the man out of Heaven) is representative when demonstrating the manner in which Dinu Păturică instruments power, through Chera Duduca and Costea Chiorul, another representative of the new parvenu's evil power. These are, as the author argues, "evidence of the artifices of the two sly men". Willing to make any sacrifice for the happiness of his concubine, Andronache Tuzluc becomes a victim of Păturică's strategy of definitively obliging him, following the cheap charade Chera Duduca enacts. She plays the role of a victim, pretending to rebuke the *postelnic* by saying that, if he loved her, he wouldn't keep her "locked like a parrot and dressed with

---

141 Cioculescu: *Prozatori români*, p. 83.
142 Pompiliu Constantinescu: *Scrieri* (Writings). Vol. 6. Edition elaborated by Constanța Constantinescu. București: Minerva 1972, p. 13–14.
143 Filimon: *Opere*, p. 33.

these rags, like a slum priestess". The woman exploits the *postelnic*'s weakness and jealousy, so that the presence of Costea Chiorul, with "the sly face of Costea Chiorul the *bogasier*", the vendor of fine clothes and jewellery, at the opportune moment, proves fatal to the *postelnic*. The latter, in order to satisfy his 'ailing' mistress, purchases the entire merchandise from the sly merchant, accumulating new debts. This action, instrumented by Dinu Păturică, a hidden witness to the entire scene, generates a visceral reaction in him, as a result of accomplishing his plan of social ascension: "That groan, resembling the cry of joy of demons when they make a saint fall into their chains, was the infernal expression of Păturică's joy, who, through this trick of Duduca became master of all that the poor Phanariot had left."[144]

It is therefore possible to identify here, returning to Lukes' taxonomy, a one-dimensional perspective on power, in the wake of which Păturică, with the help of Duduca and Costea Chiorul, determines Andronache Tuzluc to do what he would not normally do and we thus witness the fall of the Phanariot and the ascension of the new local parvenu, definitively contaminated by the actions learnt precisely at the court of his master.

Nicolae Filimon seems to confirm a certain cycle of destiny which, nevertheless, just like classicist prose, would gradate in the end its moralizing power by harshly punishing the immoral and rewarding the righteous, the marriage between Maria, the daughter of the honest boyar Ban C., to Gheorghe. However, Dinu Păturică's ascension is achieved quickly and by using the classical instruments: he falsifies financial documents and money, increases the peasants' taxes, sells lordships and takes bribes, steals from the postelnic's money and then from the country's treasury, uses the beauty and erotic magnetism of Chera Duduca, who had become his wife following the ruin of postelnic Andronache Tuzluc, as instruments in his obscure business. His ascension is rapid and determined by the parvenu's cynicism, which spares no action in order to acquire absolute power. He sacrifices Chera Duduca or is despotic with the peasants who can no longer pay the tolls he imposed, ordering Negru Rupe-Piele to torture them by coating them in hot black oil, and he no longer acknowledges his old father, having him hustled and drawing upon himself, as a voice of popular predestination, the 'parental curse'.

He gradually moves from being a bailiff at Tuzluc's court to being a *sameș*[145] and following the postelnic's elimination he will take advantage of Vodă Caragea's[146] flight and the credulity of the new ruler, Alexandru Șuțu, and through

---

144 Filimon: *Opere*, p. 164.
145 'sameș': accountant and responsible for tributes and taxes.
146 'Vodă Caragea': the Phanariot Prince Caragea.

astute intrigues he becomes a stolnic. The political intrigues the new parvenu is involved in propel him to the office of sub-prefect of two counties, Prahova and Săcuieni, assuming before Ipsilanti the decisive contribution to the elimination of Tudor Vladimirescu whom the author infinitely admires. Alexandru Ipsilanti's promise to make him *caimacam* of Craiova, the deputy of the ruler, impels him once more to be against the Phanariots' regime, which, he emphasized, "had brought only hardship and oppression to his people."[147]

Dinu Păturică's portrait becomes iconic for the modern Romanian novel, in spite of the narrative inconsistencies inherent to its beginning, ascertained by the entire literary criticism. In general, the novel *Ciocoii vechi și noi* (The Old and New Parvenus), in terms of the *autochthonization* of a new literary genre, of the novelistic epic, is inevitable in any process of retrospective recovery, in spite of the fact that, due to the distancing of the 1800 world and of the language defining it, the novel seems antiquated. But, when reading Thomas Pavel's assertions on Walter Scott, from *The Lives of the Novel. A History*, it is not possible to fail to ascertain a similarity, at least in terms of variation of the narrative formula. In the absence of the heroic register representative for Scott's novels, Filimon's novel turns Dinu Păturică into an anti-hero, because for Filimon the moralizing force of the discourse is essential. From this point of view, Filimon keeps the moral discourse of the novels from the past century, a discourse so natural at the dawn of the Romanian novel, but also brings into focus a surprising variety of the literary formula. In other words, we are dealing with a novel emphasizing the moral flaws of the parvenus, but which drastically penalizes the excesses of power, born of the inherent weaknesses of an emerging state, for:

> [...] nothing is more dangerous for a state that wishes to reorganize, than to surrender control over the government to the parvenus, who are meant since their very conception to be servants and educated how to get blood out of a stone at any cost![148]

Filimon's heroes, Gheorghe, "the former court bailiff of postelnic Andronache Tuzluc" and "the beautiful Maria, the daughter of ban C." are instruments of the final moralization that leaves us with hope regarding the future of the emergent state.

When analysing the hierarchy of the novelistic actantial roles, therefore of the authority holding control over the action and implicitly over the other characters, the novel *Ciocoii vechi și noi* (The Old and New Parvenus) is exponential. The semantic relevance of the progressive power held by Dinu Păturică is important

---

147 Hitchins: *The Romanians*, p. 151.
148 Filimon: *Opere*, p. 5.

when demonstrating both the novel's anchoring in history, denouncing the excess of active power of the Phanariots and the consequences of their rule, as well as a category of novel. In regards to this category, Dinu Păturică perfects his power instruments, exceeds his Machiavellian education in order to exert total power in favour of his own interest to rise. His path, described by Filimon, from his humble appearance at the *postelnic*'s court, to his office of High Steward, is that of the active Subject exerting a gradual power on the others and to whom the entire narrative flux is reduced to. The omniscient author's focus on the gradually active actions of the character demonstrates his intention of moralization. The critical discourse, sometimes hidden behind irony, also has a general, historical nature over the Phanariot period and the impact of this period on Romanian society. This intention to depict a coherent image of the society undergoing modernization responds to the interest of the autochthonous forces in autonomy, unity and emancipation, which had animated the Principalities in the 19th century and which also dominate other texts, such as Ion Budai-Deleanu's *Țiganiada sau Tabăra țiganilor* (*Țiganiada or The Gypsies' Camp*).

The final image of Dinu Păturică, who transformed his active power to excess, preserves the moralizing nature of the novel and speaks implicitly of the fact that, in the equation of power, the Subject relates only to his own selfish interests, using the leverages of the offices acquired progressively in order to gain increasing power. The active nature of his power is directly proportional to the hierarchy the Subject possesses. The climax of his power however, just like in a fatalist equation of history, is the moment of his decline as well. The intriguer, the cunning, therefore the parvenu who until now has used his power in a rational manner, in order to emphasize it, finds himself eventually reduced to the instinctual, symbolically thrown to the entrails of the Earth: "The dense darkness, the loneliness, his pallet and the poorly nourishing food had brought him in a dire state of paroxysm and rage to such extent that the prison resounded with his groans and whines."[149]

At the Rise of the modern Romanian novel, Nicolae Filimon exposes and denounces through his Subject the practices of excesive power that produces the death of his character. Caught between total ambition of absolute power and the ethical norms of the society, he is smashed by the author who became for the first time the voice of the public moral sphere. As a consequence, the novel became a *medium* which uncovers the disproportions between 'power on', as an active form of endless power, and 'power to', as a form of transgressing the limits of the individual ethical status, subjugated by the instinctual need of domination, of those who obtain and practice the active form of power.

---

149 Filimon: *Opere*, p. 251.

3 The Reflexive Power of the Subject

"How splendid, how sublime it is to be mad! I used to say to myself, and I realised with unimaginable regret how many powerful, familiar, stupid habits [...] separated me from extreme freedom [...]."¹

3.1 In Search of Power Authenticity

"Don't respect anything, believe only in yourself, in your youth, in your biology, if you want to... He who fails to start like this, in what regards himself or the world-will not create anything, will remain barren, fearsome, overwhelmed by truths. To be able to forget the truths, to have so much life in yourself that the truths cannot permeate, nor intimidate you-this is the calling of a hooligan."²

The national metaphor of 'România Mare' (Great Romania), coined after the 'Treaty of Versailles', in 1920, designates a phase of radical transformations, embedded in the historical memory of the Romanians as the absolute point of reference of modernity and rapid social Romanian modernization. In compliance with social modernity, the interwar period has been or still is a defining point of reference of the cultural memory, the effects of its transformations and those of the interwar liberalism being felt in art, therefore in the manifestations of aesthetic modernity. The first chapter analysed the fact that the *canonical battle* regarding the novel reaches at a certain point a defining moment during this period,³ from the psychological realism of a naturalism essence to the practice of Lovinescu's modernism, the Romanian epic confirming the general social tendency of searching for authenticity, i.e. of its own formulas of expression.

The pinnacle of the interwar period is confirmed both socially, as a result of the concretization of the national ideal pursued during various historical moments of the past century, since 1848 and especially prepared by the 'Mica Unire' (Small Union) of 1859, as well as artistically, as a distinct and representative moment in Romanian canonical memory. The two perspectives, that of social modernization and that of aesthetic modernization, were phenomena circulating

---

1 Max Blecher: *Occurence in the Immediate Unreality*. Translated by Alistair Ian Blyth. Plymouth: University of Plymouth Press 2009, p. 54.
2 Mircea Eliade: *Aspecte ale mitului* (Aspects of the Myths). Translated by Paul G. Dinopol. Preface by Vasile Nicolescu. București: Univers 1996, p. 168.
3 Carmen Mușat: *Romanul românesc interbelic. Dezbateri teoretice, polemici, opinii* critice (Romanian Inter-War Novel. Theoretical Debates, Polemics, Critical Opinions). București: Humanitas Educațional 2004.

in synchronicity during the 19th century as well, from the 1848 discourse on the specificity of national art, to Maiorescu's theory of forms searching for content. Also, aesthetic modernity, as proven by the critical discourse on culture, occurs as an emergent phenomenon, a result of social reforms. The effervescence of the Romanian interwar epic is a similar result of the emergence of the idealistic and metaphysical theories, according to which spontaneity and unpredictableness are qualities of the procedural nature of development. Just like these theories, the novel can also be regarded as an emergence of the social transformations taking place in the '30s of the 20th century, as a true model of interaction.[4] It is surprising that the pinnacle was reached in counterweight with what was happening in Central Europe as a result of the First World War. "After the First World War, Central Europe was therefore transformed into a region of small, weak states, whose vulnerability ensured first Hitler's conquest and ultimately Stalin's triumph. Perhaps for this reason, in the European memory these countries always seem to be the source of dangerous trouble."[5]

This is also the perspective of the inconsistent development suggested by historian Bogdan Murgescu, who demonstrates in his comparative analysis of Romania and Europe during the interwar period that, "overall, the interwar period brought about very different national or regional evolutions or an increase of the economic divergence within Europe."[6] The contrast is also visible when comparing Central Europe and Romania during the '30s.

The case of Greater Romania is a discussion of the consolidation of the national consciousness through the union, but also of a unitary social development, stimulated by rapid transformations, such as the demographic growth, a result of the territorial enlargement, the feeding of the public's conscience, through electoral reform and the multiplication of political parties and the modernization stimulated by the agrarian or school reform. The interwar Romania is the result of coagulation and not of fragmentation, a sudden and unplanned coagulation, therefore a spontaneous and unpredictable emergence. Such features are proved also by the birth of virulent antinomic visions, foreshadowing and thus preparing the power excesses, the anti-humanistic horrors of Communism.

The image of Greater Romania is nevertheless a nostalgic and ideal Arcadia, crystallized of course in the imaginary of the post-war man, defeated by the

---

[4] See Nicolae Sfetcu: *Fizica simplificată* (Simplified Physics). București: Createspace 2014.
[5] Milan Kundera: The Tragedy of Central Europe. In: *The New York Review of Books*, Apr 26, 1984; 31, 007, p. 34.
[6] Bogdan Murgescu: *România și Europa. Acumularea decalajelor economice (1500–2010)* (Romania and Europe. The Accumulation of Economic Gaps. 1500–2010). Iași: Polirom 2010, p. 210.

political *Gorilla* of Communism, to paraphrase Liviu Rebreanu's 1938 novel. This imagological construct[7] belongs especially to the '60s, which were years of relative liberalization, of the illusion of liberation of art from the pressure of the political. In fact, the disillusion of the extremes and of the insurmountable hiatus during this period between the material needs of a society affected by the effects of the war and the necessity of an authentic culture that would consolidate and confer meaning to this modernization is explained by a character of Rebreanu's novels. Professor Cumpănașu, "with his didactical patheticism", fully depicts this schism, this disparity between social modernity and the cultural one or, better said, between the ideal and the necessity of social transformations and the neo-traditionalism of the period:

> Around us, all the peoples are reajusting their powers [...] Our people have no ideal left and only believe in a full stomach... Is that a good thing? Do you think that through this ideal of full stomachs we will be able to maintain the unity of our people and build the genuine Romanian culture that would confer meaning to our existence? A full stomach cannot be the ideal of a people.[8]

The victory of the political *gorilla* over the cultural elites, a central theme in the non-canonical novel by Rebreanu, is a proof of that period, also visible in the alternation of extreme nationalistic ideologies, an obvious risk of this emergent culture. When outlining the image of interwar Bucharest, Ioana Pârvulescu, speaking about the "Political options of the literates", confirms that:

> Writers are most of the times defeated in the great political game, regardless of their good intentions. If the writer chooses the political career, in the meantime neglecting his vocation, he has two possibilities: either to compromise himself in a spectacular manner or to fail discretely, tasting the uselessness of the gesture.[9]

The discomfort of placing the writer in the public space, according to the nationalistic ideological options of the period, has culminated most of the time with his withdrawal and, implicitly, with a crisis of the public, educative and formative activism of the elites. The crisis of the elites is dualistic, not being therefore determined by their inexistence, but either by their adhesion, sometimes lamentable, to the extremist-nationalistic discourse, or by their withdrawal to a romantic

---

[7] Lucian Boia: *"Germanofilii". Elita intelectuală românească în anii Primului Război Mondial* (The Germanophils. The Romanian Intellectual Elite in the years of the First World War). București: Humanitas 2010.
[8] Liviu Rebreanu: *Gorila*. București: Minerva 1985, p. 89.
[9] Ioana Pârvulescu: *Întoarcere în Bucureștiul interbelic* (*Return in the Inter-War Bucharest*). București: Humanitas 2003, p. 39.

'ivory tower' of creation, to use Sainte-Beuve's metaphor regarding Alfred de Vigny's isolationist attitude.

Thus, the interwar period proves, first of all, a crisis of the elites, in the meaning that part of the of the eminent public figures involved in the political life of the *republic* opt for what was called 'Kulturkritik',[10] as a direct expression of the Spenglerian neo-traditionalism and of the differentiation between culture and civilization, which argues for the resistance of the intellectuals to the process of democratization of Romania. This is the main divergence of the interwar ideologies that led to the weakening of the effects of modernization and even to the segregation of Romanian public space, allowing for extreme clashes during the period. Florin Țurcanu confirms that this political criticism of the Romanian neo-traditionalists "occurs as a logical consequence of this *Kulturkritik*."[11] Eminent public figures of that time, such as Nae Ionescu, Nechifor Crainic, Cezar Petrescu or Pamfil Șeicaru had distinct critical positions against democracy, parliamentarism and liberalism and in favour of royalty. "Their political ideology was nationalist or *extreme right* (Nae Ionescu), *nationalist traditionalist* (Pamfil Șeicaru), and the press or the leftist intelligentsia found similarities with the ideology of the *French action* or with Italian fascism."[12]

At the same time, the political journalism practiced by *Ora, Cuvântul, Neamul românesc, Hiena* or *Gândirea* oriented part of its articles around anti-liberalistic, anti-parliamentaristic themes, intensely supporting the authoritarian monarchism.[13] The neo-traditionalist criticism conducted by Nichifor Crainic in the pages of the *Gândirea* magazine tries to argue for the idea of ethnic conservatism and of organic nature of the traditional culture, to the detriment of democratic modernization. The 1930 moment, when Carol II comes to power, determines Nae Ionescu to foresee the birth of an *organic* state. But "what was called the *restoration* of June 1930 seems to be a new meeting between culture in both its meanings and politics from now on *organic*, therefore acceptable."[14] This obsession with organicity that has led to the two world conflagrations and the absolutistic idea of the 'New Man', fascist or communist, has also had an entropic effect on interwar

---

10 See Zigu Ornea: *Tradiționalism și modernitate în deceniul al treilea* (Traditionalism and Modernity in the Third Decade). București: Eminescu 1980; Armin Heinen: *Die Legion "Erzengel Michael" in Rumänien. Soziale Bewegung und Politische Organisation*. München: R. Oldenbourg Verlag 1986; Florin Țurcanu: *Intellectuels, histoire et mémoire en Roumanie: de l'entre deux-guerres à l'après communisme*. București: Editura Academiei Române 2007.
11 Țurcanu: *Intellectuels, histoire et mémoire en Roumanie*, p. 16.
12 Țurcanu: *Intellectuels, histoire et mémoire en Roumanie*, p. 17.
13 See Țurcanu: *Intellectuels, histoire et mémoire en Roumanie*, p. 17.
14 See Țurcanu: *Intellectuels, histoire et mémoire en Roumanie*, p. 26.

Romania as well, due to the triumph of monarchic absolutism, practically cancelling out the results of that period and leading to an excess of anti-humanistic power that basically culminated with the Stalinism of the 'Obsessive decade'.

The political *Gorilla* annihilating the democratic elites was denounced through the subversive power of literature and by Mircea Eliade, in his 1935 novel, *Huliganii* (The Hooligans), where the pupil Nae Ionescu denounced, through his character, "the primacy of the pure collective, against any elite" which thus means a "return to zoology". This attitude "of considering intelligence, culture and genius to be subversive means of disdain and oppression of the others" has generated the dictatorship of organicity to the disfavour of individualism which seemed to characterize and mark this bright Arcadia. "We, the intellectuals, as you like to classify us", says Eliade's character, "are isolated and few in our destiny. He who cannot bear such loneliness can go ahead and join an assault battalion". But the political assault of the '30s against the democratic elite was possible by means of a neo-traditionalistic excessive exertion of power that only widened the gap between art and society, art often times becoming, as it happens throughout the 'Obsessive decade', an instrument of ideological manipulation.

The interwar democratic project, initiated rapidly at the end of the First World War, through the territorial integration and sealed technically through the liberal *Constitution* of 1923, through the clash with the neo-traditionalist resistances that have been presented, proves the eclecticism of Romanian modernity in the 20th century, by 'burning through' certain phases of development and a disagreement between social reality and technical, legislative and economic changes at the beginning of the century. Lovinescu's synchronicity had a cultural effect first of all, due to its openness towards Western models, the Romanian modernity of the third and fourth decade demonstrating that this process was not completed.

The constitutional monarchy during the reign of the Prussian king Ferdinand, co-artisan of a liberal type of project of balance and separation of powers within the state, held a significant role in articulating the national project that set the interwar period in the Romanian collective memory. Unlike his father, King Carol II, during his second reign between the 1930s and 1940s, he instituted an authoritarian regime, with harmful effects on Romanian society, which was called the 'Carlist dictatorship'. This monarchic excess of power culminated in 1938 with the dissolution of the political parties, a historical fact specific to dictatorships, and this absolutism is recurrent during Romanian communism. In the 3rd article of the *Constitution of Romania* of 1965, the Romanian Communist Party was defined and stated as "the leading force of the entire society in the Socialist Republic of Romania". The excess of power had a devastating impact on the spiritual life of society and literature, a direct expression of freedom of speech and of the critical spirit, therefore ceasing to represent an exercise of the balance of forces. The results of the Carlist absolutist sovereignty created an acute political instability, leading to the weakening of the historical parties and to the consolidation of ideologies and extremist movements. The personality cult, instituted by Carol II, definitively counterbalanced the liberalism and relative democratization at the beginning of the period accredited to his father, King Ferdinand.

In the political battle between neo-traditionalists and democrats, the values that have accredited the idea of a rebirth of the modern spirit together with the national spirit have often been cancelled out by the defeat of the critical spirit of democratization. These are some of these values of the *Romanian Constitution* in 1923,[15] which were the basis for the birth of the modern spirit of interwar Romanian society, principles which many times during the interwar decades were reduced to an inefficient rhetoric. The articles underlining the idea of the freedoms of the Romanians' enjoyed a privileged place in the new Constitution, as follows:

> Art. 5. – Romanians, regardless of their ethnical origin, language or religion, enjoy the freedom of consciousness, the freedom of education, the freedom of press, the freedom to gather, the freedom to associate and all the freedoms and rights established by the law.

Also, the freedom of expression and the right to publish without any official censorship, which might therefore interfere with the freedom of the press, allow for the liberalization of the public space. This is demonstrated by the article below:

> Art. 25. – The Constitution guarantees to everyone the freedom to communicate and publish their ideas and opinions orally, in writing and through the press, every person being responsible for abusing such liberties in the cases determined in the Criminal Code, which will by no means limit the right in itself. No prior authorisation from any authority is needed for the occurrence of any publication.

Another article refers to the settlement of state powers, in order to avoid authoritarian excess:

> Art. 33. – All State powers emanate from the nation, which can only exert them by delegation and in compliance with the principles and rules set in this Constitution.

It also contains a standardization of the monarchical powers by relating royalty to the letter of the Constitution and its limitations:

> Art. 91. – The king only has the powers granted to him by the Constitution.

An overview of interwar Romanian society and especially of the result or impact that the metamorphoses, allegedly democratic and modernizing, should have

---

[15] The text of the "Constitution of 1923" was consulted at the following web address: http://www.cdep.ro/pls/legis/legis_pck.htp_act_text?idt=1517 [27.04.2018].

had on the post-war period raises the question of what the conditions of the (un) functionality of this modernizing project were. Beyond its impression on the post-war image imaginary, especially in the conditions of the relative liberalization in the '60s, the interwar period represents a new age, that of Greater Romania, of modernization through reforms, the birth of the public space and ideological repositioning. It is a world in search of authenticity, of socio-cultural autonomy, in the context of a new European neo-nationalist formula. Romanian modernity had been given the trial of its absolute youth, in the context of a Europe of fragmentism and nationalistic sideslips during the post-imperialistic period. The paradox of this image resides precisely in the selectivity of the images and perhaps in their imagological overuse. The historians who have reconstructed with precise instruments the image of the Romanian interwar period, such as Lucian Boia[16] or Bogdan Murgescu,[17] follow with convincing arguments both "the contradictions of the interwar world",[18] projected in a global context, as well as the imagological overuse of this world, often seen as a genuine 'golden era' of humanity.

Although he ascertains that the 'nostalgia' of the interwar period was at the beginning of Romanian communism in contradiction with the criticism against the "bourgeois-landlordly regime", Bogdan Murgescu appreciates that "when shifting to national-communism, the attitudes of the regime towards the interwar period got nuanced themselves, the elements of positive appreciation gradually overshadowing the negative ones."[19] The accomplishment of the national ideal achieved through the Union of 1918, the agrarian reform and the distribution of land to peasants or the acceleration of industrialization have indeed constituted real arguments in the configuration of this ideal construct. As has been previously established by Vlad Georgescu, Bogdan Murgescu reconfirms that the "principles or foundations on which Greater Romania had been erected had been good: economy or culture progressed constantly. The interwar years were years of development, as it was in fact throughout Eastern Europe."[20] The impact of culture was determined and, in this regard, the power field of the cultural elites was often the predominant battlefield of that period as well. The intellectual elites played a

---

16 See Boia: *"Germanofilii"* and Lucian Boia: *Capcanele istoriei. Elita intelectuală românească între 1930 și 1950* (The Traps of History. The Romanian Intellectual Elite between 1930 and 1950). București: Humanitas 2011.
17 Murgescu: *România și Europa*.
18 Murgescu: *România și Europa*, p. 205.
19 Murgescu: *România și Europa*. p. 212.
20 Vlad Georgescu: *Istoria românilor. De la origini până în zilele noastre* (The History of Romanians. From Origins to Present Days). București: Humanitas 1992, p. 222.

determining role in the process of economic transformation of Greater Romania and of standardized freedoms assumed, therefore legitimised, through the *Constitution* of 1923.

This is the starting argument for the majority of those who analyse the Romanian 'myth' of the interwar period, such as the critical, demythologizing perspective of Lucian Boia in his book, *Capcanele istoriei. Elita intelectuală românească între anii 1930–1950* (The Traps of History. The Romanian Intellectual Elite Between 1930–1950) (2011), or the descriptive and generalizing one of Dan Dungaciu in his *Elita interbelică. Sociologia românească în context European* (The Interwar Elite. Romanian Sociology in a European Context).[21] Boia's critical perspective starts from the argument that "in Romania, between the two world wars, the intellectual elite expands considerably: a consequence of progressive democratization."[22] Upon configuring this Arcadian image of Romania as an "idealized image of the period between the two world wars",[23] the defining contribution belonged to the intellectual elites from the new Romanian public space who highlighted more clearly than ever, in an era of relative freedom of expression, the discrepancy between neo-nationalistic conservative traditionalists and the young reforming modernists. In an attempt to identify "the members of the Romanian intellectual elite, in the strict meaning of the term",[24] Lucian Boia considerably narrows down the 'list' of those who played a decisive role in the configuration of the interwar world and, especially, of its utopian image. The historian refers to the "almost 200 university members from the two national universities (Bucharest and Iași), a few tens of front-rank writers and publicists, other cultured wits with authority in various fields and, of course, the members of the Romanian Academy (selected from previous categories)."[25] He intransigently and too restrictively limits the categories of the artisans of the interwar Romanian society, claiming that: "Two categories of intellectuals played a very special role in the Romanian society during the modern age. Writers and historians."[26]

It is obvious that the image of interwar Romania has been configured and imposed in a manner similar to a literary canon, i.e. through the sedimentation in the historical memory of an absolute model, recognized as such, therefore legitimised by the elite of the period, and rememorized and consolidated by the

---

21 Dan Dungaciu: *Elita interbelică. Sociologia românească în context european* (The Inter-Wars Elite. Romanian Sociology in European Context). București: Mica Valahie 2011.
22 Boia: *Capcanele istoriei*, p. 21.
23 Murgescu: *România și Europa*, p. 212.
24 Boia: "*Germanofilii*", p. 63.
25 Boia: "*Germanofilii*", p. 63.
26 Boia: "*Germanofilii*", p. 63.

elites of the historical moments that followed it. The legitimisation of the historical canon of the interwar period was a process of elite reformation as a result of the global democratic transformations, but also a process of imaginary historical sedimentation, in the context of the conditions of democratic reversibility during the following age, of power excess during the communist period. Thus, memory functioned in a compensatory manner, consolidating the illusion of pre-existence of a mythologized world.

The interwar elites, as well as the ones that stratified this image, operated in compliance with the type of mythological thinking Mircea Eliade spoke of when admitting the function of 'exemplary model' of the interwar national myth,[27] the 'story' of interwar Romania thus being the "story of a *genesis*: we are told how something was produced, how it came into being".[28] The evolution of this exemplary canon is determined by the conjunction of the two histories included in the myths, that is 'true history' and 'false history', and the fundamental role in counterbalancing the relations belonged indeed to the interwar intellectual elite. The role of the writers and that of historians in the configuration of this ideal construct of an identity and national nature was indeed a determining one, with these two categories of public personalities erecting and counterbalancing excesses, historians marking the ideal moments with a nationalistic impact, such as the Union of 1918, while the writers maintained and promoted the idea of the new literature, such as those from Lovinescu's 'Sburătorul' group, dreaming of a literature synchronised with the European literature of that time. Aware or not of the "seducing danger of journalism",[29] the writers constructed the image of a genuine battlefield within the pages of several important magazines during that period. Across their pages genuine insurrections were being waged against conservative movements at the beginning of the century, such as 'Sămănătorism' or 'Poporanism'.

The young writers were waging genuine battles for power with the old neonationalistic generation, although their position was not always in favour of democratic values, liberalization and Europeanization, but sometimes rather in favour of autochthonism, later on ideologically confiscated by the legionary movement as well or by the communist one. The interwar intellectual elite constantly maintained including "the tension of the dictatorship-democracy relation",[30]

---

27 Eliade: *Aspecte ale mitului*, p. 8.
28 Eliade: *Aspecte ale mitului*, p. 6.
29 Pârvulescu: *Întoarcere în Bucureștiul interbelic*, p. 237.
30 Zigu Ornea: *Anii treizeci. Extrema dreaptă românească* (The '30s. The Romanian Rightist Extreme). București: Fundația Culturală Românească 1996, p. 53.

with some of them[31] being supporters of certain radical ideas, such as "the parliamentary anti-democratism built on the corporate ideas",[32] and the superannuation of the multiparty politics in favour of the absolutism of the sole party, as demonstrated by Mihail Manoilescu's studies.[33] In fact, even the construction of the elite ideal of the nation, as described by Manoilescu, reuniting the general criteria of social value, such as economic, political, military, cultural and even aesthetic,[34] has a pretty homogenizing and nationalistic perspective.

The autochthonic ideas clash virulently with the liberalist-democratic ones,[35] supported by convicted pro-Europeans such as Mihail Ralea or by the circle of intellectuals from 'Sburătorul', where Eugen Lovinescu played a determining role. For example, Mihail Ralea argued in his article of 1930, entitled "Misiunea generației mele" (The Mission of My Generation),[36] for the necessity to promote certain European cultural values to the circle of intellectuals at the *Viața Românească* magazine, such as rationalism, democracy, Europeanism. Such ideas were spread in spite of the ethnic-autochthonic phases of the magazine, in fact recurrent also on the pages of other magazines, such as Alexandru Vlahuță and Nicolae Iorga's *Sămănătorul* at the beginning of the century or Nichifor Crainic's *Gândirea* in the '30s. Zigu Ornea, in his exemplary synthesis dedicated to the 1930's and to the manifestation of the Romanian rightist extreme, rightfully confirms the idea with regards to autochthonism:

> [...] the difficulty is not to defend it, but to grant it that overly accused restrictive and even normative nature. In the field of literature and culture in general, those meeting the autochthonic normative criteria were recognized and promoted. The modern movement of renewing the Romanian literature was condemned with rare violence, being considered foreign to the autochthonous spirit, an aimless imitation and promoted by the allogenes.[37]

---

[31] It is of course the case of Emil Cioran or Mircea Eliade as well, amply commented upon by Zigu Ornea in his book dedicated to the extreme orientations during the 1930s: *Anii treizeci. Extrema dreaptă românească*.
[32] Ornea: *Anii treizeci*, p. 49.
[33] See Ornea: *Anii treizeci*, p. 48–50.
[34] Also see the observations, perhaps overly descriptive and poorly analytical, of Dan Dungaciu regarding "Perspectiva corporatistă și teoria elitelor. Elitele profesionale și elitele totale (M. Manoilescu)" (The Corporate Perspective and the Theory of the Elites. Professional Elites and Total Elites). In: Dungaciu: *Elita interbelică*.
[35] Ioan Scurtu: *Din viața politică a României, 1926–1947* (From Romania's Political Life). București: Editura Științifică și Enciclopedică 1983.
[36] See Mihail Ralea: The Mission of My Generation (Misiunea generației mele). In: Mihail Ralea: *Scrieri* (Writings). Edition by Florin Mihăilescu. București: Minerva 1989, p. 195–196.
[37] Ornea: *Anii treizeci*, p. 102.

The criticism of the 'sămănătorist' foundation of this type of autochthonic idealization of the past was the main weapon in the battle for the power of the new aestheticism to the detriment of the restrictive formulas of tradition.

The iconoclasm of youth does not emerge, as Lucian Boia believed, from the rebelling of the young people in the face of typically Romanian 'complexes' of marginalization and subordination,[38] but precisely from the democratic values to which they have access due to Romania's openness during this period. They find themselves *waging war against everybody,* to paraphrase Eugen Ionescu, but not because of a complex of inferiority, but rather because of a complex of inauthenticity. The Romanian culture at the beginning of the past century, however devoid of synchronicity with the predominantly modernist European one, an ideal expressed and supported by Lovinescu, is first of all in disagreement with the Romanian social modernity, and the efforts of the youth to have a culturally authentic discourse are suffocated by the lack of adherence to their ideas in this stiff public space. In other words, culture was in a different phase than society, still dominated by the autochthonous discourse, the revolt of the young people often ending in oblivion or drastic exclusions from the public space. An eloquent example in this case is the the avantgarde group arround the *Alge* magazine, encouraged by Geo Bogza's ostracism following the publication of 'Poemul invectivă' (The Invective Poem), and in general by the Romanian literary avant-garde, or by Mircea Eliade, Eugen Ionescu, Mircea Vulcănescu, Constantin Noica or Emil Cioran's generation.

In fact, an article from 1932 by Mircea Eliade is definitive for the iconoclastic position of the youth within this war for the modernizing cultural power of Greater Romania. The article, entitled "Tendințele tinerei generații" (The Tendencies of the Young Generation), was published in the 268/1932 issue of the *Vremea* newspaper, and Eliade hereby seals the different mission of the youth culture, unlike the autochthonous ideals that still dominated the market of interwar cultural ideas. Below is the manifesto of withdrawal from this battle of the youth, whose discourse appears to the elites at the beginning of the century firstly as inauthentic:

> That is why I was saying that this generation should have avoided politics precisely because their inner battle is still full and effervescent. They haven't yet solved anything, but have merely experimented... I believe this generation is the first one in Romania that can say without exaggerating that it has risked its own skin for the truth. There have been other heroic generations before us that created this country and enlarged its borders: the generation of the Union, the generation of liberalism, and the generation of war. But all these generations had an exterior goal: the country, the nation, the state... Young people no longer have, nor could they, nor should they have such ideals anymore. That explains the

---

[38] Boia: *Capcanele istoriei*, p. 32.

success of orthodoxy around 1927–1928, a movement that has failed lamentably (historicizing dogmatism, neo-Byzantinism, excess of decorative elements, autochthonism at any cost, reduction of Christianity from a cosmic vision of humanity to a historical phase etc.). While *experience* and *direct living* are the first characteristic of the young generation-its corollary is humanism.[39]

There are other apostles of the withdrawal of the youth from the political battle in favour of art, especially aestheticism, in the group of 'criterionists'. In favour of the idea of the generation renouncing political activism, Zigu Ornea also mentions an article from 1932 belonging to Constantin Noica in which the author spoke of the aggression of history, advising young people to adhere to the collective ideals invoked by Eliade as well. Noica's article is dedicated to those who want "to reconcile aestheticism with national exigencies", thus preaching, as a central idea of the modernist aesthetic centric discourse of that period, the idea of separating the aesthetic from the social. The 'cleverness' of the new generation of elites would consist of accepting "as fatality this *absurdness* of ours to think individualistic" themes or "the painful *Hic et nunc* of individual consciousness and to live our life as orphans in a dignified manner [...]."[40] These orphans of history are in fact the nonconformists, the immoral, the arrogant without complexes, the brutal and the irreconcilable hooligans from the same category as the Petru Anicet character in Eliade's novel, *Huliganii* (The Hooligans), published in 1935. *The hooligan vocation*, if the metaphoric formula from Eliade's novel is to be adopted, that is indeed the distinctive feature of the young generation, was eventually defeated by the excessive power of history. The effects of this withdrawal of the young elites from the public space led to a segregated image of the interwar period: on the one hand, we have an idealized image of the socio-political modernization, a canonized image, still dominated however by the nationalistic autochthonism and an authentic image of the literary modernization, in which the Romanian novel has excelled, precisely by returning to the authentic sources of reflexivity. The *experience* and *direct living* Eliade spoke of are essential coordinates in the aesthetic program of the youth as well, who thus discover the authenticity of the reflexive power, in the context in which on the outside they feel defeated by the active power of the political 'gorilla'.

Nevertheless, the imaginary memory of the interwar period has engrained itself so well in Romanian culture due to an obvious fact: the cultural canon in general and the literary one in particular was set and circulated more freely and more fuzzily at that time than during any other period of Romanian's young and

---

[39] Apud Ornea: *Anii treizeci*, p.176.
[40] Apud Ornea: *Anii treizeci*, p.177.

'unsettled' culture. The role of literature and especially that of the novel, which experienced a revival around the war time and especially during the '30s, defined as genius years, is evident, through the writers being in charge of initiating and promoting an almost inexistent genre. This genre becomes the manifesto of the interwar period, the active image of its modernizing culture.

The memory of the interwar period functions in a similar manner to that of the Occidental West during this period. What Milan Kundera defined as the cultural image of the West would also be valid for the literary image of interwar Romania. "The last direct personal experience of the West that Central European countries remember is the period from 1918 to 1938, *Kundera confirms*. Their picture of the West, then, is of the West in the past, of a West in which culture had not yet entirely bowed out."[41] Therefore, the canonical image of interwar Romania is partially determined by the canonical image of interwar literature as well, in the forms and through its reflexive formulas, of withdrawal into creation from the excesses of aggressive history and of the political 'gorilla'. The reflexive power of the interwar novel is proved by the authentic proses of writers such as Mircea Eliade, Camil Petrescu, Anton Holban, Hortensia Papadat-Bengescu or Max Blecher. The aesthetic centric formulas of this interwar canon are therefore the result of a modernity defeated on the outside. Subversive with the public environment of the period to the extent of depersonalization, the interwar novel ends with the return of the writer to the inner universe, in its turn exposed to the erosive nature of power. The disillusion of active power transforms into an illusion of the all-encompassing and allpowerful reflexivity.

3.2 The *Power* of the Interwar Novelistic Canon

Speaking about 'The paradox of reactionary modernism',[42] Jeffrey Herf relativizes the existence of modernity as a universal, general and uniforming paradigm, talking about the fact that "There is no such thing as modernity in general. There are only national societies, each of which becomes modern in its own fashion."[43] Such dichotomies, characteristic when defining the specificity of the beginning of the 20th century, such as tradition-modernity, community-society, progress-reaction, invoked by the American historian, have been assimilated differently by European modern societies. Jeffrey Herf starts from the

---

41 Kundera: The Tragedy of Central Europe, p. 37.
42 Jeffrey Herf: *Reactionary Modernism*. Cambridge: Cambridge University Press 1984, p. 1.
43 Herf: *Reactionary Modernism*, p. 1.

national-identity assumption of modern 'Germanism' defined in the 1944 discourse of Thomas Mann, entitled "Germany and Germanism". Herf's objective is to demonstrate the theory of the German novelist on the "technological romanticism" of modernity, generated by the encounter of that German *Innerlichkeit* with the robustness and accentuated technologization of modernity.

But such a reactive modernity is specific to several worlds in which on the doorstep of the previous century, lived the same type of incompatibility, the same withdrawal into a national romanticism, in a context of a crisis of humanity meeting the horrors of history and of modern civilization. The art of the first half of the century reflects the complexes of the man who no longer has the 'features' needed to adapt to the change in sensitivity of those times. For example, the British prose writer, Virginia Woolf, believed that the moment of representation of a modification of 'human nature' through the explosion of sensitivity specific to modern art took place in 1910, with the first post-Impressionistic exhibition. This exhibition included paintings by artists such as Cézanne, Matisse, Van Gogh or Picasso, the last two also being the recognized representatives of the historical avant-garde, therefore of the aesthetic insurrection at the beginning of the last century. However, there were several factors that contributed to this triggering moment, such as the microscopic observation of the depths of human psychism through the Freudian psychoanalysis at the beginning of the century, through the conscious-unconscious equation or Einstein's theory of relativity, with its redefinitions of space-time relations, or the increased interest in quantic spatiality etc. The scientific context has been doubled by the historical context, by the shock produced by the consequences of the First World War which, in addition to the humanitarian disaster that came upon Europe, has also had identity-related effects, due to the disintegration of the great empires and the attempt of national repositioning of constituent identities.

In this context of relativization of theories, beliefs and human consciences, "psychic determinism replaces social determinism; the concepts of absolute time and space are substituted with the concepts of a space and time continuum, time thus becoming the fourth dimension of space."[44] The impact of this psychological determinism is decisive for the novelistic art as well, which undergoes a radical change of focus, shifting from the exterior setting, from the continuous, certain and dominant environment, to the discontinuous stream of consciousness, perceived at least in the offering totality of its authenticity. The relation seems to be almost of transposition or at least of simultaneity with the scientific theory of De Broglie, regarding the discovery and argumentation for the undulatory nature of

---

[44] Mușat: *Romanul românesc interbelic*, p. 14.

matter, i.e. in a fluctuant, bipolar dynamic. Modern literature, propelled by the scientific discoveries of the beginning of the century, discovers the paradoxical truth in the relativity and discontinuity or in the fluctuations of human psychism. But this is not merely the role of psychoanalysis or of the physicist relativism that are part of and which fuel the climate of the period, but is also the consequence of a long process within the history of the novel. Following the social determinism that placed man in a relation of dependency with the environment, unveiling his psychological flaws, the mechanisms of adaptation to the environment he came from and its implicit reflection on his processes of consciousness, the modern novelist acknowledges the superfluous and rudimentary character of this referential automatism.

The socio-cultural changes representative of the interwar period function similarly to a 'scientific revolution', in the meaning given by Thomas Kuhn in 1970, who considered 'scientific revolutions' as "scientific revolutions are here taken to be those non-cumulative developmental episodes in which an older paradigm is replaced in whole or in part by an incompatible new one."[45] Following this assertion, it can be seen that during the interwar period we witness an aesthetic 'revolution' of art in general and of literature in particular. However, this assertion became a cliché of the end of the last century, and the spectre of this aesthetic 'Golden Age' still floats above the current literature. The image is tributary to a canonizing, aesthetic-centrical manner of thinking, and the explanation is pretty obvious in the context in which this short period of approximately twenty years was the first genuine autonomization of Romanian society and, implicitly, art.

'La Belle Époque', in the autochthonous Romanian variant, is the interwar so-called 'Golden Age', therefore a shifted period pushed to the interwar moment, as an effect of social transformations of the legitimation of the national spirit following 1918. The national context is the one allowing the birth of the interwar national literary canon and, on the other hand, the modernization through liberalization of the Romanian public space allows for such an iconoclasm against traditional art which no longer corresponds to the sensitivity of the modern artist aggressed by history and its redundant and manipulative mechanisms. The paradigm of the interwar modernization, with the legitimisation of the public space as an arena for canonizing battles, causes the modern artist to ultimately seek refuge, ascertaining the incompatibility of this aggressive world with the unstable and discontinuous forms of its psychology. In accord with this conflict,

---

[45] Thomas S. Kuhn: *The Structure of Scientific Revolutions*. Second Edition. Chicago: The University of Chicago Press 1970, p. 92.

the modern novel radically changes its manner of depicting the relation of the writer with the world, an incompatibility between his sickly sensitivity and the insensitivity of the space he lives in. Insensitive and impassive to his egocentric needs, the new world, modernized, impersonalized and polarized, has lost its innocence, determining a crisis of literature, of the novel in particular. The novel adopts an indirectly critical discourse against dehumanization and impersonalization of the modern public space, adopting the strategy of self-referentiality.

The novels of discontinuity and relativity of consciousness place in the centre of investigations a psychology that often reflects rather the variability of relations with reality and the diffused world generated this time by the human psyche and not by the outer world. It is indeed a 'psychological determinism' around which the great novels of the first half of the century gravitate, and novelists such as Marcel Proust, Virginia Woolf, Thomas Mann, Robert Musil, André Gide, James Joyce and others shift the centre of gravity towards the sensitive indetermination of the psyche, aggressed by its contact with the environment, denouncing or renouncing its contract with history. The reactions to the anti-humanistic excesses of history, to its aggressive and manipulative power, are firstly visible especially in the novels describing the fracture between the exterior environment, of war, and the interior one, of consciousness and sensitivity. For example, this break is obvious in the canonical war novels such as *A Farewell to Arms*, by Ernest Hemingway, *The Good Soldier Svejk*, by Jaroslav Hasek, *All Quiet on the Western Front* by Erich Maria Remarque, *The Radetzky March* by Joseph Roth, *Lesson in a Dead Language* by Andrzej Kusniewicz or even *Pădurea spânzuraților* (Forest of the Hanged), the 1922 novel by Liviu Rebreanu.

The Romanian novel finds itself on the barricades of this aesthetic 'revolution', experiencing a genuine birth around the 1930s, as a result of a genuine debate on the importance of urban subjects that should be determinant as a formula of this mutation of sensitivity. The avant-garde of this battle includes for certain the insurrection against the past-ridden currents of a traditionalistic orientation, led by important critics such as Eugen Lovinescu in the pages he dedicated to *Istoria literaturii contemporane* (The History of Contemporary Literature*)* or George Călinescu and his generalizing perspective on traditionalism and modernism in *Istoria literaturii române de la origini până în prezent* (The History of the Romanian Literature from Origins to Present Day). The ideological battle is supported in the pages of certain important magazines of that time, such as *Revista fundațiilor regale*, *Adevărul literar și artistic*, *Convorbiri literare*, *România literară*, *Viața Românească* and especially *Sburătorul*, except for the last one, all them mirror the inconsistencies of that time and the doctrinaire eclecticism. The battle is gradually transformed, in the spirit of that time, into a debate displaying the counter-arguments for the necessity to *synchronise* Romanian prose with

European urban prose, especially French, and to give up the rural themed novels. In other words, the period witnesses a conservative *reactive modernity* visible especially in the realistic novels of the Romanian interwar period which had a greater success than the modernists responsible for the *impersonated, imitated modernity*.

Speaking of the 'spirit of that time', we evoke the insurrection of the *modernizers* of the interwar period, such as Eugen Lovinescu or Ștefan Zeletin, against the rural world and the promotion of popular culture at the centre of the artistic preoccupations at the beginning of the 20th century, a direction actively supported by the elites of that period, the 'reactive' Constantin Dobrogeanu-Gherea, Nicolae Iorga or Constantin Stere. It is about the rebellion against conservatism that characterized the discourse of these personalities at the beginning of the century, and the radicalization of this doctrinaire resistance is memorable within the programmes of the first Romanian avant-garde, that of the artists arround the *Alge* magazine, stimulated by Geo Bogza's spirit of insurrection or within the manifestations of the 'Generation 30'. Expressions such as 'the belated of history', 'the eternal villagers of history', 'the eternal, patriarchal, rural, ahistorical Romania', 'minor culture' or 'biblical lamentation' are included in the multitude of *Pagini despre sufletul românesc* (Pages on the Romanian soul),[46] belonging to the generation denouncing Romanian apriorism and imperatively requesting as a sole form of cultural subsistence, *Schimbarea la față a României* (The Transfiguration of Romania).[47]

These young people proclaim 'an actual Romania', denouncing the ahistorical 'eternity' of the Romanian peasant and their insurgence often resorts to extreme formulas. The challenge of the 'peasant identity' is the result of the 'crystallization of image' or better said of the rustic national-identity pre-construct during 1821–1883.[48] What is therefore being discussed is an image of an image of the 'peasant' in the proximity of the 20th century, a fact remarked in an exemplary chapter of Alex Drace-Francis, dedicated to the representation of the Romanian

---

[46] Constantin Noica: *Pagini despre sufletul românesc* (Pages on the Romanian soul). București: Humanitas 1991.
[47] Emil Cioran: *Schimbarea la față a României* (The Transfiguration of Romania). București: Humanitas 1990.
[48] A complex perspective on the crystallization of this stereotypical identity 'imaginary' in the Romanian culture is offered to us by Alex Drace-Francis' research, in the chapter entitled "The Tradition of Invention. Representation of the Romanians. Peasant from Ancient Stereotype to Modern Symbol" from his book centred on Romanian ethnical and social stereotypies, *The Traditions of Invention. Romanian Ethnic and Social Stereotypes in Historical Context*. Boston; Leiden: Brill 2013.

peasant.[49] The history of this image is doubly determined, national in terms of the formation of the modern state beginning with the end of the 19th century, and European, according to historical coordinates. In fact, Alex Drace-Francis confirms the double status of the imaginary construct, by stating: "If the creation of a peasant identity within Romania is a modern affair, then the identity of the Romanians as peasants has a rather older history in certain writings in wide circulation in the rest of Europe."[50] His argumentation starts from the agrarian cult of Romans, up to the Enlightenment and the reforms of the Romantic revolutionaries. The negative perception of this culture can be explained through consideration of the clash between the identity image of the peasant, consecrated at the end of the 19th century and implicitly of the ideologizing implications from the beginning of the following century, with the sudden democratization and industrialization of interwar Romanian society. This complex is certainly due to the major changes that took place during the interwar period, changes of a cultural and elite nature, of sudden modernization, an identity complex due also to the formation of the urban literary canon, in synchronicity with the European tendencies.

As usual, Eugen Lovinescu is 'trenchant' in this regard as well, translating the dispute on the rural literature versus the urban literature into coordinates of an aesthetic nature i.e. into the necessary shift from the objective to the subjective. In the chapter dedicated to 'Evoluția Prozei literare' (The Evolution of Literary Prose),[51] the critic understands the 'reactionary' significance of modernism, in the meaning of a movement "against traditionalism and as an expression of the synchronicity of the contemporary civilization."[52] He underlines the "Contribution of *Sburătorul*" to promoting the subjective novel, and places at the centre of his argumentation prose texts belonging to G. Brăescu, F. Aderca or H. Papadat-Bengescu to whom he in fact dedicates an ample and eloquent chapter on the argumentation of modernist techniques.

The critic's motivation for placing the prose of Hortensia Papadat-Bengescu at the centre of his argumentation is determined precisely by its translation from the objective into the subjective, in a discrete manner, through narrative progressivity and style. Exponentially, Lovinescu appreciates "this power of analysis, as well as the sincere attitude, to the extent of cynicism, towards the psychological phenomenon and, in particular, towards femininity", which "takes the writer's

---

49 Drace-Francis: *The Traditions of Invention*, p. 11–59.
50 Drace-Francis: *The Traditions of Invention*, p. 16.
51 Eugen Lovinescu: *Scrieri 5. Istoria literaturii române contemporane* (Writing 5. The History of Contemporary Romanian Literature). Edited by Eugen Simion. București: Minerva 1973.
52 Lovinescu: *Scrieri 5*, p. 156–157.

literature out of the common Romanticism and subjectivism of feminine literature, which is struggling between the lyrical explosion and sensorial exuberance of the Countess of Noailles, for example, and the aerial sentimentalism and the discrete sensitivity of most female writers." The importance of her prose is that "passion is accompanied by the scientific interest of knowledge by dissecting feelings to their ultimate adherences."[53] We thus identify in the Lovinescian analysis the explanation for the power of analysis, the meaning of the reflexive power of the prose writer who succeeds in an authentic manner to progressively, tacitly and discretely return the analysis, from the fresco social to the dissection of the ultimate subjective processes. In other words, what we notice in prose texts such as *Ape adânci* (Deep Waters), *Sfinxul* (The Sphinx), *Femeia în fața oglinzii* (The Woman in front of the Mirror) or *Concert din muzică de Bach* (A Concert of Music by Bach) is a shift from the objective, active power of characters such as Lică Trubadurul, to the interior reflexes of their reflexive power, such as Prince Maxențiu. It is about a new technique in Romanian literature, that of searching for the sources of power in these 'deep waters' by 'dissecting feelings' to the extent of the dissolution of the Self.

But the search for reflexive authenticity, i.e. of the voice that brings to the surface, with a specific aggressive dramaticism, the particularities and especially the paradox's of the modern caught in the conflict between nostalgic past admirers, reactionaries, i.e. modern romantics, and the modern reformers, often filled with a frenzy of influence and not at all by its 'anxiety', does not always have the anticipated results. The successful novelistic typology during the interwar period remains nevertheless the realistic novel, the modernist one being perceived more like an experimental epic category. The authentic modernist novels, aesthetically innovative due to their change of narrative perspective, or which elude the suffocating pragmatics of the realistic novel, banking exclusively on the hypertrophy of consciousness, such as *Patul lui Procust* (Procrustes' Bed) (1933) by Camil Petrescu, *Ioana* (1934) by Anton Holban or *Întâmplări în irealitatea imediată* (Occurrences in the Immediate Reality) (1936) by Max Blecher still lack their deserved canonical success. From this point of view, Paul Cernat's opinion in his essay, *Modernismul retro în romanul românesc interbelic* (Retro Modernism within the Interwar Romanian Novel),[54] according to which this phase of the novel is no longer justified solely "through the filter of Lovinescu's theories, dominant in the post-war Romanian studies",[55] is justified.

---

[53] Lovinescu: *Scrieri* 5, p. 241.
[54] Paul Cernat: *Modernismul românesc retro în romanul românesc interbelic* (Romanian Retro Modernism in the Romanian Novel between the Wars). București: Art 2009.
[55] Cernat: *Modernismul românesc retro*, p. 7.

The canonization of the interwar Romanian novel reduced to Lovinescu's ideas, starting from the transition from the lyrical to the epic, from the objective to the subjective, from the conservative, past-admiring rural to the visionary urbanism "are necessary conditions, but not sufficient for a valid theory of the modernization of the species."[56] The Lovinescian ideas played a considerable role during the period, but their impact on the evolution of the novelistic species was limited by the recurrence of anachronisms in a society modernized overnight. The 'mortifying' and 'refractory' tradition has often been regarded as "a dangerous arresting factor" (Ion Pillat), ultimately ignoring precisely the specificity of the Romanian modernism, the doctrinaire eclecticism. The ideological interbreeding, the conflict between the practice of the new novel and the persistence of the 'retro' novel, the sudden transition from the lyrical model to the epic one and the nostalgia of the Old Regime has led to a symbiosis of traditionalism and modernity during the third decade of the century. The air of the time between 1918 and 1930 is of a permanent conflict between the innovative tendencies and the excessive conservative tradition. In fact, Zigu Ornea's idea is precisely that this novelistic canon was prepared in the laboratory of the second decade of the century, therefore after the achievement of the national ideal of 1918 and the modernizing reforms that followed after that. The critic confirms that:

> From any perspective we choose to contemplate the picture of the interwar period, we ascertain that the load is on this third decade (which in fact lasted twelve years, because it started in November 1918 and ended in 1930). In almost all the compartments, 'the games were played' (if we are allowed to say that) in the 1920s. In the following decade previously-stated intentionalities were asserted, accents were modified. But the map remained within its characteristic data, set after the overthrows from the third decade. This happened in the context of political scenery and of political ideology. In the context of literature and art, practically, the 1930s only add a few new values. But the essential had already been consumed during the third decade.[57]

Moreover, the ideological interbreeding, a fact argued for by Ornea and subsequently reconfirmed by Cernat, of Romanian modernity has not been assumed exclusively by the *Sburătorul* group through Camil Petrescu, Ion Barbu or Camil Baltazar, but also by adepts of the *Gândirea* current or young avant-gardists, such as Ion Vinea, Ilarie Voronca, B. Fundoianu, Gherasim Luca or by the group of *Viața Românească*, under the guidance of Alexandru Philippide. Therefore, the modernization of Romanian literature was not solely the attribute of the modernist Lovinescians, but also of modernizers from the first half of the previous century.

---

56 Cernat: *Modernismul românesc retro*, p. 7.
57 Ornea: *Tradiționalism și modernitate*, p. 22–23.

In the second decade of the century, the battle for the cultural canon was not focused solely on Eugen Lovinescu and Garabet Ibrăileanu, but also on the young people from the post-war generation such as Nichifor Crainic, Mihail Ralea, Tudor Vianu, Felix Aderca or Cezar Petrescu, who animated this confrontation in the public space through polemic articles in the pages of literary magazines such as *Gândirea, Hiena, Cuvântul liber, Mișcarea literară, Viața românească, Ideea europeană*. The publishing in 1924 and 1925 of *Istoria civilizației române modern* (The History of Modern Romanian Civilization) by Eugen Lovinescu only aggravates the debate regarding the balance between national values and the assumption of Occidental models in the cultural foundation of the Romanian national state.

In such a context, of formative and reformative debates regarding the tendencies and cultural foundations of the Greater Romania moment, the modernist novel often was a certain victim of conservatives who, at numerous times, regarded it an example of 'imitation'. But the 1930s are favorable for novelistic experiments precisely because the battles for cultural power had already been waged in the previous decade, so that the atmosphere of the third decade of the century, of relative moderation of previous asperities, becomes favourable to narrative experiments. Constantin Pricop[58] also refers to the reorientation of the active-revolutionary energies of the previous decade when he claims and comments on the 1934 study of Mircea Vulcănescu, eloquently entitled 'Generație' (Generation). For certain it is not exclusively about the generation of the 'criterionists',[59] but also of the young writers, coming from eclectic literary directions but who had already made their debut in the second decade, with the feeling of actively participating to the literary foundation of the new Romania. If the first phase, that of the '20s, is one of "hope of the youth in their powers",[60] the second phase, at the beginning of the '30s, is of "spiritual fall, of defeat, of deception, of perplexity, of victorious affirmation that lend to the youth the illusion of living a moment of grace, decisive in the destiny of Romanian culture."[61] This phase is characterized by fundamental binders of the young generation, revealed by Mircea Vulcănescu as well, such as "dramatic tension, tragic nature, crisis, which are undoubtedly the crucial point of the experience shared by the young generation."[62]

---

58 Constantin Pricop: *Seducția ideologiilor și luciditatea (rigoarea) criticii. Privire asupra criticii literare românești din perioada interbelică* (The Seduction of the Ideologies and Lucidity (Rigour) of the Critics. Overlook on Romanian Literary Criticism in the Inter-War Period). București: Integral 1999, p. 347.
59 The young writers formed arround the *Criterion* magazine (1932–1933).
60 Pricop: *Seducția ideologiilor*, p. 347.
61 Apud Pricop: *Seducția ideologiilor*, p. 347.
62 Apud Pricop: *Seducția ideologiilor*, p. 348.

The constitutive tragic nature of the youth, a result of a feeling of failure to adhere to the process of modernization of interwar Romanian literature, is a considerable force that "leads some to negativism, others to agony, and still others to despair". In order to save themselves from this existential but also existentialist blockage, in the spirit of the decade, "some blindly throw themselves into action, while others proclaim their despair with pathos, searching for quietness, for a lull in their language."[63] It is for certain a refuge in the only functional reality, the reflexive one, a power still unexplored at that time within Romanian literature, a compensation of the failed experimentalism of the past year.

In the process of analysis of the metamorphoses of the interwar Romanian novel, Carmen Mușat places at the centre of the preoccupations of the novelists of that time the 'reflection' of the world and of the soul, as a proof of the modernizing diversification of the species. The polymorphism of the interwar Romanian novel is proven by the different 'ages' of the species, Carmen Mușat confirming that the Romanian novel shifts "from epic *realism*, oriented exclusively towards the outer world, to *subjective realism*, interested in discovering the infinitely more complex reality of the spirit, experimenting at the same time with novel formulas, such as musical structure, the journal, the antinovel or the novel with a mythical substratum."[64] The points of reference of the interwar Romanian novel vary from the "epic and descriptive Realism" of Liviu Rebreanu, to Călinescu's 'Balzacian Realism', to the 'psychological Realism' or the phenomenological one of certain prose writers such as Hortensia Papadat-Bengescu, Camil Petrescu, Anton Holban, to the "symbolist and aestheticizing Realism" of Mateiu I. Caragiale.

At the same time, novelists rediscover the primary sources of the supernatural irrational, creating the 'mythical novel', such as the Sadovenian one or the fantastic, central in certain novels of Mircea Eliade. While the 'antinovel', represented during this period by the Urmuzian experiment, manifests hostility towards the pragmatism of recurrent realism, 'the indirect novel' suggests that the reader takes refuge in the omnipresent authenticity of living, also as an alternative to the realistic novel. This category of novel, reproduced after the general taxonomy proposed by Carmen Mușat in her analysis of *Romanul românesc interbelic* (The Interwar Romanian Novel),[65] would represent the emblematic feature of the 'experimentalist' generation, as Petru Comarnescu characterizes the young leading writers of the 1930s, such as Mircea Eliade, Anton Holban, Mihail Sebastian, Horia Bonciu or Max Blecher. "The dramatic tension, tragic nature

---

[63] Apud Pricop: *Seducția ideologiilor*, p. 348–349.
[64] Mușat: *Romanul românesc interbelic*, p. 18.
[65] Mușat: *Romanul românesc interbelic*, p. 17–37.

and crisis" that Mihail Sebastian spoke of are distinctive features of these prose writers who find their refuge in subjectivity, in uncensored reflexivity, the last resource of power of living and writing.

More than "autobiographic",[66] as characterized by Carmen Mușat,[67] Blecher's prose is the fundamental point of reference in the attempt to rebuild the effects of self-reflexivity on the interwar Romanian novel. Even the scarce reception of that time to his prose proves the particularities and obvious originality of the formula. The autobiographic, as a technique of the indirect novelistic discourse, is merely an antinovelistic formula, in the meaning of yet another opposition against the obsessive recurrence of the realistic novel. In the case of Blecher's prose, and especially in regards to his 1936 novel, *Întâmplări în irealitatea imediată* (Occurrences in the Immediate Unreality), reality does not disappear to the detriment of the biographic, but rather its power is weakened, obscured by the autobiographic, that is, by an invisible and variable psycho-sensorial map.

What is witnessed then is a narrative experiment, following which reality is hypertrophied by the exacerbated senses of the Subject. This reality is controlled, manipulated and therefore weakened precisely through the Subject's reflexive power, as a last solution to the incompatibility and lack of adherence, this time biographical as well, to the real. The captivity of the author "in a body ground by sickness"[68] is merely a biographic instrument that allows the microscopic exploration of the otherwise unsuspected force of subjectivity to conquer the captivity of the real by matter and the terror of the biographic. The reflexive power proves a determining characteristic of an authentic novel, a complementary solution of autonomization of the narrative in the face of the immobile realism and, implicitly, an ignored modernization of the species.

3.3 From the *Literaturisation* of the Autobiographical Trauma to the Reflexive Power

"Não o prazer, não a glória, não o poder: a liberdade, unicamente a liberdade."[69]

---

66 Doris Mironescu makes some clarifying specifications "against the Blecherian biography", i.e. regarding the exceeding of the autobiographic status of his prose, in *Viața lui Max Blecher. Împotriva biografiei* (The Life of Max Blecher. Against Biography). Iași: Timpul 2011.
67 Mușat: *Romanul românesc interbelic*, p. 34.
68 Mușat: *Romanul românesc interbelic*, p. 35.
69 Fernando Pessoa: *Livro do Desassossego*. Org. Richard Zenith. São Paulo: Companhia das Letras 1999, p. 70.

3.3.1 The Surrealist Dare. The Autobiography of "[...] a man cut in half by a window"

In his *Jurnal*, Mihail Sebastian recomposes Blecher's image, between life and death, on the edge of bearing suffering, a being frailed by spine tuberculosis, for whom literature ultimately becomes just an instrument exorcising the violent reality. We encounter, in the pages of the diary, the image of the man weakened by the gap between the aggressive reality and the memory of an artist isolated in his world, with his senses more acute and hypertrophied. Within the proximity of imminent death and within an agonising life, most of the time Blecher's destiny is exemplary for his fellow writers, such as Geo Bogza or Mihail Sebastian, as "Everything becomes absurdly pointless when facing such pain."[70] The biographical element is a devouring force, an exemplary feature for Sebastian:

> Blecher's life at Roman continues as I have seen it. Will I ever again have the nerve to complain about anything? Will I ever again be so brazen as to have caprices, bad moods, or feelings of irritation? He is living in the intimate company of death. It is not a vague, abstract death in the long term, but his own death, precise, definite, known in detail, like an object.[71]

In such a liminal existential context, literature seems to be of secondary importance or divided from the extreme living. Mihail Sebastian invokes Blecher's confession regarding the relation between life and literature and the priority of life: "Listen, I've begun to write a novel. But I don't feel that I absolutely must complete it. If I die first, I don't think I'll even regret not having finished it. What a minor thing literature is for me! And how little of my time it takes up!"[72]

The secondary role of writing related to the intensity of living such a reality and its total assumption makes "the biography of an author so actively involved in the fight against self-biographical narration"[73] be admirable in the epoch, transmitting the message of that total, existential assumption of living. Being a generation that sets the 'experimentalism' Petru Comarnescu talked about at the centre of the artistic programmes, it is not possible to refrain from observing that Blecher is an exemplary writer for the interwar period. Even his extreme 'souffrance', which we encounter in his prose, could not be understood only by reference to his biographical drama. The narativity of exasperation is also a reaction and a response to this paradoxical 'Zeitgeist' of interwar modernity. In

---

[70] Mihail Sebastian: *Jurnal* (1935–1944) (Journal). Gabriela Omăt (ed.). Preface and notes by Leon Volovici. București: Humanitas 2002, p. 120.
[71] Sebastian: *Jurnal*, p. 86.
[72] Sebastian: *Jurnal*, p. 102.
[73] Mironescu: *Viața lui Max Blecher*, p. 202.

fact, David Le Breton[74] is right when he speaks about the attitude of the subject face with his pain: "L'attitude du sujet face à sa douleur, et même le seuil dolorifiè auquel il réagit sont liés à la culture somatique de son groupe social et à sa propre psyché."[75] Through the nature of his tragic biography, he sets the experience of suffering at the centre of his life. The author is a model of the interwar writer, placed between the acute living of history, biography in his case, by experimenting its violence, and writing as a comprehensive form, as forced self-exile because of the absurd of the adherence to reality. Out of this incompatibility Blecher's surreal images crystallized through the narrative exercise. Although the fact that, when measured against the feeling of the deadly sickness, literature occupies a secondary place in the hierarchy of the author makes literature a vital act, a refuge from a secondary reality, the purgative function of writing which has two functions: a self-comprehensive one and a compensating one. We observe a transfiguration of the biography, a circumstance which allows the complex understanding of the reality crises and therefore writing becomes an instrument meant to activate the reflexive power which assures the transgression of the limit.

As an example, a moment of Sebastian's existential panic, fear of death, as can be read in his *Jurnal* (Journal), makes him think about Blecher or, better said, about the reflexivised Subject of the *Inimi Cicatrizate* (Scarred Hearts) but also of *Întâmplări în irealitatea imediată* (Occurrence in the Immediate Unreality) in which he demonstrates his self-comprehensive functionality: "I saw again the whole first chapter of *Inimi cicatrizate* (Scarred Hearts). 'Cold abscess', 'hot abscess', 'fistula', 'fistular abscess', at deaths' door-Blecher's vocabulary. At last I understood how a fistula digs in, how it makes room for itself, how it can sink through flesh 'right into the buttock' as Blecher put it, and how I was never able to understand."[76] Understanding the exceptional character of the transgressed biography, Sebastian's note on the date of 5th June 1938, the moment of Max Blecher's death, has the role of speaking directly about the refuge within himself in search of the reflexive power, an inexhaustible and authentic source of the novel:

> Blecher has died. His funeral was on Tuesday at Roman. I thought not of his death, which was a merciful release in the end, but of his life, which has been shaking me to the core. His suffering was too great to allow compassion or tenderness. That young man who lived as in another world because of his terrible pain, always remained something of a stranger. I could never completely open up and show a real warmth toward him. He scared me a little, kept

---

[74] David Le Breton: *Corps et sociétés. Essai de sociologie et d'antropologie du corps*. Paris: Méridiens Klincksieck 1988.
[75] Le Breton: *Corps et sociétés*, p. 94.
[76] Sebastian: *Jurnal*, p. 144.

me at a distance, as the gates of a prison that I could not enter or he leave. And each time we said goodbye, where did he return to? What was it like there?[77]

The awful/bad places of Blecher's refuge under the fatal force of autobiography are visual forms, representations of the action turned towards the polymorphic encounter between memory-sensation, that of the writing placed under the domination of the explosive sensorial. As in Surrealism, the physical is just a pretext, biography is only a developing framework for a trans-psychological perspective on the world. Blecher's 'world' within a world, which Sebastian discusses, is a drastic change of perspective from immediate exposures, provoked by the interaction with reality, towards the sensorial recoil of memories which give a more authentic image of the man, as they operate selectively, keeping active only the emotionally laden images. The pure, crystalline image of Blecher's Subject is an eclectic one, formed out of fractions of sensations from reality, memorised through the sensorial filter, a memory snip around some determining, therefore powerfully self-reflexive sensations.

'The strangeness' of the relation biography writing astonished the readership of Max Blecher's prose, as well. His placement within or outside the post-war canon was fluctuant also because of the unique character of his prose, seldom perceived as 'experimental'. The late reception of his prose is interpreted by Nicolae Manolescu as a consequence of the short and superficial analyses done by Călinescu in *Istoria literaturii române de la origini până în prezent* (The History of Romanian Literature from Origins till Present) (1941), therefore the result being his historical necanonisation. The Romanian literature historian seems incapable of overcoming the biographical sources of the writing out of paradoxically subjective reasons, a fact which would undoubtedly mark his analyses:

> I know a famous case in which a writer was out of the canonical list and hasn't re-entered till today, only because that who made the canon at that time hated writers and books which spoke of disease, I mean Blecher and Călinescu. Călinescu did not like books about disease. He could not stand *The Magic Mountain* by Thomas Mann. He thought it was a stupid book. Because Blecher was sick and his literature reflected this, he wrote about Blecher ten rows in *The History of Literature*...dismissing him. The result was that Blecher is not even today a canonical writer. He's becoming, he's starting to be one, but he is not yet.[78]

Moreover, if attention is redirected from another 'case' of critical evaluation, already observed in the analyses of Lovinescu's critical role in imposing the modern post-war canon, that of Hortensia Papadat-Bengescu, the circumscribing

---

[77] Sebastian: *Jurnal*, p. 164–165.
[78] Apud Ada Brăvescu: *Max Blecher-un caz de receptare problematic și spectaculos* (Max Blecher-a problematic and spectacular case of reception). București: Tracus Arte 2011, p. 13.

of the action around the disease obsession in her novels can be observed in Călinescu. What still creates a strident image in these analyses is the dominant character of the physiological degeneration in determining the epic conflict, of mainly external actions. In other words, disease is an activating pretext of the actions of characters, observation which determines the admittance that the famous historian of literature does not surpass the actantial level, considering that Hortensiei Papadat-Bengescu's prose presents a panoply of sick people who create a type of specific action:

> First, we observe in it the horror of promiscuous and degenerate, therefore a whole gallery of physical and moral crippled (paralytics, hysterical, twins, hybrids, illegitimate children). Character analyse is replaced with the sanitary exam. Heroes are well born or degenerate, healthy or sick. Disease is mostly the climate in which the characters live and the predilect place of the action is the sanatorium. Cerebral congestion, neurasthenia, septicaemia, tuberculosis, cancer, stomach ulcer, pernicious anemia, here are just a few of the sicknesses around which intrigues are built.[79]

Nevertheless, as in the case of Lovinescu's analyses, 'psychologism' seems to be the fundamental criteria of imposing this prose within the modern post-war canon. The perspective is reductionist regarding the rapport exterior-interior, simplifying the narrative strategy of the prose-writer who does not include certain sick characters, such as Maxențiu, in Breughel's picture of grotesque characters. Ion Bogdan Lefter's observations, referring to Călinescu's analyses which seemed limited to psychologism are justified. We notice not only the inappetence of the historian for the category of 'diseased', but also a limitation of the vision and a justified critique of its reductionism when facing the originality of the two writers' perspective, Bengescu and Blecher, in which themes such as the environment, sick people, the sanatorium etc. are instruments of extrapolating a reflexivity which surpasses the limit of conventional rationality. The reflexive power of these characters is the one which overpasses the prose of the two, demonstrating the saving retreat within the depth of the conscience aggressed by the reality which remains a simple pretext.

The interpretative split of the author is between the debut years (1936–1939) and the years of his true affirmation or recognition (1966–1978), a fact observed attentively by Ada Brăvescu (2011) in the research in which she details more distinctive stages in the reception and canonisation of Blecher. The eight stages analysed by Ada Brăvescu, I. 1930–1935, II. 1936–1939, III. 1941, IV. 1942–1965, V. 1966–1979, VI. 1980–1989, VII. 1990–2000 and VIII. 2001–2008, are relevant regarding

---

[79] George Călinescu: *Istoria literaturii române: compendiu* (The History of Romanian Literature. Compendium). București: Litera 2001, p. 291.

the argumentation of the experimental and novel character of Blecher's prose. Truly, the reception of the prose-writer in the '70s presupposes a terminological revival and a change of critical paradigm, being understood in the terms of the fantastic (Crohmălniceanu), or in an existentialist key (Pillat, Negoițescu) and a fashionable trend during the period which is along the line of a new realism, in hallucinatory key.

The critical reconsideration of Blecher's prose in the years of the relative ideological relaxation, a metaphor which cannot be here and now ignored, is another proof of his experientialist, self-reflective prose formula. The reclusion when facing 'the terror of history' permits the critics of the '70s to see in his prose an indubitable proof of literature's aesthetical-centrist autarchy towards the realist excess of the '30s. Doubled by the self-biographical blockage, Blecher's prose is understood as a form of rejection of the immediate history, as a declaration of authenticity and absolute liberty, an implicit 'war' with the realist prose of the time. As an answer to active characters, which put pressure on the hierarchy of power in a public space represented by the tableau of social modernisation, Blecher's character discovers reflexivity as an ultimate redoubt to defend when faced with the intrusions of the active power. The conceptual recalibration synthetized by Ada Brăvescu, from "the concepts of *psychological analyses, confession, intimate diary*"[80] to those "of *fantastic realism* (Crohmălniceanu), *lucidity, existential fever* (Pillat), *existential drama, existence defect, the exploration of the unconscious* (Horodincă), *ontological or ontic crises* (Balotă, Protopopescu), *spectacular, theatrical, objectual* (Horodincă, Balotă), *existentialist writer through structure* (Negoițescu)", completed by a terminology specific for the period, such as "*dreamy, oneiric and Surrealism* (Horodincă, Eugenia Tudor Anton)",[81] reconfirms the idea of the focus of Blecher's prose around the reflexive nucleus.

"The memorable singularity"[82] of Blecher's prose, according to Dinu Pillat in the *Preface* of the 1970 volume, *Întâmplări în irealitatea imediată* (Occurence in the Immediate Unreality), is conferred by the almost strange peculiarities of this type of writing and of the vision of the author. Also, Dinu Pillat observes a certain "sensitive and nervous exacerbation" of the prose-writer facing reality and this obsession of the artificial resuscitated can be explained through the acute need to amplify it, a need also determined by the crises of the writer's physical immobility, therefore of the double blockage, ontological and existentialist. On one side the autobiographical, ontological crises determine a refuge in a minimal

---

80 Brăvescu: *Max Blecher*, p. 120.
81 Brăvescu: *Max Blecher*, p. 120.
82 Dinu Pillat: Foreword. In: Max Blecher: *Întâmplări în irealitatea imediată. Inimi cicatrizate* (Occurence in the Immediate Unreality. Scarred Hearts). București: Minerva 1970, p. X.

and redundant reality. On the other side, the Subject acutely lives the feeling of estrangement, of the existentialist rupture from any exterior reality and favouring a minute analyses of his conscience anchored in the past. The image resulted here is an eclectic one, an artistic prolific eclecticism.

On the other side the "Conscience of the reflecting subject has a refraction angle totally novel in his morbid acuity, leading to a vision which seems partially oneiric",[83] hallucinated, in the full spirit of Surrealism. Moreover, the placing of this ultra-confessive novel within the varied ideologies of the period is evidently full of contradictions and ambiguities. This is partially owed to the authenticity of Max Blecher's confession and his capacity to transcend models and doctrinaire types any time. Blecher's prose definitely surpasses the contours of the dilated reality "in fantastic forms" (E. Lovinescu), fully recuperates a certain "ontological tension of the Ego" (N. Balotă) and not one of psychological aspect. "Typologically, *affirms Radu G. Țeposu*, Blecher's prose belongs therefore to the authenticist and experimentalist direction, subjective, confessive literature promoted and theoreticised in our literature by Camil Petrescu."[84] The critic recognises the directions observed in the typology of Blecher's writing already traced by George Călinescu, Octav Șuluțiu, Camil Baltazar, Ovid S. Crohmălniceanu.

Nicolae Manolescu considers, in *Arca lui Noe* (Noe's Arch) a "hypertrophy of reality"[85] regarding Blecher, placing the novel in the category of the 'Corinthic', motivated by the presence of a world of the artificial and kitsch, with the statuettes of the fair, wax puppets and counterfeit objects. This is the obsessional universe, omnipresent in his prose, one imposed by the diseased sensitivity of the writer. His obsessions are minutely surprised by the same Radu G. Țeposu, who reminds us of the "imaginary of subjectivities, phantasms of interiority, depth of the unconscious, the terrifying spectacle of the abyss."[86]

Therefore, beyond the Surrealist predilection for dream and the hallucinatory, overpassing the exhausted and exhausting forms of Kierkegaardian existentialism and of the introspection and analyses prose, Max Blecher's novel *Întâmplări în irealitatea imediată* (Occurence in the Immediate Unreality) marks a formula of authenticity and absolute confession in post-war Romanian literature. The unique character of this work resides in the author's total involvement being unconditioned by fashions, in an experience totally assumed, that of the

---

[83] Pillat: In Max Blecher: *Întâmplări*, p. X.
[84] Radu G. Țeposu: *Suferințele tânărului Blecher* (The Sufferings of Young Blecher). București: Minerva 1996, p. X.
[85] Nicolae Manolescu: *Arca lui Noe* (Noe's Arch) III. București: Minerva 1983, p. 61.
[86] Țeposu: *Suferințele tânărului Blecher*, p. X.

experientialist writing laden with grave lyricism, a fact that contributes to the inclusion of the novel in the frontier zone of the literary genres.

Blecher's prose exposes an image of a Subject which observes its own precarious ontological status by pitting itself against the predictable failure of its 'activism' in mundane relations. The exhausted active powers of the Subject are replaced in this context with the formula of reflexive exasperation, of minute search for a power which assures its survival, which gives the true measure of authenticity. As in the case of the surreal image in the Bretonian dream of the man cut into half by a window, in Blecher's case it is possible to observe a problematic situation of the Subject split between the unwillingness of faraway reality, either historical or biographical, and the immediate reality, inferred, of mnemonic sensorial depth, which comes to the surface with unthought power, of some reflexive images so powerful, that waking up to reality is impossible. The magnetism of this reflexive power is so great, that even the dream within a dream of the Subject has an unimaginable force which changes the trajectory of the reader's glance towards the sensory abyss generated by this reflexive vortex. Finally, woken up from the dream within a dream, the Subject notices the gradual separation from the 'sense of reality', but also the 'authentic feeling' of this force:

> What I now see around me differs very little from what I saw only a second before, but somehow it has an air of authenticity, which floats in things, in me, like a sudden cooling of the winter air, which all of a sudden magnifies all sonorities... In what does my sense of reality consist?[87]

The 'sense of reality' is the sense of his reflexivity, as an internal reaction to external overpowering cause.

3.3.2 The Occurrence of the Subject in the Immediate Reflexivity

Taken over by reality, in whole "ontological crises",[88] the Subject of the novel *Întâmplări în irealitatea imediată* (Occurrence in the Immediate Unreality) lives a true existentialist reinvestment, at the moment he discovers his own photography in the artificial, depressing world of the fair. The striking image, similar to the strange image-like representations of the Surrealist, functions as a real activator, a sensorial stimulant. 'The sense of reality' of the fair is blurred, the place of the

---

[87] Blecher: *Occurence in the Immediate Unreality*, p. 111.
[88] Alexandru Protopopescu: *Volumul și esența* (The Volume and Essence). București: Eminescu 1971, p. 58.

artificial object being taken over gradually by the powerful sensory which gives it a Proustian sensation of 'immortality', similar to that of the madelaine cake. It is certainly an overriding of the ontological blockage, a real objectual metaphor:

> I used to like to linger for hours in front of the photographers' booths, contemplating the unknown persons, in groups or alone, petrified and smiling, in front of grey landscapes with cataracts and distant mountains. All these personages, due to their common backdrop, seemed members of the same family on an excursion to the same picturesque place, where they had been photographed one after another. On one occasion, in such a display case, I came across my own photograph. That sudden encounter with myself, immobilized in a fixed attitude, there at the edge of the fair, had a depressing effect upon me. Before arriving in my town, it had, of course, also travelled through other places unknown to me. In an instant I had the sensation of not existing except in a photograph. This inversion of mental positions often happened to me in the most diverse circumstances. It would sneak up on me and all of a sudden transform my body from within. In an accident on the street, for example, I gazed for a number of minutes at what was happening as though at a hackneyed performance. All of a sudden, however, the entire perspective changed and – as in that game which consists in descrying a bizarre animal in the paint on the walls, which one day we can no longer find, because we see in its place, made up of the same decorative elements, a statue, a woman or a landscape – in that street accident, although everything remained intact, it was suddenly as if I was the one who was lying stretched on the ground and saw everything from my position as the person knocked down, from below, from the center to the periphery, and with the vivid sensation of the blood trickling out of me. Likewise, without any effort, as a logical consequence of the mere fact that I was looking, I used to imagine myself in the cinema, experiencing the intimacy of the scenes on the screen[...] The whole of my life, the life of the one standing in the flesh and blood outside the glass display case, all of a sudden appeared to me indifferent and insignificant, just as to the living person behind the glass the voyage of his photographic 'I' through unknown towns also appears absurd.[89]

The photographic self discovered by Max Blecher respects, reconfiguring the vast Surrealist pathways, the projection of the being within the affective objectuality. At the same time, the fair becomes a *bad place* for the character, a repository and vast labyrinth of its supra-mobile representations. The memory of the fair signifies another certitude of existence, a concrete fact through the abundance of artificial and kitsch, a necessary presence for prolonging freedom. The discovery of his own photography in this environment determines him to operate with a phenomenological reduction, a crucial moment of being frustrated by the lack of movement, an absconded immediate reality in favour of the objectual Unreality, which figures as a constant equation of the *Întâmplări în irealitatea imediată* (Occurence in the Immediate Unreality), maintaining a permanent division

---

[89] Blecher: *Occurence in the Immediate Unreality*, p. 60–61.

and dilution of corporeality and its representation, in favour of a profound ultra-sensitive conscience.

Le pacte autobiographique[90] proposed by Max Blecher in this novel, starting from the ample cited fragment, is that of doubling the image, foregoing inclusively the fictional pact or the autobiographical one,[91] in order to provoke the empathic reading act which would become an authentic involvement act of the reader and of getting over the tragic nature of the diseased, over autobiographical immobility. This is also the explanation Radu G. Țeposu offers when he talks about the evident transition of Blecher's autobiographical element from "the simple referential note to reflexive narration."[92] The non-referential character is sustained by the narrator through a subtle and tensioned sensorial relation proposed to the reader, o "delectatio morosa", or what Eco calls "lingering in the woods"[93] on a certain subjective, reflexive, sensorial time which becomes the substance of the narrative.

The reader projected by the author of the *Întâmplări* (Occurrence) anticipates a project of Reader Response Criticism, the fact that "Interpreters do not decode poems. They make them.",[94] meaning that the images of the narrator Subject, reconstructed from memory, have meaning just through their unconditional assumption by the reader who contributes as a resonance box to the sensorial construct. It is a participative formula, 'making sense' in Fish's formula,[95] which assures the transgression of the tragic biographism, within whose limits we might be tempted to articulate the meaning of the novel. Imagining himself "at the cinema, living in the intimacy of the screen scenes" or "in front of the photographer's barrack replacing the one who watched me still from the carton", the author lives and relives the relation reality-representation as a living one, as an active, progressive doubling, as he does not perceive himself, the photographical self, as a representation of his physical form, but as another strange entity coming from a different time, invading and seemingly aggressing his identity. The strange self-detachment, exposed in the fragment read by invoking a situation recovered through affective memory, has depth and an unsuspected fertility for the being seemingly entirely transformed, but as another strange entity, coming from a different time, invading and almost aggressing his intimacy. The strange Self detachment, exposed in the cited fragment through the invocation of a situation recovered from the affective

---

90 Philippe Lejeune: *Le pacte autobiographique*. Paris: Seuil 1996.
91 See Mironescu: *Viața lui Max Blecher*.
92 Țeposu: *Suferințele tânărului Blecher*, p. 42.
93 Umberto Eco: *Six Walks in the Fictional Woods*. Cambridge and London: Harvard University Press 1994, p. 49.
94 Stanley Fish: *Is There A Text in This Class?* Cambridge: Harvard University Press 1980, p. 327.
95 Fish: *Is There A Text in This Class?*, p. 327.

memory, has depth and an unsuspected fertility for the being transformed integrally in nervous and sensorial terminations in an ample process of hypertrophy of the senses. "The reality crises",[96] similar to that of Bruno Schulz, produces a detachment, a rupture and a refuge within reflexivity, with prolific effects on the imaginary level of the Subject who perceives matter and implicitly the physiological self from the outside, with detachment and dialectic objectivity.

The prose texts of Max Blecher, *Întâmplări în irealitatea imediată* (Occurrence in the Immediate Unreality), (1936), *Inimi cicatrizate* (Scarred Hearts) (1938) and *Vizuina luminată* (The Enlightened Den), the sanatorium journal written between 1937 and 1938, in the last months before death, herald a new epic direction in post-war Romanian literature, that of the confessive novel which voluntarily makes the relation between the biographical self and empirical one ambiguous. The narrator's favorite method is that of dominant introspection and of complex anamnesis, necessary in order to outperform and compensate a living deficiency in the present, due to the biographical blockage of an ontological nature.

In a 1937 letter addressed to his friend, Geo Bogza, Blecher claims even more intensely the drama of the modern Creator face to face with the immobility of the matter. The delirium of the writing, similar to the surrealist hallucinatory states, determines within the author a sort of automatic 'dicte' such as that of Dada, in which the being is instrumentalised and the unconscious is invested with absolute power. The oneiric Surrealism is one of the fashionable formulas of the period which, associated with existentialism, provokes a hallucinatory 'living' which is the essence of the writing:

> For me, *affirms Blecher*, literature, poetry and even the whole reality, have lost all attraction without trace for a long time, and if I continue to live, do something, write, is because I have nothing better to do, in this condition of my life (…) All I do, all I «am living» is within a state of dizziness and hallucination as if I had taken opium. In the end life is the same, as noctambulist as if I had taken opium or not.[97]

The Subject discovers, as Hermann Broch's *Noctambulists*, "the world behind the mirror" although Max Blecher's formation cannot be dissociated from the poetics of the Avant-garde, Surrealism especially and its atmosphere through his friendship with Geo Bogza. This friendship with the theoretician of "dream rehabilitation", the text of which was published in the avant-garde magazine *unu* (one), with one of the generators of the Romanian avant-garde movement, had a major effect in the evolution of young Blecher, adept at parting from Reality

---

[96] Nicolae Balotă: *De la Ion la Ioanide* (From Ion to Ioanide). București: Eminescu 1974, p. 161.
[97] Apud Mădălina Lascu: *Max Blecher, mai puțin cunoscut* (Max Blecher, lesss known). Preface by Ion Pop. București: Hasefer 2000, p. 140.

and of literary reduction to the authentic and exasperating sensitivity. His friendship with Geo Bogza, demonstrated by their prolific correspondence,[98] has the role of catalyzing the becoming of the experiment novel *Întâmplări în irealitatea imediată* (Occurrence in the Immediate Unreality). Furthermore, one of Blecher's letters towards Bogza describes the creation process of the novel and the tensioned situation of the author towards writing, ample process of restructuring his senses tragically ground by disease. Blecher would confess to his friend:

> Roman, 24.V.1935
> My dear Geo Bogza,
> Here is what has been going on with me ever since I haven't written to you. It is warm, awfully warm, in the morning I spend some time on the terrace and then sitting, on the wood platform where it's cooler. The heat is not good at all for my upset stomach; I am also harassed even during the day, but not as much as before. Moreover, I am allowed to eat everything, to feed myself as good and as substantial so I get better and come to my senses. Here is what happens with the *Exercises* (Occurrence). Generally, I can say I have finished the first version. I still have a few pages to add-twenty-but these are already written and I will complete and transcribe them later, for the moment not feeling the 'vibration' necessary for them, but it is a matter of a day or two and when I will feel 'possessed' I will describe them in a single writing style. I've written the last chapters without being in a mood and for now this is visible; but I hope in a revision, as in exchange I started the version for the typing machine (the sequel to what you have read) and here I have pretty great intimate satisfaction, I don't know what will come of it, but I am working with a sort of joy which builds things as it should. In certain moments the manuscript itself seems to organize and define itself, I only retouch here and there and some completions and unsuspected corrections come to my mind when I first wrote the rough variant. Finally, you will see and judge.[99]

Furthermore, the process of creation and sublimation of the physical pain in writing is described with absolute accuracy by Geo Bogza as well, in a sentimental and commemorative confession, at his friend's premature death:

> I know we have loved each other equally and we have influenced our lives in an equal measure, Geo Bogza would affirm. I have brought many things to M. Blecher and he has brought many things into my life. After I met him in 1934, we remained three months together in Brașov. We talked to each other, every day, for hours, almost without saturation. It was the most beautiful period in our lives. M. Blecher had behind him five years of disease and sanatoriums. After so much suffering he could be tired, exhausted. But, look, in our evenings of discussion, a steel strength was awakened in him, the wish to write a real book. Since that epoch he had had the idea of the *Occurence in the Immediate Unreality*. After five years of atrocious disease, M. Blecher's book could have honestly been a painful litany, a lament on the world. How could such heroism be within this man? Not even a bray, not an allusion to the curse that hit him. Calm and lucid, M. Blecher analysed life rationally,

---

98 Lascu: *Max Blecher, mai puțin cunoscut.*
99 See Lascu: *Max Blecher, mai puțin cunoscut*, p. 64.

in clear and precise sentences, as mathematical formulas. Everything in him and around him would have entitled him to be pathetic, nebulous, incoherent. How did he defeat these dangers, how was he protected from them? I think here lies the superior essence M. Blecher's being was made of.[100]

Max Blecher succeeds in the novel *Întâmplări în irealitatea imediată* (Occurrence in the Immediate Unreality) to surpass the climate and the experimental Avant-garde tendencies. His novel is not a simple experiment or a protest against the stale traditional forms, not having anything out of the activist-declarative formulas of the historical avant-garde. This novel, or better said this bio-novel, to keep something of the revolutionary climate of the avant-garde generation and to distinguish Blecher's prose from the methods of the traditional epic, synthetises in "long and precise phrases", with tragic lucidity, the introspective experience of a being blocked in the immediate Real. This blockage is no doubt determined, as the critics observe without hesitation and by the *sufferings of young Blecher*, by the ontic crises prematurely determined by disease. It is possible to observe what has been called the intentional confusion or the interdetermination between the biographical self and the artistic one. The disease is filtered within the work through the retrospective Subject, predisposed to an eternal limit confession, a tragic existence transformed in sensorial abundancy, a compensatory prose.

Citing André Gide with his *Journal*, Radu G. Țeposu, in the 'Preface' to the *Întâmplări în irealitatea imediată* (Occurrence in the Immediate Unreality), evokes, as in Blecher's case, the 'valences' of suffering. Gide's affirmation, which states that "We value only what separates us from the others, idiosyncrasy is our valuable disease", seems to have a major role in Blecher's case. Therefore, considering the disease differentiates us on an ethical and gnoseologic stage we can understand the value attributed to suffering by our author, as "the self-scopic vision"[101] is the one that permits the access to the resorts of the reflexive power, the understanding key of the entire prose of M. Blecher. The anthology of great sick men, put up also by Gide in the same *Diary* (prophets, Saint Paul, Saint Joan, Jean-Jacques Rousseau, Nietzsche, Dostoievski, Flaubert) is evoked by Radu G. Țeposu who cited the list of the great sick writers in the Romanian space, realised by Camil Baltazar and George Călinescu. In Romanian literature the following writers are mentioned: Gib I. Mihăescu, B. Fundoianu, Ș. Petică, B. Nemțeanu, M. Blecher, N. Milcu, I. Cioránescu, D. Iacobescu, A. Sahia.[102] In such a context of the great diseased, Blecher succeeds to surpass this ontological limit, making

---

100 See Lascu: *Max Blecher, mai puțin cunoscut*, p. 322–323.
101 Țeposu: *Suferințele tânărului Blecher*, p. 72.
102 Țeposu: *Suferințele tânărului Blecher*, p. 13.

3.3 From the *Literaturisation* of the Autobiographical Trauma to the Reflexive Power — 143

reflexivity an inexhaustible resource of his power. This is the supreme magnetism discovered by Blecher, who therefore surpasses that of the disease.

The narrator character of the *Occurrences*, diagnosed with paludism (malaria), will experiment through the trauma of permanent fever, manifested through delirium, a world resembling that of the Surrealist opium addicts in which the forms of reality are either obscured or hypertrophied. 'The cursed places' such as the panopticon the fair, theatre and mud all have a major importance in the existence of the young man who recovers from memory the spectacular moments which have definitely marked his diseased sensitivity since childhood. No matter how artificial to the point of being grotesque that reality is, it is animated by an ultra-sensitive self, oscillating between liminal moods. He confesses that:

> Besides the wax museum, the August fair brought me many other occasions for sadness and exaltation. Its sweeping theatrical performance would swell like a symphony. It commenced with the prelude of isolated dioramas, which arrived much earlier than all the rest and set the general tone for the fair, like the scattered and drawn-out notes that announce at the beginning of the concerto the theme of the composition as a whole. The grandiose finale, on closing day, was an explosion of shouts, firecrackers and brass bands, followed by the immense silence of the deserted field. The few dioramas that came early comprised, in essence, the fair as a whole and represented it with exactitude. It was sufficient for only the first of them to set up in order for the entire colouring, the entire sparkle and the entire carbide odor of the fair as a whole to seep down into the town.[103]

The effect produced by these artificial spaces is a 'hallucinatory' one, as he is impressed by "everything that is imitated", by the reproduction of reality in forms more or less faithful. The sensation described in these cursed spaces, "a bizarre sensation of poignancy and detachment" explains the need for the represented artificial, the dependency of spaces which stimulate the senses. Such as the photography in the shop window, imitations, copies (wax figures, trinkets etc.), they explain the sensation of strangeness when facing the authentic. Doubling represents, for the being aggressed by the Real, an escape solution, an ample digression through a secondary reality, in which bollards are sensible and exhausting. "For me, *confesses the author*, the fair thus became a desert island, girdled by desolate auras, altogether similar to the indistinct and nevertheless limpid world into which my childhood crises bore me."[104] These are, therefore, 'cursed spaces', 'bad places', prolongations of the dream or the delirium provoked by the disease, isolations within a reality searched for with accuracy, in the immediate unreality. Convinced of the fact that "In the end, there is no

---

[103] Blecher: *Occurence in the Immediate Unreality*, p. 58.
[104] Blecher: *Occurence in the Immediate Unreality*, p. 62.

well-defined difference between our real self and our various imaginary inner characters",[105] therefore in a process of multiplication of the self, the hyper-sensitive being will be continuously searching for the "interior imaginary characters", a process which allows the exploration of the depth of the self through memories and hypertrophied senses. Reflexivity is irradiant, emits an unsuspected imaginative power which determines a permanent rebirth and infinite emotional multiplication.

The fear induced by the panopticon, therefore by this vulgar reproduction of the physiological, is completed by a strange pleasure of identifying the double, therefore of the sensorial dilatation. The sensation described is that of a repeated experience. The profoundness and strangeness of the emotions determined by the wax figures provokes the feeling of identifying with them in order to recuperate the lost corporeality. The coldness and artificiality of the figures predispose him towards a grave meditation on existence:

> I think that if the urge for an aim in life were ever to arise in me and if this impulse had to be bound to something that is indeed profound, essential and irremediable in me, then my body would have to become a mannequin in a wax museum and my life a simple and endless contemplation of the display cases of the dioramas.[106]

In other words, if the meaning of the existence would be a precise, determined, objective one, therefore ontologically assumed, the Subject would become artificial, eviscerated from the entire and unsuspected force of the unconscious. The existence described by the narrator character is one forever contradictory, always under the menace of entropy caused by the meeting between an excessive fragility and the real seizure through its active power.

> A single and supreme desire remains alive for me: to witness the incineration of a wax museum; to see the slow and scabrous melting of the waxwork figures, to gaze petrified as the yellow and beautiful legs of the bride in the glass case writhe in the air and a real flame takes hold between the thighs, burning her sex.[107]

The dreamed fire of the panopticon and the melting of the wax figures also signifies an exacerbation of the senses, of the visual, and olfactory, as supreme gesture of extrapolating his reflexive 'Berghof'. Burning means here also purification and not least, by burning the sex of the bride in the glass box, an exacerbation of the destructive sexual desire, a supreme victory of the reflexive power over the active one.

---

[105] Blecher: *Occurence in the Immediate Unreality*, p. 53.
[106] Blecher: *Occurence in the Immediate Unreality*, p. 54–55.
[107] Blecher: *Occurence in the Immediate Unreality*, p. 57.

3.3 From the *Literaturisation* of the Autobiographical Trauma to the Reflexive Power

The experiences invoked by the narrator have, as has been shown, a profound exploration of corporeality. The vision over his own body oscillates between the outside view, the Chagallian autoscopy Țeposu talked about[108] and the one within. This within view culminates with the imagination of a miraculous journey within his own corporeality, as revealed in a suggestive fragment in *Vizuina luminată* (The Lit-up Burrow). "The moment I am writing, on small obscure canals, in lively wriggly rivets, through the dark cavities carved in flesh, a small gurgle rhymed by the pulse overflows the night of the body, circulating between the flesh, nerves and bones, my blood."[109] The fabulous journey in the organic micro-universe of the being signifies a real exploration of life, a projection of the self in the universe of corporeality. And here it is possible to observe a projection of autobiographical type, as the lost motricity of the body is recovered through a hyperactive imaginary, motivated to find ample resorts of the necessary dynamics, self-reflexively this time.

Another reinvention of corporeality can be found in Blecher's prose, the body being a source of rich explorations of the surrealist type. A dissonance, a re-anthropologisation of the body is observed. The traditional relation between the body and spirit, an extrapolation of the faith in equilibrium, is reversed here, and the body becomes a discovery object, but also generator of existential confusions without precedent. David Le Breton confirms that: "L'homme du commun projette sur son corps un savoir composite qui ressemble à un manteau d'Arlequin, un savoir fait de zones d'ombre, d'imprécisions, de confusions, des connaissances plus ou moins abstraites auquel il prête un certain relief."[110] The body becomes, in Blecher's case, a real laboratory in which the real experiences of the being are experimented on, sometimes the being having entered this heteroclite game of the recomposition of such an emotive puzzle. The relation of man with the world is fundamentally modified according to the body and the capacity of the body to adhere to the world and communicate. Although it is convincing that though Blecher's prose "ce qu'on lui retranche ou ce qu'on lui ajoute modifie son rapport au monde de façon plus ou moins prévisible."[111] The imprecitable change of the relations between Subject and Reality is reinforced by the impredictible power of literature, which gives infinite reflexive energy to the Subject.

The harlequin cloak that dresses the body of Blecher's subject is a projection of some obsessions which are adjusted with the dominant power in the depth of the

---

[108] Țeposu: *Suferințele tânărului Blecher*, p. 72.
[109] Max Blecher: *Vizuina luminată. Jurnal de sanatoriu* (The Lit-Up Den: Sanatorium Journal). Postface by Nicolae Manolescu. Edition by Florin Ioniță. București: Art 2009, p. 68.
[110] David Le Breton: *Antrhopologie du corps et modernité*. Paris: Presses universitaires de France 1990, p. 88.
[111] Le Breton: *Antrhopologie du corps et modernité*, p. 262.

unconscious. Therefore, we can understand the place of these happenings and their role in the configuration of a veritable universe, through the authentic nature of the emotions he is invested with. The instruments that articulate this reflexive universe are "the imaginary of subjectivity, the phantasms of interiority, the hallucinate unreality of the psychic depth, the profoundness of the unconscious, the terrifying spectacle of the abyssal."[112] A world similar to the Surrealist one, but more powerful just through the hallucinate force of the diseased emotional burden. Blecher's imagism, in which the reader is also involved, is not a simple architecture of torn representations, but they compose the figure of an extremely powerful Subject through the unsuspected and incontrollable force of his reflexivity. It is a *cinetic reflexivity*, assumed sensorially and imagistically, with that of the Surrealist cinema.

3.4 The Cinetic Anamorphosis of the Reflexive Power

"I try to define my crises precisely and all I can find are images."[113]

A refuge in a complex world, Blecher's subject finds its power exclusively in "the intimate resorts of the unconscious."[114] Even more, Țeposu invokes in his essay, *Suferințele tânărului Blecher* (The Sufferings of Young Blecher), a very important note of the author ever since school years, referring to the predomination of the reflexive power when dealing with antic crises:

> The power of the subconscious is great. An unconscious well organised [...] can bring us ideas to which our conscious would never have reached. Therefore, I quote two characteristic manifestations of this power: revelation and inspiration.[115]

Following this path of the subconscious, together with part of the critical studies on Blecher,[116] it becomes apparent that this type of novel proposes a different type of referentiality, one whose contours melt under the dominant power of the subconscious. He is among the first post-war prose writers who practice such a narrative strategy of the non-referential, excluding here the "forerunner Urmuz", as Geo Bogza named him,[117] the one who, unlike Blecher, dynamites intentionally

---

112 Țeposu: *Suferințele tânărului Blecher*, p. 23.
113 Blecher: *Occurence in the Immediate Unreality*, p. 31.
114 Țeposu: *Suferințele tânărului Blecher*, p. 25.
115 Apud Țeposu: *Suferințele tânărului Blecher*, p. 25.
116 See Manolescu: *Arca lui Noe*, p. 59 and Țeposu: *Suferințele tânărului Blecher*, p. 25.
117 Apud Marin Mincu (ed.): *Avangarda literară românească* (The Romanian Literary Avant-Garde). Introduction, antologie and bibliographical notes by Marin Mincu. Translation from French by Ștefania Mincu. Constanța: Pontica 2006, p. 535.

and completely referentiality as a form of poetic protest to the pragmatic formulas of realism and naturalism of the beginning of the century. The reflexive power discovered by Blecher's Subject within the abyssal folds of the subconscious help him to surpass the ontological blockage that was previously discussed, assuring the reader a determining, participative role. Revelation and inspiration are the kinetic imaginative forces which help build the 'bad places' together with the Subject and his experiences rememorized and reinstituted affectively.

In a letter addressed to his friend Sașa Pană, dated in the period of the construction of the novel *Întâmplări în irealitatea imediată* (Occurence in the Immediate Unreality), Max Blecher sets forth a real Surrealist kind of poetics which forms the basis of its construction. The absolute model is nobody else but Salvador Dali and his ontological ruptures and breakthroughs in the order of the Real:

> The unreality and illogism of quotidian life are no longer for me vague problems of intellectual speculation: I am living this unreality and its fantastic events. The first freedom I have given myself was that of the irresponsibility of my interior acts one towards the other-I have tried to break the barrier of consequences and, as honesty towards myself, I tried to make of equally lucid and voluntary value any temptation of the hallucinatory. But as to how much and how sur-reality develops its tentacles within myself, I don't know, I couldn't know… The ideal of writing would be to me the transposition in literature of the high tension which is released from Salvador Dali's painting. Here is what I would like to realize-that cold dementia, perfectly readable and essential.[118]

Blecher searches for an instrument with which to operate the experiencing of the world, meaning a certain "lucidity more profound and more essential than that of the brain", similar to Surrealists who observed the limits of the rational. Apparently, Blecher's technique is one of empiricist origin, based on sensible experimentation, with aprioric results, as it happens with the surrealist technique, which is opposed to the rational manner of knowledge. The experimental method, of the observation and a posteriori conclusion, is the one which comes first in the empiricist approach which rejects the unique method of rational, deductive knowledge. Nevertheless, Surrealist hazard, placed in the centre of his anti-rationalism, is more situated in the phenomenological type of system of Merleau-Ponty's analyses, who conceives the man as a result of a discontinued conscience reactivated through rememoration. The discontinued conscience is the true sensible nature of man who reconstructs and lives in the present according to the flux of the anterior conscience.

Discontinued images render this irrational, incoherent flux of human nature. The sensible human nature can expose the authenticity of its nature

---

[118] Apud Pillat: Foreword. In: Max Blecher: *Întâmplări în irealitatea imediată*, p. X.

inclusively through broken, discontinue images. Rationalism, especially Surrealists believe, has warped the image of man, creating false expectations about its essence, inducing the illusion of the discursive coherence, of formal logics, of structural equilibrium. The consequence of this position on art was that art represented a coherent, clear, imaginative world, therefore an illusion. Art was preponderantly descriptive and this made man further gradually from his sensible, reflexive nature. The sensibility mutation Virginia Woolf observed at the beginning of the 20th century, attests just the transfiguration of art in accordance to the artists' exacerbated sensibility. A referentiality reversed towards the subconscious presupposed not only a sensorial reinvestment of art, but also a new kind of poetics.

The historical Avant-garde of the beginning of 20th century proposes such a radical mutation. For example, Surrealism produces a visual shock, with impact on the human conscience altered by the linearity of the rationalist perspectives or even the empiricist ones. The shock provoked by Surrealism is firstly of a visual nature, whether talking about poetry, novel or even the cinematographic experiments of the '30s. The discontinuous visual, reflecting the true nature of man, replaces the coherent and predominantly descriptive linearity of conventional art. The anti-canonical formulas of surrealism are generated by his revolt against a redundant way of knowledge of exclusively rationalist type, set out in conventional discourses after the clear formulas of the referential discourse. Against any conventions, Surrealist poetics is shocking because it appears as anti-natural because it seeks shock at any price, in order to establish some hyper-real relations. The sensible mutation is of a phenomenological nature, reflecting another image of human nature, which reinvents itself according to the form searching for content. Similar to a family photo album, the human conscience recovers out of memory the broken images of the past which, reinvested sensorially, compose the present discontinuous, ondulatory nature, of the being. This technique was not exclusively the property of the Surrealists, the Proustian method or that of Joyce or Virginia Woolf, practically constituted out of the same recomposition of the present through bits of the subconscious. It is a perspective of self-reflexive recomposition of man and one of the predilect techniques of epic modernity.

The visual energy of Max Blecher's prose,[119] as that of the Surrealists, describes therefore a reflexive power of the man who turns towards himself to describe the

---

[119] See also Florin Oprescu: *Les espaces maudits chez Max Blecher et dans le film surréaliste des années 30*. In: Sabine Krause; Heide Flagner (eds.): *Räume und Medien in der Romania-Espaces et médias dans les cultures romanes-Spații și medii în culturile romanice*. Hildesheim, Zurich, New York: Georg Olms Verlag 2018, p. 183–196.

truthful sensible image, hidden in the mnemonic discontinuity of conscience. To have power over the self, therefore over his own conscience, means a turning back of the artistic eye from the interiority observed exclusively through artistic speculation. It is not self-control, but a self-reflexive refuge in the process of identification and defining one's own existential status. In this process the sensorial occupies a central place, determining the verosimility of the limit situations, recovered through memory and which confer intensity to the existence. In Max Blecher's prose 'the bad places' or 'cursed spaces' are existential benchmarks coming directly out of the author's sensorial memory, being selected according to their intensity. This sensorial memory ensures for the author a certain distancing from the world, the real, as in the case of Surrealists, a detached perspective with a radical confusion of the focalisation degrees. It is neither the zero focalisation of the Realist omniscient narrators, although sometimes bad places are minutely and objectively observed and described, nor the external one, as the narrator knows more than the character, although sometimes gives the sensation that he cannot give any precise explanation referring to the impact of reality on its senses.

The prevalence of internal focalisation is also an illusion most of the time as just for the identity narrator-character the search of the enantiomorphosis, of the match for identity, the filler of reflection and reflexivity is anamorphotic, meaning that the image is deformed as in a concave or convex mirror. This is the explanation given to the binary Subject between the abstraction of the character and the person. The intense gaze of the fixed point at the beginning of the novel and the dualism resembles one Bretonian image: "l'homme coupé en deux par la fenêtre".[120] It is about "a bizarre phrase" which animates the Bretonian Surrealist sensitivity in the 1924 *Manifesto of Surrealism*. The explanation the theoretician of Surrealism gives to this phrase reconfirms the fact that the mutation proposed by the poetics of the avant-garde has to the fore a repositioning towards reality, the creation of a visual shock, of a visual dislocation. Therefore, the interest of the Surrealists for the cinematographic image. This image:

> [...] était de la faible représentation visuelle d'un homme marchant et tronçonné à mi-hauteur par une fenêtre perpendiculaire à l'axe de son corps. A n'en pas douter il s'agissait du simple redressement dans l'espace d'un homme qui se tient penché à la fenêtre. Mais cette fenêtre ayant suivi le déplacement de l'homme, je me rendis compte que j'avais affaire à une image d'un type assez rare et je n'eus vite d'autre idée que de l'incorporer à mon matériel de construction poétique.[121]

---

[120] André Breton: *Manifestes du Surréalisme*. Paris: Jean-Jacques Pauvert 1962, p. 35.
[121] Breton: *Manifestes du Surréalisme*, p. 35.

Breton's conclusion referring to this bizarre image has not necessarily a connection to the empiricist explanation of it, consisting in observing the laws of optics which deform or recompose the image, but also to the way reason works, or more with the irrational flux which dictates the operation of thinking, as his conclusion is "la vitesse de la pensée n'est pas supérieure à celle de la parole, et qu'elle ne défie pas forcément la langue, ni même la plume qui court."[122] The automatic message will then constitute, besides objective hazard, one of the nodal points in Surrealist poetry, of suspension of the linear flux of thinking, in favour of discontinuity and authenticity of the irrational. It is also the kind of observation Blecher starts the discovery of this 'immediate unreality':

> When I gaze for a long time at a fixed point on the wall, what sometimes happens is that I will no longer know who I am or where I am. I sense my lack of identity from afar, as though I had, for an instant, become a complete stranger. With matching strength, this abstract personage and my real person vie to convince me. In the following instant my identity is regained, like in those stereoscopic views when the two images sometimes separate by accident and only when the projectionist readjusts them, superimposing them, do they all at once provide the illusion of depth. Then it appears to me that my room is of a freshness it did not previously possess. It regains its prior consistency and the objects in it fall back into place, in the same way as in a glass of water a lump of crumbled soil will settle in strata of different, well defined and variously coloured elements. The elements of my room stratify into their own outlines and into the colouring of the old memory I have of them. The sensation of distance and loneliness in the moments when my everyday self has dissolved into inconsistency differs from any other sensation. When it lasts longer, it becomes a fear, a terror of not being able to regain myself ever again. Afar, an uncertain outline lingers in me, encompassed by a great luminosity, in the same way as objects sometimes loom from the mist. The terrible question "Who exactly am I?" then dwells in me like an entirely new body, having grown in me with skin and organs that are wholly unfamiliar to me. The answer to it is demanded by a deeper and more essential lucidity than that of the brain. All that is capable of stirring in my body writhes, struggles and rebels more vigorously and more elementarily than in everyday life. Everything begs for a solution.[123]

This uncertainty generates a certain "alienation from the world" which generates a being suspended between worlds "a clear and suave melancholia, like a dream, which we will remember in the power of the night". The dissipation of identity is a nucleus generating sensations similar to those associated to "my falling in the cursed spaces in the past". The narrator, similar to Breton's description, or to the broken images in Dali's or De Chirico's paintings, establishes that this oscillation between the farther away reality and the immediate and marking unreality of the 'cursed places' is similar to some hallucinating trances. The fever or the state of

---

[122] Breton: *Manifestes du Surréalisme*, p. 37.
[123] Blecher: *Occurence in the Immediate Unreality*, p. 26.

mood for writing, therefore of literature, is characterised by the dizziness or the noctambulist hallucination Blecher described to Bogza. Blecher is not far from the Surrealist strategies of the negation of matter. Therefore, the Surrealist projection of the self is within a contemplation object, in the ambiance of a reality dislocated from the descriptive logic so far. It is an evident split of the real passed through the filter and fractured sensibility, as happened for example to Giorgio de Chirico in *Il grande metafisico*, from 1917, where the straight lines and the urban architectural equilibrium is reduced to the metaphysical void of man and/or his heteroclite image. He is the man cut or fractured in half by reality, by the physical and mechanical rationality of the immediate.

The preponderance of the hallucinating, stereoscopic image, which seems to come out of a lucidity "more essential than that of the brain", is recurrent in the art of the beginning of the 20th century, due partly to the changes of aesthetical nature, on the other side due to those of social nature.

The arts which react rapidly to the reversal of modern sensibility are literature, the novel and especially the film, a new art which proposes the replacement of the linguistic code or its completion with a visual one, an image code. Gradually, last century becomes the "century of the cinematography", the attendance of cinemas being fashionable in this period as a mondenity act of the modern society. "The film fascination"[124] is evident in post-war Romanian society, interested in all that meant the spirit of 'Occidentalisation'. The fact is also confirmed by Ioana Pârvulescu, who noticed that in 1933, there were not less than fifty cinemas in Bucharest, which in 'good days' could offer even "seven representations".[125]

In this contexts of the explosion of cinema, of the evident and growing interest for the new art of the beginning of century, it is evident that:

> Although it had entered the back door of art, as journalists consider, cinematography has won. The same phenomenon happened last century with the novel, which took the place of lyrical, epical poetry and dramaturgy and established itself without remorse on the first place in literary hierarchy.[126]

In the complex cinematographical analyses in *Cinema 1* (1983) and *Cinema 2* (1985), Gilles Deleuze distinguished two categories of images characteristic for the 20th century:

---

124 Tudor Vlad: *Fascinația filmului la scriitorii români (1900–1940)* (The Fascination of Film at Romanian Writers). Cluj-Napoca: Fundația Culturală Română 1997.
125 Pârvulescu: *Întoarcere în Bucureștiul interbelic*, p. 135.
126 Pârvulescu: *Întoarcere în Bucureștiul interbelic*, p. 135.

a. *the movement image* is an image of the action-reaction type, meaning that the action determines a reaction. In this case the action decides and determines the time and the examples can be found either in action films, or in westerns, where characters act according to an action on temporality implicitely determined. We can understand that it is a cinematographic construction, a 'quadrage' on an empirical model;
b. *the time image* is an image in which the length of the plane is not decided by the action, time being therefore independent. In Deleuze's opinion this is an image "qui renvoie plus à une situation globalisante ou synthétique, mais dispersive".[127]

Deleuze's considerations start from Bergson's analyses and from the appreciation of a dead end in humanities, the same anticipated by Virginia Woolf or of the same nature with what has been defined here as a transition towards reflexivity. It is about the impossibility of psychology to maintain active and valid a position. Concerning the time-image: "ce qui a cassé, c'est la ligne ou la fibre d'univers qui prolongeait les événements les uns dans les autres, ou assurait le raccordement des portions d'espaces."[128] Out of this disequilibrium between the discontinuous flux of conscience and the coherent image, continuous and logical of the movement, the conflict between the realist novel and the modernist one in the post-war period [the conflict] arises. Starting from this distinct and autonomous character of the time image, we can consider that such an image cannot be centered only on the natural processuality of the conscience, offering us the image of the Subject searching for reflexive power in order to dominate or control the excesses or the impure pressures or the real in a crisis of inauthenticity.

The time image is for Deleuze a pure image, because this image is not from the present, as Merleau-Ponty affirms, it is a recovery of a past fragmented in the present. It is the result of an anamorphosis, a different perception of the self recovered from the past, especially through the senses. The equation Action-Reaction continues to exist in the representation of image-time, but the Reaction is not logical anymore, seldom in contrast to Action, determined by intimate, sensorial resorts which assure the Subject a force position over the impure 'quotidien' through excessive and formative organisation. The French philosopher situates this modality of conceiving the image-time equation in the period following the Second World War, when the schemas Action-Reaction were not credible anymore. His favourite cinematographic references inwhich there is an effective

---
[127] Gilles Deleuze: *Cinéma 2. L'image-temps*. Paris: Les Editions de Minuit 1985, p. 279.
[128] Deleuze: *Cinéma 2*, p. 279.

refuse of the Reaction are *La Dolce Vita* (1960) by Federico Fellini, *Last Year in Marienbad* (1961) by Alain Resnais or *Death in Venice* (1971) by Luchino Visconti.

The narrative ambiguity and the direct refusal of the relation reality-dream make these films be considered representative for the projection within the image of a discontinuous, reflexive dimension, with notable impact on time. Speaking about Resnais, we observe that Deleuze places the 'New Wave' of French cinematography of the '60s, the time-image extrapolated in the films of directors such as Truffaut or Godard. In other words, a favorable context in the '60s permitted a mutation of the cinematographic art towards the logic of movement with external referentiality, towards the illogism of the movement with internal referentiality. Such an affirmation allows for a clearer analogy with the situation of the revival of Blecher's reception in the '70s, understanding the novel *Întâmplări în irealitatea imediată* (Occurence in the Immediate Unreality) in terms of the narrative imagine of the type invoked by Deleuze.

The context of the reception of the '70s is predisposed to the understanding of this type of novel, focused on a kinetic sensorial narrative scheme, meaning that the action centres on the image of time, recovered out of the tragic reflexivity, composed imagistically of the Subject. Although, in order to associate even more of Blecher's narrative image with the articulation manner of the cinematography world, a similar intention at the beginning of modern cinema would need to be identified, between the period at the end of the First World War and the '30s. This type of image is the harsh nucleus of the Surrealist cinematography of the period. Surrealism discovers this new form of expression, the film, which corresponds to Breton's artistic programme, of extrapolating the subconscious and of artistic syncretism.

Films such as that of Germaine Dulac, *La Coquille et le clergyman* (1928), after the screenplay of Antonin Artaud, of Luis Buñuel and Salvador Dalí, *Un Chien Andalou* (1929) (1929), Man Ray, *L'Etoile de mer* (1929) (1929), Luis Buñuel with the help of Salvador Dalí, *L'Age d'or* (1930) or Jean Cocteau, *Le sang d'un poète* (1930), are built in accordance to the Surrealist experimental poetic formulas. Knowledge and representation of the space are questioned, as reason with its linear logic is no longer a credible instrument, while this heteroclite combination of directors, painters, writers seek the true duration of thought and invoke the hazard and arbitrariness of the dream. 'The solution' reclaimed by Blecher in contemplating the interiour image is to be found in building pure Deleuzian images, which are fragments of a subjective time, intentional and provoking dislocations of the man of empirical logic, based on Action-Reaction. Time is exclusively determined by the heteroclite character of memory revealed rapidly and fragmentarily in dissonant images. Suddenly time frees itself from action, relativizing through reflection.

The 'cursed spaces' of the novel *Întâmplări în irealitatea imediată* (Occurence in the Immediate Unreality) or the Surrealist film of the '30s appear as discontinuous images which produce a fracture within Self and Reality. The favourite equation of this type of imagery, either of narrative or filmic nature, is based on the principle that to know cannot be just a rational empirical activity, but a question of representation and arbitrary association of the images projected within the Self. Out of the formulas specific for this type of anamorphotic imagism, the perception of the body as a 'bad place' or 'cursed space' is primordial in defining the introduction of the observer into the depth of reflexivity. In this regard we identify two perceptions exterior to the body space and an interior one, as follows:

a. *the visual corporeal shock*, perceived either from the outside, as in the case of the photographic image analysed anteriorly, as an affective external and distant stimulus, either as a presence within absence, a true anosognosia.[129] In a similar manner, Merleau-Ponty's thesis of phenomenological perception starts from the question: "Mon corps, n'est-il pas, exactement comme les corps extérieurs, un objet qui agit sur des récepteurs et donne lieux finalement à la conscience du corps?"[130] Starting here, Blecher's perception is similar to those of people having the anosognosia condition, the mysterious neuro-vegetative sickness which makes sick people be unaware of their condition. Their body is mostly perceived from the outside, as an external stimulus which fuels a complex series of reflexive reactions, almost uncontrollable. The own body in the photography or the exorcisation of interior pain through the exterior, physical one, are appropriate examples in this respect. In moments of sadness, the character narrator of the *Întâmplări* (Occurence) resorts to such an external stimulus which deflects his attention from the real and profound suffering: "Fire purifies all. I always used to keep a box of matches in my pocket. When I was very sad, I would light a match and pass my hands through the flame, first one, then the other."[131]

b. *the split, fragmented or deformed corps* till the sensation of the artificial is Blecher's second exterior projection. As with Giorgio de Chirico or Dali, the body is seldom for Blecher a clear image, Surrealist projection of anamorphotic type of the fracturation of the empiric coherence of reality. The difference towards Chirico's or Dali's representations is that Blecher has a dysmorphic perception of this exterior representation, meaning that an obsessive fear of being ugly or malformed comes out of the incontrollable depth of the conscience. The obsession of the monstrous body is characteristic for these diseased who have a degraded and/or deformed image of their own body. This is also the source

---

[129] Coming from gr. *nosos*, 'maladia' and *gnosis*, 'knowledge', is defined as a neurovegetative sickness which makes the patient unaware of his maladive situation. Consulted at the web adress: http://www.larousse.fr/encyclopedie/medical/anosognosie/11206 [25.04.2018].
[130] Maurice Merleau-Ponty: *La Phénoménologie de la perception*. Paris: Gallimard 1945, p. 90.
[131] Blecher: *Occurence in the Immediate Unreality*, p. 33.

of their blockages of social nature, living with the rejection obsession because of their physical deformities. The dysmorphia of the character narrator is compensated by a rich interior life, invested with exuberant imagism. The refuge is in itself a consequence of the fear from the aggressed or aggressive body. The strange perception of the Surrealist body is similar to that of Cocteau who, in the film *Le sang d'un poète* (1930), imagines a character to whom a moth is transferred or transposed in his palm, a moth he had just erased with his palm from the canvas of a painting. The perception and contemplation of the bizarre talking hand becomes the first step towards the projection in a hallucinatory world, coming out of the fractured imaginary of the character, the one who will gradually observe discontinuous theatrical images, extracted from his subconscious aggressed by the real.

The body perceived as an exterior object induces the fear, the fear of the foreign body, distant at first but which gradually becomes an aggressive and/or aggressed body. The strangeness of the hand at Cocteau or the double hermaphrodite with fur in its mouth, the aunts coming out of the hand or the lovers devoured by insects in the end of *The Andalusian Dog* by Luis Buñuel and Salvador Dali or the head of the cleric in the glass bowl in Dulac's film are also images of a distorted body and which are forms of aggression of the equilibrated body of the anterior representations. *Un Chien Andalou* starts with a shocking image, of the dissection of the ocular globe of the woman who speaks directly, through an ostentatious Surrealist gesture, about the transgression of the physical dimension of the gaze, such as in Dali's or de Chirico's painting. The classical physical body remains a compromised image for Surrealists, which cannot reveal the distortion of reflexivity and the loss of the Subject within the interior abyss.

In Blecher's case, the uncomprehended body is a continuous threat, perceived as an exterior aggressive form with a double function, terrorising but also attractive for his natural character. The image of the panopticon of the wax figures is relevant and the speculative character is reminiscent of the theater-like strange hotel rooms, contemplated through the key-hole by Cocteau's character. The time images in Cocteau's film, the successions incoherent from the point of view of SAR scheme (Situation-Action-Reaction) offer pure images born with the character's entering through the mirror. In every room different limit situations, with absurd characters who act isolated from any meta-reality. With Blecher the wax spectacularity of the panopticon transforms into a real 'terror' doubled by a sensation of pleasure of this pure image, of domination of the exterior and of exclusively artificial construct. The fragment of Blecher's surrealist solution is representative for the ability of the reflexive power to re-project reality:

> It was a fear mixed with a tinge of vague pleasure and somehow with that bizarre feeling we each sometimes have of previously living in a certain setting. I think that if the urge for an aim in life were ever to arise in me and if this impulse had to be bound to something that is indeed profound, essential and irremediable in me, then my body would have to become a mannequin in a wax museum and my life a simple and endless contemplation of the display cases of the dioramas.[132]

Blecher's solution is that this exterior inoffensive wax theatrical body would be doubled by the passing from the perception dimension to the contemplation one, therefore a real focalisation on the reflexive power. This is also the motif for which the Subject intentionally weakens the objectual nature of the exterior world, filtering it through a process of mineralisation, freezing, through the instrument of subjective memory but also through the taste for artificial. He still appears as a speechless spectator of this artificial and immobile spectacle of imitated objects. It is a secondary world, dominated by the Subject's powerful reflexivity:

> I used to be impressed by everything that was an imitation. Artificial flowers, for example, and funeral wreaths, especially funeral wreaths, forgotten and dusty in their oval glass cases in the cemetery chapel, framing with old-fashioned delicacy anonymous old names, submerged in an unechoing eternity. The cut-out pictures with which children play and the cheap statuettes from flea markets. In time, these statuettes would lose a head or an arm and their owners, repairing them, would surround the delicate throat with the white scurf of plaster. The bronze of the rest of the statuette would then acquire the significance of a tragic but noble suffering. And then there are the life-size Jesuses in Catholic churches.[133]

c. *the refuge or the isolation in a terrified, hypertrophied body*, which is an unreal natural paradise of perceptions is the third successive image proposed by Blecher's Surrealism visionary perspective. This reclusion is generated by the insufficiency of the real regarding the senses and searching for authenticity. The withdrawal to the corporal universe corresponds to what Cocteau observed, referring to the surrealist experiment in *Le sang d'un poète*. For Cocteau this is only:

> [...] une descente en soi-même, une manière d'employer le mécanisme du rêve sans dormir [...]. Les actes s'y enchaînent comme ils le veulent, sous un contrôle si faible qu'on ne saurait l'attribuer à l'esprit. Plutôt à une manière de somnolence aidant à l'éclosion de souvenirs libres de se combiner, de se nouer, de se déformer jusqu'à prendre corps à notre insu et à nous devenir une énigme.[134]

---

132 Blecher: *Occurence in the Immediate Unreality*, p. 54–55.
133 Blecher: *Occurence in the Immediate Unreality*, p. 56.
134 Jean Cocteau: *La difficulté d'être*. Paris: Editeur Paul Morihien 1947, p. 891.

Blecher's prose is an exploration of the fascinating physiological universe, an unhoped motricity for the image of the fragmented body. Providing a real corporal network which fundamentally leads to an abyss of the so dreamt of absolute reflexivity. Antonio Patraș[135] saw a similarity between the journey within physiology, within the body, on the waves of blood in *Vizuina luminată* (The Lit-up Den) and some similar images in Mircea Cărtărescu's *Orbitor* (Blinding). In order to consolidate the association to Cărtărescu's prose we remark the fact that not only is this this image relevant, but also the set of places which determine an exacerbation of the senses and a minuteness of observation, whether in discovering Herman's skull, the room of the silk worms, the broken image of the twins' photography. The observation of the writing as almost a physiological reality is disconnected from the personal detail with Cărtărescu, in a similar way to Blecher's description. Here is also Blecher's centrifugal journey, towards the Self, where the search of reflexive power till the ultimate configurations of the globules becomes the fundamental search of survival:

> The moment I am writing, my blood floods within the night of my body, circulating through flesh, nerves and bones through small obscure cannals, in living wavy rivelets, through dark cavities dug in flesh, with a little gurgle of rhythmed pulse. In the darkness it flows like a map with thousands of rivelets, through thousands and thousands of pipes and, if I imagine I am miniscule enough to float on a raft down one of these arteries, the roar of the liquid which leads me fills my head with an immense roar in which ample blows beneath the waves, as those of a gong, of the pulse, [...] waves wrap me quickly in the darkness and an unimaginable roar throws me in the waterfalls of the heart. [...] I am burying my arm down to its elbow into the river that is carrying me. It is dark and I am trapped in the steams of my own blood.[136]

Of course the association, at least from an aesthetical point of view, of the progressive detail in discovering the hypersensitive Self occulted within the body, with Cărtărescu's prose is evident. Nevertheless, Blecher's journey within the body may be associated with the vision from inside, the surprising instrospection of prince Maxențiu in the novel *Concert din muzică de Bach* (Bach Musical Concert) (1927) by Hortensia Papadat Bengescu. "The torture of the febrile nights" of the sick Maxențiu culminates as a dream in which he visualises the cause of death, "a small bacillus", as a "sinister cone [...] projected onto a blue background, as the huge sapphire" engagement ring given to Ada Razu. "In the same dreams you could see, on the immaculate sheets the red drawing of some palm leaves with

---

135 Antonio Patraș: Interpretări: În lumea lui Max Blecher (Interpretations: In the world of Max Blecher). In: *România literară*, anul 2000, nr. 47. Consulted at the web adress: http://www.romlit.ro/n_lumea_lui_m._blecher [26.04.2018].
136 Blecher: *Vizuina luminată*, p. 68–69.

painful fibres which changed their place as he moved his agitated hands." At the same time, Maxențiu's existence is doubly determined, divided, fractured, as it happens with Blecher's character, between "the exterior hygiene: bath, massage" through which he "recomposed the decomposed countenance after he woke up" after diseased dreams. Of a special importance there is "the other hygiene, within the interior of the same body":

> For him the interior was accessible. He didn't see him as a surgeon saw an open body, he saw it with a kind of tactile ability, as if on each side of the body sensitivity developed thousands of eyes turned within. Even in sleep he followed what went there, vigil in the dark. The doctor, thought Maxențiu, knew little, knew only the great, evident processes of the disease. But he knew every trembling of the fiber, he knew the connection through which that fiber will resonate within other centres [...] There were there, indeed, caverns and abysses, and torrents of red waters and drift canals and ditches, which Maxențiu, as a tragic tourist, visited in detail every day on different climates.[137]

The exterior paripatheticism of the body, which now discovers the theatrical artificiality of the world in its motricity, is now replaced with an interior peripatheticism, a projection within the depth of the body, searching for a greater power than the active-exterior one, exercised on the things in the world panopticon. The journey within the body revels the fascination of motricity, "son corps phénoménal"[138] and its power on the objectual body. We observe that "Le corps n'est qu'un élément dans le système du sujet et de son monde [...]"[139] and the turn within becomes an imaginary construct specific for literature which reconfigures the world of the subject in the limits of the body but in the unlimitless reflexivity. The interior of his own body becomes an unknown expressive universe and "Le corps est notre moyen général d'avoir un monde",[140] of detaining the power over us, reporting the objectual world to a reflexive, phenomenological one.

According to this reflexive reduction we can understand the exterior projection, in Blecher' Subject 'cursed places'. The interior anamorphosis of the body are doubled by some exterior ones, after a process of occultation-epiphany, these cursed spaces being representations of the subjective anguishes linked to the threats of the own body. Beyond the real identity of Blecher's "fantasmatic places",[141] this is the meaning of the narrative world described here, as "the final

---

[137] Hortensia Papadat-Bengescu: *Fecioarele despletite. Concert din muzică de Bach. Drumul Ascuns*, (The Disheveled Maidens. A Concert of Bach's Music. The Hidden Road). Post-scriptum by Doina Modola. Cluj-Napoca: Dacia 1986, p. 171.
[138] Merleau-Ponty: *La Phénoménologie de la perception*. p. 123.
[139] Merleau-Ponty: *La Phénoménologie de la perception*, p. 123.
[140] Merleau-Ponty: *La Phénoménologie de la perception*, p. 171.
[141] Mironescu: *Viața lui Max Blecher*, p. 26.

montage values more than the hypothetical depiction of all the origin points."[142] So, the 'cursed spaces' are only subjective coordinates, dominated by the expansive, peripathetic, reflexivity of the narrator.

The childhood objects, the piano in which a dead mule was hidden, in Bunuel and Dali's film, the empty symbolism of Dulac's shell, the living statues or the hotel rooms with suspended gravity with Cocteau or the panopticon the fair as a "deserted island" or the accumulation of the artificiality of the kitsch are elements of a sur-reality in which reality and dream mix, according to Breton's project. The aim is that of escaping the terror of the uniform realist objectual and to face a subjective reality, according to the logic of the objective hazard of reflexivity, these images being in the sphere of Deleuze's "crystalline images". The change of perspective, the re-focalisations of the characters, has the role of offering another perspective on the real world and controlling it this way. In Dulac's film, the character walks like a dog through the city, looking at the world upside down and the revolutionary cinematographic frame of the '30s is in continuous movement, reducing the objectual world, as a vertigo, to that of the animal.

As in the case of Blecher's *Occurrences*, the Subject contemplates the effects of rain on the city and observes the "houses unfolding as fans", "the muddy paste" of the "dirty lane" and all these while "heavy drops of rain lingered on the sparkling facets". These images washed by the autumnal rain uncover the "heart-breaking void which floated over the city", but also provokes the wish to re-focalise, similar to that in Dulac's Surrealist film: "Sometimes I wanted to be a dog, to see that wet world from the oblique perspective of animals, from below, lifting my head. To move more closely to the ground, with my eyes fixed upon it, closely bound to the livid colour of the mud."[143]

Blecher's state which is associated with the 'cursed spaces' is 'dizziness', a genuine crisis of the real, being therefore a crisis of perception, a sensorial crisis, similar to the process described by Merleau-Ponty, a process finalised at the supra-position of times, the past of the limit experience, with the present of evocation. In all these times, the preponderant state associated to these projections is a "suave melancholia, as a dream we remember in the power of the night", meaning that through the reflexive burden of the image the author surpasses the Surrealist 'impasse' of a simple overlapping of dream and reality, the 'cursed spaces' being interior coordinates. The crises of the Subject are provoked by "the same places in street, house, or garden". He observes that:

---

[142] Mironescu: *Viața lui Max Blecher*, p. 26.
[143] Blecher: *Occurence in the Immediate Unreality*, p. 88.

> Whenever I used to enter their space, the same faintness and dizziness would overwhelm me. They were invisible traps dotted around the town, in no way distinct from the air that encompassed them. They would ferociously lie in wait for me to fall into the trap of the special atmosphere they contained. If I took so much as a single step and entered such a cursed space, the crisis would inevitably come.[144]

The power of the fractured image comes from within the peripathetic interior of the Subject who recomposes the interior universe stimulated by the memories of the 'bad places'. The vertigo of the dance in Dulac's or the progression of the snowball fight in the schoolyard in Cocteau's film are also spaces of the crises, cursed spaces, artificial, impersonal, but also generating a certain melancholia by reducing them to the coordinates of reflexivity. This is Cocteau's cinematographic illusion or Blecher's autobiographical narrative illusion rendered through a process of the type imagine-time. The exterior world appears therefore as mystified, an illusion. We observe a falsification of the natural in favour of the artificial which becomes the true nature of reflexive reduction.

> In ensemble, objects formed stage sets. The impression of the theatrical everywhere accompanied me with a feeling that everything was unfolding in the midst of a factitious and sad performance. When I sometimes escaped from the tedious, matte vision of a colourless world, its theatrical aspect would then appear, emphatic and old-fashioned. Within the framework of this overall theatricality, there were other, more astonishing theatrical performances which drew me more because their artificiality and the actors playing in them seemed genuinely to understand the mystifying meaning of the world. They alone knew that in a stage-set universe of theatrical performance life had to be acted artificially and ornamentally. Such performances were the cinema and the wax museum.[145]

Blecher's "irrational fracture" is similar to that of the Surrealists. But the process is more complex, similar to Bergson's phenomenological process, the fragmentation of the real is produced through the "image-memory", not through the irrational deconstruction of reality. The Subject recomposes in/through the novel a powerfully individualised image of the world, and the objectual world remains only a pretext. The force of Blecher's prose, more than in the case of the surrealist film of the '30s, comes from the reflexive burden behind the images which are anamorphosis of the being, which in Surrealist film is sometimes images and time are artificial forms of deconstruction of reality, without reflexive fundament, being most of the times void semiotically, which in Blecher's prose observing an extrapolation of his reflexive power on the world. As compensation, through his reflexive power, the Subject of the *Întâmplări* (Occurrence) succeeds

---

144 Blecher: *Occurence in the Immediate Unreality*, p. 27–28.
145 Blecher: *Occurence in the Immediate Unreality*, p. 59.

in overcoming the incapacity of the world to change, its sterile immovability. He lives with the conviction that:

> Now something was for sure: the world had its own habitual outward appearance, into the midst of which I had fallen by mistake, I would never be able to become a tree, or to kill someone, and nor would the blood ever spurt in torrents. All things, all people, were enclosed in their sad, petty obligation to be precise, nothing more than precise. In vain might I have believed that there were dahlias in a vase, when it was a scarf. The world did not have the power to change in the slightest; it was so ignobly enclosed in its precision that it could not allow itself to mistake a scarf for flowers.[146]

This *insignificant world* is, for Blecher, the real, objective one, while the Immediate Unreality, the reflexive one, keeps only rhizomatic links to reality, either biographical or historical in nature, to the actual one. In the context of the cultural myth of post-war Romanian literature, sometimes oppressive on the modern artistic sensibilities through the divergent magnetism of the public space, the regain of the reflexive power was a priority. *Occurrence* is a representative novel for the poetics of the reflexive power, even if in the period it was not recognised and understood from such a perspective. Through the aesthetics of the reflexive narrative reality with its active-aggressive forms is put between the brackets, the novel regaining its autonomy, and the Subject its reflexive power as a form of final deliverance from the excess of physical terror.

---

146 Blecher: *Occurence in the Immediate Unreality*, p. 104.

4 The Passivity of the Subject faced with the Power of History

"A renúncia é a libertação. Não querer é poder."¹

4.1 The Teratology of Totalitarian Power. The Romanian Case

"The absolute power of the Sun-King is acknowledged null when compared to that of the contemporary atheist dictator, who truly enacts lord Acton's saying: absolute power corrupts absolutely. It is too scarce. Absolute power becomes undoubtedly dementia."²

4.1.1 The 'Cultural Revolutions' and the Illusions of Mass Power

Referring to Plato's censorship, applied to the poets who freed their creativity too easily and too sincerely, there is no reason to understand that those texts are literature only when they serve a moral purpose within society. This is not literay evaluation of literature but a moral one. Plato did not chase away free poets from the fortress because they did not write literature, but because their literature was not in accordance to the ideology of the Republic. Moreover, if we analyse the specific discourses of the last century totalitarianisms, the representative texts for the aberrant ideologies of the totalitarian power, could we affirm that they are not literature? They responded to a certain political identity and whether they were or not the result of the will of their creators, these texts were considered literature by the representatives of those political regimes.

For example, in Romania in he 1950s, a period recognised according to the formula used by Marin Preda, the 'Obsessive decade', this was the only literature officially accepted, as an instrument of representativeness of the new socialist reality. The illustrative texts of the totalitarian Republics represented the political culture of their worlds. They were the official literature of the period. If today we have the chance to affirm that these texts are not literature, it is done by being

---

1 Pessoa: *Livro do Desassossego*, p. 144.
2 Nicolae Steinhardt: *Jurnalul fericirii* (The Diary of Happiness). Argument by P.S. Justin Hodea Sigheteanul; ed. by Virgil Bulat; notes by Virgil Bulat and Virgil Ciomoș; with a dossier by George Ardeleanu. Iași: Polirom 2008, p. 635.

conscientious of other criteria, the aesthetic or the critical one, which were determinant for literature.

The Romanian proletcultist literary canon[3] meant an exercise of ideological power over literature which was written till the '50s and that was considered later as decadent, bourgeois, representing 'the capitalist world' which was the source of all evil. Over a number of years, official literature meant the representation of the ideal world and served as a tool in the 'class struggle' in order to destroy any other type of literature that started from other categories than those of communist practices.

Terry Eagleton is just partially right when, in trying to define literary theory and its object, literature, he states that:

> [...] is most useful to see 'literature' as a name which people give from time to time for different reasons to certain kinds of writing within a whole field of what Michel Foucault has called 'discursive practices', and the if anything is to be an object of study it is this whole field of practices rather than just those sometimes rather obscurely labeled 'literature'.[4]

The incomplete validity of the affirmation consists in the fact that this is often the case of literature under communism, when investigating the field of 'discursive practices' of the period and trying to determine what would be the mechanisms that decide the consideration of certain texts as literature. It can be observed that these cannot be defined as literature according to the discursive practices of our world or any other world, except the one in which these texts have been produced. The legitimation of the official literature of an oppressive political regime was produced only through a repressive operational system. It was a dominant Machiavelic power strategy, as Bourdieu names it, having a 'functionalist' role, serving the interests of the dominant class. In this case:

> The dominant culture contributes to the real integration of the dominant class (by facilitating the communication between all its members and by distinguishing them from other classes); it also contributes to the fictitious integration of society as a whole, and thus to the apathy (false consciousness) of the dominated classes; and finally, it contributes to the legitimation of established order by establishing distinctions (hierarchies) and legitimating these distinctions.[5]

---

3 See also Florin Oprescu: The Power and Subversiveness of Literature: The Romanian Case. In: *Art and Intercultural Dialogue* (Eds. Susana Gonçalves and Suzanne Majhanovich). Rotterdam/Boston/Taipei: Sense Publishers 2015, p. 97–112.
4 Terry Eagleton: *Literary Theory. An Introduction.* Minessota: University of Minnesota Press 1996, p. 178.
5 Bourdieu: *Language and Symbolic Power*, p. 167.

The domination of the oppressive class has made the literary discourse an official one. Regarding texts written by anonymous writers that belong to popular culture, the texts of the literature which are dominated by politics have used the illusory schemes of the political, annulling the literariness and the arbitrariness of the significant. The civilizing heroes of these texts and their utopian worlds appear today as involuntary caricatures. It is the violent effect of the political power on literature. Culture has become an official propaganda instrument of manipulation and ideological education in totalitarian systems. In other political circumstances during the Greek and Latin Antiquity and with another stake than Plato's *Republic*, literature has served the idealization of a society under the influence of certain groups or persons that have understood that in the imagined dystopic city, of totalitarian absolutism. In such times art, especially literature, played the determining role of canonizing subliminally the spiritual life of people who were controlled. The example of post-war Romania is relevant regarding the ideological suppression of literature under totalitarian regimes. Although in the period between the two World Wars, the period of a rapid modernization of Romanian society, communist totalitarian regimes could be anticipated, the dictatorial regimes that followed the Second World War had a devastating effect on Romanian literature. Since the '60s, in synchronicity with the militant pacifist movements of the Western world, liberty was felt in Romania as well, partial liberty due to destalinization and temporary removal of the cult of personality and a new hope of the creative forces.[6] In Romanian literature this corresponds to an "ideological break up" that permitted the recognition of the interwar literary canon, of the authors that in the previous decade had been forbidden, reason for which the critic Nicolae Manolescu named the '60s "a modernist remake".[7]

The illusion of the art free of ideology, of the dictatorial power and the power of the nomenclature lasted a very short time, as in the '70s we witnessed the fierce comeback of the dictatorial authoritarianism, as a consequence of the influences of the visits in the Popular Republic of China, North Korea, North Vietnam and Mongolia on Ceaușescu. 'The June Theses' from 1971, of the dictator Ceaușescu, in front of the Executive Committee of the Romanian Communist Party (PCR),[8] contained a set of ideological 'Maoist' measures,[9] a new cultural revolution

---

[6] Dennis Deletant: *Ceaușescu and the Securitate: Coercion and Dissent in Romania, 1965–1989.* London: Sharpe, 1995, p. 182–183.
[7] Manolescu: *Istoria critică a literaturii române*, p. 1000.
[8] These theses were called "Proposals to improve the political-ideological activity, of Marxist-Leninist reeducation of the party members, of all working people".
[9] Adrian Cioroianu: *Pe umerii lui Marx. O introducere în istoria comunismului românesc* (On Marx's Shoulders. An Introduction in the History of Romanian Communism). București: Curtea Veche 2005, p. 489.

meant to impose a new realism socialism in which literature and art played an essential role. The title of these theses, atrocious for the liberty of the artists was: "Exposing people to the PCR (Romanian Communist Party) programme in order to improve ideological activity, raising their general level of knowledge and promoting socialist education of the masses, for establishing relationships in our society based on principles of ethics and communist and socialist equity".

The relevant example of this socialist neorealism can be found in Romania of the '70s and '80s when, in the process of communist industrialization imagined by Nicolae Ceaușescu, literature had to reflect the image of the New Man and not the Romantic illusions of the Western capitalist society. The role of the writer, the artist in general, was that of synchronising art to social reality, imitating, in a propagandistic rhetoric, realist to trivialising language and extreme clichés, a uniform and mechanized society. Art was the effect of the cult of a personality of the ideal leader, artisan of the ideal society, industrialized and dehumanized.

In reality, masked by the official literature, the results of the totalitarian power were the creation of a pogrom country, a result of hunger and darkness, individualization, censorship and especially generalized fear. Therefore, if on the barricades of the Western world in the '60s and '70s a new social discourse was born, young people protesting for humanistic lost ideals, together with the intellectuals of the movement Michel Foucault, Jacques Derrida, Pierre Bourdieu and Jacques Lacan, after the Iron Curtain a radicalization of the socialist discourse was discovered. 'May '68' is seen by its critics as an eclectic amalgam of Trotskyism, feminism, anti-capitalism, anti-bourgeois and sexual liberation, energization and revitalization for the young spirit. The slogans of the French barricade in 'May 1968' ("Fin de l'Université!"; "L'art est mort, libérons notre vie quotidienne!"; "L'art est mort, ne consommez pas son cadavre!" etc.), filled with latent socialism, were replaced in the East by a censorship similar to the 'Obsessive decade'. However differently oriented, the Paris movement and the other movements behind the Iron Curtain were determined by the will of political power, being different just as forms and public development of exercitation of power. An essay such a Luc Ferry and Alain Renaut's, *La pensée '68. Essai sur l'anti-humanisme contemporain*,[10] may reveal, in spite of its excessively polemic aspect, the intellectual battles for power in the '60s and '70s.

---

[10] See Luc Ferry and Alain Renaut: *La pensée '68. Essai sur l'anti-humanisme contemporain*. Paris: Gallimard 1985. This essay is, in its turn, too radical regarding the role of Foucault, Derrida, Bourdieu, Lacan, Lévi-Strauss, Deleuze or Barthes in the ideological movements of May 68. The majority of these intellectuals distanced themselves from the public excess of the street. A relevant article can be read in the magazine *Observator cultural*, of Andrei Poamă: "About May 68:

In Romania, art, as a result of the 'Theses of June 1971', had to reflect the socialist transformations, the neostalinist cultural revolution. Gradually, censorship and cultural uniformity become more acute in the '80s, literature being totally under the control of the communist propagandistic ideology.

Nicolae Ceaușescu's discourse about art within the 'Talks at Mangalia', on the 3rd August 1983, is relevant:

> Why do we put on stage and on the market so many films which present the reality of our society, working people, youth or other categories of working people in a diformed manner? We do not need such cinema and such theater in our country. We need an art, a cinema which represents the essence, the model of the man we need to build. The people, within whom youth has an important role, have realised everything we obtained in the socialist development of our country, they are the heroes who should have the main roles in film, theater, poetry, art, literature, painting, in all art domains. We should represent them.[11]

Therefore, art represented an essential instrument in the depiction of the communist Orwellian dystopia. The history of the 40 years of communism constitutes a fundamental background of questioning the role, the function of literature in the society. When literature loses its critical function, a fundamental attribute, causing the aesthetical discourse, it becomes a transitive manipulative discourse, ideologist and artificial. The sterility of the propagandistic literature, of proletcultism, for example, comes from the fact that the world of literary texts is reduced to language and schemas and is nothing but empty rhetoric, devoid of life. "The heroes of socialist struggle" are, as we will see, characters without a destiny, simple ideological marionettes, as propaganda literature was an absurd puppet theatre.

In this theatre, most of the time absurd till derisory, history's lack of meaning is just one of its subjacent messages. The main message is that in a universe in which the excess of power is so visible and overwhelming, the Subject is a passive victim, projected from 'the ivory tower' of the creation of the defeated writer.

4.1.2 Victims and Heroes of the Socialist Battle

In such a context, of manipulation and ideological control, a real theory of socialist art is born. The Marxist idea of class antagonisms is taken from the literary

---

How the police of the mind is born", nb. 425/2008. Consulted at the web adress: http://www.observatorcultural.ro/articol/despre-mai-68-cum-se-nasc-jandarmii-mintii-2/ [26.04.2018].
11 Discourse consulted at the web adress: https://www.youtube.com/watch?v=YthLx3nxar8 [26.04.2018].

ideology of the system, which designed literature and involved it in the discourse of the propaganda. In the definition of an ideologist of the artistic realist-socialist system, Ion Vitner, literature must reflect, sustain and accentuate the "vision of the scientific socialist world".[12] In his vision, which is the project of the party, "the idea generated by scientific realism was that of smashing and replacing the bourgeois hierarchy, not of a simple bettering by exercising the critical spirit."[13]

In other words, the function of literature would be to serve in the 'class struggle', passing from critical aestheticism to direct and factual social criticism. Literature is seen as social language with propagandistic power, without an aesthetical stake. This declared 'socialist humanism' promoted by the totalitarian communist regime presupposes not just the use of literature and art in general in the national 'class battle', but also the ambiguity through denying the humanist Western values. Western literature was considered decadent, anti-humanist, as every artistic activity not engaged ideologically in the configuration of the 'New Man' was considered, an ideal result of socialism, as opposed to the man surprised by Western literature, submitted to "the degradation under the pressure of the morbid and pathological", according to the affirmations of the same ideologist.[14]

An attentive observer of the socio-political context that has generated the forty year drama of Romanian literature under communism, Ana Selejan explains the "betrayal of the intellectuals" in the first years of the Romanian totalitarian system, starting from Julien Benda's 1927 book, *La trahison des clercs*. "The force lines"[15] of Benda's demonstration are, considers the researcher, viable and explanation of "the betrayal of the Romanian intellectuals" in the communist period. It is about the political passions (race, class, nationality) in the interwar period, these shifting the attention and the efforts of the intellectuals from their natural destiny and pushing them into a battle of dominating ideologies. This conversion generates an eclectic literature, due to the combination of literary and politics, determining the apparition of poets, political novelists etc. But, with the proliferation of communism, what could the position of intellectuals, people who have made a public career ever since the interwar period, have actually been? The attitudes of the writer in an ideal, liberal world, believes Ana Selejan, could be three: "to cover generalities, to be silent or to have a fighting conscience. But there is a

---

12 Ion Vitner: *Formarea conceptului de literatură socialistă* (The Formation of the Concept of Socialist Literature). București: Editura pentru literatură 1966, p. 588.
13 Vitner: *Formarea conceptului de literatură socialistă*, p. 590.
14 Vitner: *Formarea conceptului de literatură socialistă*, p. 591.
15 Ana Selejan: *Trădarea intelectualilor. Educare și prigoană* (The Betrayal of Intellectuals. Education and Persecution). Second edition. București: Cartea Românească 2005, p. 113.

fourth one: the right of the artist to write what he wants, what he feels, to express his truth or, unconditionally, and without being sanctioned by the contingent."[16] The communist power didn't leave many variants of the kind to the writers. Because literature was an integrating part of the educational process/realist-socialist ideology, its relation to the new world therefore had to be essential. There were two clear possibilities:

a. the writer submitted to the official discourse, therefore to the political power and then his literature became propaganda literature, devoid of any attributes of good literature, without any trace of critical discourse implicit towards the degeneration of the man, but just factual and explicit regarding the progress;
b. the writer refused the control of his literature, of the official censorship apparatus; he either did not write what the political power commanded and did not publish or he retired from the public battle, gave up creating. In both cases, especially if the writer had a recognizable, iconic, canonical image from the interwar period, he had to suffer implicit political persecutions, his attitude being considered a defiance of the system, a riot against official literature.

The attacks on some writers who played a decisive role in interwar Romanian literature, such as Tudor Arghezi, Lucian Blaga, or the literary critic George Călinescu, who were between 1944 and 1948 in sequences that would culminate with six articles of the same ideologist lacking scruples, Ion Vitner, published in the magazine *Contemporanul*, in January 1948. Călinescu was considered a decadent result of the aestheticism promoted by Maiorescu and therefore a metaphysical idealist in disagreement to the regime. He would also be dismissed from the University of Bucharest in 1949 and his position would be occupied by the official ideologist of the party, Ion Vitner. After 23rd August 1944, the expurgation of the books in Romania was completed according to a Soviet model. "Printing, importing and disseminating periodical and non-periodical publications in Romania, presenting theatre shows and films, the functioning of the stations TFF, Postal Office, Telegraphy, Telephony would be executed in accordance to the Allied High Commandament (sovietic)."[17] Therefore, censorship is an essential instrument in maintaining power, simply for promoting the literature engaged politically in realist-socialist education. In the year 1922, in the USSR the *General Direction for Literature and Imprinting* (Glavlit) was set up, which would only be dissolved

---

16 Selejan: *Trădarea intelectualilor*, p. 114.
17 Apud Gheorghe Grigurcu: Gulagul cărților (The Gulag of Books). In: *Viața românească*, nr. 9–10/ 2013. Consulted at the web adress: http://www.viataromaneasca.eu/arhiva/87_via-a-romaneasca-9-10- 2013/10_cronica-literara/1618_gulagul-cartilor.html [26.04.2018].

in 1991 and after the war, in the countries under the political domination of the USSR, such as Bulgaria, Poland and Romania similar institutions were set up. Liliana Corobca, the author of a very precise piece of research on the *The Expurgation of Books in Romania* (2010) observes that:

> [...] the *General Direction of Press and Printing* had operated for 28 years in Romania, from 1949 to 1977, since a large part of censors had been transferred to the Council of Culture and Socialist Education, where they continued their activity. After the institution was abolished, the censorship communist system regarded the editorial activity, censorship attributions having the Writers Union, followed by Security and at the peak of the hierarchy the Section of Propaganda and Agitation of the Communist Party and the country's principal censor, Nicolae Ceaușescu.[18]

But censorship as a manner of exercising the power of a system in order to consolidate its power position and of promoting the dominant ideology is not only an exercise of direct, aggressive, violent force, that culminates with the burning of books or with indexing thousands of volumes considered immoral or harmful due to their anti-systemic character in general, the essence of literature, but also an exercise of indirect force such as the forbidding of authors and banishing of those who did not toe the line.

In 1949, the famous interwar prose-writer, Mihail Sadoveanu turned 69 years old, having an impressive literary career, together with Liviu Rebreanu, another important Romanian realist prose writer. But that year, Sadoveanu published his most controversial novel, *Mitrea Cocor*, assuming directly the realist-socialist ideology. The epic canon was imposed by Sadoveanu in Romanian literature through the realist literature of social inspiration *Hanul Ancuței* (Ancuța's Inn) (1928) or the realist historical novels *Neamul Șoimăreștilor* (Șoimăreștilor's Kin) (1915), *Creanga de aur* (The Golden Bough) (1933) or *Frații Jderi* (Jderi Brothers) (1935–1942). From the fascination of popular traditional culture and the founding history in the spirit of other canonical models, such as Costache Negruzzi or Ioan Slavici, the change of narrative history is fatal for Sadoveanu's prose. Its realist socialist canonization is an example of the practice of the totalitarian power on literature. The hyperbolical contrast comes from the renunciation regarding the aesthetical stake of his writing or by projecting an ideologized discourse into the civilizing history and in the morality of timeless models. The fake Sadovenian writing comes from the 'Machiavellic' temptation of power,[19] out of the will to

---

[18] Liliana Corobca: Instituțiile cenzurii în regimul comunist (The Censorship Institutions during the Communist Regime). In: *Revista 22*, Anul XXIV (1231), 22–28 October 2013. Consulted at the web adress: http://www.revista22.ro/institutiile-cenzurii-n- regimul-comunist-32615.html[26.04.2018].

[19] Nietzsche: *The Will to Power*, p. 407.

maintain social power, which happens as he becomes one of the new hallmarks of the new Romanian literature.

Here we witness a transfer, fatal for Sadoveanu, a fact proven by his dying interest for actual literature, a transfer from the powerful position in literature that he had obtained in the '30s through the mechanisms of the aesthetical canon, to the forced position of ideological Marxist-Leninist, gained by making an aesthetical compromise. Texts such as *Lumina vine de la răsărit* (Light Comes from the East), a volume of reports from USSR (1945), *Păuna mică* (Little Păuna) (1948) or *Mitrea Cocor* (1949) are written in the spirit of 'proletcultist' propaganda, the place of the historical characters represented from collective memory and from the need of ideal models being taken taken by sterile ones that participate actively in class-battles and the construction of the socialist world. The mythology of history is replaced by the realist-socialist mythology and in 1955, the author himself was awarded the distinction *Hero of Socialist Work*.

The change is really significant regarding the topic, the style, but also the evident ideological direction that is imprinted to his character, Mitrea Cocor, so that parts of the specialized literary critics tried to attribute the novel to another writer. In *Păuna mică* (Little Păuna) the propagandistic discourse shows a weak author, although the idea of the refugees in Păuna village, all of 'healthy origin', who transform the village through work and become a new and prosperous collective, is of proletcultist source. The images of the swamp terrain in Brăila Field and their transformation into a fertile land by industrious workers who have become successful agrarians is a topic that anticipates the more radical ideological discourse in the novel *Mitrea Cocor*. The birth of the ideal collective which changes the destiny of people would become a leitmotif of the proletcultist literature. The intervention of the party in the birth of the new man and world is not direct in the new land. This would be criticized by the ideological forces, due to which the text does not have literary value, even in the mediocre world of the proletcultist literature.

Sadoveanu became a realist-socialist epic model, projecting an ideal canon of militant literature for the communist utopia. Sadoveanu's scheme was simple and revealed a power exercise of the ideologized social aspect that took control over literature. The main character, Mitrea, was the one who transformed himself and then transformed the collective. Therefore, the novel portrays an ideal setting with ideal characters, with powerful conflicts always won by *the civilizing hero*, the socialist 'Good' prevailing, a classic recipe of formal stories. The orphan Mitrea, who revolted against the bourgeois from Malu-Surpat, Cristea-Trei-Nasuri, worked till exhaustion, and was humiliated and exploited, is a model of class battles. He is mocked by the boyar, revolted by the immorality and lack of patriotism of the army officers, forms his Marxist-Leninist convictions in the Soviet prison, becomes literate with the help of a fireman, fights against fascism, marries a 'healthy origin' girl and succeeds, through his revolutionary character, to participate in the agricultural, collectivist reform and to impose the new class order in Malu Surpat, becoming a model of the 'new man', punishing and humiliating vengefully the boyar who had humiliated him.

Imposed in the school syllabus of the time, an example of the new creation, the novel became the canon of the new power. Literature functions as a power instrument, as a third dimension of power,[20] when the dominant group imposes a model of behaviour on the community, which is considered useful to preserving power. The novel, as all his critics would remark later, lacks any literary value, has a sterile artistic language, strident in ideological expressions and violent slang, clearly ideological, that it is a classical analysis of the manner in which politics mutilates literature. The representation of the 'class battle' so direct and propagandistic, through such artificial characters that seem to quote Marxist-Leninist texts when speaking, has unfortunately as a result an involuntary caricature of the author. In this case it is obvious that the author and his novel have been invalidated by the obsession of power in the 'Obsessive decade' (1947–1960). The result of this rapport between the suffocating political power and literature is that it becomes an ideological instrument. The certain fact, not anticipated by the representatives of the system, is that, in this case literature, through its sterility caused by the obligatory monographic of the social, is a caricature probe of a sterile and utopian system.

The betrayal is implicit and obvious even in the contradiction or incompatibility between literature and society, the artistic writing being a formula to surmount the daily life and not reproduce it. If literature copies the social practice or, even more, if it becomes a vehicle of it, the risk of caricaturizing is considerable. And the novel *Mitrea Cocor* is an involuntary absurd image of the totalitarian system and its benign ideals. Unlike his historical novels, the social or natural ones, which are filled with shrill lyricism. The style is direct and tough, dominated by an artificial, propaganda rhetoric. The novel pictures the sterile thesis and the unconditional submission of the writer and literature in front of the totalitarian Power. The critical authority of the writer yields to the authority of the system. If discussing Gramsci's theory from his *Notebooks from Prison* (1978–1992), it could be stated that in Sadoveanu's case he becomes an organic intellectual, after he has perpetuated the image of the traditional intellectual, the moralizing wise man in traditional communities through his literature. He

---

20 See Lukes: *Power. A Radical View*.

becomes an organic intellectual meaning that he is closely related to the Marxist system and participates in its surplus and excess of power.

The recipe, Sadoveanu's proletcultist canon, is fervently followed throughout the 'Obsessive decade' of young organic writers who want to be part of the power system. Out of all these the most controversial example is that of prose writer Petru Dumitriu who in 1951 published a controversial novel of almost 700 pages, *Drum fără pulbere* (Road without Dust). Here, an extermination camp through forced labour appears as an ideal of the new world, the Danube-Black Sea Channel, as an example of human victory upon nature, in Marxist-Leninist spirit. Petru Dumitriu's chronicle about the happiness of the new man is a dramatic example for the devastating effects of the political power on literature. A concentration camp, of forced labour, a camp of death, as is today known the Danube-Black Sea Channel, is presented as a real achievement of the Orwellian system that civilizes the entirely empty space in arid Dobrogea. Petru Dumitriu's case is useful for the discussion, with the evaluation of his prose before and especially after the novel *Road without Dust* being positive, as he was considered one of the most important postwar writers.

For example, the novel *Cronică de familie* (Family Chronicle) is appreciated and has European echoes, being published in 1959 at Seuil. The novel impresses the critics of the period through its epic vitality set forth on successive narrative and historical planes with a style that synthesizes the great European prose, from Balzac's social descriptions to the Proustian introspection filled with memories. This is in fact the great creation of Petru Dumitriu, published in 1957, just three years before his emigration to Germany. Petru Dumitriu's case is the typical one of a young writer who, at 27, lives the fascination of collective power, the group dominated ideologically. Being part of the power's camarilla, the talented prose writer makes an infamous compromise, ideological political literature, foregoing the curative position of literature by reporting himself to its necessarily critical function. Literature, in this case, is a propaganda instrument and does not differ in anyway from the motivational discourses of the dictators. Novels like that of Dimitriu and *Oțel și pâine* (Steel and Bread) by Ion Călugăru were perceived, when they appeared, in the chronicle of the time, as "hymns dedicated to the creative work of the new man"[21] or as evident demonstrations of Marxist-Leninist victory in the class struggle.

The defeat of diverse obstacles is the main idea of the novel, from those of the character Mateică, the saboteur, in his permanent attempt to stop the "grandiose

---

[21] See the article: Books that appeared in order to honour the party. Two novels of building socialism (Road without dust by Petru Dumitriu and Steel and Bread by Ion Călugăru). In: *Flacăra*, nb. 19 (175), 10 May 1951.

realization" to the transformation of the savage wilderness, till the ideological education of the engineer Pangrati who is forced to fight against his passion for the boyar's daughter, Dona Vorvoreanu. To Mateică and Dona, nature is a hostile element which is isolated and defeated through self-denial, in both collective and communist conscience. Both the desert in the biblical Genesis and characters are the representations of the subversiveness of the totalitarian system, irrational forces that deny and denounce the system and are defeated by the power of collectiveness, retrained in a communist spirit. Their symbolic disappearance lets the reader focus on the channel, the amorphous volume of water and the crowd. Their subversive destiny is exemplary for the totalitarian power.

The term 'subversive' defines the positioning against the order imposed in a state, putting it in danger, undermining it through a strategy with an evident public effect and also risky for the power of the dominant group. In oppressive systems the sense of the term can be enlarged, applying it as an example to the cultural creations which had a subversive strategic discourse, of official anti-rhetoric, a critical discourse, even implicit towards the system. This is also a form of representation of power, much more natural to literature, therefore a critical representation. In a totalitarian system, such as the communist one, literature develops narrative strategies of subversiveness, either masked strategies or strategies justified by the 'game' of literature with language, for its metaphorical vitality, which is the reader's expectation universe. This analytical perspective in the emergency zone of contemporary pragmatism[22] could offer the instruments that probe just the subversive character of the narrative language in totalitarian epochs. Very few prose-writers succeeded in doing that, behind the imaginary scenarios induced, and suggested the true anguish behind the 'perfect world'. Communist utopias were seldom contradicted by the images of the degradation of Man, through isolation or refuge inside, as interior exile, silence, social and affective shock, death. These are forms of denouncing totalitarian power but the formulas, when they existed, were the results of complex narrative strategies. Only through the discursive practices of the official culture have writers tried to publish such texts to deconstruct the illusions of these worlds.

But there was a subversive literary discourse, specific to the art, a reaction to such cultural atrocities, to the propagandistic discourses which had become the official culture and an instrument of ideological control. The subversive discourse of Romanian literature in communism succeeded to confirm the fact that literature has a major role in denouncing the excess of power. The writer in the

---

[22] We could discuss the pragmatic analyses of the literary discourse proposed by Dominique Maingueneau: *Pragmatique pour le discours littéraire*. Paris: Dunod 1994.

Romanian subterranean succeeded to save himself through the aesthetical and, even more than that, succeeded in maintaining a subversive project finalized in 1989. It is obvious that for such a subversive text to appear, favouring factors had to exist, particular contexts that would allow the editing of such texts. Paraphrasing Nelson Goodman and his *Languages of Art* (1976), it is not a question of "What is literature in communism?", but especially "When do we speak about literature in communism?" because, going back to Eagleton's theory, liberated of the constraints of political power, the precise role of the dominant literature can be distinguished.

Such a favourable context appears halfway through the 'Obsessive decade', during the first moment of outward destalinization, when the censorship of power is more permissive. Novels that reaffirm the hope that literature can avoid political control, that the novel can find its literariness appear. Novels such as *Bietul Ioanide* (The Pitiable Ioanide) (1953) by George Călinescu, *Moromeții* (1955) by Marin Preda or *Groapa* (The Hole) (1957) by Eugen Barbu. "The democrat popular regime was searching for new legitimising acts and, after Stalin's death, it needed (at least for Kremlin's attentive eyes) the proof (at the visible level of culture) of the initiation of de-dogmatization and renewal."[23] This action was translated in discursive practices which legitimize topics forbidden just a few years before, although political power did not permit the direct criticism of the past, but just the diversification of the themes and narrative methods. The epic tradition recovered is that of interwar realism, an Arcadia lost and dreamt about permanently and this relation would also be a reality of the '60s. If the predilect place of the action is not the yard or the foundry and the character of this new world does not hold interminable Marxist-Leninist discourses, the novel should remain engaged in a class battle, subtle, either against the capitalist bourgeois or against the legionaries, the extreme-right forces.

In the year 1953, the Balzacian novel, *Bietul Ioanide* (The Pitiable Ioanide) of prose writer George Călinescu was published. He is a canonical personality of Romanian literature, especially through his activity as a literary critic in the postwar period, activity that culminated with the publication of *Istoria literaturii române de la origini până în prezent* (The History of Romanian Literature from Origins till Present) (1941). The appearance of this novel is surprising, especially because George Călinescu had been dismissed from literary life and contested in different periods.[24] After the novel was published, in 1960, George Călinescu would have a meeting with Gheorghe Gheorghiu-Dej, the communist leader of

---

23 Negrici: *Iluziile literaturii române* p. 118.
24 Selejan: *Trădarea intelectualilor*, p. 397–423.

Romania from 1948 till 1965, at the writer's request for discussions regarding the late publishing of his next novel, *Scrinul negru* (The Black Chest-of-Drawers). In the context of denouncing the legionaries who had been infiltrated in the Romanian Communist Party, it seems that the communist leader reproached the prose writer even with the wrong approach of the legionary movement in the novel *Bietul Ioanide* (The Pitiable Ioanide), suggesting the rewriting of the novel. "The meeting, *says Lavinia Betea*, – till the next archivist discoveries-may count as an example of a new style of power working with writers."[25] and the interdictions of Călinescu can appear due to the insufficient criticism he had levelled at the legionaries in *Bietul Ioanide* (The Pitiable Ioanide).

The records of the dialogue between the ideologist of power and the prose writer are an example of a veritable manner of imposing the perspective of the party in literature. The critic of the novel in 1953 focuses on the permissive context of its publishing and the non-ideological position of the central character, Ioanide the architect. The communist leder, Gheorghiu-Dej, becames an official interpreter of the novel:

> I have read the first part of the book *Bietul Ioanide* (The Pitiable Ioanide), did not like the form of the critics regarding this [...] Here there are aspects related to the legionaries, there are interesting things, but it depends how they are presented so they do not leave the impression to anyone that we would make the apology of some mystical manifestation. We are facing a cultural man and he cannot be the apologet of some mystical persons.[26]

If, at the beginning of the totalitarian communist system, such a novel that approached, among other topics, the problem of the legionary movement, but was insufficiently critical, could not have appeared due to censorship, the discourse of political power changed in the '60s, the strategy of suggestion being preferred in accordance to the reward for the revision. The prose writer is advised to review the novel and radicalize the discourse of the main character on the legionary movement, seen as a class obstacle in the new world.

Therefore, the novel, censored by the power, is a confusing result of incompatible discursive practices, between the focalization on a romantic character who isolates himself and who feels indifferent to the society with its conflicts and the gaining of the conscience of victim or his interior ideological discourse. But even the ideological excesses in the novel *Scrinul negru* (The Black Drawer), the one which follows *Bietul Ioanide* (The Pitiable Ioanide), a novel of the 're-educated'

---

25 See de transcription of the discution between Gheorghiu-Dej sand George Călinescu by Lavinia Betea. In: *România literară*, nr. 11/2003. Consulted at the web adress: http://www.romlit.ro/stenograma_discuiei_dintre_gh._gheorghiu-dej_i_g._clinescu_-_2_martie_1960_- [26.04.2018].
26 See Betea: In *România literară*, nr. 11/2003.

and converted prose writer to the canon of the power, is a vivid contrast of the anti-system discourse, therefore subversive, in spite of the censorship effects in Ioanide's novel.

It may be stated that such novels as *Bietul Ioanide* (The Pitiable Ioanide) are "key novels",[27] subversive ones that demasked, through the subjacent power of literature, its devastating force. The examples from Romanian literature could be given from the '80s period and the novel *Cel mai iubit dintre pământeni* (The Most Beloved Man on Earth) (1980) could be discussed. This is the last novel of Marin Preda, maybe one of the final and the most powerful voices of freedom under the power of Romanian communism.

4.2 *The Most Beloved Man on Earth* and the Passivization of the Subject, Faced with Excessive Power

4.2.1 The Preda Case. *The Raving* of the Most Contested Prose-Writer

The image of the writer Marin Preda continues to be disputed in the Romanian literary space, due to the polarization in his prose, between the novels that contain an implicit critique of the effects of the 'Obsessive decade', like *Moromeții* (I–1955; II–1967) or *Cel mai iubit dintre pământeni* (The Most Beloved Man on Earth) (1980) or even novels in which a direct critique of the excess of power can be observed, such as *Delirul* (The Raving) (1975) and proses in which the adherence to or at least the explicit discourse of the writer in promoting the communist ideology, such as *Ana Roșculeț* (1949) or *Desfășurarea* (The Unfolding) (1952).

His profile is a typical one in the monochrome landscape of the post-war Romanian prose of the '50s, aggressed by the excesses of totalitarian power, obeying the Stalinist pressure of placing the unique ruler at the centre of the cult of personality. The 'Preda case' is more subtle than that of Mihail Sadoveanu or George Călinescu because of the oscillated adhesion to the ideology of the time or through his image, representative for the postbelic generation and much more productive through the analyses of the subversiveness of literature in relation to power, than that of Petru Dumitriu. This is largely a result of the double artistic discourse of his prose and the subtlety of the refuge in a world that seemed still atemporal at the end of the war, the rural world.

---

27 Manolescu: *Istoria critică a literaturii române*, p. 963.

4.2 The Most Beloved Man on Earth and the Passivization of the Subject — 177

In the dispute of the critical 'revisiting' of the author, his fall in the darkness of history is evident, another *Zeitgeist* of his contemporaneity, because of the fluctuations between the ethical, moral representativeness of the author and the aesthetic one of his work. For instance, Nicolae Manolescu observed, in an article in *România literară*, that he noticed "only rare aesthetic (and systematic) revisions of the works published during communism",[28] expressing his amazement that after 1989 "authors' moral guilt" seemed more important in the process of the revisions, which therefore became moral revisions, rather than aesthetic ones, in the spirit of Lovinescu. Nevertheless, the literary historian reconsiders the idea of critical revising in 2008, in the article on Marin Preda in the *Istoria critică a literaturii române* (Critical History of Romanian Literature), this time in polemics with Eugen Simion. Manolescu argues that Simion "is the greatest authority of those who rejected any attempt to revise the novel *Moromeții*."[29] The inconsistency makes Nicolae Manolescu counterbalance Preda's 'revision' from the critical-aesthetical criteria towards the biographical one, that of the 'author', with reference to Preda's 'collaboration'. Although he admits the term may be too 'strong', Manolescu refuses this time to exclude, for any reason, 'pudicity', the ethical slips, including those in his articles, such as the semantic detouring of the concept 'Obsessive decade', in *Imposibila întoarcere* (The Impossible Return) (1971):

> [...] but it is not normal to close our eyes with pudicity, warns us Manolescu. All the revision definitely does is to lay the foundation of an impressive and unequal work, victim to a lesser extent to the inherent errosion of time than to its own artistic and moral limitations.[30]

Furthermore, *Imposibila întoarcere* (*The Impossible Return*) announced, in the context of the triumph of Ceaușescu's 'July Theses', a powerful comeback of the cult of personality, of communist nationalism and of the proletarian ideals of an egalitarian society which is not only materially uniformed. Gabriel Dimisianu sees Preda's book as an indirect form of protest when facing the impossible return to the crimes of the 'Obsessive decade'. "The entire spirit of *Imposibila întoarcere* (The Impossible Return) makes the legend of threatening to kill himself not only plausible, but confirms it. Some readers later on wanted to see in the title of Marin

---

[28] Nicolae Manolescu: Revizuirile critice (Critical Revisions). In: *România literară*, nb. 6/2003. Consulted at the web adress: Consulted at the web adress: http://www.romlit.ro/revizuirile_critice [26.04.2018].
[29] Manolescu: *Istoria critică a literaturii române*, p. 951.
[30] Manolescu: *Istoria critică a literaturii române*, p. 951.

Preda's book a polemical reference to the 'July Theses' which stipulated, by falsifying history, an impossible turn back, which was unacceptable."³¹

Falsifying history seemed to be one of the 'obsessive' themes of Marin Preda, not only ontologically, but also aesthetically assumed, his prose containing a real teratology of the disastrous effects of the power excess on the world he thought atemporal. The entire moral of Ilie Moromete, the one who believes in strong ethical values, is that time is endlessly patient with people, a position that reflects the utopian perspective of the writer at the end of the dramatic war.

But the question of morality in art is a constant preoccupation of the writer, a sign that he lives under the pressure of acute awareness of powerful immorality, a fact visible especially in some of his fellows, the example of Petru Dumitriu being relevant. From the act of reading to the act of writing, Preda's existence evolves around major examples of 'moral' novelists, and the constant models are those of Tolstoi and Dostoievski. Their readings provoke "the first moral convulsion",³² while his commentaries referring to the example of Tolstoi's morality,³³ are relevant. Having regrets that "we have few works reflecting the life of the working class, the life of the party and of the work in the party, the history of great constructions",³⁴ as can be read in the interview given in 1956 to S. Damian, leading to the conviction that Tolstoi was right when he emphasised "the irrational character from the point of view of people, of historical events" or that "from the point of view of human morals, the great historical characters cannot be cleared of guilt",³⁵ as his later affirmations, in 1975 show, the need for the moral revising of the writer more than necessary can be be seen. Furthermore, Preda's moral philosophy has certain extrapolations in his work, from the stories in *Întâlnirea din pământuri* (The Meeting between the Lands*)* (1942) to *Moromeții I* (1955) the feeling of tragedy that surrounds the rural world, which do not overcome the boundaries of immediate existence. It is reduced to the immediate practical existence, having a mundane function, being reduced to the immediate relations of the peasant to its own world. On the other side, in the second phase of his creations, from *Moromeții II* (1967), to *Delirul* (The Raving) (1975) or to *Cel mai iubit*

---

31 See Gabriel Dimisianu: Recitind *Imposibila Întoarcere* (Re-reading the *Impossible Return*). In: *România literară*, nb. 42/2010. Consulted at the web address: http://www.romlit.ro/index.pl/recitind_imposibila_ntoarcere [23.05.2018].
32 Florin Mugur: *Convorbiri cu Marin Preda* (Conversations with Marin Preda). București: Albatros 1973, p. 67.
33 See Mugur: *Convorbiri cu Marin Preda*, p. 62–63.
34 Marin Preda: *Timpul n-a mai avut răbdare cu oamenii* (The Time wasn't patient with people anymore). București: Cartea Românească 1981, p. 520.
35 Preda: *Timpul n-a mai avut răbdare cu oamenii*, p. 540.

dintre pământeni (The Most Beloved Man on Earth) (1980), we witness a transfiguration of the tragic that affects people, not just the man in the individuality of his existence. It is a political category of the tragic which makes man abandon his resistance when facing history. From the utilitarian morals of the first writings, to the existentialist one of Plato's *Republic*, exposed and victimized by the excess of power, Preda's image is a representative one. Between the portrait of the artist as a young man, in *Moromeții*, and the one in *Delirul* (The Raving) or in the novel *Cel mai iubit dintre pământeni* (The Most Beloved Man on Earth), we see the exponential image of a writer in successive phases of the 42 years of Romanian communism, as Preda is one of the few prose writers who covers a tragic history in all his phases.

Beyond the empty rhetoric formulas, in the socialist-communist key, which must be seen as an escape from censorship, Marin Preda's destiny, in the context of "the literary war generation"[36] is more complex than the one of the next generation, of those known as the "sixties' generation".[37] Then, when in 1953 he wishes, at the end of a letter to Geo Dumitrescu "Marx and Engels be with you. Agâp!",[38] the ironic code of the wish, of evident recognition of replacing dogmas and entering the political area which will annihilate the spirit can not be ignored. Moreover, in 1975, he still believed, in reminiscence of the anterior period, that of ideological relaxation, that "All human beings existent on Earth make history",[39] and this is visible in *Delirul* (The Raving) and, even more than that, literature is considered an effect of history, anticipating the effects of the neo-historians, led by Stephen Greenblatt, who saw the context of power, under Foucault's influence, as being determining, functioning as a complex relationship that influences even literature. Preda's epic phases reflect, more than other writers of the period, the understanding of history in its discontinuity, being of the same conception with the epistemic fracture between the phases of history that Michel Foucault also uses in his philosophy, a concept that forms the basis of the theory of the neo-historians, who propose literature as reflection on the historical episteme. Preda belives that "The concept of literature evolves differently from one generation to the other. Not aesthetically. But it is linked to the

---

36 Emil Manu: *Generația literară a războiului* (The Literary Generation of War). București: Curtea Veche 2000.
37 See Gabriel Dimisianu's article, suggestively entitled: Generația mea în anii 60 (My Generation in the 60's). In: *România literară*, nb. 13/2008. Accessed at the web adress: http://www.romlit.ro/index.pl/generaia_mea_n_anii_60 [23.05.2018].
38 Preda: *Timpul n-a mai avut răbdare cu oamenii*, p. 518.
39 Preda: *Timpul n-a mai avut răbdare cu oamenii*, p. 537.

mentality and prejudices of all times."⁴⁰ In this context, of becoming conscientious and accepting social pragmatic change, the imagination exercise proposed by Preda in 1974, that of estimating Sadoveanu's re-appearance in the 70's, would lead to an incompatibility. The feeling of the natural, so predominant in the first part of Sadoveanu's works, would be troubled. But not only the feeling of the natural, but also of historical iconicity, of its dogmatic character would seem troubled in Sadoveanu's work. If the natural feeling of the 1970s would have been incomprehensible for Sadoveanu, when compared to the one in *Țara de dincolo de negură* (The Country beyond Mist) (1926) or *Împărăția apelor* (The Kingdom of the Waters) (1982), the historicism of these years would have been absurd, the canonical prose-writer being in a certain misunderstanding of the historical episteme. The anti-humanism of the history of the '50s seemed incomprehensible to the one who militated implicitly for the recognition of the equilibrium of man with nature and history, and their reconciliation in the first half of the century. So, the difference between his novels at the beginning of the century, such as *Neamul Șoimăreștilor* (The *Șoimărești* Kin) (1915) and those of the '50s, such as *Mitrea Cocor* (1949) or *Nicoară Potcoavă* (1952) can be explained.

At the same time, Marin Preda's abiding conviction is that the role of art is to transgress reality, to free us from the whirlings of history,⁴¹ therefore to transcend the social, ethical gridlocks of totalitarian power, and denouncing them subversively, which happens explicitly in *Delirul* (The Raving) or in *Cel mai iubit dintre pământeni* (The Most Beloved Man on Earth). The poetics of subversiveness presupposes, therefore, to denounce the excesses of officialized power, through allusive, indirect techniques of the novel, from suggestion to allegory or parable, using the formulas of indirect writing or the instrument of irony, comparable to the poetics of the Barthian 'un-told' from *A Lover's Discourse: Fragments*. The novel in aggressive epochs contains silent knowledge which is expressed through allusions and suggestions. This way the 'un-told' is a symptom of conscience and knowledge, but also of becoming aware of the limits imposed by coercive power.

An exercise of the un-told is the novel *Moromeții*, "a novel of silences, of things half said, of presuppositions: an iceberg with a small part above, floating deeply sunken in the water of an entire linguistic universe, of an entire ideology, of a spirituality which all are ours and on the bases of which the novel is constructed."⁴² With Ilie Moromete, Marin Preda proposes the "theme of the

---

40 Preda: *Timpul n-a mai avut răbdare cu oamenii*, p. 535.
41 See Mugur: *Convorbiri cu Marin Preda*, p. 72.
42 Vasile Popovici: *Marin Preda-Timpul dialogului* (Marin Preda-Time of Dialogue). București: Cartea Românească 1983, p. 42.

contemplative man"[43] or of the one who lives with the same conviction as Sandu, Tita's husband, that the 'disease' which infiltrated the Romanian village would be fatal to him, too. For the first time, the prose-writer is aware of the 'vice' of contemplation and understands, in the context of the 'Obsessive decade', the risk of all major misfortunes which were brought with this one, therefore the risk of passivization, which would become a certainty in *Cel mai iubit dintre pământeni* (The Most Beloved Man on Earth).

Ilie Moromete's contemplative state can be associated with a type of passivity of the Subject when faced with excessive power, an attitude that is precursory to the passivity in the second volume, which leads to his death and therefore gains a symbolic function. The passivization of the subject is a progressive process of history which is dominated by active Subjects, such as Dinu Păturică, a power that turns into aggression. The Subject is in an evident process of passivization, and the association to Don Quijote is contradicted by the author.

"My Moromete is also contemplative, and his drama is the drama of contemplation, which I have mentioned earlier. His illusions are present, true, but he does not act. To be a Don Quijote, Moromete should have acted in the spirit of his illusions."[44] Within the profile of Moromete the character, the struggle with illusions or utopias can be observed, for example with the illusion of a world without money, a society of exchange in which the peasant can keep his freedom or dependency on his land, his work and the goods exchange mechanism. Exclusively preoccupied with life as "a miracle to contemplate",[45] his track describes a tragic trajectory of contemplation failing in passivity and isolation.

The tragedy of the subject facing the excess of power denounces a 'sin' of the last century which attains a threshold of human cruelty, unimaginable even by the dystopias of the beginning of century. This 'sin' of the century is that of "having proved that things we thought unimaginable, beyond the limits of human meanness, are yet possible."[46] In other words, the capital guilt of his century is that "it has made doubt towards man slip into human consciousness."[47] This is the critical point of Marin Preda's morality, practised in his epic models, sometimes invoked and exersized in his novels. The moral of oppressive history, or the excess of power performed by his puppets till the passivization of the Subject is the down layer of his novels. "The polemical

---

[43] See Mugur: *Convorbiri cu Marin Preda*, p. 84.
[44] See Mugur: *Convorbiri cu Marin Preda*, p. 86.
[45] See Mugur: *Convorbiri cu Marin Preda*, p. 89.
[46] See Mugur: *Convorbiri cu Marin Preda*, p. 128.
[47] See Mugur: *Convorbiri cu Marin Preda*, p. 128–129.

substratum",[48] evident in *Intrusul* (The Intruder) (1968), *Marele singuratic* (The Great Loner) (1972) or *Delirul* (The Raving) (1975) is fundamental to Marin Preda's poetics, which practiced an indirect message, engaging a critical message of political excesses.

But the surcharge of this polemic substratum, critical to the excesses of political power, generates the polemic overabundance in Preda's novels. Moreover, the surplus of immediate, factual history seldom creates the impression of submission to the canon of manipulated history, a fact which accentuates the dilemma of placing Preda in the category of subversive or obedient writers. At a certain point, if taking into account *Cel mai iubit dintre pământeni* (The Most Beloved Man on Earth), there aren't any clues that will endorse the subversiveness of the discourse, in spite of the ample debates between Ion Micu and Victor Petrini about the morality or immorality of history. The extreme anchorage in the obscurity of the fifth decade of the century, situational and polemical, reducing the entire moral discourse to the immorality of the excess culture of these years, makes us believe that the novel exposes, in the spirit of the '60's, the crimes of Stalinism in contrast to the 'illuminated' despotism of the period during which the novel was written. Plus, the improbability of the path of the Subject in *Cel mai iubit dintre pământeni* (The Most Beloved Man on Earth) is evident and reminds us of the second volume of *Moromeții*, especially due to the direct critical intention, non-implicit, which forms the basis of the novel.[49] This time we have the impression of confirming past history and, nonetheless, negating the history contemporary to the author. The unrealistic disequilibrium of the novel consists in the intentional evidence of configuring a process of Stalinism and to demonstrate its excess of power. This historical exaggeration, visible also in the ample debates of political philosophy, is to be found in artificial situations, be they either of social nature or erotic, or also in the political and philosophical comments placed in the dissenting actions of certain situations.

The caducity of the epic in the second part of his creation is noticed by literary critics, exactly there wherein Preda has the intention to replace the natural morals of Moromete with historical ones, of a political nature. Manolescu, for

---

[48] See Mihai Ungheanu (ed.): *Marin Preda*. Argument and anthology by Mihai Ungheanu. București: Eminescu 1976, p. 8.

[49] See, for example, the commentary of Alex Ștefănescu: La o nouă lectură: Marin Preda-*Cel mai iubit dintre pământeni* (Towards a new reading of Marin Preda – *The Most Beloved Man on Earth*). In: *România literară*, nb. 10/2004. Consulted at the web adress: http://www.romlit.ro/marin_preda___cel_mai_iubit_dintre_pmnteni_[26.04.2018]. He observes the neverosimility of the biographical path of the character, the ample carceral description and the possibility to write "a relation towards God" or towards a judge of 1200 pages in a communist prison.

example, accuses the lack of actuality of the epic flow, invoking facts, such as "In communist prisons convicts did not have pencil and paper", therefore the non-conformity of fiction to reality, Petrini's impossibility to write a "written record" being an implicit critique of history in prison. But the "Era of the Villans" has greater reference, with an extensive subversive meaning, as the action is placed in the '50s. It is what the critic names "novel with a key". The key derives from all these:

> Injustices, persecutions, political prisons, sometimes linked to historical personalities (although, unlike *Delirul* (The Raving), none of them with the real name, as at least for a generation of readers, *Cel mai iubit dintre pământeni* (The Most Beloved Man on Earth) can be considered, such as *Bietul Ioanide* (Pitiful Ioanide) or *Scrinul negru* (The Black Chest-of-Drawers), a novel with a key.[50]

But the inauthenticity of the novel consists in the hybridisation of the genre, mixing the exposing novel, that of social critique, and the adventure novel, the erotic one or the essay meditation type, as an X-ray of an aggressed conscience, owing moral explanations. The counterbalance between action and essay accentuates the impression of inauthenticity due to the aesthetical and situational hybridisation.[51] The fact that History tends to become an active Subject of the novel and to dominate a subject that becomes an actant, such as Petrini, contributes to this impression of inequality and improbability. Nevertheless, the author does not accept the historical interpretation of his novels, even where the historical reference is obvious, such as in *Delirul* (The Raving) (1975), in which the issues of the devastating effects of absolute power are followed explicitly. The interest of Preda was to deconstruct the idea of the fatality of history.

Preda mentions that in the novel *Delirul* (The Raving) historical characters are named without avoidance strategies or strategies to avoid a too direct implication in the immediate reality. Therefore, the inclusion of the novel in the category of historical novels would be inappropriate. The justification is that in order to fulfil the "theme of the storyteller" who lives in an aggressive history, he must expose and denounce a precise context which has generated the excess of power, or he is forced to decipher "the paroxism of political history".[52] The justification of the context of the excess of power and for dashing authentic, moral destinies, arises as an arch-theme of *Delirul* (The Raving) and *Cel mai iubit dintre pământeni* (The Most Beloved Man on Earth).

---

50 Manolescu: *Istoria critică a literaturii române*, p. 963.
51 See Ștefănescu: La o nouă lectură.
52 See Ungheanu. In Preda: *Timpul n-a mai avut răbdare cu oamenii*, p. 538.

In *Delirul* (The Raving), the young journalist Paul Ștefan, Niculae Moromete's cousin, a character which could be included in the post-war category of characters, such as Toma Pahonțu in Rebreanu's *Gorila* (Gorilla), who is the hypostasis of the political effects of the gorilla on the individual. As in Rebreanu's case, *Delirul* (The Raving) is a novel of contemporaneity, in spite of the fact that it refers to a 1945 reality, therefore 30 years before the moment of the publishing. It is, says Eugen Simion, "The novel of a collective destiny in a troubled and tragic epoch" which portrays "the contagiousness of history".[53]

In *Delirul* (The Raving) we encounter two hysterias, two ravings: one of erotic instinctiveness, provoked by the beauty of a woman, Luchi, loved by three men and the other, an aggressive one, of violence till extreme cruelty, antihuman, represented by the character Hitler. The latter type is 'delirium furens', "without limits of ferocity and revenge" of the tragic history provoked by the excess of power which leads to enthropy. Delirious history generates unconscious hysteria, without any perspective, felt by the 'delirious man', capable of atrocious crimes, such as the novel tells us:

> A delirious man smashes and destroys everything in his way. But what can a man find in his way? His own house and at least the neighbourhood in which he could run thoughtless with a knife in his hand. He is quickly caught and thrown by human arms, just like his, in a van which has recently been called. But if we replace the neighbourhood with a continent and the individual orders with powerful weapons? His words and decisions become historical acts. Through his delirium history is expressed in its own delirium... So thought, shivery, all those present sensing their will melting and their thought failing once again when facing the decisions of this bizarre man, without identity, almost abstract through his total lack of reason and humanity... They were all with him, adhering to his expansion ideas on the surface of the earth and through fear his killer gestures could cost their lives... Yes, they were there with him, but where was he taking them, towards which abysses?![54]

So, the raving or the delirium of history describes the causes and passivization process of the Subject under the pressure of devastating fatalism. Preda's interest is to reveal the sources of evil through the instrument called literature. The prose writer exposes, through the evolution of his characters, a transition from the firm opposition facing evil, to the excessive and absolute power which ends in enthropic, devastating power, towards passivization, by renouncing every reaction, to the acceptance of the status of victim. The failure in *Delirul* (The Raving), similar to that one in *Cel mai iubit dintre pământeni* (The Most Beloved Man on Earth), consists in the excess of oppressive history, to the detriment of

---

53 Eugen Simion: *Scriitori români de azi* (Romanian Writers Today). Vol. II. București-Chișinău: Litera 2002, p. 251.
54 Marin Preda: *Delirul* (The Raving). București: Cartea Românească 1987, p. 367.

the character, therefore in the excessive dramatization of history. Furthermore, Eugen Simion observed this insufficiency of the novel, or even of the novels, in spite of the refusal of the author to interpret his novel as a historical one: "The objections that can be brought to the prose-writer are not the fact that he brought history into the novel, but something else: that history tends to dominate fiction, in an overwhelming way."[55]

History and its puppets become the Subject and the Subject, Paul Ștefan or Victor Petrini, are passive actants, silent observers of the individuality crises, of the delirium of 'the new man'. The impersonalization of the actant in the collectivist mass translates exactly the success of oppression methods. Inevitably, the process of history or "the era of the scoundrels" is the central nucleus of his novels in the second part of his creation period, a fact which supports the idea of reading Preda as a subversive author. Also, in the process of the excess of power, the author sacrifices involuntarily the Subject, passivizes it gradually till his disappearance, through impersonalization. Most often the excessive dramatizing of the concrete, the explicit exposure of some given historical situations and the minuteness of the descriptions keep the historical contact and make Preda's novel a novel of its time. It is a genre similarly improbable to that of Camil Petrescu and Lucian Blaga in their historical dramas. Anchored excessively into an excessive, anti-humanist history, characters tend to become artificial, to become simple transmitters of preconceived messages. This puppet theatre steals the power of the Subjects to act individually, becoming passive when faced with an excess of power of a time which they only complain about, such as the Shakespearian Hamlet 'out of joint' time. The only one who dramatizes history is the author, the Subjects being defeated, passive, totally addicted to their puppeteer author.

4.2.2 The Most Passive Man on Earth. Illusions, Isolation and Passivity

In September 1977, Marin Preda stated that, after the novel *Delirul* (The Raving), his intention was to offer a sequel to it. After *Viața ca o pradă* (Life as a Prey), the prose-writer affirmed that he worked intensely on another project, "another novel, which is not easy at all. The surprise is total for me too, especially that I am working on the novel with passion, meaning with all the strength, it is not, in other words, an expectation or a transition book. It might be, as we usually

---

[55] Simion: *Scriitori români de azi*, p. 254.

think, the most important book I am writing after *Moromeții*."⁵⁶ The stake of this project is confessed in an interview given to Geo Șerban in which we find out that he is not writing a second volume of *Delirul* (The Raving), "but something that has resulted out of the intention of taking the reader onto another route."⁵⁷ This intention of the prose-writer is born out of the obsession of the total novel, of a novel that synthesises all the existential, historical and aesthetical experiences accumulated so far. It is what Marin Sorescu saw in this novel, "a book of a conscience and an epoch".⁵⁸

The poetics of "the complete novel" is one of experiential unveiling, meaning an attempt "to reveal an entire experience", a direct synthesis of limits and excesses exposed till then in Preda's novels, as he invokes the experiment *Delirul* (The Raving). He would confess here that he projected a novel in which "I want to say everything [...] with the risk of agglomerating things". This dreamt of genre, a poetical utopia, no doubt, is, as Eugen Simion argued, in the first edition of the 1987 preface, "the novel of a destiny that assumes a history, the novel of a history which lives through a destiny."⁵⁹

The historical process started by Marin Preda in the novel *Delirul* (The Raving) and continued in this "complete novel", *Cel mai iubit dintre pământeni* (The Most Beloved Man on Earth), is instrumented this time with the discursive arms of an apparent distancing from reality, those of anonymity, the camouflage of real identities of the characters and those of the meditative distancing from the evoked time. Petrini's long meditative process reminds us of Preda's first epical texts. Furthermore, analysing the texts written during 'his youth', so in the first part of his creation, Vasile Popovici observed that "they are all animated by a unique spirit and a unique narrative technique and, furthermore, the common feeling of parting from their world."⁶⁰

Thematically, we observe a repetition of the topics already used by Marin Preda, from the effects of history to the denaturization of human individuality, as in *Moromeții* or *Marele singuratic* (The Great Loner), to the failure of family or affective relationships and also at the loss of individuality in collectiveness. The novel, written in ten parts, follows the destiny of the university professor Victor Petrini related to two kinds of liberties he tries and does not succeed in

---

56 Marin Preda: *Creație și morală* (Creation and Morals). Edition by Victor Crăciun și Corneliu Popescu. Preface and notes by Victor Crăciun. București: Cartea Românească 1989, p. 518.
57 Preda: *Timpul n-a mai avut răbdare cu oamenii*, p. 565.
58 See Preda: *Timpul n-a mai avut răbdare cu oamenii*, p. 30.
59 Eugen Simion: Preface. In: Marin Preda: *Cel mai iubit dintre pământeni* (The Most Beloved Man on Earth). București: Cartea Românească 1987, p. 7.
60 Popovici: *Marin Preda-Timpul dialogului*, p. 7.

preserving: civic liberty, escaping prison, being innocent, and affective liberty, related to the types of love relationships with which he experiments, with Nineta, Căprioara, Matilda or Suzy.

The central position in this biographical pathway is attributed to Victor Petrini, whose biography is segmented by the juxtaposition of dramatic events, such as the death and suspect disappearance of Căprioara, his arrest on the eve of his daughter's baptism ceremony, having been accused of collaboration, his self-defence murders and his divorce from Matilda. The erotic plot is dominated by Victor Petrini's relationship with Matilda, the wife of his colleague from the Faculty of Philosophy, Petrică Nicolau, while the social level shows Petrini being accused of complicity to the actions of a counter-revolutionary group, 'The Black Cloaks' and he is sentenced to hard labour in the lead mine in Baia-Sprie. Petrini murdered the guardian who threatened his life, working as a rat catcher, as a turner in the tractor factory or as an accountant in the moment of illusory freedom, all being exponential phases meant to illustrate the process of the elimination of intellectuals from public life. The supreme argument of Petrini's political condemnation is to be found in the phrase "Waiting for your orders!", spoken ludically by a character in his correspondence with a friend from his youth. It is a formula over-interpreted by security, a kind of 'misreading' of the active power till oppression, similar to that of Dinu Păturică in the reading of Machiavelli's *Prince*.

But the excess of power is denounced by the author in many directions, starting with the sinuosity of the character's biographical destiny, including the juxtaposing of the levels, erotic and social. While working as an accountant at the package collecting factory, Petrini falls in love with the daughter of an inter-war ex-factory-owner, Suzy Culala, who was excluded from the social scene, expelled from college due to her 'unhealthy origin', a central point in the communist levelling ideology, of a valid unique social class, i.e. the working class. Therefore, the affective and social destiny intermingle, Preda trying to bring forth the image of the victims, the excluded who meet at the margins of society in trying to survive at least through love, a climax of the novel, but also a sign of final passivity. Committing a new murder, also in self defence, when they are attacked by Suzy's ex-husband, Petrini dreams of a reduction of the sentence. This salvation is moderated by his ex-wife Matilda, married to Mircea, a representative of power who, upon her insistence, could intervene in his favour in front of the judge. Victor Petrini writes a plea in which he attempts to provide an ultimately conscience clearing and illusory explanation.

The authenticity of the confession of Petrini's last memoir consists of going back to the first person narrative and creates the illusion of the authenticity of memory. Sliding towards the third person narrative of the dramatic events that definitely mark his existence and the first person narrative of the ending, he has the aim of creating at least the illusion of an assumed, authentic destiny, ultimately overcome through the act of confession.

The narrator subject is shocked by the "barbarity of the concrete", which dominates this fake journal. The formula of journalistic authenticity is not representative for the '80s but it has anticipative power, announcing the explosion of the prison memoirs of the '90s. The sincerity of the saved memory seems a valid mechanism of recomposing the effects of the Stalinist terror of the '50s and not only of exposing any excessive history.

Petrini's confession functions as a salvation from the epic improbability of the epic blend. His confessional memoir is a return to the written record of his own conscience at the interference with history, but also a final record of the passivization of the Subject oppressed by the excessive power of the system and the lack of love. Crohmălniceanu talks about the same "outstanding victory of authenticity" when he refers to "the style in *Moromeții*".[61] The reduction of the perspective to the Subject, on his pathway of withdrawing from love and forced out of the world, proves just the poetics of passivization, the recognition of the status of the excluded, of the status of the Subject as victim, who therefore becomes the Agent.

> The voice we are listening to no matter how auctorial, is relativized slowly, in a permanent scenic style. We are constantly offered the possibility to judge things with our own mind, independently of Petrini. The confession becomes a played monologue, allowing its situation in the space of the realities evoked by the narration. It is the stunning victory of authenticity.[62]

We are not dealing with the struggle of staying or surviving at any price within the social structure and of conserving it, such as in *Moromeții*, with the attempt to keep the active force, and neither with the process of accentuated reflexivity in *Intrusul* (The Intruder). The trajectory of the subject in *Cel mai iubit dintre pământeni* (The Most Beloved Man on Earth) is followed, as a natural consequence of the historical effect, by passivity as a unique and surviving formula. Passivity appears as a natural effect of an imperfect human nature, but also as a result of exercising abusive power, sometimes problematized by Ion Micu and Victor Petrini in their attempt to articulate a new moral code, a natural code offering the possiblility of humanity's salvation. This time the subject distances himself from active oppressiveness of collective power, and also the cheating and illusory haloes of its reflexivity.

Passivization is a continuous 'estrangement' of Ilie Moromete or of Vasile Catrina's 'confusion' in the short story *Colina* (The Hill). This is the true code in

---

61 Preda: *Timpul n-a mai avut răbdare cu oamenii*, p. 386–393.
62 See Crohmălniceanu: In Preda: *Timpul n-a mai avut răbdare cu oamenii*, p. 393.

which the Subject of Preda's final novel can be read. The acceptance of defeat, the passivization of the last Moromete defeated by an oppressive and absurd power, is the hidden manifesto of the novel *Cel mai iubit dintre pământeni* (The Most Beloved Man on Earth). The subversiveness of the novel consists only directly in "attacking the forbidden areas of the obsessive decades-political inquiry, manipulation, the degradation and mutilation of the individual in a system which was politically fanatic, the detention and horrors of the oppression, the persecution of the intellectuals."[63] The real 'subterranean code' is the one of the Subject exponentially defeated, who passively witnessed the dismembrance of a world and even to the dismembrance of his own conscience. The shift towards confession, towards the relativized, estranged and confused voice of Petrini, in one last effort of reconstruction of the human morality in a completely immoral world, is a stage of the passivization process. Certainly Preda's scholarly resources are to be found in Descartes and Kierkegaard, as Alexandru Paleologu observes, and reprojected in "the later-ego of the philosopher Petrini".[64]

Marin Preda proves his abilities in reconstructing an atemporal, matrix-like history, as Blaga would call it, therefore without the historical chronophagy and the classical descriptions of the prose-writer immortalizing a frozen, archaic world. This is also the reason for which it reminds us of a theme's recurrence or of an archaic background, as "My favourite themes are those taken from the peasants' world. I have been dominated all the time by the feeling of the universe of my peasant childhood, which I wanted to reconstruct."[65]

The characters in *Întâlnirea din pământuri* (The Meeting between the Lands) and *Moromeții* seem sometimes more authentic from this point of view than those of the novel *Cel mai iubit dintre pământeni* (The Most Beloved Man on Earth). The impression Petrini gives is that he is part of the Moromete family, that he is one of the sons of Ilie Moromete, who has regained his paternal conscience to see it diluted in the end, when facing the excesses of time. Petrini's inertia suggests not only the passivity in front of excessive power, but also the artificial novelty of the character, the fact that he is history. A victim of time, Petrini becomes a victim of the prose-writer, losing his important position in the epical construction in favour of a hostile unfolding of the world. The anticipation of the last Ilie Moromete, powerful when facing his rebellious sons, according to which the world would crash when the Subject did not self-determine his destiny, but would obey the world, is the spectrum of passivity which dominates Marin Preda's last novel.

---

63 Rodica Zane: *Marin Preda. Monografie, antologie comentată, receptare critică* (Marin Preda. Monography, commented anthology, critical reception). Brașov: Aula 2001, p. 35.
64 See Paleologu. In: Preda: *Timpul n-a mai avut răbdare cu oamenii*, p. 57.
65 Preda: *Creație și morală*, p. 320.

Ilie Moromete could not understand his conflict with the excess of power which unfolded threateningly around himself, while Victor Petrini did not have anything else to understand in a world taken over by oppressive power:

> I did everything I had to, Moromete started again with effort, I gave everything there was, I gave each what they wanted… What else was I supposed to do and I didn't do? What was to be done and I stood aside and didn't care? Did they tell me to give them something and I said no? Did anybody ask for something from me and I said no? Did anybody show me a better way for them that I avoided because I wanted so? They did what the world said, they didn't do what I said! And if the world is as they say and not as I say, what's left to be done?! Let them sink! First the world and then they will go with it.[66]

Petrini's opposition towards the world in which he cannot find himself betrays the acceptance of a limited situation that he cannot transgress. The Subject accepts his defeat, meaning that he is passive in relation to the history that unfolds over him as a wave, within the sunken world. And this passivization is produced even against the author's will, because "Preda does not like defeated people and he does not like the perspective of subduedness in literature."[67] Even so, in his discussion with Suzy, Petrini explains to her and to us "the salvation of the defeated" during a time of crisis. Cynically, Petrini concludes that "The salvation of the defeated, I said: no chance!", which paraphrases inclusively the death of the last man with a free spirit.

The discrepancies between the rural novels and the urban ones, are stylistic but also of a calibration of the conflict according to a new historical reality. Also, Eugen Simion explains the differences related to the fact that rural novels "are more open to a world in which values are calmer, rounder, they are perfect."[68] The subject of the urban novel does not assume the object entirely (which is also not possible), the tension of the idea hindering the calmness of the style. For the critic the character is searching for a new religion or a new ideology, as the harsh rural moral does not satisfy him anymore, being defeated by time with which it is in conflict. The attempt to assume this new world, and also the moral recalibration in accordance with the social raving are meant to fail.

Petrini's defeat reminds us of other parabolas of passivization in the context of the '70s, of Ceaușescu's 'cultural revolution'. For example, Mihai Bogdan, the character in the novel *Absenții* (The Absents) (1970), by Augustin Buzura, has a trajectory similar to that of Victor Petrini. The researcher Mihai Bogdan is forced by authorities to lie for years, giving the results of his research to the doctor Ion

---

66 Marin Preda: *Moromeții*. București: Cartea Românească 1981, p. 452–453.
67 Simion. In: Preda: *Timpul n-a mai avut răbdare cu oamenii*, p. 142.
68 Simion. In: Preda: *Timpul n-a mai avut răbdare cu oamenii*, p. 142.

4.2 *The Most Beloved Man on Earth* and the Passivization of the Subject — 191

Poenaru, who is given recognition for it, assuming it in a dishonest manner. The psychiatrist Mihai Bogdan is outraged, but his revolt is translated just in the reaction of a defeated, passive man:

> I, in reality, was only an object which could have been easily moved here and there, a dynamic furniture piece, tamed, having a cassette recorder and which wondered with certain anxiety, quickly, according to the situation: what role am I supposed to interpret now? An idiot? A deaf and dumb? An indifferent one? A closet? When daily, for at least about a decade, I have been lying to myself, alone, violently, why do I have to ingest other people's lies, and even spread them as truths? But do I know if I have the right to shout that nobody cares about anybody's psychological structure, as I was running from myself?[69]

But Victor Petrini's torn destiny does is not reminiscent of Mihai Bogdan's destiny, but also of an entire category of these passivized Subjects faced with the excess of communist power. More novels after the '70s describe characters looking for a form of survival, such as Ion Cristian in the novel *Orgolii* (Vanities) (1974) by Augustin Buzura, Gabriel Dimancea in the novel *Vara baroc* (Summer Baroque) (1980) of Paul Georgescu or even Mitică and Nela in the novel *Balanța* (The Balance) (1985), of Ion Băieșu, or even the characters of teachers or doctors exposed to the oppressive power who end up in a passive state is much higher. The prevalence of this category makes us believe that we are dealing with an archi-character of the novels of the time which translates the denouncing of a challenging time, of a real "time of the scoundrels".

This time, which leads to the defeat of the Subject, produces an overthrow of the tragic, as the effects of the power on people are more acute and more dehumanising, the more the understanding of the tragic seems to be worn off. The subjects do not seem to understand the tragic in itself, as a consequence of the ideologization and of the threat of the supreme tragic, death, generalised entropy. At the same time, a society without the tragic element is a passivized society. Mircea Zaciu, who comments on the fragment in the novel that refers to the disappearance of the tragic, admits that we are facing a real occultation of death in conscience. He says death is "a source of tragic, more present as anytime in this century, is hidden in the conscience, it is occulted."[70] Furthermore, Ion Micu confirms to Petrini that the lack of the tragic makes the tragedy even greater. Therefore, the tragic offers the pulsation of life, the awareness that a fundamental evil, that of history, is aggressive, powerful and threatens the human definitively. The absence of the tragic in the characters' lives, its misunderstanding and translated into a passive attitude when faced with the conflicts of life, therefore with an

---

[69] Augustin Buzura: *Absenții* (The Absents). București: Litera 2008, p. 233.
[70] Mircea Zaciu. In: Preda: *Timpul n-a mai avut răbdare cu oamenii*, p. 265.

excess of power. Such is Petrini's ataraxy translated, which is in fact a passivization of the Subject faced with a hallucinate power which functions eventually as a generalized paralysis of collectiveness.

The generalization of passivity confers eventually a historical character, either political or historical, reconstructing indirectly some concealed truth, composed inclusively of truthful details. Commenting on the fragment from the novel which refers to the escape from the mine, a fragment which has a real echo, told by Ion Ioanid in his detention memoirs, *Închisoarea noastră cea de toate zilele* (Our Everyday Prison), Nicolae Manolescu transgresses again the limits of the fictional pact towards biographic or historicism. "Preda transforms the escaped inmates in his novel into notorious snitches who, once caught, are taken to Pitești and re-educated to become tormentors. It is hard to understand why the novelist mixes things in this dishonest manner."[71] Beyond the fact that 'dishonesty' cannot be a valid evaluative category, the episode of the escape has the role to invoke history, in its factological fragmentariness, to intensify the feeling of atrocity. For the sake of the fictional pact, the escaped are not the characters of Ioanid's memory; neither is the image of the "great philosopher" that of Lucian Blaga, nor is I. D. Sârbu's, "the athlete of misery", with his tragic Periprava destiny in the communist prison, identifiable with Victor Petrini. The distinction between history and fiction is one of the fundamental characteristics of the criteria for "signing the fictional pact", the meta-literary pact, exposed by Eco, therefore a fundamental condition of objective distancing. Even in the case of the novel which shows the anti-humanism of the aggressive history, placing the true fact between the brackets is essential. Therefore, Umberto Eco affirmed:

> [...] to read fiction means to play a game by which we give sense to the immensity of things that happened, are happening, or will happen in the actual world. By reading narrations, we escape the anxiety that attacks us when we try to say something true about the world.[72]

Taken over by the anxiety of the impossibility to reconstruct the truth of the history accurately, the prose-writer operates with narrative distance, necessary to find the meaning of the history, besides concealed biographies. Maybe the most important function of the story in general, and of the novel in particular is "the consoling function of narrative", the spring of the Italian theoretician's wanderings through "the narrative woods". This formula explains "the reason people tell stories, and have told stories from the beginning of time. And it has always been the paramount function of myth: to find a shape, a form, in the turmoil of human

---

[71] Manolescu: *Istoria critică a literaturii române*, p. 964.
[72] Eco: *Six walks*, p. 87.

4.2 The Most Beloved Man on Earth and the Passivization of the Subject — 193

experience."[73] Through myths, novels are confronted with the disintegrating and atomizing power of history, and tend to find "a formula to give meaning to our existence".[74]

Preda's novel dramatizes a situation in which a specific power became epistemological,[75] meaning that the prose-writer follows the destiny of the Subject in the panopticist society, from correctional institutions (security, salt mine, prison) to the working institutions of an oppressed society (deratisation, factory, state socialist industry). The case is more an exponential one, exposing the excess through a thematic synthesis, such as: "political investigation, manipulation, degradation and manipulation of the individual in a fanatic political system, detention and the horrors of the oppression, the subjugation of the intellectuals."[76]

Towards the passivization of the character, the key moment is that in which we witness the debate between Ion Micu and Victor Petrini, with reference to the meanings of power and its equilibration. Here the two intellectuals revise the philosophical ideas that are the basis of a philosophy of power which is in the benefit of the person. This is Marin Preda's epic strategy, through which the author tries to continue the critique of the excess of power in *Delirul* (The Raving), a novel which not only denounces the absurd background of social power, but also absurd ideology, therefore lacking the practical function that is the basis of the oppressive communist system. A double critique is at the basis of the novel, one of 'epistemic' nature, mentioned by Foucault, and one of ideological nature, demonstrated by the debate between the two characters. The contribution of the two excesses leads to passivization, the refuge of the Subject into a state of paralyses faced with the excess of active power, meaning the denouncing of a major disequilibrium in society and at the eminency of enthropy. This debate is possible since the first volume of *Cel mai iubit dintre pământeni* (The Most Beloved Man on Earth), in which oppression is being constructed, appeared orchestrated. The dialogue between Micu and Petrini functions as an auctorial argumentation of the instruments of excessive power, the author borrowing the voice of the two characters to explain the path of passivization. If here the characters still problematize the function of the tragic, therefore ascertaining the effects of power, in the following volumes Petrini would be exclusively interested in survival and the erotic instinct, the ending of the memoir being passive.

Ion Micu explains "the power of the masses" starting from Ortega y Gasset who formulated the theory referring to the supremacy of the masses in *The Revolt*

---

[73] Eco: *Six walks*, p. 87.
[74] Eco: *Six walks*, p. 139.
[75] Foucault: *Dits et Ecrits*, p. 619.
[76] Zane: *Marin Preda*, p. 35.

of the Masses. In fact, Micu's theory functions also to explain the illusion of "the power of the working class", the utopia of a classless society, without power relations and without the risk of excesses. All masses are left with is:

> [...] to take political power, too and the great financial and economic power, which they will not use liberally. The masses are fed up with liberalism, which has no humour. They want absolute and real power, are not interested in parliamentary democracy, for example, with elections and democratic trifles. The absolute sense of power is that you are in charge of other people's fate. In elections you will get 99,80 per cent and you will be the only party that candidates. Bourgeois liberals are imbeciles, oppressed masses imposed this liberalism, now they are oppressed and they have other appetites, they are not interested in freedom any more.[77]

The absolute power of communism, meaning "power, absolute and total power" is defined by Ion Micu in the context of the absoluteness of power and in the capacity of those who possess it in order to instrument mediocrity in their favour. The background of power in the '50s is evident, but Micu's thesis is not contextualized exclusively in that period. The absolutism of power is born out of some people's capacity to exercise active power, till the excess of absolutism, meaning the power of making:

> The masses will curl at your feet, with hysteric adoration screams and you, as a 'parent', to give them laws on paper, extracted from humanity's utopian views and in reality to break them with some individuals belonging to the masses, but selected out of the most primitive, cruel, fanatic and to terrorize these masses, to anticipate their obscure accesses of authority and domination, this is what power means to some people in modern times.[78]

If in Nicolae Filimon's novels we observe the denouncement of the excesses of active power and the critique of the hierarchisation of power through the immorality of those who have it, a critique exemplified through the historical context of the act of 'misreading' Machiavellic power. Within Marin Preda's writing it is easy to notice a harsh critique of modern Machiavellianism of the excess of aggressiveness and its instrumentalisation. The debate between Micu and Petrini denounces "the Jdanov moment" of Soviet socialism and of the aggressive ideology orchestrated through terror by the ideologist of murder, Andrei Aleksandrovici Jdanov (1896–1948). In the first volume of *Cel mai iubit dintre pământeni* (The Most Beloved Man on Earth) we identify a position against the constant anathemisation of cosmopolitanism, formalism, Western decadence in their dialogue, as it was orchestrated by the Stalinist ideologists of the '50. Vladimir Tismăneanu

---

[77] Preda: *Cel mai iubit dintre pământeni*, p. 289–290.
[78] Preda: *Cel mai iubit dintre pământeni*, p. 290.

describes, in an article in 2014, the disastrous responsibilities of 'Jdanovism' on the whole socialist camp:

> As a member of Stalin's intimate circle in the years of the Great terror, he was directly responsible of mass massacres. As a supervisor of the ideology after 1945 he led enraged campaigns against those accused of 'liberalism' and 'cosmopolitism'. As exponent of the external Stalinist policy, he formulated the 'Jdanov doctrina' which divided the world manicheistically in 'two camps'. Eastern Europe belonged to the socialist one, a real and mental camp.[79]

The publishing of this novel in the '80s is possible also because of this explicit critique and therefore the novel seems to be distanced from the context of its appearance. But if following closely the destiny of the Subject and the stages of his 'passivization', overlapping the reading to the analysis of the history of communism, including the progressive re-deterioration of the economic, social situation, or of the equilibrium of power after the '1971 July Theses', we observe an implicit critique of the 'cultural revolution'[80] of the period. The Maoist spirit of Ceaușescu's 'cultural revolution' is in fact the hard nucleus of the critique of the excess of power in the novel *Cel mai iubit dintre pământeni* (The Most Beloved Man on Earth). It is also about the promotion of a critical idea referring to the equivalence between the cult of personality and 'the cultural revolution', a Stalinist metaphor of mass oppression, an umbrella formula which meant the tyranny of the personality who oppresses masses in order to preserve absolute power:

> A great leader, I continued, receives something in the form of a divine sparkle; he does not even govern, he hands over the power received from the people back and he only watches so that nobody with an appetite for the liberty he has given back will appear and to make the others kneel. He will eradicate those without mercy. Modern tyrants, the ones you are talking about, do not have this divine spark in them. If we should continue the analogy and ask ourselves what their power consists in, I would affirm that I agree with you that it is received from the masses, but they do not give it back, this kind of power is a nightmare, troubles the sleep of the tyrants and tortures them through infernal solitude… Anytime some daring people could kill them as some featherbrain wretches they are and they know this.

---

[79] For more see Vladimir Tismăneanu: Cine a fost Andrei Jdanov? Marele inchizitor și teroarea stalinistă (Who was Andrei Jdanov? The Great Inquisitor and Stalinist Terror), from 5 February 2014. Consulted at the web adress: http://www.contributors.ro/global-europa/cine-a-fost-andrei-jdanov-marele-inchizitor-si-teroarea-stalinista/ [24.05.2018].

[80] To exemplify the process of Romania's re-stalinisation durin Ceaușescu's epoch, see the documents from *Istoria comunismului din România* (The History of Communism in Romania), Volume II, entitled "Documents Nicolae Ceaușescu (1965–1971)". Mihnea Berindei, Dorin Dobrincu and Armand Goșu (eds.). Iași: Polirom 2012.

> And the masses are repressed not out of the pleasure of power, as you say, but out of the fear that these masses can revolt. Terror continues so it is necessary to discourage any idea of dignity and liberty.[81]

The terror of history, of a unique and illegitimate personality who lives the illusion of legitimacy, supported by oppression in order to preserve the absolutism of power is a direct denouncing of the context of the '80s. Gradually, Petrini's incapacity of reacting to this excessive, totalitarian power is transformed in a terror of the Subject who becomes an exponential victim of a nightmarish system.

But beyond an evident denouncing of history in Preda's novel,[82] the observation of the pathway of the Subject demonstrates the expositive character of the historical facts and the symbolic function of this torn destiny. At the beginning Victor Petrini lives under the "terror of history", then under the "terror of biography", dissolving under that of power. His final profile is that of the passive Subject facing oppressive history and regressive biography. He finally returns, when he evokes the assertion of the Saint Apostle Paul about love to one of the necessary abstractions referring to power. Petrini's destiny seems to be marked by the inactive character of power, observing an ample paradox: to be powerful means to have power but not exercise it, to have the power on yourself, absolute self-control, and the only effect of this passive power being the effect of amazement, contradiction. This confusion created in the masses by the fatalism of passivity does not ultimately mean lack of action, absence, but the fuelling and development of an elementary tension in society regarding power. The one who holds passive power, the novel teaches, increases the perplexity of the masses regarding the relation between the active and the passive of the verb 'to make', either in the sense of 'to exert' power on somebody, either to exert power on its own person and 'to be made'. This passivity means the first and last power for the Subject, in the sense exposed by Ion Micu:

> The power of the truly strong manifests like this: to know that you can destroy somebody and not do it and the other will not know. Power is of divine origin, naïve people think the God is 'angry', that he 'punishes'. Not at all![83]

Coming back in the end to the conviction of the last Preda, set forth in an interview in 1980 in the magazine *Vatra*, that the "political has its place in art",[84] especially

---

81 Preda: *Cel mai iubit dintre pământeni*, p. 292.
82 For the explanation of the 'camouflaging' of history in the novel of Marin Preda see Damian Hurezeanu: Istoria în opera lui Marin Preda (II) (The History in Marin Preda's work). In: *Apostrof*, year XXI, nb 3 (238), 2010. Consulted at the web address: http://www.revista-apostrof.ro/articole.php?id=1117 [24.05.2018].
83 Preda: *Cel mai iubit dintre pământeni*, p. 291–292.
84 See the article of Marin Preda in: *Timpul n-a mai avut răbdare cu oamenii*, p. 554.

in a period which he perceived as obsessed by the political, but not only without integrating it into the aesthetical. We observe that the novel exposes a subversive attitude of the writer on absolutist politics. The pathway of the passivization of the subject means not only a radiography of an absolute power, anti-humanist and implicitly an oppression of it, but also a form of salvation when facing these excesses. The passive power of the subject presupposes a survival form of the Romanian intellectual in communism, a conservation of power and this solution of passive power means a transgression of any system, an implicit synthesis of survival in the communist camp, possible in the '80s some years before communism fell and Steinhardt's solutions in *Jurnalul fericirii* (The Happiness Diary) appeared. Victor Petrini's memoir is, in this matter, a diary of passivity of the Subject before excessive and entropic power.

5 The Impersonalization of Power in Contemporary Novel

"I think the road to heaven is paved with *sarmale*."[1]

5.1 The Memory of Power, the Power of Memory and the Narrative Typology of the Postcommunist Novel

5.1.1 Memory, History, Novel-a Variable Balance

"Don't ever forget that only by opposing History in itself we can face history nowadays."[2]

In his iconic text about *The Tragedy of Central Europe*,[3] which is fundamental in defining Central European specificity at the crossroads of the centuries, Milan Kundera admits that the illustrative texts, configuring this diffuse identity, are Hermann Broch's *The Sleepwalkers*, Robert Musil's *The Man without Qualities* or Jaroslav Hasek's *The God Soldier Schweik*. The perspective of Broch, Musil or Hasek is an entropic one, therefore foreshadowing partly the ending of history, partly the refusal of memory. Thus, Kundera says:

> [...] In Hermann Broch's *The Sleepwalkers*, History appears as a process of gradual degradation of values; Robert Musil's *The Man without Qualities* paints an euphoric society which doesen't realise that tomorrow it will disappear; in Jaroslav Hasek's *The God Soldier Schweik*, pretending to be an idiot becomes the last possible method for preserving one's freedom; the novelistic visions of Kafka speak to us of a world without memory, of a world that comes after history time. All of this century's great Central European works of art, even up to our own day, can be understood as long meditations on the possible end of European humanity.[4]

The end of humanity is consensual to the concept of the "End of history", intensely problematized in 1989 by the American politologist Francis Fukuyama and extrapolated in the volume *The End of History and the Last Man*,[5] starting from the reinterpretation of Hegel's texts about history by Alexandre Kojeve and postulates the

---

1 Horia Ursu: *Asediul Vienei* (The Siege of Vienna). Iași: Polirom 2012, p. 286.
2 Witold Gombrowitcz. In: Kundera: The Tragedy of Central Europe, p. 36.
3 Kundera: The Tragedy of Central Europe.
4 Kundera: The Tragedy of Central Europe, p. 36.
5 See Francis Fukuyama: *The End of History and the Last Man*. New York: The Free Press 1992.

idea that gradual, coherent, logic 'evolutionism' of history, as it was conceived during the last century, is not actual any more. The democratic-liberal society is, in Hegel's opinion, at the climax which would mark the end of history, and Fukuyama, operating similarly to Gaston Bachelard's empirical demonstration in *La formation de l'esprit scientifique* (1983) endorses the same idea: modern science was the one who assured coherence, continuity and the logic of history, through its empiric-cumulative character. Therefore, we can understand that modernity's valid 'memory', having a progressive, therefore evolutionary character, can be only of scientific nature in the political context of the liberal democracies at the end of the 20th century. History used the mnemonic instrument frequently in order to exercise pression and power excesses, more or less discretely, over the public space in order to manipulate the masses.

The disappearance of social classes, of state unity or even of the Romantic idea of 'nationality', key concepts anticipated and analysed by Fukuyama, were not strong enough arguments for generalizing ideas "at the end of history". After the fall of The Iron Curtain, the former communist states had the first direct confrontation with History. After several years this has replaced any form of collective memory, configuring and norming existence in the public space. The incapacity to chart the mnemonic map of the communist horrors betrays this annihilating effect of history on memory and the necessity of immediate distancing from the traumas it has provoked.

In Romanian literature,[6] the explosion of prison journals, of subterranean memoirs and the sudden success of texts such as that of Nicolae Steinhardt, *Jurnalul fericirii* (The Diary of Happiness) (1991), *literaturize* the experience of communist history, reducing it to a reflexive-spiritual coordinate which proves exactly the contrary, the incapacity to end the deal with history definitively, as a consequence of winning the happy new democrat-liberal world. The process of history appears as much more complicated than a simple examination of the Actants of aggressive history and of its coercion panopticon. The recovery of memory is the most complex process of Romanian post-communism. The fact that the literary legitimisation of memory[7] was realized only in the form of the journal, a frontier genre, therefore through the voices of individual memories, biographic, which is fundamented only on the accentuation of the authentic character, proves the

---

[6] Some parts of this chapter, regarding the relations between memory and contemporary Romanian novel, could be found in Florin Oprescu: Das Gedächtnis der Macht – die Macht des Gedächtnisses im rumänischen postkommunistischen Roman. In: *Kulturelles Gedächtnis–Ästhetisches Erinnern: Literatur, Film und Kunst in Rumänien*. (ed.) Michèle Mattusch. Berlin: Frank und Timme 2018, p. 229–249.

[7] Pierre Nora (ed.): *Les lieux de mémoire. I La République*. Paris: Gallimard 1984, p. XLII.

fact that the role of literature was minimalized, the role of history remaining the preferred one. The low interest in the post-revolution period in the novels which marked the traumatisation of memory indirectly, therefore subversively, such as *Animale bolnave* (Sick Animals) (1968) of Nicolae Breban, *Principele* (The Prince) (1969) of Eugen Barbu, *Absenții* (The Absents) (1970), *Fețele tăcerii* (The Faces of Silence) (1974) of Augustin Buzura or *Cel mai iubit dintre pământeni* (The Most Beloved Man on Earth) (1980) by Marin Preda, explain the persistency of history in communism.

Moreover, covering history, the contemporary novel preferred a certain indifference to the complex processes of memory, seldom choosing to follow immediate reality, the manner in which society reacted to the transition phenomenon. Therefore, passing from the direct obsession of History from the excedentary memoirs of the '90's, to a neo-realist pattern, detached to impersonalization, masking history and the reflexivity of the authors. A part of the contemporary success novels of 2000s project, the harshness of the present, from Petru Cimpoeșu with *Simion liftnicul* (2001), Dumitru Țepeneag, with *Maramureș* (2001), Radu Aldulescu, *Proorocii Ierusalimului* (Proorocii Jerusalem's Proorocs) (2004), Dan Lungu, with *Raiul găinilor* (The Heaven of the Hens) (2007) or Horia Ursu, with *Asediul Vienei* (The Siege on Vienna) (2007). A harsh universe, de-individualized, in which characters become shadows of the past, is still living under the still active power of the alienating history.

Spectral memory had already beed discussed by Freud under the form of 'shadow of the object' that is lost which led to "an *identification* of the ego with the abandoned object."[8] The Viennese psychoanalyst identifies similarities between the labour of melancholy and the mourning of a "loved object",[9] reducing, one can say, the nature of melancholy to the univocal probing into the subconscious. Moreover, at the intersection of literature and history, Pierre Nora, in the '80's, discusses a real "le deuil de la littérature",[10] a symptom of historical recurrence, anticipating the imagological debates of the end of millennium. He suggests that literature in general and the novel in particular, as has already been observed in the opening of this typology, has a *symptomatic* function, reflecting indirectly the manner in which society reacts to excess. This function of the novel

---

8 Sigmund Freud: *On the History of Psycho-Analytic Movement. Paper on the Metapsychology and Other Works*, Vol. IV. Translated from the German under the General Editorship of James Strachey, In Collaboration with Anna Freud, Assisted by Alix Strachey and Alan Tyson. London: Hogarth Press 1971, p. 249.
9 Freud: *On the History of Psycho-Analytic Movement*, p. 50.
10 Nora (ed.): *Les lieux de mémoire*, p. XLII.

also translates the monumental character of the genre, meaning just its capacity to preserve its memory.

The significance of the term *monument* is relevant regarding literature as a representative phenomenon for the culture and time in which it was produced. If the adjective monumental has already gotten superlative qualifying meanings, such as *grandiose, great, imposing* through its proportions, or *remarkable*, therefore an incompatible literary qualification, when referring to the figurative meaning, then the noun *monument* reminds us of the initial discussion referring to the establishment of the canonical memory of literature. The monument, with reference to the architectural construction, is defined as "a sculptural or architectural work destined to perpetuate the remembrance of an event or a remarkable personality" or, in a larger sense, he has the following definition: "Any work, historical document or cultural creation of national or international significance."[11] Outside the semantic area of the term it must be rememberd that a monument has a certain meaning concerning the conservation of historical memory, therefore the monument stimulates any type of knowledge of history and especially its problematization.

The historical literary canon preserves a monumental aesthetic, remarkable memory, of high importance or national representativeness, referring to texts that are considered an aesthetic mark of a certain period, which emphasize the aesthetic and cultural norms of a certain historical period. Ultimately, the process of monumentalizing the historical literary canon is one that follows the coordinates of power, as it was defined in the first chapter. Therefore, the monumentalizing of the historical canon is a result of the canonized historical majority of the literary, cultural groups, which detain accredited or legitimate power, formally or informally, in order to decide on canonical texts. In arguing this point of view, Romanian literature had a representative evolution, from the belated introduction of Deleanu's *Țiganiada* in the canonical list, due to the absence of the context of power and therefore of its promotion as a representative canonical work, to Titu Maiorescu's major role and the cultural policy promoted by 'Junimea' or by Eugen Lovinescu with 'Sburătorul', which stimulated the debate about modernism and implicitly instituting the modern canon. A similar *monumentalizing*, reversed this time, existed in the post-war period as well, with reference to the excesses of the proletcultist canonisation but also to the neo-modernist canon or the postmodern one of the '80's. The battles for the historical canon within Romanian literature manifested with a recurrence which explains a paradox: on the one side a new need of literary and cultural identity and, on the other side, a permanent need for

---

[11] See *DEX*. Second edition. București: Univers Enciclopedic 1996, p. 652.

the autonomy of dominant models or the pressures of history, a fact which led to the obsessive, recurrent autonomy of the aesthetic.

Avoiding the frontal meeting with history and becoming isolating in art, the modernist novel assumes the risk of self-sufficiency. It is only an apparent withdrawal, the power with which history exercises pressure on the novel, determining sometimes an adverse reaction of ultra-subjectivity, such as in the cases of Max Blecher, Camil Petrescu or Gib Mihăescu, history having the role of epic cathalyst. The novelist, when confronting history, finds an authentic world within the folds of memory, which he exposes only to demonstrate the authenticity of the being faced with the artificiality of history. The fake discourse of manipulating history is replaced by the veridicity of a discourse on lost time and on instability, as constitutive attribute of the modern being. The novels of Dostoievski, Kafka, Mann, Proust or those of Virginia Woolf are arguments of the (in)utility of history in modernity.

In his *Untimely Meditations* (2007), Friedrich Nietzsche makes some important observations "On the Uses and Disadvantages of History for Life".[12] The German philosopher proves to be a precursor of the contemporary debate on power, as was shown in the theoretical chapter, and also an attentive observer of the historical phenomena in the track of humanity.

The category of the ahistorical, characteristic especially for animals due to the fact that they live in a unique present, and the category of the historical, specific for man who defines himself according to these, are analysed by Nietzsche in a dialectical rapport, both very necessary for life. But Nietzsche's conclusion is that man needs "beside the monumental and antiquarian modes of regarding the past, a third mode, the critical: and this, too, in the service of life. If he is to live, man must possess and from time to time employ the strength to break up and dissolve a part of the past."[13] He admits that there were epochs in which the excess of history was against man, the philosopher speaking of *the malady of history*. Overpowering history generates this disease of modern times. "Excess of history has attacked life's plastic powers, it no longer knows how to employ the past as a nourishing food."[14]

The excess of the critique of history and the power pressions of the cultures that gravitate in a given culture that annihilate history are the risks of disappearing ones. The example of the Greeks is eloquent for Nietzsche. This culture "was, rather, for a long time a chaos of foreign, Semitic, Babylonian, Lydian, Egyptian

---

[12] Friedrich Nietzsche: *On the Uses and Disadvantages of History for Life*. Cambridge: Cambridge University Press 2007, p. 57.
[13] Nietzsche: *On the Uses and Disadvantages of History for Life*, p. 75.
[14] Nietzsche: *On the Uses and Disadvantages of History for Life*, p. 120.

forms and ideas, and their religion truly a battle of all the gods of the East."[15] But the salvation of the Greeks comes from "the Apollinic oracle", due to which teaching and thinking "[t]he Greeks gradually learned *to organize the chaos*",[16] this being owed to their remembrance of themselves and their real needs, in which they included history. The practical need of real, immediate things led to the elimination of the risk of decorative, inherent where cultures amalgamate. Imitation is, therefore, for Nietzsche, the scourge which makes the historical disease be malign to extremely flexible cultures. This nietzscheean thesis reminds of the premises of Maiorescu's 19th century theory, referring to the 'imitations' for a culture without history or, anyway, without its memory. But the question remains: if "modern man suffers from a weakened personality."[17] or his shattered or camouflaged memory anyway? The 20th century, with its traumatic events has proved that the pressures on history were catastrophic, history seldom becoming a manipulation instrument according to the interests of the power detainees, a fact observed by Nietzsche, at the beginning of the new century, and later in *The Will to Power*. The instrumentalization of history by the detainers of power had a considerable impact on the accentuation of the need for memory, a fact exploited in the last century by the sciences (psychology, sociology, philosophy) or by literature through their avoidance and camouflage formulas facing historical pressures. Therefore, literature functioned through its allegoric formula as a representation of the 'coursed places' of history, or as a heterotopia, in Foucauldian manner,[18] as literature, especially the novel as literary genre, is the one that uses the synthesis of the divergent spaces of history, about which the French philosopher already spoke in 1967.

Michel Foucault opposes heterotopia to utopia, which is "les emplacements sans lieu réel", therefore unreal, but which maintains "un rapport général d'analogie directe ou inversée" with the real space of history. He observes that heterotopias are invariable to any culture, meaning that "[...] des lieux réels, des lieux effectifs, des lieux qui sont dessinés dans l'institution meme de la société, et qui sont de sortes de contre-emplacements, sortes d'utopies effectivement réalisées."[19] These are seen as "espaces différents, ces autres lieux, une espèce de contestation à la fois mythique et réelle de l'espace où nous vivons."[20] Examples of such spaces, which preserve a certain part of history, are military colleges or

---

15 Nietzsche: *On the Uses and Disadvantages of History for Life*, p. 122.
16 Nietzsche: *On the Uses and Disadvantages of History for Life*, p. 122.
17 Nietzsche: *On the Uses and Disadvantages of History for Life*, p. 83.
18 Foucault: *Dits et Écrits*, p. 752.
19 Foucault: *Dits et Écrits*, p. 755.
20 Foucault: *Dits et Écrits*, p. 756.

those destined to girls' education, psychiatric asylums or old peoples' asylums, prisons, orphanages or even cemeteries, receiving the crises labels or those of deviation heterotopias. Romanian heterotopies are exponential in this matter, the example of the salt pit prison in the novel *Ciocoii vechi și noi* (The Old and New Parvenus) of Nicolae Filimon, the theatre, borough, panoptic in Blecher's *Întâmplări în irealitatea imediată* (Occurence in the imediate unreality), or the factory, the universities and the labour prison during communism in the '50s represented in Preda's novel are relevant for the argumentation of the *Other Places* which are camouflages of the crises in the present of the narrative. Moreover, Foucault does not exclude the theatre or cinematography from this category of heterotopias, which "le pouvoir de juxtaposer en un seul lieux réel plusieurs espaces, plusieurs emplacements qui sont en eux-mêmes incompatibles."[21] These are antagonic examples, but dialectics of the heterotopias of artistic representation.

The constitutive principles of Foucault's heterotopias have certain validity when analyzing the manner a novel functions as an instrument of representation for history through the filter of memory. The first principle is that of the cultural universality of heterotopias, identified in every culture, while the second principle is that throughout history a society can determine the particular functionality of such a heterotopic space. The example given here is that of the heterotopia of the cemetery, that, throughout history, had different significations according to the cultural and especially religious ideas of the period. As mentioned previously, theatre and cinema are Foucault's favourite examples to determine the third principle, that of the juxtaposition of initially incompatible spaces, or apparently impossible to associate. Another favourite example is that of the garden which, "depuis le fond de l'Antiquité, une sorte d'hétérotopie heureuse et universalisante."[22]

There is also the principle of archivist accumulation, that of conserved memoir, here the libraries and museums being a relevant example. But the theatre, the cinema, the museum or the library are first of all mnemonic heterotopias, which function as spaces within space, as compensatory places of our worlds which tends to conserve the memory aggressed by history. These are shelters par excellence. The symbolic image of the ship, "un morceau flottant d'espace, un lieu sans lieu, qui vit par lui-même, qui est fermé sur soi et qui est livré en même temps à l'infini de la mer" is for Foucault "l'hétérotopie par excellence".[23] In this mechanism of heterotopia, if the museum and library are metaphors of preserved

---

21 Foucault: *Dits et Écrits*, p. 758.
22 Foucault: *Dits et Écrits*, p. 759.
23 Foucault: *Dits et Écrits*, p. 762.

memory, therefore passive, then theatre and cinema, or even representations of the novel, are, in the context of our analyses, heterotopies of reactivated memory, provoked to undermine the authority of history. This eternal antagonism between literature/novel and history reveals the dual forms of legitimising memory. It is an argument sustained by Pierre Nora at the end of his study in the collective monography on *Lieux de mémoire*.[24]

In this introductory study, entitled "Entre Mémoire et Histoire. La problématique des lieux", he arguments that, starting from the literary references to Michelet or Proust:

> L'histoire est notre imaginaire de remplecement. Renaissance du roman historique, vogue du roman personnalisé, revitalisation littéraire du drame historique, succès du récit d'histoire orale, comment s'expliqueraient ils sinon comme le relais de la fiction défaillante? L'intérêt pour les lieux où s'ancre, se condense et s'exprime le capital épuisé de notre mémoire collective relève de cette sensibilité-là. Histoire, profondeur d'une époque arrachée à sa profondeur, roman vrai d'une époque sans vrai roman. Mémoire, promue au centre de l'histoire : c'est le deuil éclatant de la littérature.[25]

The projection of memory in history and the resurrection of the literary genres which are at the interference of fiction and history through the mediation of memory demonstrates, in Nora's vision, the end of literature. The balancing of the authors' interest towards memory is not yet a sample of the death of literature and its fictional specificity, but a proof of the pressures history exercised on literature. The literary discourse reflects and portrays the change of historical paradigm of the 20th century, in the way this was marked, especially in its second half, by traumatising reality. When Nora affirms that history is a substitute of our imaginary, this happens because manipulated history replaces collective memory. Moreover, even Jaques Le Goff starts in the analyses of the relation History and Memory[26] from the premise of the existence of historical dualism: "celle de la mémoire collective et celle des historiens". Starting from this distinction he admits that "La premiere aparaît comme esentiellement mythique, deformée, anachronique", and the second one "doit éclairer la mémoire et l'aider à rectifier ses erreurs."[27]

Nevertheless, on the background of the power excesses of the last century, history appeared as a defining propagandistic benchmark, communism or fascism for example, focusing on the effects of mythologised history on the

---

24 Nora (ed.): *Les lieux de mémoire*, p. 43.
25 Nora (ed.): *Les lieux de mémoire*, p. 43.
26 Jacques Le Goff: *Histoire et Mémoire*. Paris: Gallimard 1988, p. 194.
27 Le Goff: *Histoire et Mémoire*, p. 194.

human imaginary, imposing its monumental status. History has done nothing but amplifed the confusions of memory. Even replacing memory, history has taken the form of a spectrum coming from the past and adapting to the need of our expansive imaginary of identification, of representation and protection. In this context texts such as those which intentionally distorted the effects of communist 'accomplishments' appeared, presenting them as 'strong' identity formulas, legitimating the power discourse in favour of the collective historical identity. Seldom, as could be seen in the chapter on passive power, literature has become one of the predilect formulas of arguing anti-humanistic ideals of the excessive power. Following the Soviet models of the period, such as *The Defeat* (1927) of Fadeïev or *On the Slow Don* (1928–1940) of Sholokhov, the Romanian novel of 'the obsessive decade' has a nucleus of the recently manipulated history, with fiction being replaced with falsified historical memory. This history is an imaginary construct which creates the illusion of an ideal reality, which has instantly become history, in which class equality is important and the purist civilisation effects of the 'New Man'. The examples of this type of literary camouflage are significant, from *Mitrea Cocor* by Sadoveanu, to *Bărăgan* by V. Em. Galan, *Oțel și pâine* (Steel and Bread) of Ion Călugăru or *Drum fără pulbere* (Road without Dust) by Petru Dumitriu, as we have already demonstrated in the previous chapter.

Therefore, it can be understood why the issue of memory has been situated in a privileged position in the contemporary novel. Not only history has been the interest nucleus of the post-communist positionings, but the individual and then collective memory too, and when referring to memory we refer to its manner of working the mechanism which allows the recovery of a past well camouflaged within falsified history.

The mechanism of resetting collective memory has been understood by contemporary prose-writers as reflection on exponential individual destinies which survived the pressures of the excess of power. It is still exceptionalism, but a revealing one this time, the prose-writers who have placed memory at the centre being interested in observing the physiognomy of *The Survivor* of this substitution. The psychological, sociological, politological or philosophical instruments seemed insufficient for this attempt of rehabilitating history through memory, so that literature became a predilect instrument of implicit exposure of the falsification of history in the years 2000 again. This was particularly due to the reflexive character and the authenticity of the personal memory which participated in the remake of the puzzle of collective memory. In the background of fiction there was not necessarily collective history, which happened in proletcultist novels, but the reflective history of the characters which show the manner in which they succeeded or not in escaping collective history, through simulation or withdrawal. The Romanian post-communist novel rediscovers the role of literary memory, exposing falsified characters which deconstruct falsified history and its effects on man.

The expectation horizon of the historical post-revolutionary public is therefore baffled due to the incapacity of the historians to probe the authenticity of narrated history. The 'credibility pact', which made history a fundamental discourse of the national construct is therefore under question. Historians will speak for doubting readers who expect a sort of autentification of their narrative.[28] Starting from this, Ricoeur notices that history replaces the subject of action with anonymous actants,[29] and this is the process of passivization till the disappearance of active subjects. The incredulity of history and its inauthenticity have brought our era to the acute need of authentic memory, reconstituted and credible, which will replace the process expositive and presumptive and the sequential nature of history. The need of a politics of "mémoire equitable"[30] is expressed by Paul Ricoeur who, in his book, *Mémoire, Histoire, Oubli* (2000), discusses the three "mnemonic modes" introduced by Edward Casey in *Remembering. A Phenomenological Study* (1987), this constituting in fact, in the French philosophers' vision, a transition between reflexive and mundane levels of memory.[31] Casey's three modes are:

a. *Reminding* which is a remembrance process through remembering indices of certain facts, persons, phenomena. This remembering process is between the demarcation limit between interiour and exterior, external signs reminding us of current daily requirements;
b. *Reminiscing*, reactivating moments of the past within collective memory through the simultaneous and complementary evocation of the same set of memories by more people. Regarding this, Ricoeur discusses an interiorisation of this process "sous la forme de la mémoire méditative", given by that German *Gedächtnis*, represented in the diary, memoires and autobiographies "où le support de l'écriture done matérialité aux traces conservées, réanimées, et à nouveau enrichies des dépots inédits."[32]
c. *Recognizing*, seen as an overlaying process of the past event to the present, an identification through memory, a recognition of some present, recurrent events through memory.

---

[28] Paul Ricoeur: *Time and narrative*. Volume I. Translated by Kathleen McLaughlin and David Pellauer. Chicago and London: The University of Chicago Press 1984, p. 176.
[29] Ricoeur: *Time and narrative*, p. 177.
[30] Paul Ricoeur: Penser mondial. In: *Le Nouvel Observateur*, 2–8 June 2005, p. 12.
[31] Paul Ricoeur: *La Mémoire, L'Histoire, L'Oubli*. Paris: Gallimard 2000, p. 56.
[32] Ricoeur: *La Mémoire, L'Histoire, L'Oubli*, p. 46.

The process of remembering described by Ricoeur has the role to support the operation mechanisms of the human memory in the philosopher's attempt to find the pathway towards the explanation of that 'equitable memory'. Literature, especially the novel, offers us the possibility to identify these memory benchmarks which Ricoeur operates with, in Casey's theory. These memory stages are in fact processes which can be identified in post-communist Romanian novels which place memory at the centre of their interests. Even novels that apparently focus only on the present, such as *Profeții ierusalimului* (The Prophets of Jerusalim) by Radu Aldulescu or *Asediul Vienei* (The Siege of Vienna) by Horia Ursu, implicitly follow the effects of history on the past, dominating the present as a spectrum. The process of *Reminding* is one through which the novel recuperates in the present, following subtly the effects of the power of history on present, this dominating the present as a spectrum. The course of *Reminding* is one through which the novel recuperates hints of history in the present and makes the passing from the exterior background to the interior one, being similar to Blecher's panopticum of the wax figures. Reminiscing means a method of identification of common elements in crosswords and the inflation of memoirs in the post-communist period confirms this. Recognising means the recognition of history in the present and when it is camouflaged. Even the net cleavage between past and present, as the one in a novel like *Asediul Vienei* (The Siege of Vienna), by Horia Ursu, does not demonstrate anything else but the dialectical link between history and present.

The contemporary novel is, therefore, a full novel of memory, of different ways of accessing unfalsified history or a novel of indirect reconstruction of history through the mnemonic instrument. It is not a memoir, because memoirs continue the perplexity of self-reflexiveness which would place it at the interference of genres, but a novel of different mnemonic processes, more or less direct, more or less evidentiated or occulted in quotidian. The first impression is made through a generalising optical exercise, therefore with an implicit relativisation of the contemporary novels. Therefore we recognise a resurgence of the daily life in the foreground, the immediate dominating the narrative outline. Kept at a distance by immediate reality, the novel rediscovers it obsessively and many times it can be considered a neo-realist novel and this is the case of all the representative texts of the period, from the novels of Herta Müller, Norman Manea or Cristian Teodorescu to those of Filip Florian, Dan Lungu, Radu Aldulescu, Horia Ursu or even the turn into reality in 'Aripa dreaptă' (The Right Wing) of the trilogy *Orbitor* (Blinding) of Mircea Cărtărescu. The discourse of the novel proves authentic for the fixation of memory in its different forms and implicitly for the fixation of memory in its different forms and for the formation of gender identity.

Aleida Assmann admits the fact that there is a variability of the access paths to memory, difficult to trace or define being the way which is linked to "the link between memory and identity-a connection that entails cultural acts of remembrance, commemoration, eternalization, past and future references and projections, and, last but by no means, forgetting, wich is integral to all of these actions."[33] Literature can fill this mnemonic void within collective memory, when personal, autobiographic memory or not, but moreover a reflexive memory fictionalizes history selectively. Maybe literature compensates and re-establishes a connexion between personal memory, collective memory and historical memory.

Literature functions as 'memory place', especially there where collective and individual memory have been aggressed by historic memory. A relevant argument in this matter is the one that literature functioned and functions as a compensation and submination of memory aggressed by the power excesses of communism in Romania. In this matter, not only the publishing of numerous memoirs that describe the limit of prison experiences, such as those of Nicolae Steinhardt, Ion Ioanid, Constantin Noica, Doinei Jela, Lena Constante, but also the novels that place histories in the communist past, such as *Provizorat* (Provisional State) by Gabriela Adameșteanu, *Matei Brunul* by Lucian Dan Teodorovici or even *Orbitor. Aripa dreaptă* (Blinding. Right Wing) by Mircea Cărtărescu, demonstrate the role of literature in historical mediation. Plus, historical memory was manipulated and confiscated by the communist power. The rewritings of national history are classical, which was called communist historic nationalism, the rewritings of literary history etc., the literary mythologizing of history.

The meeting point of memory with literature is where literature presupposes the fixation of 'memory places', as they are defined by Pierre Nora, and the resemblance consists in the fact that these places are self-referential, distinctive literary elements. Furthermore, literature includes history which, being reconstituted from memory is implicitly excluded, as long as literature retains, through its mnemonic instrument of 'the memory place' just what is relevant and with self-referential character. Therefore, the novel is a place of memory and historical purification, not having an immediate referent, but one far away in history.

In Nora's conception, memory is life in perpetual transformation, while history is a constantly problematic and incomplete reconstruction or, as could be said, in a continuous negotiation and rewriting according to the authority which is in power. From this point of view the assertion according to which memory exposes a perpetual phenomenon is a connection with our eternal present and the history is just a representation of the past.[34] Which means the novel surpasses the simple

---

33 Aleida Assmann: *Cultural Memory and Western Civilization: Functions, Media, Archives.* Cambridge: Cambridge Universiy Press 2011, p. 18.
34 See Nora (ed.): *Les lieux de mémoire*, p. 8.

representation relation, especially in the case of the contemporary novel founded on memory, in which case we can talk about the osmosis, which is unfalsified and not manipulated by history, filtered through an eternal self-reflexive, personal gesture. Such a gesture, of recognition of the history, reduced to the unicity of the characters, gives the novel a specific status in the hierarchy of the mnemonic instruments of reconstitution of the past into the present. The novel is therefore a *heterotopia* (Foucault) or a *memory place* (Nora), not necessarily situated between memory and history, but using memory as a defence instrument when facing the excessive power of history or the selection and emphasis of lived history. Citing Maurice Halbwachs, Pierre Nora reminds us the fact that memories have not only an individual, subjective character, but also a multiple, collective one. Nevertheless, the same Aleida Assmann suggests that in the attempt to make the difference between memory and history, Halbwachs operates with the empirical instruments of the sociologist, observing "the importance of shared memories as a mode of cohesion."[35] In this context he speaks about group memory. As a consequence of this discussion Assmann synthesises the major points of the differences between collective memory and historiography in Halbwachs' (1992) thesis:

a. Collective memory assures the unicity and continuity of a group, while historical memory tries to neutralise the dimenssions of the affective aspect and of identity;
b. Collective memories, exactly as in the group they are connected, are always plural, while historical memory, which offers a universal background for more histories, is singular;
c. Collective memory tries to join, to reject change, while historical memory is specialised in change.[36]

Starting from these delimitations, it is possible to ask if there has ever been an autochthonous 'group memory' and if this can be observed through the study of literature, of the novel as an aesthetic formula of group identity. If looking at the 2000's novels, both through the return of the novelist 'groups' (postmodern eighties writers or young novelists) to the novel, as also through the interest of the 'groups' of readers (amateurs or professional) in the novel, then we can claim that the revival of the novel is real. The eloquence of the 'return of the novel' also signifies a rising interest not only in the aesthetics of the genre, but also in the complex manner in which this instrumentalizes memory and in history. Even if

---

[35] Assmann: *Cultural Memory and Western Civilization*, p. 121.
[36] Maurice Halbwachs. In: Assmann: *Cultural Memory and Western Civilization*, p. 121.

most of the time group memory excludes history, preferring the confrontation with the present, the link between memory and history cannot be rejected, especially after the epic syncope of the '90's transition. The Romanian novel of the 2000's rebuilds that lost connection in the last decade between memory and historical identity, and its access ways are multiple and complex. Even so, when talking exclusively about the present, the novel camouflages a latent collective memory which speaks indirectly about the effects of history on the Subject, from its passivity towards impersonalization, therefore to its dissolution in collectivism.

Consequently, it is ppossible the path of the actual novel connected to recent, communist history and the transition one, which leads from stigmatization and passivity to impersonalization, meaning an indifference (at least apparent) towards history and its identity function and till the intentional dissipation of the power poles. Power exists, it is emergent from every character relation of the novel, its effects on the subjects being relevant, only that it is impersonal and this is a symptom of transition. Impersonalization was an avoidance process of memory faced with the aggressions of history, starting from the observation that forgetfulness is impossible and has a stigmatizing effect, the only solution being de-personalization, meaning the intentional destruction of Subjects' identities. Folowing a case study of impersonal power, of this paradox of power, such as *Asediul Vienei* (The Siege of Vienna) of Horia Ursu, we observe that the novel makes a cartography of the polarization and impersonalization of power in contemporary society and its effects on the Subjects.

Subdued to a mnemonic void, therefore without any problematization instrument of history, they are living with the obsession of emptiness, a historical crisis and this is due to an *impersonalization* which is translated into an identity blocking. The Subjects of the novels who set the plot in contemporaneity are living a temporal crisis, without present and future, but being bogged down in an obsessive past, camouflaged in all their actions. Symptomatologically, a series of novels of the period focus on this social actantial model of Romanian transition and the dissipation of power is a constant which reminds and continues the paradox of the anterior novels, of the passivization of power under the excessive pressures of delirious history.

5.1.2 Contemporary Novel as a Novel of Failed or Reclaimed Memory

Discussing the case of the psychological and the historical novel, Milan Kundera observes in *The Art of the Novel* that Hermann Broch mistakenly adopts the term 'poly-historical' novel, in trying to dissociate from the aesthetics of the psychological novel. In Kundera's vision, Adalbert Stifter, considered "the founder of Austrian prose",[37] created such a 'poly-historical' novel, a real anticipative diorama of the end of 19th century, out of which the pulsation of life or even the human being is missing. In the case of Broch, the specific of the novel presupposes "mobiliser sur la base du récit tous les moyens, rationnels et irrationnels, narratifs et méditatifs, susceptibles d'éclairer l'être de l'homme."[38] This archeology of humanity, as "archeologie du savoir",[39] would be the generative center of the modern novel which proves "la conscience mélancolique d'une Histoire qui s'achève dans des circonstances profondément hostiles à l'évolution de l'art et du roman en particulier."[40]

Nevertheless, if we think about the status of contemporary memory we observe there is a negotiation in the public space between individual and collective memory. Postmodern art, which according to Lyotard's thesis, does not trust any more the legitimising 'metanarratives'[41] that is macro-stories which define a mnemonic pattern generally accepted in modernity, escaping into a fragmented and polarised memory, without the intention of reconfiguring History. Reconstituting the past does not seem to be a major objective of the 20th century, and even less of our beginning of century, but the configuring and describing of an aggressed History, torn from the past, therefore without its nostalgia, an eclectic identity, which accepts the present as only form of multiple existence. The present aggresses the memory of the postmodern and not History which has fulfilled its meaning, becoming occult in the present. In this context, Lyotard admits, "The narrative function is losing its functors, its great hero, its great dangers, its great voyages, its great goal. It is being dispersed in clouds of narrative language elements-narrative, but also denotative, prescriptive, descriptive, and so on."[42] If modernity has a melancholic conscience of the finite history, postmodernity is more passive about the end of History, adopting a neutral position.

Such melancholic conscience and not a nostalgic one of the immediate History can be observed at contemporary Romanian novelists, as well, being a characteristic of a generation, a *Zeitgeist*. If in the '80's of the last century the novel was a seldom ignored genre, this phenomenon is also an effect of the pressures exerted by the communist power on art during that period and a result of the postmodern fragmentary aesthetics. After the success of the novels in the '70's, having as

---

37 Kundera: *L'Art du roman*, p. 85.
38 Kundera: *L'Art du roman*, p. 86.
39 Michel Foucault: *L'archéologie du savoir*. Paris: Gallimard 1969.
40 Kundera: *L'Art du roman*, p. 90.
41 Jean-François Lyotard: *The Postmodern Condition: A Report on Knowledge*. Translation from the French by Geoff Bennington and Brian Massumi. Foreword by Fredric Jameson. Manchester: Manchester University Press 1984, p. XXIV.
42 Lyotard: *The Postmodern Condition*, p. XXIV.

leitmotif the recovery and critical reevaluation of the 'Obsessive decade', of the excess of power in the '50's, taking advantage of the ideological breach manifested through retaliations on writers, and the novel *Cel mai iubit dintre pământeni* (The Most Beloved Man on Earth) (1980) of Marin Preda, with its contested destiny is an argument in favour of those affirmed above. Even the relatively late appearance of the contemporary Romanian novel, having the consistency only after tens of years after the fall of the communist regime, proves the fact that the novel has been excluded from history, due to its capacity to discover, reveal the human being in the artificiality of its historical diorama, meaning to expose the negative effects of the excess of power on man. The novel, to come back at the Aristotelian understanding of fiction, is more authentic in this case than history, because it can refer both to its contemporary history, but also to the present it speaks about. Therefore, the authenticity of the novel is that of exposing history through the authenticity of memory, even when it speaks about the present.

Plus, the complexity of the Romanian novel resides just in the development of subversive strategies, of counterbalancing the control manifested by the excess of history, in the effort of conceiving poetical instruments, aesthetic sidesteps through which the archaeology of human will continue and the revelation of evil imposed by power.

This resistance was manifested within Romanian modernity especially in the post-communist period, as a belated revolting, ostentatious, neo-avantgarde formula. The history of Romanian literature is marked by real 'survivals' through the aesthetic, when facing the ideological aggressions of the 19th and 20th century. We better identify a reversed image of Romanian literature across time: through the aesthetic, literature resisted the contact with history. The representative case in this sense is one of the Romanian novels which evolved contrastively. We have, on one side, the direct narratives of the confrontation of the individual with history and its aggressions, and the examples are numerous, from *Ciocoii vechi și noi* (Old and New Parvenues) by Nicolae Filimon, to *Gorila* (The Gorilla) of Liviu Rebreanu, to *Cel mai iubit dintre pământeni* (The Most Beloved Man on Earth) by Marin Preda. This is the direct novel which marked history within memory. On the other side, we identify the indirect novel, a novel which takes refuge in the aesthetic to override the block of history and in this key we can read novels such as *Întâmplări în irealitatea imediată* (Occurence in the Immediate Unreality) by Max Blecher, *Groapa* (The Hole) by Eugen Barbu or *Zenobia* by Gellu Naum. These avoided the memory of ideological pressure, by running away from history and isolating themselves in the labyrinth of the imaginary levels of reality.[43] Seldom do we identify a problem of

---

43 Calvino: *The Uses of Literature*.

the occulted memory in the immediate in the Romanian novel, especially when this novel's action takes place in the present. It is mostly the case of the contemporary novel which, although describes plots in/from the transition period, hides a collective memory overloaded with the aggression of history and which has a bearing on the destiny of the characters. It is an indirect strategy which, for example, we identify in a novel such as *Asediul Vienei* (The Siege of Vienna) by Horia Ursu, in which we can observe such an occulted memory within immediate history.

Noticing the situation of the 2000 Romanian novel through its meta-literary extrapolations, through the critical formulas that fixed and provided its success in contemporaneity, we remark that it is enrolled in the general tendency statistically-hierarchizing the period. Consequently, in March 2010, the magazine *Adevărul literar și artistic*[44] proposed a provoking decade, at least through the immediate character of the analyses, therefore through the focalisation risking close to the object of observation, referring to the 'Novel of the Century' or, better said, to the novels of the century. We remember that such an interest in Romanian society is not new and the remembrance of the interwar rhetoric, starting from Mihail Ralea's question "Why don't we have a novel?" is relevant. The process of the Romanian novel is a complex one, exactly for the fact that the novel seems to have functioned as a barometer of the modernisation of Romanian society at a certain point or, at least the Romanian novel seems to be a certain mirror of a culture in its historical process. Active literary critics have answered this question, therefore we have a complete perspective on the contemporary Romanian phenomena, such as Paul Cernat, Marius Chivu, Al. Cistelecan, Daniel Cristea-Enache, Mihai Iovănel, Ion Bogdan Lefter, Dan C. Mihăilescu, Simona Sora, Andrei Terian sau Alex Ștefănescu. The 'top' contains novels published between 2000 and 2010 and *Adevărul* mentions the five titles designated by each literary critic, so that, after this relative axiological 'quantification' there is a canonical hierarchy, as follows:

1. *Orbitor* (Blinding), by Mircea Cărtărescu - 23 points
2. *Asediul Vienei* (The Siege of Vienna), by Horia Ursu - 17 points
3. *Teodosie cel Mic* (Teodosie the Little), by Răzvan Rădulescu - 16 points
4. *Pupa Russa*, by Gheorghe Crăciun - 15 points
5. *Povestea Marelui Brigand* (The Story of the Great Brigand), by Petru Cimpoeșu - 10 points

Without any doubt, the novels hierarchized through the mathematical method of the magazine, even if we do have the argumentation of the persons who

---

[44] The survey could be consulted at the web address: http://adevarul.ro/cultura/arte/romanul-deceniului-1_50ad559c7c42d5a663932de6/index.html [25.04.2018].

propose the personal top, are some of the representative novels of the contemporary Romanian novel landscape. Moreover, the reaction of Mircea Cărtărescu is partially justified in accordance with the arguable character of the hierarchy, through the facile argumentation asked by the rule of the survey game:

> [...] such surveys are the area of 'little talk', gossip and society games of the critical act. Interesting because sometimes, as in the case above, they say something about the state of the critical act (more than about the state of the literature) at a certain point about the manner in which the literary space is configured, about the idiosyncrasies and the rumours of the literary world. But in no case are these worthy of being taken seriously as a literary diagnosis.[45]

No matter how hard we might try to ignore the canonical hierarchy, dreaming of the "pure air that follows it",[46] what the survey does is only to re-establish a canonical hierarchy, rarely fundamental for the novel. Taking a double convention, that of the 'tops' but also a "tacit convention of the type one man-one (single) book" (Terian), the critics asked by the survey in *Adevărul* invoke relative and succinct criteria of the selection, as the formula remains subsidiary but dominant, which was invoked by Nemoianu, who considered the canon as "a best-seller of the historical majority",[47] or of the contemporary critical *establishment*. This time the formula is that of a better critical and historical representativeness. Arguments such as "the span and exemplarity of every volume" (Cernat), "Cărtărescu's trilogy as being one of the most ambitious, complex and important novels in our literature" (M. Chivu) or "five authors in full artistic maturity and with high creative powers" (D. Cristea-Enache) are all general formulas, part of the media arsenal of canonical generalisation. The critical argumentation is invoked by Mihai Iovănel who associates "the axiological criteria with the typological ones", admitting that "The result is relative and axiological and typological". But the critical argumentation of the selection, with the risk of its aesthetic-centrist argumentation belongs to Dan C. Mihăilescu, who starts from the inherent limitations of the hierarchies which reduce the classification and sometimes the canon "to the melting pot of the total novel". Nevertheless, the criteria of the critic are arguments for the impersonal character of the selection, as possible:

> Ingenuity, calophilia, filigree textures, but also Dostoievskianism, picturesque cases, cruelty, ceremonialism, neo-existentialism. Visionary energies in the context of macerated

---

45 See Mircea Cărtărescu. In: *Adevărul*, 23 March 2010. Consulted at the web address: http://adevarul.ro/cultura/arte/mircea-cartarescu-desfiinteaza-critici-sunt-groaza-nu-legatura-literatura-1_50ad79ba7c42d5a66395dc94/index.html [25.04.2018].
46 Alexandrescu: *Privind înapoi, modernitatea*, p. 154.
47 See Virgil Nemoianu. In: Nemoianu; Royal (eds.): *The Hospitable Canon*, p. 232.

derision. Alchemical symbolism, satirical, argotical dimensions, depth and individual destiny, unfulfilment, sublime, grotesquely tragic, moral parable.[48]

All these categories belong to the analyses of the novel in its historicity or they are "Great themes of the great prose forever, but grafted onto the hypersensitivity of a narrative being which in the '90's seemed close to apoplexy, surprising us then through a vitality sometimes hypnotising" confirms Dan C. Mihăilescu. This is basically the central idea of the prolixity of selection, a certain rebirth of the 2000 novel after the precarity of the genre in the transition period. The situation is similar to the one in the '30's of the last century when, after the inexistence of the novel at the beginning of the century, out of the battle between the conservatism of *poporanism* and *sămănătorism* and the modernist reformers, the victory belongs to the novel. In other words, preoccupied with the confrontation with the communist history and the neo-communist one of transition in the '90's, novelists withdraw from literature. The reclaiming of the memory in the 2000, therefore the escape from the aggressive realism of transition, equals the rediscovery of the genre, a genre which offers a critical distancing towards the power pressions exerted by history. The transition novel is not a novel of direct memory, one rediscovering the narrative instrument of focalisation and critical distancing from the effects of history on men. Seldom, this is a novel of impersonalization, of the reflection of a diffuse conscience, "a moral parable" (Mihăilescu) of the disappearance of the Subject.

A typology of the novel of this period, after the criteria of the relation between memory and history, not of a hierarchical kind, a practically impossible one, would reveal a unity specific for the genre, as an expression of the extrapolation of the problem status of the Subject in the field of power. The unitary character of the Romanian contemporary novel is given by the distorted link between memory and history, both hidden through the epic strategies of the avoidance of the direct discourse. The literary Romanian discourse offers a sample of indirect reconstruction of history and of the identification of its effects in the immediate present. Memory offers therefore an essential background for the critics of the effects of historical power on the Subject. Without memory and without history, the power of the Subject is dissipated into a disoriented world, searching for lost values. The solution of the impersonalization translates the failure when facing history, the attempt to escape from its authoritarianism and the acceptance of an impersonal status as being one ontologically fundamental in the process of identity affirmation.

---

48 See Dan C. Mihăilescu in the cited survey from *Adevărul*, consulted at the web adress: http://adevarul.ro/cultura/arte/romanul-deceniului-1_50ad559c7c42d5a663932de6/index.html [25.04.2018].

5.1.3 The Transitional Novel. A Modular Typology

Taking into account the equation Memory-History-Subject and starting from the necessity of a contemporary Romanian typology, we can go back to the signification Michel Foucault attributes to the other spaces "des espaces autres"[49] and from the statement that the great challenge of the 19th century was history, with its variable provocations, associated to the development, cyclicity, accumulation or the past. On the other side, the perspective of the philosopher on our present reveals the fact that:

> L'espace dans laquel nous vivons, par laquel nous sommes attirés hors de nous-même, dans laquel se déroule précisément l'érosion de notre vie, de notre temps et de notre histoire, cet espace qui nous ronge et nous ravine est en lui-même un espace hétérogène.[50]

Michel Foucault inquires into the link or the connector which makes or remakes the spatial unity of our world, and all these spaces which have "the curious propriety" to maintain connections to all the others, like utopias and heterotopias. The heterotopia of the mirror is the incipient example in Foucault's essay, just because the mirror is a metaphor which offers a double status: ontological and spatial: either that of the real space taken over at the moment of the projection, or the virtual, ireal space of reflection. The metaphor of the mirror or of the ship can be replaced today with that of the novel which becomes "un lieu sans lieu"[51] and a time without time, therefore without history we would say, meaning a means of transport, conservation and extrapolation of a heterogeneous world. Starting here, the contemporary novel represents a real space of heterotopic memory, which discovers or covers the places which marked the identity of the authors aggressed by history. The metaphor of the heterotopic novel is useful in the case of the contemporary novel only to demonstrate the fact that beyond its critical neo-realist assumption till total exhaustion, there is a common layer, a coagulating element which describes just the heterogeneous character of transition under the domination of the excessive power of history.

Starting from the interference analysed here, linked to the uncertain ontological status of history and memory in contemporary novel, we can identify at least three categories of novels specific for the post-revolution period in Romanian literature:

1. *The heterochrony prose texts* of personal memory are those writings that reconstruct histories from memory, by overlapping immediate time, objective

---

49 Foucault: *Dits et écrits*, p. 752.
50 Foucault: *Dits et écrits*, p. 755.
51 Foucault: *Dits et écrits*, p. 762.

with the anterior subjective one, recovered completely out of personal memory. These are the analepse novels, with analeptic effect, having a fortifying, tonic role through the attempt of the prose-writers at confronting directly with a remembered History. They preserve in memory an anterior time passage, such as the museum or the library, history being reduced to the Subject and its biographical trajectory. Biographism meets a historical collective memory and the intention of this kind of novels is to mark the meeting between the subjective and collective memory, to describe the reactions of the Subject to the group effects of collective memory. Novels such as *Niederungen* (The Low Inlands) (1982, 2012), *Herztier* (The Animal of Heart) (1993) by Herta Müller, *The Hooligan's Return* (2003) by Norman Manea, *Pupa russa* (2004) al lui Gheorghe Crăciun, *Cartea șoaptelor* (The Book of Whispers) (2009) of Varujan Vosganian, *Medgidia, orașul de apoi* (Medgidia, the City Thereafter) (2009) by Cristian Teodorescu, *Provizorat* (Provisional State) (2010) by Gabriela Adameșteanu are at the frontier between personal memory, therefore subjective, and historical, collective memory. This category of novels is therefore fundamented on personal memory, with its help collective memory, the process of affective reconstruction being criteria of authenticity being reconstructed progressively. The role of the heterochronic novel is to rebuild a time through the exclusive mediation of personal memory, contributing so to the attestation of the authenticity of collective memory. Novels are complementary 'spaces' which compose hetero-histories or alternative histories meant to grant veridicity to the collective memory through the personal memory of artistic reflexivity.

Herta Müller and Norman Manea are the exponential prose-writers for this category of novels, both trying to recompose a collective memory through personal memory. They intentionally maintain the confusion of the textual genres proposed, between fiction and autobiography, just to distance themselves from the two temptations, one of excessive biographical subjectivity and the one of convention of the autonomy of fiction. Their fiction belongs to the category of biographical novels, of narrations that recompose a time from memory. Furthermore, the fragmentation in *Niederungen* (The Low Inlands), the apparently autonomous structure of the stories and even the lyric-evasive style are the favourite instruments of extraction from the personal memory of a collective memory. Moreover, Herta Müller's affirmation according to which "You can have a country only based on a biography and my biography is as valid as the biography of a security officer or of a dictator. But I left and they stayed and this lack of equality, this loss of biography discomforted me."[52]

---

[52] Herta Müller: Capcanele memoriei (The traps of memory). In: *Dilema Veche*, 24 January 2011. Consulted at the web adress: http://dilemaveche.ro/sectiune/dilemateca/articol/capcanele-memoriei [25.04.2018].

The trauma of lost biography is compensated through the recovery of personal memory and its fictionalisation, the novel construct being a hybrid. And Norman Manea starts from the premise that "Memory is a process that you cannot detain. You do what you can, use any memory that you have, but the past is not exactly what you think it is", naming the text as 'hybrid', a mixture between fictional type and memoir, fact observed accurately by literary critics. He admits that his writing is a combination of genres:

> The American editor has catalogued it as *memoir*, but in Germany it appeared as *self-portrait*, in Italy it was called a *life* and in Spain it was a *novel*. It may be read in different ways. In Romania, where I had to make the decision, I told them not to use subtitles, but only *The Hooligan's Return*.[53]

These heterochronies are more than simple anamneses, histories of a collective disease provoked by the Subjects by the excesses of History and its pressures to manipulate collective memory. The biographical novels of the two authors are biographical, subjective reconstitutions of an authentic memoir and the gender frontier becomes a privileged instrument because this only shows what has been hidden in the search for an authenticity of the past.

Gheorghe Crăciun, in *Pupa russa* (2004), oscillates between interior monologue and conversation or mundane dialogue, with the intention of consolidating the sensation of authenticity. G. Crăciun's textualism, in the sense of textual imagery, is evident, and the "Fake Journal to a Novel" reminds of moral combustion, therefore of the placement of the action within the depth of the conscience, as we can notice with Marguerite Yourcenar in her *Carnets de notes de Mémoires d'Hadrien* (1977). This descent into the epic laboratory has as basis the intention of consolidating the authentic gesture of narrativity in order to recompose a lost time.

On the other side, Cristian Teodorescu, in *Medgidia, orașul de apoi* (Medgidia, the City Thereafter) (2009), proposes a succession of histories and the reader is provoked to recompose the great History through the small history of a town in picturesque Dobrogea of the last century. The modular structure of the 100 stories has as linking factor a nucleus of characters to which others are progressively added. Theodorescu Family, Fanică and his wife, Virginica, the administrators of the station and the waiter Ionică, major Scipion who is the commander of the unit in Medgidia and his lover, doctor Lea, the judge of the town, the seller Haikis, are

---

[53] See Norman Manea: The Great Work and the Compromised Man: An Interview with Norman Manea. In: *Los Angeles Review of Books*, 2 February 2014. Consulted at the web adress: https://lareviewofbooks.org/article/great-work-compromised-man-interview-norman-manea/ [25.04.2018].

only some of the characters who recompose seemingly from aesthetised personal memory this Foucauldian 'different space'.

The dialogue with history is provoking through its sequentiality and through the maintenance of a temporal and authentic indecision, intentionally practised by the author. Therefore, we see on the one side a discrete process of history and an evident interest for its demythisation after the mythologizing abuse in communism and, on the other side, a personal memory, subjective through the recomposition of individual destinies.

The junction between subjective and collective memory are realised through the articulation of the macro-image of the city, this disappeared arch-Medgidia, "the afterwards city" or in a dissolution process and through the maintenance of the tension between autobiography (Theodorescu family) and fiction. In *Provizorat* (Provisional State) (2010) by Gabriela Adameșteanu, the feminine character, Letiția Arcan, will affirm exponentially that for this category of heterochronic novels "The future will not bring the best surprises, but the past which we do not stop to reread throughout our life."[54] It is the exponential voice of the implicit author, a powerful demonstration of the revisiting of the past through personal memory, in order to reconstitute what was left of History and to assure an identity of the Subject. Oscillating between the years 70 and 40 Adameșteanu proves the condition of a provisional state of history and the effects produced on it by personal and collective memory. Reactivating a complex image of the social life from the communist period out of the collective memory and overlapping it on Letiția's intimacy, the prose-writer grants relevance to the idea of heterochrony, a construction in the present of the future.

2. *The utopia proses of the personal imaginary* are those that evade history by avoiding the present of the narration, using sur-real images. These novels avoid the direct contact with reality, overcoming the obsession of the social diorama of the present or of the past by building parallel worlds in which we observe a translation of the panoramic view towards a utopic vision. Utopia novels are those that offer:

> [...] les emplacements sans lieu réel. Ce sont les emplacements qui entretiennent avec l'espace réel de la société un rapport général d'analogie directe ou inversée. C'est la société elle-même perfectionnée ou c'est l'inverse de la société, mais, de toute façon, ces utopies sont des espaces qui sont fondamentalement essentiellement iréells.[55]

Therefore, we discover ideal, imaginary universes in which we observe an escape from reality, a reclusion or a refuse of the direct confrontation with it, in which either an agglutinated memory persists, or one exulted by an explosive imaginary.

---

54 Gabriela Adameșteanu: *Provizorat* (Provisorate State). Iași: Polirom 2010, p. 194.
55 Foucault: *Dits et écrits*, p. 755.

As in Blecher[56] unreality takes the place of reality becoming another utopic form of placement of the Subject. Memory and history become therefore simple pretexts in the searching trail of those possible worlds.

From *Orbitor. Aripa stângă* (Blinding. Left Wing) (1996) by Mircea Cărtărescu, to Petru Cimpoeșu with *Povestea Marelui Brigand* (The Story of the Great Brigand) (2000), Florina Ilis with the novel *Cruciada copiilor* (The Crusade of the Children) (2005), to *Teodosie cel Mic* (Teodosie the Little) (2006) by Răzvan Rădulescu, to the novel *Cine adoarme ultimul* (Who Sleeps Last) (2007) by Bogdan Popescu, or even *Matei Brunul* (2011) by Lucian Dan Teodorovici, these complex narrations proposes such parallel worlds in which the functioning principles of reality are reversed. These kinds of narratives which propose utopian spaces as amnesic solutions to the conflict with History, which voluntarily reverses the recurrence Reality-Memory-History, correspond to the general principles of utopias, either as critical positions towards reality, either as the offer of different worlds in which flaws or disfunctionalities of the precedent world are not longer to be found or are eliminated.[57] Moreover, this type of novel compensates the loss of collective memory and/or the personal one with parallel worlds in which Subjects defy the norms of the real, eliminating therefore the excesses of the power of History. Utopias have a communicative-compensatory function, fulfilling an emptiness of the real which is of prosaic nature, which can not constitute matter for fiction. The reconstitution of the past, as in heterocronias novels, or of the present, such as in heterotopias, does not reveal an objective for this group of writers. They only observe the aporia of the referential novels and propose spaces with compensatory and constitutive function, novels which rewrite History in a utopic manner.

In the *Orbitor. Aripa stângă* (Blinding. Left Wing) by Cărtărescu, largely considered "the novel of the decade",[58] we identify a world which is not at all similar to Max Blecher's 'panopticon', in which the wax figures are this time multiplications of the Self and journeys into complex worlds that come from the explosive imaginary of the author. Cărtărescu's images have only rhizomatic links to immediate reality, his characters coming down to a world in which there is a postmodern diorama, a view of from the Writer-God, a world that is exclusively born in and through the author-narrator and which remains the only acceptable dimension of the real. The ultimate purpose of this complex world is the one of Writing, as a complex process of ocultation into the text. The oniric perspectivism is one of the main points of this novel, the reshape of sight into vision and identification of

---

56 See *infra*. chap. 3.
57 Anne Staquet: *L'utopie ou les fictions subversives*. Zurich, Québec: Grand Midi 2002, p. 7.
58 See *infra*. cap. 5.1.2.

the world from the interior, as for 'Black Romantics',[59] fact which offers complexity to the oniric utopias of *Orbitor*.

The *Left Wing* is the first part of the trilogy building a surrealist parallel, thus compensating a parallel surrealist world, balancing something towards the role of History, but which makes personal memory a projection instrument in this complex world. The intentional confusion of the levels of reality is one of the current practices of the author, close to Blecher's distancing as a consequence of the contemplation of the fixed point. The oniric utopia of Cărtărescu's *Orbitor* (Blinding) presupposes a co-substantiality between the Subject and the projected universe, or a projection of the narrative ego in reality, a world in which Bucharest is "my city, my alter-ego". The city and therefore Cărtărescu's world are parallel to reality, at least in *Left Wing* and *The Body*, that is in the first two parts of the trilogy, which allows the extrapolation of the hallucinatory world created in the author's imaginary or of some characters like Hermann, on reality. It is certain that by looking at these two parts of the trilogy *Blinding* in contrast to the third part, we observe a reversed focalisation, from the real towards the imaginary, and we understand completely the functionality of the oneiric utopias proposed by the author. It is truly a resonance solution, of concrete descendence from Blecher's prose, of transgression of the concrete devoid of meaning, aggressed by the history which instrumentalised collective memory. The complexity of this compensating universe is the one observed by Carmen Mușat:

> The monozygotic twins, dreaming embryos, the author and his character are placed on the one side and the other of the textual mirror which functions as a fascinating kaleidoscope: with every switch the image changes, the pieces of the puzzle are reorganised, making up imaginary funambulist geographies, bursting many times in full realism of descriptions (see the incursion of Ionel in *Blinding* in the depth of Puskin's statue).[60]

Even Florina Ilis' novel, *Cruciada copiilor* (The Crusade of the Children) (2005), although it proposes a situation with roots in the communist collective memory, that of the departure of the pupil pioneers by train for a school camp in Năvodari, develops around a utopia. Doubled by the historical utopia of "Crusade of the children" from 1212, the allegorical utopia of Florina Ilis presupposes that, as in the case of *Lord of the Flies* (1954), by William Golding, there is another *mise en abîme*, a world in another world, in which children will take over the power over the train.

---

59 See Mario Praz: *The Romantic Agony*. Translated from the italian by Angus Davidson. Oxford: Oxford University Press 1954.

60 Carmen Mușat: *Strategiile subversiunii. Descriere și narațiune în proza postmodernă românească* (Subversion Strategies. Description and Narration in Romanian Postmodern Prose). Postface by Mircea Martin. Pitești: Paralela 45 2002, p. 274.

Simona Sora's intuition regarding the utopian resources of the novel confirms the fact that Florina Ilis exploits a historical topic on which she juxtaposes a utopia in order to avoid contact with history. She uses collective memory in a utopian present, in which the innocence of the children becomes an illusion:

> The crusade of the children is a story about the loss of innocence, fatal, certain, mathematical loss in the world. A heroic-mystical-satyric epopee, treated simultaneously with the weapons of the utopia and with those of high 'reportage', which seems linked-paradoxically-with the tradition of *Țiganiada* or of Iocan's clearing, but also with Andrei Codrescu's metatextual postmodernism in Mesi@. The subject, purely utopian, seems taken out of the hottest and most aberrant journalistic reality: a special vacation train leaves Cluj for Năvodari, but it never arrives there. Through a conspiracy of the entire universe (novelistic and Romanian), the train is conquered by the school children, each with his own drama, led by a street child, the nephew of 'the last witch' in Ferentari. The story goes on, as in time and space unity, the classical hijack, firing in Posada (where else?), the re-grouping and then the predictable failure, the reintegration in the realist circuit of hierarchies and abuses.[61]

Moreover, Lucian Dan Teodorovici starts from an apparent heterochrony in his 2011 novel *Matei Brunul*. Matei is the amnesic political convict who partially loses his memory after a battle in the detention period, remembering just the years before 1937. After such a physical shock he appears as an ideal image, the model convict who believes in the ideology of power, in the ideal metaphor of the New Man, being the perfect puppet in the hands of the system represented by the security officer Bojin. Matei's amnesia functions as a sort of memory allegories aggressed by power or even of the conservation instinct through forgetfulness. Therefore, the allegory of amnesia, as a solution for the ideal of Lukes' tri-dimensional power or of Foucauldian excessive power is certain. The man without memory is therefore 'The New Man', the ideal man, who is built on a collective memory, the man historically manipulated. Teodorovici's utopia consists in the narrative direction of the utopia of History, in offering a puppet theatre parallel to the world, in which the autism of Matei Brunul and his amnesia as a consequence of an aggression, is the ideal of the New World. Matei is "A man caught by history and dragged by it. A puppeteer who forgot to lead its puppet, he forgot the self. And then not knowing how to lead any more, he cannot protect himself when he is led by the others."[62]

---

[61] Simona Sora: O epopee eroi-mistico-satirică (A Heroical-Mystical-Satyrical Epic). In: *Dilema Veche*, Nb. 98/2–8 December 2005 Consulted at the web adress: http://www.romaniaculturala.ro/articol.php?cod=6788 [26.04.2018].

[62] Lucian Dan Teodorovici: *Matei Brunul*, romanul păpușarului mânuit (*Matei Brunul*, the Novel of the handled pupetter). In: *Jurnalul național*, 17 October 2011. Consulted at the web adress: http://jurnalul.ro/cultura/carte/lucian-dan-teodorovici-matei-brunul-romanul-papusarului-manuit-593889.html [25.04.2018].

The utopian-allegorical fantasia in *Teodosie cel Mic* (Teodosie the Little) by Răzvan Rădulescu, with Pisicâinele Gavril, the owl Kaliopi, Samoil the minotaurus who is in charge of the Mushroom plantation etc., the Saint Village in Bogdan Popescu's prose, with Foiște and Repetentu who self-name themselves "two moonstruck Gods" are compensatory utopian universes which abstract any historical excess. The carnivalesque and burlesque of the utopias imagined by this category of prose-writers is a sort of a Baroque ostentation of the utopian world which proposes implicitly the ushering out of history through the front door, assuring the novel the power to avoid the cliché reproduction of immediate reality. The fantasias of utopian novels presuppose an implicit process of history and memory.

3. *The heterotopian prose texts of history* are those that built histories within the present of the text, through juxtaposing and observing the impact of the remembered past on the present. These are the novels of the reminiscences, according to the definition given by Paul Ricoeur. If we were to go back to Foucauldian spaces we would affirm that we witness a generalisation of the heterotopia of crises, which is what Foucault observes primarily in primitive societies as privileged, sacred or forbidden spaces, destined to individuals in dissonance to the societies they come from. Heterotopic novels, starting from this formula, would represent the generalisation of deviation or instituting it as a norm, therefore the reversal of the functioning criteria of the society. It is the juxtaposition in the same place of some diverse, divergent or even incompatible spaces, in which the subject finds its position with difficulty.

Novels which are integrated in this category of heterotopic proses would be those of Petru Cimpoeșu, *Simion Liftnicul* (Simion the Elevator Man) (2001), of Dumitru Țepeneag, *Maramureș* (2001), of Radu Aldulescu, *Proorocii Ierusalimului* (The Prophets of Jerusalim) (2004), Dan Lungu, *Raiul găinilor* (Chicken Paradise) (2007) or *Sunt o babă comunistă* (I'm a Communist Biddy) (2007), Horia Ursu's novel, *Asediul Vienei* (The Siege of Vienna) (2007), of Radu Pavel Gheo, *Noapte bună, copii!* (Good night, children!) (2010) or of Ovidiu Nimigean, *Rădăcina de bucsău* (The Root of Weaver's Broom) (2010).

In the novel of Ovidiu Nimigean, Liviu, the reflecting Subject of the novel, is the resonating nucleus of the histories in the novel. He is not to be found in the post-communist world, trying to understand its dysfunctionalities, succeeding just to understand "that almost all that followed Ceaușescu's fall is a devilish dance on the graves of those killed in December." Here the heterotopy of crises is amplified by the fact that Liviu witnesses the agony of his mother, with all the physiological degradation associated and with the malfunctioning of the health care system associated with the acute feeling of failure. As the author observed, it is a novel "about the search for self, about love and hate, that odi et amo of couples forever, about believing and not believing at the same time, about decrepitude and dignity at the same time, about cowardice and heroism at the same time."[63]

In Horia Ursu's novel, *Asediul Vienei* (The Siege of Vienna) (2007), we have another variant of Cristian Teodorescu's Medgidia or the Abraxa town of Petru Cimpoeșu. It is the world of the little town Apud in Transylvania, in which the author gradually destroys historical clichés, such as multi-ethnicity, multiculturalism, the cult of labour and of order etc. this world is more like an unhappy Babel, suppressed by a black lethargy, with people emigrating or wanting to, old men who place ads to sell their organs or grave places, therefore a world in a never ending crisis.

The neorealism of these novels creates the impression of sinking into an obsessive reality which consumes the energies of the characters, leading to the loss of their identity. But this type of novel corresponds to the observation of Roland Barthes in *S/Z*, who talked about a literature which does not necessarily set out to reproduce reality, but to demonstrate the scholarly, therefore artificial character and, last, but not least, an impersonal one. It is what Carmen Mușat observed, with reference to Romanian postmodern prose: "The realist attitude of the postmodern writers presupposes the recognition and assumption of the prefabricated nature of reality, as the camouflaged intertextuality of any reference."[64] The feeling of artificiality of this world in crises appears as a distinctive coordinate of this category of novels. For example, the 'misters' and 'misses' in Cimpoeșu's novel (Mr Toma, Mr Vasile, Mr Ion, Mr Anghel, Mr Elefterie, Mr Eftimie or Mrs Filofteia, Mrs Alis, Mrs Gudelia, Mrs Pelaghia) composing a sometimes grotesque theatre through counterfeit and superficiality. The transfer of artificiality from real to fictional creates the sensation of naturalness, leading to the intentional confusion of the worlds.

In the same heterotopic novel, the Subject is the one who bears the immediate reality which is powerfully determined by the past, by a History which still exercises subjacent pressures, which has warped the present by manipulating collective memory. If regarding modern memory, Nora affirmed that "Modern memory is, above all, archival. It relies entirely on the materiality of the trace, the immediacy of the recording, the visibility of the image. What began as writing

---

[63] Ovidiu Nimigean: Bucuria de a constata că povestea ajunge la celălalt, că nu este doar o bizarerie autistă (The joy of acknowledging that the story reaches the other, that it is not an autistic bizarreness). In: *Adevărul*, 12 October 2010. Consulted at the web adress: http://adevarul.ro/locale/timisoara/interviu-ovidiu-nimigean-bucuria-constata-povestea-ajunge-celalalt-nu-doar-bizarerie-autista-1_50aeb10c7c42d5a6639f2db7/index.html [25.04.2018].
[64] Mușat: *Strategiile subversiunii*, p. 193.

ends as high fidelity and tape recording."⁶⁵ Whereas, the heterotopic contemporary novel proposes a camouflage of the memory behind the real and a determination of this one. Therefore, the neorealism of these novels is defined as a memory place, a real *mise en abîme*.⁶⁶

Therefore, the heterotopic novel is the predilect genre of the contemporary novel, exposing and denouncing the artificiality of the world in two distinct stages, occulting history in the deepness of the mundane labyrinth and then suddenly revealing it, in a process of epiphany of collective memory, which shows itself and lives its representative moments, demonstrating its dependence on history. The moment of transition, the predilect space of these novels is, in its generality, a heterotopic frame of the crises in which the characters prove that the rupture from history is impossible, fact which provokes their inadaptation. The strategy of the impersonalization of power is a favourite instrument of the demonstration of social desagregation. Collapsed in the illusion of the unity of collective memory, manipulated by history, the Subjects of the heterotopic novels express an ontological block, as their actions lack span and perspective. In Horia Ursu's imaginary heterotopic town, Apud, everything 'is said', 'is talked about' and 'is even done' neutrally, vague and impersonally, facing the dissolution of power under the thin ice of Romanian transition nightmare.

5.2 The Impersonalization of Power and the Stigma of Historical Memory

> "It is difficult to talk simply when you are good with words."⁶⁷

5.2.1 The Novel without Memory and History in the Ecuation of Impersonalization. From Apud to Vienna and back

In the relevant radiography of 'the dark literary decade', Radu G. Țeposu observes that the accuracy of the epic images on reality come from the 'disillusionment' of the prose writer related to the arch-contemplated real. Therefore, we observe

---

65 Pierre Nora: Between Memory and History: Les Lieux de Mémoire. Translated by Marc Roudebush. In: *Representations*, No. 26, Special Issue: Memory and Counter-Memory. Spring 1989, p. 13.
66 Nora: Between Memory and History, p. 20.
67 Ursu: *Asediul Vienei*, p. 85.

the Weberian of "eine Entzauberung der Welt", projected to the centre of the narrative process. The narrative unravelling of the '80s writers has an aesthetic effect as, "The real effect has to be one of writing, as well", an effect which has, besides "the dismantling of the real into cinematographic sequences",[68] constitutes some of the reference points of the postmodern poetics of Romanian prose. Moreover, the observers of the literary phenomenon post '80s, interesting as literary formula, just because of its passing and adaptability to a history or another and/or from a generation or another, observe a return and a progressive metamorphosis of postmodern textuality which culminated in the 2000s, through the novels of writers such as Mircea Cărtărescu, Cristian Teodorescu, Gheorghe Crăciun.

The phenomenon of adaptation to the conditions of the new time has created a beneficial situation for the Romanian novel, specific to the new transition aesthetics, through which the margin, peripheral worlds start to become attractive and replace centrality gradually. It is obviously the case of the referential reversal, of the described worlds but also of authors.

If the epic voices of the authors of the '80s, such as Ioan Groşan, Bedros Horasangian or Ştefan Agopian are blurred, others such as Petru Cimpoeşu or Cristian Teodorescu, or even less well-known, such as Horia Ursu, initially placed "at the margin of the canon start to weigh a lot in the eschatology of the trend."[69] Also, in an interview given to Iolanda Malamen, Petru Cimpoeşu claims his vocation of a 'marginal', 'outsider' writer, which grants him authenticity in the public show of the time: "To signal a small paradox: all my books have received important prizes, although I am still an obscure author, I am, as I have said, a writer without backup, provincial, or, if you prefer, an outsider through vocation. To be honest, it is more comfortable that way."[70]

Through his 2000 novel, *Povestea Marelui Brigand* (The Story of the Great Brigand) and the 2001 novel *Simion liftnicul* Cimpoeşu's comeback, initially integrated by Radu G. Ţeposu in the category of "the mythology of the derisory",[71]

---

[68] Radu G. Ţeposu: *Istoria tragică şi grotescă a întunecatului deceniu literar nouă* (The Tragic and Grotesque History of the Dark Nineth Literay Decade). Third Edition. Preface by Al. Cistelecan. Bucureşti: Cartea Românească 2006, p. 26.
[69] Alex Goldiş: Despre mediocritate şi alţi demoni (About Mediocrity and Other Demons). In: *Cultura*, nb. 95/2007-10-25 Consulted at the web adress: http://revistacultura.ro/cultura.php?-articol=1803 [27.04.2018].
[70] Petru Cimpoeşu: Materia primă a creaţiei este libertatea (The Raw Material of Creation is Liberty). Interview given to Iolanda Malamen. In: *Ziua*, 24 August 2006. Consulted at the web adress: http://www.9am.ro/stiri-revista-presei/2006-08-24/materia-prima-a-creatiei-este-libertatea.html [25.04.2018].
[71] Ţeposu: *Istoria tragică şi grotescă*, p. 197.

together with prose-writers such as Bedros Horasangian or Cristian Teodorescu, constitute, without doubt, a revelation in contemporary prose. He succeeds a metamorphosis of the textual poetics on one side, but also an avoidance, an escape from the neo-realism of the crises in the transition period, on the other side, demonstrating the fact that the coming back to literature is not a calculated fact, projected, with pragmatic stake, but a necessity of subjective nature, with an aesthetical stake.

Starting from the subjective considerations, but also from the vocational category of writing, we observe that *Povestea Marelui Brigand* (The Story of the Great Brigand) contains a sort of "failed metanoia",[72] being implicitly "a reflection, a meditation about the relationship of man with the transcendent"[73] in the context of Romanian utopia in the city of Abraxa. On the other side, *Simion liftnicul*, "The novel with angels and Moldavians" is the anti-novel of neo-realist transition, through its caricaturization, contrary to Mircea Iorgulescu's[74] affirmation, through the religious pastiche, but also the dark irony which statues the tolerant parodic level of the immediate reality. Cimpoeșu's epic sanguinity defies the phlegmatic pattern of the other novelist heterotopias, including some excessively anchored in the real, such as *Proorocii Ierusalimului* (The Prophets of Jerusalem) or *Sunt o babă comunistă* (I'm a Communist Biddy). Cimpoeșu's return to the novel is more than an ironical radiography of transition, it is a search for the complementary meanings of the immediate. From this point of view, unlike *Povestea Marelui Brigand*, a "utopian-imaginative"[75] novel, *Simion Liftnicul* does not totally give up the meeting with reality, as the level of the parable is profoundly anchored in this, a parable-realist mise-en-abîme, in which the focalization is progressive, from the city to the communist block of flats, the staircase of the block and the lift. The prose-writer demonstrates here "the acute sense of reality",[76] just that reality is not the main stake, but its parabolization. From here the meta-realist character of Cimpoeșu's heterotopic novel. The block lift, Simion's space of isolation, is,

---

[72] See the observations of the author in an interview entitled: Scriind, ordonezi lumea (By writing, you order the world differently). In: *Contemporanul*, May 2007, p. 15–16.

[73] Petru Cimpoeșu in the interview given to Ovidiu Simonca, entitled: Eu sunt un om cu umor (I am a humorous man). In: *Observator cultural*, nb. 112 (369)/2007. Consulted at the web adress: https://www.observatorcultural.ro/articol/eu-sint-un-om-cu-umor-interviu-cu-petru-cimpoesu-2/ [26.04.2018].

[74] Mircea Iorgulescu: Viața la români după Evenimente (Life for Romanians after Events). In: *Revista 22*, nb. 51/December 2001, p. 15. He claims that Cimpoeșu's world, with "permanent ambiguity", "never has a caricatural aspect", but is seen with warmth and understanding.

[75] Manolescu: *Istoria critică a literaturii române*, p. 1368.

[76] Manolescu: *Istoria critică a literaturii române*, p. 1368.

first of all, another space of reality, a heterotopia of transition where Memory and History are suspended.

In this background, Simion is the image of a caricature camouflage of the sacred into profane, or better said a camouflage of Memory into History. It is about the communist memory, of the reflexes and automatisms, in the history of the '90's transition. Cimpoeşu's novel formula is notable exactly for the avoidance of the direct critical register, the prose-writer using the instruments of caricature and the search or camouflage of the Christian spiritual meaning behind the mundane scheme. The prose writer is consistent with "the incisive, alert, economical style" or "the narrative travesties" and "the naive-ironical description", which consecrated him as an important writer of the '80s generation, and the "depth of perception"[77] is doubled in recent novels by the dimension of parable and religious pastiche. These two create and entertain the faith that behind the temporal and mundane suspension of the characters there is meaning, even mystical.

In this epic landscape of the meta-real universe, Cimpoeşu's Abraxa is not the only parabolic place, of searching and dissipation of meanings, being followed by Horia Ursu's Transilvanian Apud, a fact which supports the need of these writers to use the instrument of parabolic analogy or even allegorical fantasy[78] to avoid the excess reality of the heterotopic novel, by situating itself in its shadow. Therefore, in the context of the discussion about the return to the '80s writers, Horia Ursu is the novelist who succeeds to make a comeback at least as spectacular as that of Cimpoeşu in the eclectic landscape of the novels of the 2000s and equally, influenced by the time without history of transition. Horia Ursu's comeback to the centre of the contemporary epic novel, as in Cimpoeşu's case, is so much spectacular as Horia Ursu has not been placed in the centre of the '80s poetics and he succeeds in marking contemporary prose by not assuming its neorealist formula. He appears as an author who reinvents writing, avoiding subtlety, using aesthetic strategies. He was a member of 'Echinox' circumstantially, a marginal '80s writer and a 2000 generation writer without the predisposition of the miserability of the last generation.

The image here is of a prose-writer with three ages or which, only after the success of the novel *Asediul Vienei* (The Siege of Vienna) was assumed by three generations, who was classified by critics in at least two generations, a prose-writer whose writing, as in the case of Petru Cimpoeşu, can only be partially associated to the generational programmatic criteria. In the larger view of postmodernism, both Cimpoeşu and Ursu can be associated to a type of rhetoric

---

77 Ţeposu: *Istoria tragică şi grotescă*, p. 202.
78 Ţeposu: *Istoria tragică şi grotescă*, p. 43.

specific to the end of the century. Moreover, the contact with history, through the memory or the metamorphosis of history into reality, makes the prose-writer accept the authenticity of history which can be regained through discourse or the rhetoric of art, of the novel. "Postmodern man cannot be freed of the past, as it comes back automatically into his consciousness, through discourse, through rhetoric. And to suppress rhetoric means at least to refuse the own human substance transmitted by memory through language."[79]

Horia Ursu makes his debut in the collective volume *Debut 86*, with the short stories *Scrisoare acasă* (Letter Home) and *Iarbă de august* (August Grass) and individually with the 1988 volume, *Anotimpurile după Zenovie* (Seasons after Zenovie), at the same publishing house, Cartea Românească, republished in 2001, at the publishing house Paralela 45, with the title *Anotimpurile dupa Zenovie și alte proze* (Seasons after Zenovie and Other Short Stories). He publishes short prose in the volume *Generația 80 în proză scurtă* (The '80s Generation in Short Prose) from 1998, which appeared again at the same publishing house. In 2008, he published at Eikon a monographic volume entitled *Milan Kundera: teme, variațiuni, paradoxuri terminale* (Milan Kundera: themes, variations, terminal paradoxes). But notable critical reactions appeared with the publishing of the volume *Asediul Vienei* in 2007. Once this novel had favourable reviews, it also got distinctions that placed him among the most prized contemporary prose-writers, the author being distinguished with the 'Ion Creangă' Award of the Romanian Academy, with the Prize of the Writers' Union, with the Prize The Book of the Year from the Cluj Branch of the Writers' Union, with the prize of the magazines *Observator cultural*, *Tribuna* or *Familia*.

Zenovie, the character of the short story which gives the title of the volume, is a character searching for identity, with "an heredity which predisposes him towards day-dreaming and contemplation", as can be read on the 4th cover of the 2010 volume, from Dacia Publishing House, by Marian Papahagi. Zenovie's block is that one of the lack of perspective, a real Musil's "man without qualities" and without any alternative (Papahagi) in a limited and predictable universe, of provincial monotony and degradation. Apud is the town-centre of this minor world of Checkhovian province, as the character model of Zenovie is not "the man without qualities" of Musil's central European modernity. Therefore, we observe a "contamination by the anguishes of the great novel Central-Eastern-European (from Broch to Kundera)",[80] but not a scholarly or conscientious one,

---

[79] Țeposu: *Istoria tragică și grotescă*, p. 60.
[80] Adriana Stan: Realismul palimpsest (Realism Palimpsest). In: *Tribuna*, year IX, 1–15 November 2010, p. 5.

but to a co-substantiality of decadent atmosphere, the overlapping of feelings of calmness and inutility, generated by a history in an accelerated process of entropy. Tortured by heavy memory, Ursu's characters are living the obsession of the end. This is the main association with the main novels of central-Europeanness. Ever since 1988, Horia Ursu, in the *Telquel* atmosphere of Romanian postmodernism, succeeds in avoiding the ludic excess of the period, the excess of technicism and in filtering introscopically into the details of reality, initiating the sinuous and grave path of the impersonalization of his Subject. Still introscopically he is intuitive about the sinuous and serious path of the impersonalization of his Subject. He is intuitive about Zenovie's exceptional character, without portraying him in thick and clear touches such as the naturalists, describing him as "slow, awkward, distracted, used to split hairs and dreaming". Stories such as *Maxim, Cu soarele în față* (Facing the Sun), *Iarbă din august* (August Grass), *Scrisoare acasă* (Letter Home), *În preajma țintei care cade* (Near the Falling Target) sau *Propria persoană* (The Own Person) propose images of the 'sleepy' Apud, of a world in a slow degradation process, with eclectic identities, without perspectives, clinging on to the past and remaining invariably suspended in it. These are also the Subjects objected to a complex narrative X-ray.

And to realise thoroughly such epic dioramas of a marginal and marginalised world, a different type of slowness is needed, a mechanism of narrative slowness, remembering the idea that "Every text, after all (as I have already written) is a lazy machine asking the reader to do some of his work."[81] The metaphor "inferential walks"[82] used by Eco in explaining narrative slowness at a certain point, is useful in a text such as that of Horia Ursu, because the reader is invited to make mnemonic inferences of projection into the communist history in order to understand the situation of the present. The understanding of the actuality through the past, to which Ursu's text makes reference, is one of the keys to the understanding of the text. This is the result of the delay through the narrative woods. The author freezes the present or just imprints it a strange slowness, in order to make place for a mnemonic interference from the reader which gives meaning to the described world. Suddenly, the narrative heterotopia becomes the proximal genre of the representation of transition. Hence the strangeness of this revisitation, far and still so close to our world.

Nevertheless, the narrative delay, with inferential effects, of captivating and stimulating a lethargic Memory, even paralysed by the History of the reader of our

---

[81] Eco: *Six walks*, p. 3.
[82] Eco: *Six walks*, p. 50.

time, has a correspondence in the laboratory of the epic construction. We have the explanation of the thirteen years 'slowness' of the writing, the epic construction which is therefore one of the most elaborated novels of the period. Horia Ursu, in an interview for *Suplimentul de cultură*, nb.175/2008, granted to Bogdan Romaniuc, uses one of Emil Cioran's syllogisms from *Avantajele exilului* (The Advantages of Exile), in order to explain the complex process of the epic construction: "La prose demande, pour se développer, une certaine rigueur, un état social différencié; et une tradition: elle est délibérée, construite; [...] Créer une littérature c'est créer une prose."[83]

The rigour of the epic construction presupposes for the author of the *Asediul Vienei* (The Siege of Vienna) a complex observation process and also of social analyses, as well as the necessary detachment which takes time, offers time and space for the development of an epic rationalism seen behind the complex web of the novel. This detachment permits the author to observe accurately the effects of the power of History. He identifies here the fact that "The tonic feeling of freedom coexists with its gay hysteria or with a grotesque parody."[84]

The paradox of the '90s, explained by Ursu and imprinted in the smallest details of the novel, consists in the coexistence and collision of the states and reactions facing a free rhetoric, a fact which has generated the hallucinating public conflicts of the transition:

> The year 1989 had become the Year of Romania, to be transformed afterwards through an inconsistent and carnivalesque exaltation in the Year of Universal Romania, through a sad and grandiose emigration. The real suffering, banalised through supra-exposure or supra-solicitation, had become an export product, a simple identity-publicity slogan which led neither to compassion, nor to redemption.[85]

From such an analysis of the paradoxes of our contemporaneity, the prose-writer extracts the theme of the novel, which is the engine of Eco's 'lazy car', which explores the immediate reality. This topic, the author says propedeutical, is camouflaged in the exclamation of the postman Ghereță, being:

> Inscribed in the gay-mad cry of Ghereță: 'Good people, we have won! Good people, we have died!' He announces, in fact, the death of a cardinal point, the East, with political connotations. Any loss leaves emptiness behind. This emptiness has naturally become the

---

[83] Cioran: *Oeuvres*, p. 855. See also Horia Ursu: Trei răspunsuri de la Horia Ursu (Three Answers from Horia Ursu). In: *Suplimentul de cultură*, nb. 175, 19-04-2008. Consulted at the web adress: http://suplimentuldecultura.ro/3255/trei-raspunsuri-de-la-horia-ursu/ [25.04.2018].
[84] Ursu: Trei răspunsuri de la Horia Ursu.
[85] Ursu: Trei răspunsuri de la Horia Ursu.

theme-key, as the void had a past and colours that we have explored as an archaeologist-restorer and, paradoxically, as an archaeologist -constructor.[86]

The effects of the loss of history and memory, which lead to a certain impersonalization of the Subjects, to its float in the void without escape, are to be found projected ironically in the most representative scenes of the novel. Certainly one of the representative sequences for the panoramic emphasizing of the chromatics of the void in the ironic formula is the one in which the old Jewish clockmaker Cain, the one who "provided the hour of London anytime. And of Central Europe", is about to leave Apud for Israel, the place of his future impersonal death, "without characterization", after Gheretă's sigh. Without Cain, as a woman under a sun umbrella said, the people in Apud will not know what world they are living in, and his discourse from the balcony to Carolina Market addressed to the people who "had nowhere to go", meaning to those definitely "had a difficult time", being suspended in the vertigo of the Transylvanian void, between two epochs, between two worlds. Then, as a corollary, the discourse of the mayor in Apud is held, which is in fact the ironical auctorial voice, the one who takes the "pathway of nuances, seldom ironical and not few times on counterpoint, even cruel, why not cynical, with the intact hope that I will avoid the confrontation without appeal and without return."[87]

The mayor, in his hypostasis of representative power of the majority, but also of ironical auctorial voice, in an impressive rhetoric, legitimised and legitimising, assures Cain of "eternal memory", wishing anticipatively "să vă fie țărâna ușoară" (peace to his ashes). The effect of Cain's leaving is an emptiness which reminds us of the theme of the novel:

> You leave an empty place behind in which the mayor will place a bronze memorial plaque with the inscription 'The Jewish Emptiness' which together with 'The German Emptiness' will shine forever on the frontline of our history, even fuller of void.[88]

But the scene of Cain's leaving is representative not only thematically, as an extrapolation of the novel, with reference to the effect of impersonalization left behind by the successive waves of the abandonment of space, but also by the emptiness of qualities, in the meaning preferred by Musil. Therefore, we must return to the conviction of the author, who states that "The novel does not replace History and does not subordinate it unconditionally, but it cannot turn back or mystificate, either."[89]

---

86 Ursu: Trei răspunsuri de la Horia Ursu.
87 Ursu: Trei răspunsuri de la Horia Ursu.
88 Ursu: *Asediul Vienei*, p. 129.
89 Ursu: Trei răspunsuri de la Horia Ursu.

The narrative instrument has the capacity to generate a certain tension of the rapport with History, to entertain it, inclusively through the strategy of intentional dilution of an eloquent scene, such as the one of Cain's leave. It is not only about a descriptive dilution, but also an intentional postponing which is in accord to the emotional paradox of the Subject who wants to leave but is nostalgic after this heterotopic world.

Another evoking delay who presupposes a narrative game of translation from the slowness of the description, a "lazy machine",[90] to the 'languor' of the character, is the one in which Petru follows an imaginary map, by an imaginary traveller. Reaching Vienna, which fact "the auctorial instance thinks it is the one who fissures it and sends it into derisory",[91] he is blocked for inexplicable reasons, and "there was an emptiness in his mind which fell from above, the same word: Vienna, Vienna."[92] The same suspension has an effect on his self, as a result of this emptiness: "He himself twisted in the void of his own memory as in a black hole ready to swallow him forever." The mnemonic emptiness provoked by the history which functioned as a vacuum seems to be of Cioranian origin. The fact that beyond Vienna lies the void of a province which lacks conscience and has a destiny dashed by History, an excessive and aggressed Memory, makes the author of the *Syllogismes de l'amertume*[93] observe the temporal void in which he is projected, 'the curse' of impersonalization into and under the destructive power of History.

In such a Transylvanian void, to paraphrase the same Cioran who spoke about 'neantul valah' (the Wallachian nothingness), Horia Ursu places the action of his novel, *Asediul Vienei* (The Siege of Vienna), a void which translates here through a state specific for the characters, through void and identity dispersion, of losing historical values, of amnesia till impersonalization.

> She did nothing. She lingered by. She wasted time. But only the good God knew this and did not scold her. Gave her another chance. Because she still did something: she looked. And the look gave languishes a form, even impressed it a discrete energy, such as the smoke volutes that once elevated out of Szanto's pipe. God knows that to look is a good thing, as in the seventh day of the Genesis neither he had done anything else but look at the world as we are looking at it now on Animal Planet or Discovery.[94]

---

90 Eco: *Six walks*, p. 49.
91 Ștefan Manasia: Evangheliștii resemnării (The Evanghelists of Resemnation). In: *Tribuna*, nb. 125, 16–30 November 2007, p. 14.
92 Ursu: *Asediul Vienei*, p. 222.
93 See Emil Cioran: *Syllogismes de l'amertume*. Paris: Gallimard 1952.
94 Ursu: *Asediul Vienei*, p. 222.

Gradually, this void leads to the dissipation of individuality, turning into a co-substantial 'languor' of the Subjects, a translation from the ethnic void to the emptiness of 'qualities', and finally to impersonalization.

5.2.2 The Transgressive Method of Impersonalization

In his *Maxims and Reflections*, Goethe considered that "the man who is overpowered may at least express his views in speech, because he cannot act",[95] and his manner of expression in such a liminal situation can only be indirect, allusive or ironic. Defeated by the practices of the excess of power, the Subject adopts complementary expression strategies which impersonalise him, determining him to mask his presence in the public space till dissipation. His voice is lost in the concert of the public voices, being an indirect expression of an implicit social auctorial critics.

This is also the starting point for Elvira Sorohan in an article in *Convorbiri literare*, in 2013, speaking about "Mecanismul psiho-spiritual al ironiei" (The Psyho-Spiritual Mechaism of Irony),[96] and endorsing the ideas of Philippe Hamon[97] that irony has not exclusively a social function, focusing on the 'oblique meaning', therefore hiding direct thinking. But the French author has as a basis for his theory about the meaning of hiding, about indirect, allusive or oblique thinking, the theory of Vladimir Jankélévitch, who considered that the detour practised by irony functions on the formula of litotes.[98] For Jankélévitch, the indirect method of irony has the role of stimulating the intuition of the reader, therefore of proposing an equation in which the competent reader,[99] has role of participating in the articulation of a secondary meaning. Here is what he affirms about the mechanism of irony:

> [...] elle renonce à épeler les idées mot pour mot et syllabe pour syllabe, car elle sait qu'à un morceau de phrase ne correspond pas littéralement un morceau de pensée; le long des

---

[95] Friedrich Goethe: *The Maxims and Reflections*. Second and revised edition. Translated by Thomas Bailey Saunders. London: Macmillan 1908, p. 375.

[96] Elvira Sorohan: Mecanismul psiho-spiritual al ironiei. In: *Convorbiri literare*, Oct. 30/2013. Consulted at the web adress: http://convorbiri-literare.ro/?p=1254 [26.04.2018].

[97] Philippe Hamon: *L'ironie littéraire. Essai sur les formes de l'ecriture oblique*. Paris: Hachette 1996.

[98] Vladimir Jankélévitch: *L'ironie*. Paris: Flammarion 1964, p. 91.

[99] See also Hamon: *L'ironie littéraire*, p. 71. The observations of Hamon are about the triad of the competences required for the understanding of the ironic discourse.

sinueuses périphrases, c'est encore l'intuition immédiate qu'elle recherche, la suggestion évasive et sans rapport direct avec le volume du discours.¹⁰⁰

In other words, irony is first of all a rhetoric mechanism, of hiding the signification, of coding. As a consequence of this observation, literature would have a privileged function. We realise that Hamon reduces irony to its social function and realises that the majority of those who have explained minutely the function of irony have demonstrated that this has a normative function in the community:

> 'Tout est social dans l'ironie', telle est, formulée diversement et avec des nouances, la phrase clé de la grande majorité des traités (non littéraires) qui traitent de l'ironie (Bergson, Jankélévitch, Freud, etc. Freud parle de 'processus social', Bergson de 'geste social'), et la pluspart des traités des 'moralistes', comme tous les trités et manuels de politesse et de savoir-vivre, passent leurs temps à définir soigneusement et symétriquement d'une part la liste des manières 'convenables' de faire de l'esprit en société, d'autre part la liste des conduites à tenir pour ne pas etre 'ridicule' en société.¹⁰¹

Moreover, we would complete Hamon's perspective with a transgressive function of irony, which is immanent to literature and which can be tested through its meta-real character. The novel which has irony as one of its instruments, succeeds to follow a path of detachment from reality, contemplating it and transgressing it through indirect, ironic reality. A *tel quel* reproduction of reality is not possible any more, without the danger of a recurrent realism, which also happened in the contemporary novel, and the contemporary writer, aware of the transgressive values of narrative art, disposes of irony as of a renunciation regarding the recurrences of mimesis. He lends the ironical voice to some characters who are not capable of irony and this contrast and this contract between the Author-Subject-Reader permits the transgression of reality in favour of an open meditation about the described world. For example, in *Asediul Vienei* (The Siege of Vienna), the emptiness left after the departure of minorities, but also the void left in the people by History, passes beyond the formal limits of a depopulated world, suggesting an emptiness of meaning. So, beyond the social character of irony we also identify a literary character of it, as it figures as an instrument for indirect, transgressive talk, offering a critical, gnoseologically stimulating perspective on the described and ironized world.

Hamon suggests, influenced by Bourdieu's theses called "critique sociale du jugement",¹⁰² that as a language instrument which could be associated to power,

---

100 Jankélévitch: *L'ironie*, p. 91–92.
101 Hamon: *L'ironie littéraire*, p. 9.
102 See Pierre Bourdieu: *La Distinction, critique sociale du jugement*. Paris: Editions de Minuit 1979.

irony is not "ni l'outil langagier des dominants, ni celui des dominés, mais simple production généralisée des diférenciations, donc maintien de la socialité comme champ ou se produit, simplement, de la *distinction* entre des espaces ou des aires de pouvoir différenciés."[103] The two typologies of irony identified by Hamon[104] are relevant in the observation of the mechanism of a pragmatic analysis of literary irony. 'Paradigmatic irony' undermining hierarchies by reversing the world and carnavalising it in order to dynamite the mechanisms of Power excesses. 'Syntagmatic irony' deconstructs the logics of the logical development of facts and causalities, denouncing even the "dysfunctionalities of the argumentative implications".[105]

In Horia Ursu's novel, Farkas Jenő observes, in the presentation of the novel,[106] the black humour specific for Hasek, therefore a paradigmatic irony which reverses the world and especially hierarchies, with the completion that it is humour à la Svejk, without Svejk, without Hasek's ironic uni-perspective, without the saving perspective that Hasek hides in the 'idiocy' of his character. We identify a paradigmatic Svjek, without name, therefore impersonal, in Ursu's novel. But in the novel we identify a complexity of the ironic register which has a transgressive function, as a perspective on this world which also moves theatrically, not only realistically. The roles of ironie are those of intentionally weakening the personalisation power of the characters, of casting them entirely to the roles of History victims.

In this context we observe that neither of 'the faiths' of the characters are 'tough', they do not articulate around some ideologies which guarantee the resistance and the power to overcome the emptiness of transition. These 'faiths' are part of the strategy of the author to demonstrate the incapacity of the Subjects to overcome the latent and impersonal little pleasure:

> There were times when women still believed in something. Comrade Lucreția Cristea, an illegalist's daughter, believed in the party. Madam Irina Stein in the curative powers of the apple vinegar. Mirela Strîmbu in common celandine. Sanda Tertulian in God. Elly Cazan in her husband, dead in Siberia. Ingrid Vlahovici in Laczi Kutassy, elegant footballer, but a little lecher, as she said. Madam Rațiu in signs. Salvia Dănilă in the length of her own legs. Tamara Urdă in the Five-year plans accomplished in four years and a half. Dana Răduța in promises of any kind, Roxana Bradu in coitus interruptus. Cerasela Stan in Joan Baez, Bob Marly and Bob Dylan.[107]

---

103 Hamon: *L'ironie littéraire*, p. 18.
104 Hamon: *L'ironie littéraire*, p. 69–70.
105 Hamon: *L'ironie littéraire*, p. 70.
106 See Ursu: *Asediul Vienei*.
107 Ursu: *Asediul Vienei*, p. 105–106.

Ironically, the author plays with the meaning of the 'faiths' of the women in Apud, demonstrating the hybrid and derisory character of weak faiths. The scenery of this feminine Apud is completed by the auctorial voice, which observes that "Altough small, Apud was, as we could see, a town of faithful women". The panorama of feminine characters, although they are named, they participate in the general panorama of the disindividualised characters,[108] therefore informed, impersonalized in the magma of social transition from a history to the other.

The hierarchy of the feminine 'faiths' of Apud is completed by those of 'negative' faiths, therefore making up a Breughelian panorama of Romanian transition, the social radiography unmasking a world *bric à brac*, with faiths laid out in disarray, without common fundamental values, in a generalized disorder. And "Men were generally good, diligent and party members with a register but with no political convictions. Those who came from the countryside believed blindly in chiefs. They also called them misters." Behind the informal supremacy of the urban above the rural, men are mingled in this formless, not unitary social mass to which they belong through adhesion but without convictions. The chiefs-misters equation betokens only transition, the syntagmatic link of a time span, that of landowners, to the other, that of socialism-communism. Unlike women, the landscape of men's society denounces impersonalization, by exposing the amorphous mass, without real convictions but with evident 'competences' of a patriarchal society:

> They all knew women, politics and football.... Great wine, beer and 60 degree plum brandy drinkers, they finished libations with the formula Fuck!... Then, in a changing order followed: the state, the party, the country, the Russian, the Hungarians, the Americans, the work place, public personalities of all forms, the local football team and the national one, the post, telephones, the radio, television, neighbours, rain, clouds sun, EGL, newspapers, magazines, laws, habits. In short, everything and everybody.[109]

This transition from the 'Iocan clearing' in Marin Preda's *Moromeții*, extended to the level of the entire town Apud, reinstates, in an ironic formula of a Hungarian inhabitant, the '80s attitude, the one in which "irony, sarcasm, complicity, ambiguity, pastiche and parody are at the center."[110] Unlike the fiction texts which are exclusively centred on irony, making it the stake of the writing, the aesthetical formula of the representation of reality, Horia Ursu's irony is an instrument adapted to an overrated objective, that of making a statement of the decline in its different hypostases, including the decline of the Power officially rated. It is

---

[108] See Ovidiu Pecican: Apud gloriam mundi. In: *Tribuna*, nb. 125, 16–30 November 2007, p. 13.
[109] Ursu: *Asediul Vienei*, p. 206.
[110] Țeposu: *Istoria tragică și grotescă*, p. 39.

a "kind of a happy Apocalipse *à la* Broch",[111] and the path in this Transylvania "is not only aesthetical, but also ethical", confesses Ursu to Bogdan Romaniuc, confirming both the objective of the novel, and its realization methods.

The literary stratagema behind the ironical register is the parable of the derisory, the image of a world emptied of personal memory and impersonalised. The impersonalization is an aesthetic process of weakening the power of the Subject in the actantial ecuation, of intentional diminuation of its reaction capacity in the case of tenssed situations. Its polarisation and, implicitly, the dissipation of the power of the Subject has the meaning of demonstrating its memory crises and the abandonment before History. The category of public and private derision, unlike the situation of the passive power, which makes Petrini accept and try to survive the status of victim of the excessive power of the oppressive system, betrays the lack of interest of the Subject, in search for the equilibrium of the power hierarchy. Petru or Flavius Tiberiu, who have the potential of powerful Subjects who can react through exploring personal memory, or at least through recovering reflexive power, are the victims of a world emptied by meaning, will detain the same power in the social mechanism, such as the postman Ghereță or Bejan, the organ seller.

Even more, the scene of the discussion between Petru and Bejan Iustin, "the ex-Romanian Communist Party member, actually without party, but faithful till death",[112] linked to the fact that the last sells his organs in order to buy Wellman's front land patch in the cemetery, is representative for the pathway from dark humour to irony, where death, as time without memory and history, is the only salvation in the emptiness of transition. Social hierarchy is dissipated in this world in which only the position of the place in the cementery matters. "Only the Aztecs had better positions." Or, completing Petru, 'higher'. The only supreme 'faith' of this world, expressed by 'the nomenclatura' bloke Bejan, who remembers Wellmann's wisdom, is that one that "the only place for which you deserve to give everything you have is the burial place". In these hierarchical dialectics, in which the only Power that counts is that of life over death, the position in the cemetery represents the last chance of redemption. "Because the redemption that will come, Bejan, will find you on top. Up there, close to the angels." Therefore, this is the confirmation that: "This novel, irrigated by humour (seldom black) and irony is finally a peaceful, almost convivial dialogue with Death, insinuated into the most delicate fibers of Death."

In the diorama of social transition of Romania, "the bright road of Transition",[113] as restored by Horia Ursu, we observe a dissipation of Power in this

---

111 Ursu: Trei răspunsuri de la Horia Ursu.
112 Ursu: *Asediul Vienei*, p. 201.
113 Ursu: *Asediul Vienei*, p. 365.

frantic world, a fact that results in the impersonalization of the Subject just to accentuate derisory. This derisory world is situated at the same time at the margin and in the middle, where disillusions come from, and this is an expression of confusion, blended values and disintegration of power. Therefore, what can be seen is the weakening of the implicit status of the old community authorities, in a world more and more emptied of meaning, such as the authority of the butcher Husvago who feels his apogee, to the authority of the postman Ghereță, lost in a world without letters and retrained as staff of the TV cable company, of the 'new parvenue', the corrupt business man Brândușă. For Husvago, as for the whole pig-dependent community, the 'white as snow' pig becomes an axis mundi. This auctorial strong irony supports the dissipation of values, the rudimentary, physiological existence of the community who lives without the power of overcoming the materialism of reality. It is a world which lives according to a nostalgic, historical ideal of the "socialist multilaterally developed society", as well as to the 'passeisme' of Emilia Apostoae from the novel *Sunt o babă comunistă* (I'm a Communist Biddy) by Dan Lungu. Here mathematics becomes essential, the planification of the retirement money from one month to the other being a daily exercise. The ironical-derisory formula of the author, exponential for the discussed novel, is the following:

> Who said we are a vegetal people? We are nomad mathematicians and, partially, sedentary poets, who gather once a year around the pig on Christmas, amazed and frightened at the same time, as Trojans around the cursed gift of the Achaeians. The same mercato cry resounds in their ears: '*A kingdom! My kingdom for a pig!*'[114]

If in the novel *Ciocoii vechi și noi* (Old and New Parvenue), in which as exposed earlier, the active character of Dinu Păturică's power 'the old parvenue' and his way of rising quickly to the top of social hierarchy, exercising his authority excessively. In Horia Ursu's novel the authority of the corrupt capitalist business man Brândușă is that of the 'new parvenue'. He is here the new capitalist who wants to make a party: THE NATIONAL AND UNIVERSAL PARTY TO BE BORN, which, believes Brândușă, being named so, will never die. The ideological void of such a project is deflected by the semantic force of tautological nature according to which, if something was not born, it cannot die. Continuing with the same mundane dialectics of the power of death over life, the main objective in the ideological programme of the Brândușian party is that of burying old people for free. "I am willling to bury the whole city. Even the country, if necessary. What more

---

[114] Ursu: *Asediul Vienei*, p. 366.

can you wish for?",[115] asks as a practical moralist the provincial business man who sells death to people, and creates the impression that it owns it, inclusively.

The supremacy of Brânduşă's power is another strategy of the author to operate contrastively. Faced with the impersonalization of the Subjects, he is the example of the absolute Power, who succeeded in controlling everything that happens in Apud by controlling money. "The New Years Eve with the painting sale", where people from Apud come with the convinction, similar to that of Ghereță, that "the road to heaven is paved with *sarmale*[116]", is dominated by the business man who buys all the paintings out of sheer snobbery, practicing an innocent kind of semiotics of daily life, of utilitarian banality. The collectionary businessman sees:

> Signs everywhere: look at a horse...Then a herd. Look, also a mill...Rural tourism: for foreign currency...Look and two bottles of wine...I've never thought that art is good at something and look...business deals were being made and unmade. If he succeedes, he will pray to these paintings as if they were icons.[117]

Behind his gesture there is no aesthetic taste, but the intuition of a following profit, being convinced that his power and hierarchical position in the new world are given by the monopoly guaranteed by money. In the chapter 'New Years' Eve with Sale' and not only, the whole cultural scheme of the dioramic edifice is deconstructed through the intertextual charge of the scholarly, literary references being put into contrast with Brânduşă's vulgarised till decorative world, which seems a strategic aesthetic textualist reminiscence.

Brânduşă subminates and assumes the authority of the 'cable men' inclusively, or the media authority in this transition world. We observe an abundance and authority of newspapers, a fact certified in the chapter 'Personal Column Ads', where the ad for the organ sale for buying the front place in the cemetery is run. Flavius Tiberiu's business dealing in TV aerials is destroyed by the Brânduşă's television business, whose firm 'Neuronic', will offer the multitude of TV stations which the transition man needs so much, as on Romanian TV1 people will find "nothing or almost nothing".[118] Also, Cain's leaving discourse, which leaves behind the 'Jewish void', is filmed integrally by the local television, so that "the discourse will be analysed and commented with a masoretes' passion by specialists of national rambling."[119] Society looks on passively, 'languishes' in front of the TV, which leads to interminable debates and cliche commentaries,

---

115 Ursu: *Asediul Vienei*, p. 360–361.
116 Romanian cabbage rolls dish.
117 Ursu: *Asediul Vienei*, p. 290.
118 Ursu: *Asediul Vienei*, p. 262.
119 Ursu: *Asediul Vienei*, p. 138.

generalising the shocking events. Facing 'progress', people harbour the same convictions, repositories of past history which marks their destiny forever and makes them believe more in death than in life. Iolanda lives with the prejudice that computers are "for children and adolescents or for those who condemn themselves to a never ending adolescence and loneliness." The computer fan 'religion', the one which is to be found nowadays in every house, provokes a conditioned reaction, activating the immediate memory, as "in her mind the word programming was associated with planning, or her life and everyone else's was planned in several five-year plans". The memory of the historical programming of communism makes her believe that the era of computers is "A new piece of barbarity! Or, who knows, The Last Great Migration! On the Internet!"[120]

We witness a successive hybridization of the paintings, and therefore a loss of the Subjects in the world of transition, associated to a *bric à brac*. The general background is that of a grey, bleak landscape of the Transylvanian town in transition, in which 'leaving' (emigration or death) is the only notable event. Here the characters evolve between the mythologisation of the historical memory, of the socialist communist utopia and the consummerist mythology, of the derisory of transition, which has no memory. On the temporal axis of the novel two time sequences are confronted, between which the characters slide, till the loss of temporal benchmarks and their overlapping. On one side there is the confruntation with the transition of the '90s and, on the other side, the communist anamnesis. Within this universe, the only compensatory function and immanently transgressive one is fulfilled by the oneiric and the chapter 'Notebook with Dreams and Notes'[121] is significant for the ushering out of the time of History and acceding to the time of memory. Dreams are shorthand signs of a Memory deeply hidden within the Subject and which as a reaction flows into the cruelty, the ridicule of the immediate world, dominated by an oppressive History. In a world without compensatory dreams, the death History threatens, therefore its lack of meaning is the epilogue, as "A sleep without dream is pure death". Here memory has hermeneutical responsibility, building up on the past, but avoiding the present and anticipating oneirically-narrative the individual future and therefore recomposing it after its disintegration in the collective impersonality. Dreams, placed as the memories at the center of the physiological existence, become the only transgression and personalisation modality in a diffuse world. "The place of dreams and memories could be the head of the chest."[122]

---

[120] Ursu: *Asediul Vienei*, p. 178.
[121] Ursu: *Asediul Vienei*, p. 139.
[122] Ursu: *Asediul Vienei*, p. 219.

5.2 The Impersonalization of Power and the Stigma of Historical Memory — 243

This lead back to the observation that the Romanian epic reflects an erosive social transition, with its interminable anguishes and torments, with the confusion and instability of the man just out of communism. The history of the genre confirms a profound anchorage in history, manifested even when its prose-writers propose its avoidance. The link with history, either actual or recent, is obviously obssessive, or allusive and strategic. The conscience of the Romanian fiction writer, a 'debutant' in the communist period or in post-communism, therefore belonging to both generations, is that of a heavy past which, by excessively exercizing its violent power, stigmatised society. People have obtained an excessive and mecanomorphus behaviour. From reflexivity to behaviour and language, the characters of the Romanian contemporary novel reflect through automatized living these stigmas of history.

What is left out of the textualist strategies of the writers of the '80s, out of the scholarly, theoretical foundations of their writings? What does the novel-writer keep out of the theoretic-semiotic constructs of these fiction writers, that is out of the structural categories such as "the ludic function of the writing (Jacqueline Risset), the conscious production of the meaning simultaneously with the process of text constitution (Julia Kristeva), the preeminence of the structural conscience on the semantic one (Roland Barthes), the possibility of denouncing ideology through lucid thinking in the form and textual mechanisms (Jean Luis Baudry), the pragmatism of the writing (Jean-Joseph Goux)"?[123]

Horia Ursu's novel, adapting some of the narrative strategies of the '80s Romanian prose, such as the fragmentation of the epic through numerous complementary histories or the frequent use of analepse, the ample labirynth of the texture, the dense and impersonal style, the scholarly-textual play and the refuge into a memory of history sometimes artificial, impersonal, sometimes a personal memory of dream and books, reshapes the image of the postcommunist Romanian society under the spectre of history. But this ironical reconstruction of the derisory post-revolution social transition has as its only purpose a detailed, realist reproduction of the world and the adaptation of the strategies to the new reality allows a permanent slide either into the derisory of the world or outside it, in an ironical manner. The author seems aware of the risk of the 'misery' of this world, the descriptive and superfluous redundancy of this degraded world. He offers a complex image on this world, with its anguishes and complexes, the preponderent instruments of transgression being irony, the authenticity of the dream or the refuge into the scholarly-textual world.

The model or "certificate of authentification/authenticity"[124] can only be partially regained in the hypostasis of Musil's *The Man without Qualities*. As Ulrich,

---

123 Țeposu: *Istoria tragică și grotescă*, p. 40.
124 Ursu: Trei răspunsuri de la Horia Ursu.

Petru is a man 'without nostalgia' or Ursu's world feels, up to a point, a certain nostalgic pressure, indefinite and abstract, not after something lost, but after something dreamt, feeling a breakdown, a failure of utopias. But failed utopias of Horia Ursu's world are not identitary, but personal. Therefore, the process of impersonalization of the Subjects in the Transylvanian post-historical Apud. The Romanian author resembles Musil in a certain auctorial position when facing time, either present, therefore the time of history which is articulated under our eyes, either the past, of falsified history. This position is given by the author himself by the reference to a fragment about the telling of history in the journal of the Viennese author:

> J'ai note deja qu'il s'agit de raconter des histories; a present, je sens aussi qu'il faut, d'une certaine maniere, raconter les evenements les plus banals. [...] Jusqu'ici j'ai toujours vu les choses de beaucoup trop pres, il faut se placer plus loin, d'ou une scene se reduit parfois a quelques phrases. [...] J'ai ecrit: travailler avec les elements dont on dispose librement, c'est ce que l'on voit dans la vie, lit dans le journal, les romans, etc. On ajoute simplement le jugement, le point de vue-et c'est ainsi que l'on se retrouve forme soi-meme, avec le temps.[125]

In this context, of telling history from outside of it, in order to emphasize its overwhelming power and its amnesic effects on the Subject, we mention the archtheme of the novel *Asediul Vienei* (The Siege of Vienna), that of the historical void and mnemonic and the implicit effects in the process of the impersonalization of the Subject in the ecuation of contemporary Power.

---

[125] Robert Musil: *Journaux*. Tome 1. Traduction de Philippe Jaccotet. Paris: Seuil 1981, p. 308.

Conclusions

The Subversive Use of Literature in the Field of Power

On the 7th of January 1977, in his innaugural lecture at College de France, Roland Barthes postulated a really 'scandalous' fact, at least at a first glance, which is "La langue, comme performance de tout langage, n'est ni réactionnaire, ni progressiste; elle est tout simplement: fasciste; car le fascisme, ce n'est pas d'empêcher de dire, c'est d'obliger à dire."[1] Beyond the intentionally provoked polemics through the analogy with one of the devastating ideologies of the last century, the well-known *Telquell* essayist and critic suggested, first of all, the problematization of any language in accordance to a social mechanism which produces it with utilitarian purpose. Language is seen here as a direct expression of any constitutive behaviourism of any social group which organises itself, therefore it cannot function outside of any structure, including the ones of linguistic nature. This has, eventually, the attribute of the authoritarianism of 'saying', of an affirmation, therefore of imposing an absolute expressive structure.

Barthes' lesson is about power relations, language being perceived as 'législation' or legiferation and language seen as 'code' or coding. Starting here, the French essayist considers that when it is proliferated, even in the intimacy of the subject, "la langue entre au service d'un pouvoir". This obligatory 'regimentation', lacking arbitrariness in the process of social interaction, follows two distinctive features, assertive authority and the gregarity of repetition and the logics of linguistic modality, seen as the attitude of the locutor Subject towards the content of his assertions, is not "que le supplément de la langue". The argumentation of the constitutive authoritarianism of language follows classical pathways in Barthes' vision, which were described by linguists like Saussure or Jakobson, or philosophers like Nietzsche, Kirkegaard, Wittgenstein or Deleuze or sociologists such as Foucault or Bourdieu. The conviction expressed by Bourdieu, that language expresses "the dream of absolute power",[2] only reconfirms this fact.

The solution of the essayist to get rid of this constitutive and gregarious 'fascism' of the language is that of undermining its oppressive system, of shortening its automatic pathways. The only subversion valuable in this case, through which we depart from the schematic and limited sociologist, through its literarity, is that of instrumentalizing literature within this conflict. The discourse questions

---

[1] Roland Barthes: *Leçon inaugurale de la chaire de sémiologie littéraire du Collège de France prononcée le 7 janvier 1977*. Paris: Seuil 1978, p. 14.
[2] Bourdieu: *Language and Symbolic Power*, p. 42.

any prior knowledge of the world but also its oppressed authority, 'cheating' or 'avoiding' the preconceived formulas of the social organisation and of its imprinting within language:

> Mais à nous, qui ne sommes ni des chevaliers de la foi ni des surhommes, il ne reste, si je puis dire, qu'à tricher avec la langue, qu'à tricher la langue. Cette tricherie salutaire, cette esquive, ce leurre magnifique, qui permet d'entendre la langue hors-pouvoir, dans la splendeur d'une révolution permanente du langage, je l'appelle pour ma part: littérature.[3]

Of course, at a first sight, the ludic stratagema of the language of literature reminds of the definitions offered by the formalists of the literary discourse. It is about that 'denaturation', forcement or even aggression of the language through which these theoreticians of the last past century tried to explain 'Art as Device':

> On this theory, literature is a kind of writing which, in the words of the Russian critic Roman Jakobson, represents an 'organized violence committed on ordinary speech'. Literature transforms and intensifies ordinary language, deviates systematically from everyday speech.[4]

But mainly, as Bourdieu mentions, the violence on the common language which forms the basis of literature, expresses a necessity of the literary 'device'. This necessity comes from the defensive formula of literature in the public space and from the oblique thinking it applies to the world we are living in. The obliquity thinking of literature has permitted the creation, even in hostile times, of a parallel discourse to the official one, discourse within and through which literature proved itself subversive, proposing another level of reality which simulated the total parallelism to the world of excess. The subversiveness of literature in general and especially of the novel, as a specific instrument of the construction and deconstruction of the world, comes from the fact that, along its changing history, literature exposed itself and denounced the excess forms of the world it was born in. The analyses of the novel *Ciocoii vechi și noi* (Old and New Parvenus) has proven this fact. These forms have appeared either from the social disequilibrium, as in the case of the Realist or Naturalist novel, either from the incompatibility between the Subject and the world, as in the case of the modern novel, a fact which finally determined the alienation of the Subject and its gradual and total self-reflexivisation, as in the case of the subjective-analytical novel.

---

[3] Barthes: *Leçon inaugurale*, p. 15.
[4] Eagleton: *Literary Theory*, p. 2.

Starting here, the acknowledgement that literary texts are real study materials of power relations, either of contextual relevance, containing history, either of structural or semiotic analyses, unmasking the typology of the social relations between persons is essential. This idea, of the effective utility and of the relation between social power and literature, was sometimes circulated during the last century. For example, Jean F. O'Barr strengthened the idea that the study of literary texts would contribute to the understanding of power relations in society,[5] stipulating at least four points of view, in order to substantiate this idea, out of which the most important would be the observation of birth and crystallization of a political conscience which is seldom actively reflected in literary representations.

But the novel, as has been demonstrated in the analytical chapters, is not just a historical image of a time with its morals and its relational disequilibrium. The evolution of the Realist novel and the psychological inquiries of naturalism demonstrated it thoroughly. The novel does not propose the reproduction of a history, as we have seen in the case of the contemporary novel, as the novel benefits of the trump of an individual artistic conscience which overcomes the functionality and mechanicism of any time. It is the direct expression of an assumed liberty of the writer reported to the time he lives and in which he articulates the meaning of his literature. This individualization of perspective and filtration of the world represented through the anatomy of his conscience makes the novel seem opposed to the image of the world in which it was born. The meaning of the novel is therefore more than parabolic and mediating, meaning that it does not expose coldly and impersonally a disequilibrium, but it functions as social symptomatology practiced on a particular reflexive conscience in which the excess is hidden. Blecher's novel, *Întâmplări în irealitatea imediată* (Occurrence in Immediate Unreality), stands as proof to this observation.

Liberty, affirms Steinhardt, paraphrasing Thomas Mann, "[...] is a pedant and bourgeois notion",[6] and the concept understood so "questions exactly the survival chances of liberty in the world named by Ortega y Gasset, more relevantly than anyone, of the masses."[7] It is the masses who "[...] do not care about individual liberty, freedom of speech; they love authority [...] through equality they understand the equality of oppression...just civilised individuals wish for freedom."[8] Understood this way the Subject-Liberty-Mass equation translates an

---

5 See Cheris Kramarae; Muriel Schulz; William M. O'Barr (eds.): *Language and power*. Beverly Hills: Sage Publications 1984, p. 222.
6 Steinhardt: *Jurnalul fericirii*, p. 130.
7 Steinhardt: *Jurnalul fericirii*, p. 130.
8 Steinhardt: *Jurnalul fericirii*, p. 130.

equivalence, an identification of liberty with literature or an assumable liberty by literature. In its turn the novel can be looked at as the pedantry of a certain social category which has the time, energy and competences to write, but moreover to read. The category of the novel, a modern one par excellence, was a sort of a probe of another type of modernising social contract which translated not only the reality of a certain opposition towards authoritarian excesses, but meant, implicitly, a certain risk. It is the risk Denis de Rougemont mentioned regarding the same 'liberty', cited by Steinhardt, according to whom 'Liberty is not a right, it is the assumption of a risk".[9] This fact is fundamental in the case of most analyzed novels but is evidenced especially in the case of novels from totalitarian epochs, such as *Cel mai iubit dintre pământeni* (The Most Beloved Man on Earth).

The discussion about liberty, absolute power and literature is not, as the category of the novel, a new one. In the third Book of the *Republic*, it is possible to find out about the reasons of antique censorship proportional with poeticism and the limits of literature. Poets who propose the guardian's of 'inner' literature, which could make them fear death should be repudiated. Plato states that: "[...] the more poetic they are, the less they should be heard by boys and men who must be free and accustomed to fearing slavery more than death."[10] Maybe for Plato the question of power and its will of censorship is a question of social organization of the Republic, but certainly Foucault has the reason to state, as a main idea in his studies, that excessive power is essentially repressive. The repressive form of totalitarian power could be traced in Romanian society through the representations of literature and the analysis in the 4th chapter has proved this reality. Even when speaking about 'weak literature', the communist one, it was possible to see the effect of ideological power and *the caricaturising* of literature that loses its meaning, becoming only a direct instrument of power proliferation or propaganda, as it is the case of Romanian 'proletcultism'. In the meantime, it must be argued that even literature has had its power, through its subversive strategies, imaginary constructions and discourse practices of political, totalitarian power denunciation.

But the denunciation of an excess of power which functions repressively can only be followed in novels from different historical periods, not just those of communist totalitarianism, as it is the case of the novel *Cel mai iubit dintre pământeni* (The Most Beloved Man on Earth). Opposing Victor Petrini, the passivized Subiect in Marin Preda's novel, Dinu Păturică, the character of Nicolae Filimon, in *Ciocoii vechi și noi* (Old an New Parvenu), also proves the toxic effects of devastating power. Pătruică's active power is a progressive one, the author demonstrating the

---

9 Steinhardt: *Jurnalul fericirii*, p. 130.
10 Plato: *The Republic*, p. 64.

effects of this active power, till the self-destruction of the Subject. Dinu Păturică's self-didacticism, faithful reader of Machiavelli's *The Prince*, is also a kind of proof of the semantic misappropriation of the message about the excesses of power and its effects on the Subject. Reading and rereading Machiavelli's 1532 Renaissance message, Dinu Păturică appears firstly as a 'misreader' of the Prince, interpreting his convictions just for using individual, active, hierarchising power. But, if we refer to the exclusion of moral characteristics in exercising political power, we realise that Păturică is also Machiavelli's ideal reader, proving absolute pragmatism which determines him to act exclusively in favour of active principles, of exercising power within public space. Filimon's Subject exercises his Machiavellic dominance strategies by influencing, manipulating, blackmailing, therefore exercising constant pressure, active in order to obtain absolute power, renouncing moral principles.

If in the case of Filimon and Preda the novel is a formula of denouncing a social excess which determines the activisation (Păturică) or passivization (Petrini) of the subjects according to a power specific pressure, with Blecher the concept of power changes. Blecher's reflector Subject searches for another type of power, as a consequence of an ontological block. It is the power to do, or more exactly the power to survive according to a hostile medium. The search turns within himself, his own reflexivity, which contains the pulsations of life recovered through memory. Locked inside his own body, as in a panopticon, Blecher's subject translates from the plane of the immediate unreality, over the panopticist reality, directly onto the plane of the reality of literature where liminal experiences are literaturised. This process of gradual reflexivisation corresponds to a pathway of gradual descent into the purgatory of the body in the paradise of his own senses. Blecher's imaginary pathway presupposes a discovery of reflexive power, it being saving and fertile on the level of narrativity.

The diachronic study of the Romanian novel from the perspective of the analyses of the deconstruction and reconstruction of power offers a fluctuant perspective, overcoming the historical principle of literary generations, groupings, trends and specific ideologies in specific contexts, predominant in lansonian critique and in the field of Romanian literary studies. Although *Ciocoii vechi și noi* (Old and New Parvenues) from the perspective of the active power of the Subject, the passivization of the Subject in the novel *Cel mai iubit dintre pământeni* (The Most Beloved Man on Earth) or his reflexivization in *Întâmplări în irealitatea imediată* (Occurrence in Immediate Reality) have all been analyzed, these inquiries have been made according to the criteria of evidence. This means that the explorations of these relation typologies of power can also be met in other historical periods and in other contexts, as well. We observe narrative formulas which represent social behaviours, classical patterns of human interrelations. Nevertheless, the analyzes of the contemporary novel from the point of view of the concept of power makes us consolidate the conviction of a social function of the novel, in the direction of facilitating the access to an immediate model, of the context. Horia Ursu's novel, *Asediul Vienei* (The Siege of Vienna) offered us the possibility to identify an impersonalization process in the equation of power. This time, the captivity of the Subject is not only his own and self-destructive ambition, such as in Filimon's case, in his own body as in Blecher's novel or in a repressive political system, as in Preda's case, but in a society in transition. We no longer have a Subject, but impersonalized subjects who are living a larval state, who survive without values, benchmarks or faiths, without clear representations of power. We assist in a dissolution of society, reflected as such in Ursu's novel, in which power impersonalises the subjects. They are becoming an amorphous mass, a world in an accentuated process of enthropy.

But to follow the modalities through which the world is coded within the novel till its apparent obliteration, what has been searched for is a working instrument more appropriate to the literary science, seen as a science of language. The first chapter demonstrated that the theories of the social sciences would only connect literature excessively to the social and transform it in its discourse, which would not confer it its immanent liberty, meaning the risk of total and opposite liberty we mentioned. The formula of literature as 'tricherie salutaire' when facing the unidirectional 'fascism' of language, according to Barthes' formula, induces the fact that it functions as a palimpsest, rewriting reality in specific codes and therefore opposing it. It renounces and denounces it, rewriting the samizdat of the novel, anticipated in the argument.

Also as argument what has been proposed is a terminological and operational transfer, taken from structural morphology, the concept of voice. Voice shows a relational typology, of structural nature which demonstrates the form of interaction between the participant into action and the dominant position, legitimate or not, of the one who detains the initiative 'to initiate' and 'to do'. The model of the voice reflects a typology of action and relational reaction which we can identify in the narration as well and which reproduces a social scheme of the social relations, including those of power. The usefulness of the conceptual transfer between the structural morphology of grammar, which studies the formal discursive modifications of action regarding the holder of the 'power' of action, towards narrative analyses, permits the visualization of the function of the novel in society, implicitly of reading.

Following and arguing Stanley Fish's school of pragmatism referring to "the authority of interpretative communities",[11] Scholes tries to prove through

---

11 See Fish: *Is There a Text in This Class?*

semantic analyses that readers can achieve literacy competences which lead to the understanding of texts as representative cultural products. Scholes' idea is that through competences specific to literary studies deepening what he calls 'the textual power' the reader can identify certain codes that link the text to the structures and ideologies of power in the culture represented by these texts. In other words, the development of literary competences of a semantic nature allow the understanding of the ideologies that lie at the basis of power and the avoidance of the manipulation of the reader through their reproduction. This is Scholes' initial reproduction. He observed the block of teaching literature according to the formula of the 'reverence' of Romantic aestheticism when facing the canon:

> In the age of manipulation, when our students are in dire need of critical strength to resist the continuing assaults of all the media, the worst thing we can do is to foster in them an attitude of reverence before texts. The reverential attitude, a legacy or romantic aestheticism, is the one most natural in literary interpretation as we practiced it.[12]

From this point of view, of the risk of the comfort of the given images, finite and clearly manipulated by the actual media, literature tends to become or has become, in turn, economic goods, a fact confirmed by Thomas Pavel who quoted Tocqueville, with his 1840 study about *Democracy in America*. Pavel says: "Tocqueville was right to note that in democratic times literature tends to become one trade among others."[13] Therefore, this is the risk which is synonymous to the birth of the modern novel, which is the risk of the assumed liberty within democratic times, in order to become 'one trade', pedant, bourgeois, but still so actual. To talk about the novel and the equation of power presupposes a discourse on the assumed liberty of literature and about the necessity of this instrument used to understand the predisposition of the excess which governs our existence. The culture of the novel means the culture and the practice of freedom.

---

12 Robert Scholes: *Textual Power: Literary Theory and the Teaching of English*. New Haven: Yale University Press 1985, p. 16.
13 Pavel: *The Lives of the Novel*, p. 291.

Bibliography

Adameșteanu, Gabriela: *Provizorat* (Provisorate State). Iași: Polirom 2010.
Alecsandri, Vasile: *Comedii* (Comedies). Edition by Georgeta Rădulescu-Dulgheru. Antologie by Aurora Slobodeanu. București: Minerva 1984.
Alexandrescu, Sorin : *Paradoxul român* (The Romanian Paradox). București: Univers 1998.
Alexandrescu, Sorin: *Privind înapoi, modernitatea* (Looking back at Modernity). București: Univers 1999.
Alexianu, Alexandru: *Mode și veșminte din trecut: Cinci secole de istorie costumară românească* (Fashions and Clothes of the Past: Five Centuryes of Romanian Dressing up). București: Meridiane 1987.
Altieri, Charles: *Canons and Consequences: Reflections on the Ethical Force of Imaginative Ideals*. Evanston: Northwestern University Press 1990.
Assmann, Aleida: *Cultural Memory and Western Civilization: Functions, Media, Archives.* Cambridge: Cambridge Universiy Press 2011.
Atlas, James: *Battle of the Books. The Curriculum Debate in America*. New York, London: W. W. Norton & Company 1992.
Babe, Robert E.: *Cultural studies and political economy: toward a new integration*. Toronto: Lexington Books 2009.
Bachelard, Gaston: *La formation de l'esprit scientifique*. Paris: Vrin 1983.
Bakhtine, Mikhail: *La poétique de Dostoïevki*. Paris: Seuil 1970.
Balotă, Nicolae: *De la Ion la Ioanide* (From Ion to Ioanide). București: Eminescu 1974.
Barthes, Roland: *Mythologies*. Selected and translated from the French by Annete Lavers. New York: The Noonday Press 1972.
Barthes, Roland: *Leçon inaugurale de la chaire de sémiologie littéraire du Collège de France prononcée le 7 janvier 1977*. Paris: Seuil 1978.
Barthes, Roland: *S/Z*. Translated by Richard Miller. Preface by Richard Howard. Oxford: Blackwell 2002.
Béhar, Henri; Carassou, Michel: *Le Surréalisme*. Paris: Librairie générale française 1984.
Benda, Julien: *La trahison des clercs*. Paris: Bernard Grasset 1927.
Berindei, Mihnea; Dobrincu, Dorin; Goșu, Armand (ed.): *Istoria comunismului din România* (The History of Communism in Romania). Volume II. "Documents Nicolae Ceaușescu (1965–1971)". Iași: Polirom 2012.
Blaga, Lucian: *Ființa istorică* (The Historic Being). Edition, notes and postface by Tudor Cătineanu. Cluj-Napoca: Dacia 1977.
Blecher, Max: *Întâmplări în irealitatea imediată. Inimi cicatrizate* (Occurence in the Immediate Unreality. Scarred Hearts). Foreword by Dinu Pillat. București: Minerva 1970.
Blecher, Max: *Occurence in the Immediate Unreality*. Translated by Alistair Ian Blyth. Playmouth: University of Playmouth Press 2009.
Blecher, Max: *Vizuina luminată. Jurnal de sanatoriu* (The Lit-Up Burrow: Sanatorium Journal). Postface by Nicolae Manolescu. Edition by Florin Ioniță. București: Art 2009.
Bloom, Harold: *The Western Canon. The Books and School of the Ages*. New York: Harcourt Brace & Company 1994.
Bloom, Harold: *The Anxiety of Influence. A Theory of Poetry*. Second Edition. New York and Oxford: Oxford University Press 1997.

Bloom, Harold: *Canonul occidental: cărțile și școala epocilor* (The Western Canon: The Books and School of the Ages). Translated by Diana Stanciu. Afterword by Mihaela Angelescu Irimia. București: Univers 1998.
Boia, Lucian: *"Germanofilii". Elita intelectuală românească în anii Primului Război Mondial* (The Germanophils. The Romanian Intellectual Elite in the years of the First World War). București: Humanitas 2010.
Boia, Lucian: *Capcanele istoriei. Elita intelectuală românească între 1930 și 1950* (The Traps of History. Romanian Cultural Elite between 1930 and 1950). București: Humanitas 2011.
Bourdieu, Pierre: *La Distinction, critique sociale du jugement*. Paris: Editions de Minuit 1979.
Bourdieu, Pierre: *Language and Symbolic Power*. Edited and introduced by John B. Thompson. Translated by Gino Raymond and Matthew Adamson. Cambridge: Polity Press 1991.
Bourdieu, Pierre: *The Rules of Art. Genesis and Structure of the Literary Field*. Translated by Susan Emanuel. Stanford: Stanford University Press 1995.
Brăvescu, Ada: *Max Blecher-un caz de receptare problematic și spectaculos* (Max Blecher-a problematic and spectacular case of reception). București: Tracus Arte 2011.
Breton, André: *Manifestes du Surréalisme*. Paris: Jean-Jacques Pauvert 1962.
Budai-Deleanu, Ion: *Țiganiada sau Tabăra țiganilor* (Țiganiada or The Gypsies' Camp). Edition and glossary by Jaques Byck. București: Editura pentru Literatură 1967.
Buzura, Augustin: *Absenții*. București: Litera 2008.
Călinescu, George: *Istoria literaturii române de la origini până în present* (The History of the Romanian Literature from Origins to Present Day). Edition and preface by Alexandru Piru. București: Editura Fundațiilor Regale 1982.
Călinescu, George: *Istoria literaturii române: compendiu* (The History of Romanian Literature: compendium). București: Litera 2001.
Cărtărescu, Mircea: *Orbitor. Aripa stângă*. București: Humanitas 1996.
Cărtărescu, Mircea: Mircea Cărtărescu îi desființează pe critici: "Sunt o groază care nu au legătură cu literatura!". In: *Adevărul*, 23 March 2010. Consulted at the web address: http://adevarul.ro/cultura/arte/mircea-cartarescu-desfiinteaza-criticii-sunt-groaza-nu-legatura-literatura 1_50ad79ba7c42d5a66395dc94/index.html. [26.04.2018].
Calvino, Italo: *The Uses of Literature*. Translated by Patrick Creagh. New York: Harcourt Brace Jovanovich 1987.
Canetti, Elias: *Crowds and Power*. Translated from German by Carol Stewart. New York, Continuum 1978.
Caragiale, Ion Luca: Moftangioaica. In: *Moftul român*, Nr. 5/11 February 1893. Consulted at web adress: http://www.digibuc.ro/colectii/moftul-roman-1893-c5023 [26.04.2018].
Caragiale, Ion Luca: *Opere. Teatru* (Works. Theater). Edition by Al. Rosetti, Șerban Cioculescu, Liviu Călin. Preface by Alexandru George. București: Editura Fundației Culturale Române 1997.
Caragiale, Mateiu: *Opere* (Works). Edition by Barbu Cioculescu. Preface by Eugen Simion. București: Univers Enciclopedic 2001.
Casey, Edward: *Remembering. A Phenomenological Study*. Bloomington și Indianapolis: Indiana University Press 1987.
Cernat, Paul: *Modernismul românesc retro în romanul românesc interbelic* (Romanian Retro Modernism in the Romanian Novel between the Wars). București: Art 2009.
Cimpoeșu, Petru: Materia primă a creației este libertatea (The Raw Material of Creation is Liberty). In: *Ziua*, 24 August 2006. Consulted at the web adress: http://www.ziua.ro/display.php?data=2006-08-24&id=205946 [26.04.2018].

Cimpoeşu, Petru: Eu sunt un om cu umor (I am a humorous man). In: *Observator cultural*, nb. 112 (369)/2007. Consulted at the web adress: http://www.observatorcultural.ro/articol/eu-sint-un-om-cu-umor-interviu-cu-petru-cimpoesu-2/ [26.04.2018].

Cimpoeşu, Petru: Scriind, ordonezi lumea (By writing, you order the world differently). In: *Contemporanul*, May 2007, p. 15–16.

Cioculescu, Şerban: *Prozatori români* (Romanian Prose Writers). Bucureşti: Eminescu 1977.

Cioran, Emil: *Syllogismes de l'amertume*. Paris: Gallimard 1952.

Cioran, Emil: *Oeuvres*. Paris: Gallimard 1955.

Cioran, Emil: *Schimbarea la față a României* (The Transfiguration of Romania). Bucureşti: Humanitas 1990.

Cioroianu, Adrian: *Pe umerii lui Marx. O introducere în istoria comunismului românesc* (On Marx's Shoulders. An Introduction in the History of Romanian Communism). Bucureşti: Curtea Veche 2005.

Cocteau, Jean: *La difficulté d'être*. Paris: Editeur Paul Morihien 1947.

Constantinescu, Pompiliu: *Scrieri* (Writings). Vol. 6. Edition by Constanța Constantinescu. Bucureşti: Minerva 1972.

Constantinescu, Pompiliu: in *Conceptul de realism în literatura română* (The Concept of Realism in the Romanian Literature). Alexandru Săndulescu, Marcel Duță, Adriana Mitescu (eds.). Bucureşti: Eminescu 1974.

Cordoş, Sanda: Scara Păcătoşilor (Sinners' Ladder). In: *Vatra*, nr. 11–12, December 2003, p. 159.

Corobca, Liliana: *Epurarea cărților în România (1944–1964). Documente* (The Expurgation of Books in Romania). Bucureşti: Tritonic 2010.

Corobca, Liliana: Instituțiile cenzurii în regimul comunist (The Censorship Institutions during the Communist Regime). In *Revista 22*, Anul XXIV (1231), 22–28 October 2013. Consulted at the web adress: http://www.revista22.ro/institutiile-cenzurii-n- regimul-comunist-32615.html [26.04.2018].

Cosma, Anton: *Geneza romanului românesc* (The Genesis of the Romanian Novel). Bucureşti: Eminescu 1985.

Costache, Iulian: *Eminescu. Negocierea unei imagini-construcția unui canon, emergența unui mit* (Eminescu. Negotiating an image-the construction of a canon, the emergence of a myth). Bucureşti: Cartea Românească 2008.

Dahl, Robert A.: The Concept of Power. In *Behavioral Science*, 2:3 (1957: July), p. 201–215.

Danțiş Gabriela (ed.): *Nicolae Filimon*. Bucureşti: Eminescu 1980.

Deletant, Dennis: *Ceauşescu and the Securitate: Coercion and Dissent in Romania, 1965–1989*. London: Sharpe 1995.

Deleuze, Gilles: *Cinéma 1. L'image-mouvement*. Paris: Les Editions de Minuit 1983.

Deleuze, Gilles: *Cinéma 2. L'image-temps*. Paris: Les Editions de Minuit 1985.

Deleuze, Gilles; Guattari, Felix: *Anti-Oedipus. Capitalism and Schizophrenia*. Translated from the French by Robert Hurley, Mark Seem, and Helen R. Lane. Preface by Michel Foucault. Minneapolis: University of Minnesota Press 1983.

Dimisianu, Gabriel: Generația mea în anii 60 (My Generation during the '60s). In *România literară*, 13th issue of 2008. Consulted at the web adress: http://www.romlit.ro/generaia_mea_n_anii_60 [26.04.2018].

Dimisianu, Gabriel: Recitind *Imposibila întoarcere* (Re-reading the Impossible Return). In *România literară*, nb. 42/2010. Consulted at the web adress: http://www.romlit.ro/recitind_imposibila_ntoarcere [26.04.2018].

Djuvara, Neagu: *Între Orient și Occident. Țările Române la începutul epocii moderne 1800–1848* (Between the East and the West. The Romanian Principalities at the Beginning of the 1800–1848 Modern Age). București: Humanitas 1995.
Dowding, Keith: *Power*. Minnesota: University of Minnesota Press 1996.
Dowding, Keith: Three-Dimensional Power: A Discussion of Steven Lukes' *Power: A Radical View*. In: *Political Studies Review*. Volume 4, Issue 2, May 2006, p. 136–145.
Dowding, Keith (ed.): *Encyclopedia of Power*. Los Angeles: Sage Publications 2011.
Drace-Francis, Alex: *The Traditions of Invention. Romanian Ethnic and Social Stereotypes in Historical Context*. Boston; Leiden: Brill 2013.
Dungaciu, Dan: *Elita interbelică. Sociologia românească în context european* (The Inter-Wars Elite. Romanian Sociology in European Context). București: Mica Valahie 2011.
Durkheim, Émile: *Les règles de la méthode sociologique*. Paris: PUF 2005.
Eagleton, Terry: *Ideology: An Introduction*. London and New York: Verso 1991.
Eagleton, Terry: *Literary Theory. An Introduction*. Second edition. Minneapolis: The University of Minessota Press 1996.
Eco, Umberto: *Opera aperta*. Roma: Bompiani 1962.
Eco, Umberto: *Six Walks in the Fictional Woods*. Cambridge and London: Harvard University Press 1994.
Eliade, Mircea: *Aspecte ale mitului* (Aspects of the Myths). Translated by Paul G. Dinopol. Preface by Vasile Nicolescu. București: Univers 1978.
Eliade, Mircea: *Huliganii* (The Houligans). Edition and foreword by Mircea Handoca. București: Garamond 1996.
Eliade, Pompiliu: *Influența franceză asupra spiritului public în România. Originile. Studiu asupra stării societății românești în vremea domniilor fanariote* (The French Influence on the Public Spirit in Romania. The Origins. A Study on the State of the Romanian Society during the Phanariot Rulings). Translated by Aurelia Creția. Foreword and notes by Alexandru Duțu. București: Univers 1982.
Escarpit, Robert: *Sociologie de la littérature*. Paris: Presses universitaires de France 1958.
Escarpit, Robert: *Le littéraire et le social. Eléments pour une sociologie de la littérature* (avec Charles Bouazis, Jacques Dubois, Robert Estivals). Paris: Flammarion 1970.
Ferry, Luc: *Homo Aestheticus. The Invention of Taste in the Democratic Age*. Translated from French by Robert de Loaiza. Chicago and London: University of Chicago Press 1993.
Filimon, Nicolae: *Ciocoii vechi și noi* (The Old and New Parvenus). București: Editura pentru literatură 1964.
Filimon, Nicolae: *Opere* (Works). Edition by Mircea Anghelescu. București: Univers Enciclopedic 2005.
Fish, Stanley: *Is There a Text in This Class? The Authority of Interpretative Communities*. Cambridge and London: Harvard University Press 1980.
Flonta Mircea; Keul Hans-Klaus (eds.): *Filosofia practică a lui Kant* (The Practical Philosophy of Kant). Iași: Polirom 2000.
Foucault, Michel: *L'archéologie du savoir*. Paris: Gallimard 1969.
Foucault, Michel: *Surveiller et punir. Naissance de la prison*. Paris: Gallimard 1975.
Foucault, Michel: *Dits et écrits*. I–IV. Edition établie sous la direction de Daniel Defert et Francois Ewald. Avec la collaboration de Jacques Lagrange. Paris: Gallimard 1994.
Freud, Sigmund: *On the History of Psycho-Analytic Movement. Paper on the Metapsychology and Other Works*. Vol. IV. Translated from the German under the General Editorship of

James Strachey. In Collaboration with Anna Freud. Assisted by Alix Strachey and Alan Tyson. London: Hogarth Press 1971.

Fukuyama, Francis: *The End of History and the Last Man*. New York: The Free Press 1992.

Georgescu, Vlad: *Istoria românilor. De la origini până în zilele noastre* (The History of Romanians. From Origins to Present Days). Bucureşti: Humanitas 1992.

Goethe, Friedrich: *The Maxims and Reflections*. Second and revised edition. Translated by Thomas Bailey Saunders. London: Macmillan 1908.

Goldiş, Alex: Despre mediocritate şi alţi demoni (About Mediocrity and Other Demons). In *Cultura*, nb. 95/2007-10-25. Consulted at the web adress: http://revistacultura.ro/cultura.php?articol=1803 [27.04.2018].

Golescu, Dinicu: Însemnare a călătoriii mele (An Annotation of my Journey). Foreword by Marin Bucur. Bucureşti: Minerva 1971.

Goodman, Nelson: *Languages of Art*. Indianapolis: Hackett Publishing Company 1976.

Gramsci, Antonio: *Selections from the Prison Notebooks*. Edited and translated by Quintin Hoare and Geoffrey Nowell Smith. New York: International Publishers 1992.

Greenblatt, Stephen: *Renaissance Self-Fashioning*. Chicago: University of Chicago Press 1980.

Grigurcu, Gheorghe: Gulagul cărţilor (The Gulag of Books). In: *Viaţa românească*, nr. 9-10/2013. Consulted at the web adress: http://www.viataromaneasca.eu/arhiva/87_via-a-romaneasca-9-10- 2013/10_cronica-literara/1618_gulagul-cartilor.html [26.04.2018].

Guillory, John: *Cultural Capital. The Problem of Literary Canon Formation*. Chicago: The University of Chicago Press 1993.

Guţu Romalo, Valeria (ed.): *Gramatica limbii române* (The Grammar of the Romanian Language). Bucureşti: Editura Academiei Române 2008.

Halbwachs, Maurice: *On Collective Memory*. Edited, translated, and with an introduction by Lewis A. Coser. Chicago: The University of Chicago Press 1992.

Hamon, Philippe: *L'ironie littéraire. Essai sur les formes de l'ecriture oblique*. Paris: Hachette 1996.

Heinen, Armin: *Die Legion "Erzengel Michael" in Rumänien. Soziale Bewegung und Politische Organisation*. München: R. Oldenbourg Verlag 1986.

Herf, Jeffrey: *Reactionary Modernism*. Cambridge: Cambridge University Press 1984.

Hirimiuc-Toporaş, Durnea (Ed.): *De ce scrieţi? Anchete literare din anii 30* (Why do you write? Literary Investigations from the '30s). Iaşi: Polirom 1998.

Hitchins, Keith: *The Romanians. 1774–1886*. Oxford: Clarendon Press 1996.

Hurezeanu, Damian: Istoria în opera lui Marin Preda (The History in Marin Preda's work). In *Apostrof*, year XXI, nb 3 (238), 2010. Consulted at the web address: http://www.revista-apostrof.ro/articole.php?id=1117 [26.04.2018].

Ibrăileanu, Garabet: *Campanii* (Campaigns). Bucureşti: Minerva 1971.

Iorgulescu, Mircea: Viaţa la români, după evenimente (Romanian Life, after Events). In *Revista 22*, nb. 51/2001, p. 15.

Isar, Nicolae: *Principatele Române în epoca luminilor 1770–1830. Cultura, spiritul critic, geneza ideii naţionale* (The Romanian Principalities during the Enlightenment 1770–1830. Culture, critical spirit, the genesis of the national idea). Bucureşti: Editura Universităţii din Bucureşti 1999.

Ivaşcu, George: *Istoria literaturii române* 1 (The History of Romanian Literature 1). Bucureşti: Editura Ştiinţifică 1969.

Jameson, Fredric: *The Political Unconscious. Narrative as a socially symbolic act.* London and New York: Routledge 1983.
Jankélévitch, Vladimir: *L'ironie.* Paris: Flammarion 1964.
Kafka, Franz: *Metamorphosis.* Translated by David Wyllie. Release Date: August 16, 2005 [EBook #5200]. Consulted at the web adress: http://www.gutenberg.org/ebooks/5200 [26.04.2018].
Kant, Immanuel: *Critique de la faculté de juger suivi de Idée d'une histoire universelle au point de vue cosmopolitique et de Réponse a la question: Qu'est ce que les lumières?* Published under the supervision of Ferdinand Alquié. Translated from German by Alexandre J. L. Delamarre, Jean-René Ladmiral, Marc B. de Launay. Paris: Gallimard 1985.
Kogălniceanu, Mihail: *Scrisori. Note de călătorie* (Letters. Travel Notes). Texts elaborated, annotated and delivered by Dan Simonescu. București: Editura pentru literatură 1967.
Kramarae, Cheris; Schulz, Muriel; O'Barr, William M. (eds.): *Language and power.* Los Angeles: Sage Publications 1984.
Kuhn, Thomas S.: *The Structure of Scientific Revolutions.* Second Edition. Chicago: The University of Chicago Press 1970.
Kundera, Milan: The Tragedy of Central Europe. In *The New York Review of Books.* April 26, 1984; 31, 007, p. 34–38.
Kundera, Milan: *L'Art du roman.* Paris: Gallimard 1986.
Lascu, Mădălina: *Max Blecher, mai puțin cunoscut* (Max Blecher, lesss known). Preface by Ion Pop. București: Hasefer 2000.
Lăzărescu, Gheorghe: *Romanul de analiză psihologică în literatura română interbelică* (The Psychological Analyses Novel in Inter-War Romanian Literature). București: Minerva 1983.
Le Breton, David: *Corps et sociétés. Essai de sociologie et d'antropologie du corps.* Paris: Méridiens Klincksieck 1988.
Le Breton, David: *Antrhopologie du corps et modernité.* Paris: Presses Universitaires de France 1990.
Le Goff, Jacques: *Histoire et Mémoire.* Paris: Gallimard 1988.
Lefter, Ion Bogdan: *Recapitularea modernității: pentru o nouă istorie a literaturii române* (The Revision of Modernity: for a new history of Romanian literature). Pitești: Paralela 45 2000.
Lejeune, Philippe: *Le pacte autobiographique.* Paris, Seuil 1996.
Levinas, Emmanuel: La signification et le sens. In: *Revue de Metaphisyque et de Morale,* 1964/69 (2), p. 125–164.
Lovinescu, Eugen: *Scrieri 5. Istoria literaturii române contemporane* (Writing 5.The History of Contemporary Romanian Literature). Edited by Eugen Simion. București: Minerva 1973.
Lovinescu, Eugen: *Opere* (Works). Vol. V. București: Minerva 1984.
Lull, Janis (ed.): William Shakespeare: *King Richard III.* Cambridge: Cambridge University Press 1999.
Lukes, Steven (ed.): *Power (Readings in Social & Political Theory).* New York: New York University Press 1986.
Lukes, Steven: *Power. A Radical View.* Second edition. London: Palgrave Macmillan 2005.
Lyotard, Jean-François: *La Condition postmoderne: Rapport sur le savoir.* Paris: Éditions de Minuit 1979.
Lyotard, Jean-François: *The Postmodern Condition: A Report on Knowledge.* Translation from the French by Geoff Bennington and Brian Massumi. Foreword by Fredric Jameson. Manchester: Manchester University Press 1984.

Machiavelli, Niccolo: *The Prince*. Translated into English by Luigi Ricci. London: Oxford University Press 1921.
Maingueneau, Dominique: *Pragmatique pour le discours littéraire*. Paris: Dunod 1994.
Maiorescu, Titu: *Critice* (Critiques). București: Minerva 1973.
Manasia, Ștefan: Evangheliștii resemnării (The Evanghelists of Resemnation). In *Tribuna*, nb. 125, 16–30 November 2007, p. 15.
Manea, Norman: The Great Work and the Compromised Man: An Interview with Norman Manea. In: *Los Angeles Review of Books*, 2 February 2014. Consulted at the web adress: https://lareviewofbooks.org/interview/great-work-compromised-man-interview-norman-manea [26.04.2018].
Manolescu, Nicolae: *Arca lui Noe (Noe's Arch)*. Vol. III. București: Minerva 1983.
Manolescu, Nicolae: Revizuirile critice (Critical Revisions). In: *România literară*, nb. 6/2003. Consulted at the web adress: http://www.romlit.ro/revizuirile_critice [26.04.2018].
Manolescu, Nicolae: *Metamorfozele poeziei. Metamorfozele romanului* (The Metamorphoses of Poetry. The Metamorphoses of Poetry). Edition by Mircea Mihăieș. Iași: Polirom 2003.
Manolescu, Nicolae: *Istoria critică a literaturii. 5 secole de literatură* (Critical History of Literature. 5 Centuries of Literature). Pitești: Paralela 45 2008.
Manu, Emil: *Generația literară a războiului* (The Literary Generation of War). București: Curtea Veche 2000.
Marger, Martin; Olsen, Marvin Elliot (eds.): *Power in modern societies*. Boulder: Westview Press 1993.
Marino, Adrian: *Biografia ideii de literatură* (The Biography of the Idea of Literature). Vol. IV. Cluj-Napoca: Dacia 2000.
Martin, Mircea: Du canon à une époque post-canonique. In: *Euresis*, issue 1997–1998, București: Univers 1998, p. 3–25.
Mateescu, Constantin: *Pe urmele lui Nicolae Filimon* (In Pursuit of Nicolae Filimon). București: Sport Turism 1985.
Merleau-Ponty, Maurice: *La Phénoménologie de la perception*. Paris: Gallimard 1945.
Merleau-Ponty, Maurice: *La prose du monde*. Paris: Gallimard 1969.
Metzeltin, Michael: *Semiologia puterii* (The Semiology of Power). Translated by Oana Balaș. București: Editura Universității din București.
Mincu, Marin (ed.): *Canon și canonizare* (Canon and Canonization). Constanța: Pontica 2003.
Mincu, Marin (ed.): *Avangarda literară românească* (The Romanian Literary Avant-Garde). Translation from French by Ștefania Mincu. Constanța: Pontica 2006.
Mironescu, Doris: *Viața lui M. Blecher. Împotriva biografiei* (The Life of M. Blecher. Against the Biography). Iași: Timpul 2011.
Montesquieu, Charles-Louis de Secondat, Baron de La Brède: *Lettres persanes*. Édition revue et annotée d'après les manuscrits du chateau de la Brède avec un avant-propos et un index par Henri Barckhausen. Paris: Hachette 1913.
Mugur, Florin: *Convorbiri cu Marin Preda* (Conversations with Marin Preda). București: Albatros 1973.
Muller, Claude: Diathèse et voix en français. In: *Interaction entre sémantique et pragmatique, Actes du XI Séminaire de Didactique Universitaire*. București: ASE 2005, p. 73–95.
Murgescu, Bogdan (ed.): *Istoria României în texte* (The History of Romania in Texts). București: Corint 2001.
Murgescu, Bogdan: *România și Europa. Acumularea decalajelor economice (1500–2010)* (Romania and Europe. The Accumulation of Economic Gaps (1500–2010). Iași: Polirom 2010.

Muşat, Carmen: *Strategiile subversiunii. Descriere şi naraţiune în proza postmodernă românească* (Subversion Strategies. Description and Narration in Romanian Postmodern Prose). Postface by Mircea Martin. Piteşti: Paralela 45 2002.

Muşat, Carmen: *Romanul românesc interbelic. Dezbateri teoretice, polemici, opinii critice* (Romanian Inter-War Novel. Theoretical Debates, Polemics, Critical Opinions). Bucureşti: Humanitas Educaţional 2004.

Musil, Robert: *Journaux*. Tome 1. Traduction de Philippe Jaccotet. Paris: Seuil 1981.

Muthu, Mircea: *Literatura română şi spiritul sud-est European* (Romanian Literature and the South-East European Spirit). Bucureşti: Minerva 1976.

Müller, Herta: Capcanele memoriei (The traps of memory). In: *Dilema Veche*, 24 January 2011. Consulted at the web adress: http://dilemaveche.ro/sectiune/dilemateca/articol/capcanele-memoriei [26.04.2018].

Negoiţescu, Ion: *Analize şi sinteze* (Analyses and Syntheses). Bucureşti: Albatros 1976.

Negoiţescu, Ion: *Istoria literaturii române* (The History of Romanian Literature). Vol. I (1800–1945). Bucureşti: Minerva 1991.

Negrici, Eugen: *Literatura română sub comunism. Proza* (Romanian Literature under Communism). Bucureşti: Fundaţia Pro 2003.

Negrici, Eugen: *Iluziile literaturii române*. Bucureşti: Cartea Românească 2008.

Nemoianu, Virgil: *A Theory of the Secondary. Literature, Progress and Reaction*. Baltimore: John Hopkins University Press 1989.

Nemoianu Virgil; Robert Royal (ed.): *The Hospitable Canon. Essays on Literary Play, Scholarly Choice and Popular Pressure*. Philadelphia and Amesterdam: John Benjamins Publishing Company 1991.

Nemoianu, Virgil: *Tradiţie şi libertate* (Tradition and freedom). Bucureşti: Curtea-Veche 2001.

Nietzsche, Friedrich: *The Will to Power*. Translation by Walter Kaufmann and R. J. Hollingdale. Edited, with Commentary by Walter Kaufmann. New York: Vintage Books 1968.

Nietzsche, Friedrich: *On the Uses and Disadvantages of History for Life*. Cambridge: Cambridge University Press 2007.

Noica, Constantin: *Pagini despre sufletul românesc* (Pages on the Romanian soul). Bucureşti: Humanitas 1991.

Nora, Pierre (dir.): *Les lieux de mémoire*. Vol. I. La République. Paris: Gallimard 1984.

Nora, Pierre: Between Memory and History: Les Lieux de Mémoire. Translated by Marc Roudebush. In: *Representations*, No. 26, Special Issue: Memory and Counter-Memory. Spring 1989 p. 13.

Olteanu, A. Gh.; Pavnotescu, Maria: *Limba şi literatura română* (Romanian Language and Literature). Textbook for 9th grade. Bucureşti: Editura Didactică şi Pedagogică 1984.

Oprescu, Florin: Ţiganiada, un canon littéraire manqué. In: *Perspectives contemporaines sur le monde médiéval*. Piteşti: Tiparg 2010, p. 89–92.

Oprescu, Florin: Literatură şi canon istoric (Literature and historical canon). In: *Philologica Jassyensia*, Year VII, Issue 2 (14) 2011, p. 343–351.

Oprescu, Florin: The Power and Subversiveness of Literature: The Romanian Case. In: *Art and Intercultural Dialogue* (eds. Susana Gonçalves and Suzanne Majhanovich). Rotterdam/Boston/Taipei: Sense Publishers 2015, p. 97–112.

Oprescu, Florin: Das Gedächtnis der Macht-die Macht des Gedächtnisses im rumänischen postkommunistischen Roman. In Michèle Mattusch (ed.): *Kulturelles Gedächtnis–Ästhetisches Erinnern: Literatur, Film und Kunst in Rumänien*. Berlin: Frank und Timme 2018, p. 229–249.

Oprescu, Florin: *Les espaces maudits chez Max Blecher et dans le film surréaliste des années 30*. In: Sabine Krause; Heide Flagner (eds.): *Räume und Medien in der Romania-Espaces et médias dans les cultures romanes-Spații și medii în culturile romanice*. Hildesheim, Zurich, New York: Georg Olms Verlag 2018, p. 183–196.

Ornea, Zigu: *Tradiționalism și modernitate în deceniul al treilea* (Traditionalism and Modernity in the Third Decade). București: Eminescu 1980.

Ornea, Zigu: *Anii treizeci: Extrema dreapta românească* (The Thirties: the Romanian Extreme Right). București: Fundația Culturală Românească 1995.

Panu, George: *Amintiri de la Junimea din Iași* (Memories from Junimea in Iași). Iași: Polirom 2013.

Papadat-Bengescu, Hortensia: *Fecioarele despletite. Concert din muzică de Bach. Drumul Ascuns*, (The Disheveled Maidens. A Concert of Bach's Music. The Hidden Road). Post-scriptum by Doina Modola. Cluj-Napoca: Dacia 1986.

Parsons, Talcott: On the Concept of Political Power. In: *Proceedings of the American Philosophical Society*, 1963, vol. 107, no. 3, p. 232–262.

Patraș, Antonio: Interpretări: În lumea lui Max Blecher (Interpretations: In the world of Max Blecher). In *România literară*, year 2000, nr. 47. Consulted at the web adress: http://www.romlit.ro/n_lumea_lui_m._blecher [26.04.2018].

Pavel, Thomas: *The Lives of the Novel. A History*. Princeton/Oxford: Princeton University Press 2013.

Pârvulescu, Ioana: *Întoarcere în Bucureștiul interbelic* (Return in the Inter-War Bucharest). București: Humanitas 2003.

Pecican, Ovidiu: Apud gloriam mundi. In *Tribuna*, nb. 125, 16–30 November 2007, p. 13.

Perpessicius: *Opere* (Works). Vol. 2. București: Editura pentru literatură 1967.

Pessoa, Fernando: *Livro do Desassossego*. Org. Richard Zenith. São Paulo: Companhia das Letras 1999.

Plato: *The Republic of Plato*. Second Edition. Translated with notes and an interpretive essay by Allan Bloom. New York: Basic Books 1968.

Poamă, Andrei: Despre Mai 68: cum se nasc jandarmii minții (About May 68 : How the police of the mind is born). In *Observator cultural*, nr. 425/2008. Consulted at web adress: http://www.observatorcultural.ro/articol/despre-mai-68-cum-se-nasc-jandarmii-mintii-2/ [26.04.2018].

Pop, Ioan-Aurel; Șipoș, Sorin: Despre calitățile și defectele românilor într-un manuscris redactat de Antoine François Le Clerc (On the Qualities and Defects of Romanians in a Manuscript edited by Antoine François Le Clerc). In *Familia*, issue 11–12, (469–470) November–December, p. 261–262.

Popovici, Vasile: *Marin Preda-Timpul dialogului* (Marin Preda-Time of Dialogue). București: Cartea Românească 1983.

Potra, George: *Bucureștii văzuți de călătorii străini. Secolele XVI–XIX* (Bucharest through the Eyes of Foreign Travellers. XVI–XIX Centuryes). București: Editura Academiei 1992.

Praz, Mario: *The Romantic Agony*. Translated from the italian by Angus Davidson. Oxford: Oxford University Press 1954.

Preda, Marin: *Moromeții*. București: Cartea Românească 1981.

Preda, Marin: *Timpul n-a mai avut răbdare cu oamenii* (The Time wasn't patient with people anymore). București: Cartea Românească 1981.

Preda, Marin: *Cel mai iubit dintre pământeni* (The Most Beloved Man on Earth). București: Cartea Românească 1980.

Preda, Marin: *Cel mai iubit dintre pământeni* (The Most Beloved Man on Earth). Foreword by Eugen Simion. București: Cartea Românească, 1987.
Preda, Marin: *Delirul* (The Raving). București: Cartea Românească 1987.
Preda, Marin: *Creație și morală* (Creation and Morals). Victor Crăciun and Corneliu Popescu (ed.). Preface and notes by Victor Crăciun. București: Cartea Românească 1989.
Pricop, Constantin: *Seducția ideologiilor și luciditatea (rigoarea) criticii. Privire asupra criticii literare românești din perioada interbelică* (The Seduction of the Ideologies and Lucidity (Rigour) of the Critics. Overlook on Romanian Literary Criticism in the Inter-War Period). București: Integral 1999.
Protopopescu, Alexandru: *Volumul și esența* (The Volume and Essence). București: Eminescu 1971.
Pruteanu, George: *Pactul cu diavolul (Șase zile cu Petru Dumitriu)* (The Pact with the Devil. Six Days with Petru Dumitriu). București: Universal Dalsi-Albatros 1995.
Ralea, Mihail: *Scrieri* (Writings). Edition by Florin Mihăilescu, București: Minerva 1989.
Ricoeur, Paul: *Time and Narrative*. Volume 1. Translated by Kathleen McLaughlin and David Pellauer. Chicago: Univeristy of Chicago Press 1984.
Ricoeur, Paul: *La Mémoire, L'Histoire, L'Oubli*. Paris: Gallimard 2000.
Ricoeur, Paul: Penser mondial. In *Le Nouvel Observateur*, 2–8 June 2005, p. 12.
Ronnett, Alexander E.: *Romanian Nationalism: The Legionary Movement*. Chicago: Loyola University Press 1995.
Said, Edward: *Des intellectuels et du pouvoir*. Traduit de l'englais par Paul Chemala et revu par Dominique Edde. Alger: Marinoor 2001.
Said, Edward: *Orientalism*. New York: Pantheon 2003.
Sarane, Alexandrian: *Le Surréalisme et le rêve*. Paris: Gallimard 1974.
Sasu, Aurel; Vartic, Mariana (eds.): *Bătălia pentru roman* (The Battle for the Novel). București: Atlas 1997.
Saunders, Peter: *Citizenship and Social Theory*. London: Sage Publications 1993.
Schmidt, James (ed.): *What is Enlightenment? Eighteen-Century Answers and Twentieth-Century Questions*. Berkley; Los Angeles: University of California Press 1996.
Scholes, Robert: *Textual Power: Literary Theory and the Teaching of English*. New Haven: Yale University Press 1985.
Scott, John (ed.): *Power: critical concepts*. London: Routledge 1996.
Scurtu, Ioan: *Din viața politică a României, 1926–1947* (From Romania's Political Life). București: Editura Științifică și Enciclopedică 1983.
Sebastian, Mihail: *Jurnal* (1935–1944) (Journal). Text îngrijit de Gabriela Omăt. Prefață și note de Leon Volovici. București: Humanitas 2002.
Selejan, Ana: *Trădarea intelectualilor. Educare și prigoană* (The Betrayal of Intellectuals. Education and Persecution). Second edition. București: Cartea Românească 2005.
Selejan, Ana: *Literatura în totalitarism. Întemeietori și capodopere (1945–1951)* (Literature in Totalitarianism. Founders and Masterpieces). Second edition. București: Cartea Românească 2007.
Sfetcu, Nicolae: *Fizica simplificată* (Simplified Physics). București: Createspace 2014.
Shakespeare, William: *King Richard III*. The Project Gutemberg, Posting Date: March 7, 2015 [EBook #1103]. Release Date: November, 1997, p. 12–13. Consulted at the web adress: http://www.gutenberg.org/ebooks/1103 [26.04.2018].
Simion, Eugen: Primul nostru romancier (Our First Novelist). In: *România literară*, 2nd year, issue 36, September 4th, p. 13.

Simion, Eugen: *Scriitori români de azi* (Romanian Writers Today). Vol. II. București-Chișinău: Litera 2002.

Sora, Simona: O epopee eroi-mistico-satirică (A Heroical-Mystical-Satanical Epopea). In: *Dilema Veche*, Decembre 2005. Consulted at the web adress: http://www.romaniaculturala.ro/articol.php?cod=6788 [26.04.2018].

Sorohan, Elvira: Mecanismul psiho-spiritual al ironiei. In: *Convorbiri literare*, 30 octombrie 2013. Consulted at the web adress: http://convorbiri-literare.ro/?p=1254 [26.04.2018].

Spiridon, Monica; Lefter, Ion Bogdan; Crăciun, Gheorghe (eds.): *The Post-War Romanian Literary Experiment* (Experimentul literar românesc postbelic). Pitești: Paralela 45 1998.

Stan, Adriana: Realismul palimpsest (Realism Palimpsest). In: *Tribuna*, year IX, 1–15 November 2010, p. 5.

Staquet, Anne: *L'utopie ou les fictions subversives*. Zurich, Québec: Grand Midi 2002.

Steinhardt, Nicolae: *Jurnalul fericirii* (The Journal of Hapiness). Argument by P.S. Justin Hodea Sigheteanul. Virgil Bulat (ed.). Notes by Virgil Bulat and Virgil Ciomoș. With a dossier by George Ardeleanu. Iași: Polirom 2008.

Svoronos, Nikos: *The Greek Nation*. Athens: Polis 2004.

Ștefănescu, Alex: La o nouă lectură: Marin Preda-*Cel mai iubit dintre pământeni* (Towards a new reading of Marin Preda-*The Most Beloved Man on Earth*). In: *România literară*, nb. 10/2004. Consulted at the web adress: http://www.romlit.ro/marin_preda___cel_mai_iubit_dintre_pmnteni_[26.04.2018].

Țeposu, Radu G.: *Suferințele tânărului Blecher* (The Sufferings of Young Blecher). București: Minerva 1996.

Țeposu, Radu G.: *Istoria tragică și grotescă a întunecatului deceniu literar nouă* (The Tragic and Grotesque History of the Dark Nineth Literay Decade). Third Edition. Preface by Al. Cistelecan. București: Cartea Românească 2006.

Țurcanu, Florin: *Intellectuels, histoire et mémoire en Roumanie: de l'entre deux-guerres à l'après communisme*. București: Editura Academiei Române 2007.

Teodorovici, Lucian Dan: Matei Brunul, romanul păpușarului mânuit *(Matei Brunul,* the Novel of the handled pupetter). In: *Jurnalul național*, 17 October 2011. Consulted at the web adress: http://jurnalul.ro/cultura/carte/lucian-dan-teodorovici-matei-brunul-romanul-papusaru-lui-manuit-593889.html [25.04.2018].

Tismăneanu, Vladimir: Cine a fost Andrei Jdanov? Marele inchizitor și teroarea stalinistă (Who was Andrei Jdanov? The Great Inquisitor and Stalinist Terror). In: *Contributors.ro*, 5 February 2014. Consulted at the web adress: http://www.contributors.ro/global-europa/cine-a-fost-andrei-jdanov-marele-inchizitor-si-teroarea-stalinista/ [24.04.2018].

Turner, Jonathan H.: *Societal Stratification: A Theoretical Analysis*. New York: Columbia University Press 1984.

Ungheanu, Mihai (ed.): *Marin Preda*. București: Eminescu 1976.

Ursu, Horia: Scriind, ordonezi lumea (By writing, you order the world differently). In: *Contemporanul*, May 2007, p. 15–16.

Ursu, Horia: Trei răspunsuri de la Horia Ursu (Three Answers from Horia Ursu). In: *Suplimentul de cultură*, nb. 175, 19-04-2008. Consulted at the web adress: http://www.suplimentuldecultura.ro/index.php/continutArticolAllCat/8/3255 [25.04.2018].

Ursu, Horia: *Asediul Vienei* (The Siege of Vienna). Iași: Polirom 2012.

Vărzaru, Simona (ed.): *Prin Țările Române. Călători străini din secolul al XIX-lea* (Across the Romanian Principalities. Foreign Travellers from the 19th Century). București: Sport-Turism 1984.

Vattimo, Gianni: *The End of Modernity. Nihilism and Hermeneutics in Post-modern Culture.* Translated and with an Introduction by Jon R. Snyder. Cambridge: Polity Press 1988.
Veeser, Harold A. (ed.): *The New Historicism.* New York: Routledge 1989.
Vianu, Tudor: *Arta prozatorilor români* (The Art of Romanian Prose Writers). București: Contemporanul 1941.
Vitner, Ion: *Formarea conceptului de literatură socialistă* (The Formation of the Concept of Socialist Literature). București: Editura pentru literatură 1966.
Vlad, Tudor: *Fascinația filmului la scriitorii români (1900–1940)* (The Fascination of Film at Romanian Writers). Cluj-Napoca: Fundația Culturală Română 1997.
Weber, Max: *The Theory of Social and Economic Organization.* Translated by A. M. Henderson and Talcott Parsons. Edited with an introduction by Talcott Parsons. New York: Free Press 1947.
Weber, Max: *Economy and Society: An Outline of Interpretive Sociology.* Edited by Guenther Roth and Claus Wittich. Berkeley: University of California Press 1978.
Wolfreys, Julian (ed.): *Literary Theories: A Reader and Guide.* Edinburgh: Edinburgh University Press 1999.
Yourcenar, Marguerite: *Mémoires d'Hadrien*, suivi de *Carnets de notes de Mémoires d'Hadrien*. Paris: Gallimard 1977.
Zalis, Henri: *Nicolae Filimon*. București: Tineretului 1958.
Zane, Rodica: *Marin Preda. Monografie, antologie comentată, receptare critică* (Marin Preda. Monography, commented anthology, critical reception). Brașov: Aula 2001.

Index

Adameșteanu, Gabriela 49, 209, 218, 220
Aderca, Felix 40, 125, 128
Adler, Alfred 10–11
Agopian, Ștefan 227
Aldulescu, Radu 49, 51, 200, 208, 224
Alecsandri, Vasile 41, 44, 75–78
Alexandrescu, Sorin 31, 35, 37, 43
Alexianu, Alexandru 70
Alighieri, Dante 2, 28, 50
Altieri, Charles 27
Anghelescu, Mircea 79, 86, 97–98
Anton, Eugenia Tudor 135
Arghezi, Tudor 168
Aristotel 5, 18
Artaud, Antonin 153
Asachi, Gheorghe 44
Assmann, Aleida 208–210
Austen, Jane 28

Babe, Robert E. 35
Bachelard, Gaston 199
Băieșu, Ion 191
Bakhtin, Mikhaïl 3
Bălăiță, George 46
Balotă, Nicolae 135–136, 140
Baltazar, Camil 127, 136, 142
Balzac, Honoré de 84–88, 101, 129, 172, 174
Bănulescu, Ștefan 46–47
Barbu, Eugen 45–47, 174, 200, 213
Barbu, Ion 45, 127
Barthes, Roland 1–2, 21, 165, 225, 243, 245–246, 250
Baudry, Jean Luis 243
Beckett, Samuel 28
Benda, Julien 167
Bergson, Henri-Louis 152, 160, 236
Berindei, Mihnea 195
Betea, Lavinia 175
Blaga, Lucian 44, 97, 168, 185, 189, 192
Blecher, Max 56–57, 108, 120, 126, 129–151, 153–161, 202, 204, 208, 213, 221–222, 247, 249–250
Bloom, Harold 10, 13, 27–29, 36
Boas, Franz 75

Boccaccio, Giovanni 50
Bogza, Geo 118, 124, 131, 140–141, 146, 151
Boia, Lucian 110, 114–115, 118
Bolintineanu, Dimitrie 44, 91
Bonciu, Horia 129
Borges, Jorge Luis 28
Bourdieu, Pierre 2, 4, 6, 26–27, 53–54, 163, 165, 236, 245–246
Bourget, Paul 39
Brannigan, John 18
Brăescu, Gheorghe 125
Brăvescu, Ada 133–135, 141
Breban, Nicolae 46–47, 200
Bremond, Henri 4
Breton, André 149
Broch, Hermann 140, 198, 211–212, 230, 239
Brunetière, Ferdinand 41
Budai-Deleanu, Ion 15, 36, 58, 107
Buñuel, Luis 153, 155, 159
Buzura, Augustin 46–47, 51, 190–191, 200

Călinescu, George 32, 35, 37, 42, 84, 86, 101, 123, 129, 133–134, 136, 142, 168, 174–176
Călugăru, Ion 172, 206
Calvino, Italo 5–6, 46, 213
Canetti, Elias 9
Caragiale, Ion Luca 15, 75–78, 89
Caragiale, Mateiu 46, 129
Cărtărescu, Mircea 49, 157, 208–209, 214–215, 221–222, 227
Casey, Edward 207
Cernat, Paul 126–127, 214–215
Cervantes, Miguel de 2, 28, 50
Chaplin, Charlie 1
Chaucer, Geoffrey 28
Chivu, Marius 214–215
Cimpoeșu, Petru 48–49, 51, 200, 214, 221, 224–225, 227–229
Cioculescu, Șerban 77, 86–87, 90, 96, 101–102, 104
Cioran, Emil 1, 117–118, 124, 142, 232, 234
Ciorănescu, Ioana 142
Cioroianu, Adrian 164

Cistelecan, Alexandru 214, 227
Cocteau, Jean 153, 155–156, 159–160
Codru Drăgușanu, Ion 41, 61, 71
Comarnescu, Petru 129, 131
Conachi, Costache 44
Constante, Lena 209
Constantinescu, Pompiliu 38, 104
Corobca, Liliana 169
Cosma, Anton 40
Costache, Iulian 32
Crăciun, Gheorghe 46, 48–49, 214, 218–219, 227
Crainic, Nechifor 111
Creangă, Ion 15
Cristea-Enache, Daniel 214–215
Crohmălniceanu, Ovid. S. 135–136, 188

Dahl, Robert 5, 19, 24
Dalí, Salvador 147, 153, 155
Damian, Sami 178
Danțiș, Gabriela 84
Deletant, Dennis 164
Deleuze, Gilles 11, 36, 151–153, 159, 165, 245
Descartes, René 189
Dickens, Charles 28
Dickinson, Emily 28
Dimisianu, Gabriel 47, 177–178
Djuvara, Neagu 66, 68, 73
Dobrincu, Dorin 195
Dobrogeanu-Gherea, Constantin 124
Dostoievski, Fyodor 142, 178, 202
Downing, Keith 59
Drace-Francis, Alex 124–125
Dulac, Germaine 153, 155, 159–160
Dumitrescu, Geo 179
Dumitriu, Petru 46, 172, 176, 178, 206
Dungaciu, Dan 115, 117
Durkheim, Émile 2

Eagleton, Terry 11–12, 14, 163, 174, 246
Eco, Umberto 21, 139, 192–193, 231, 234
Eliade, Mircea 38, 42, 108, 112, 116–120, 129
Eliade, Pompiliu 93–94
Eliot, Thomas Stearns 28
Eminescu, Mihai 15, 31–32, 41–42, 75
Escarpit, Robert 2–4, 6

Fadeïev, Alexandre 206
Farkas, Jenő 237
Fellini, Federico 153
Ferry, Luc 49–50, 165
Filimon, Nicolae 40, 46, 51, 56, 61, 64, 71, 75, 78–82, 84–92, 94–98, 101–107, 194, 204, 213, 248–250
Fish, Stanley 139, 250
Flaubert, Gustave 84, 142
Florian, Filip 49, 208
Foucault, Michael 11, 19, 21–23, 25–26, 28, 36, 52, 58–59, 163, 165, 179, 193, 203–204, 210, 212, 217, 220, 224, 245, 248
Frankl, Viktor 10–11
Freud, Sigmund 10–11, 28, 121, 200, 236
Fukuyama, Francis 198–199
Fundoianu, Benjamin 127, 142

Gadamer, Hans-Georg 4
Galan, V. Em. 206
Gasset, Ortega y 50–51, 193, 247
Georgescu, Paul 191
Georgescu, Vlad 114
Gheo, Radu Pavel 224
Ghica, Ion 44, 90
Gide, André 123, 142
Godard, Jean-Luc 153
Goethe, Johann Wolfgang 2, 16, 28, 235
Golding, William 222
Goldiș, Alex 227
Goldmann, Lucien 3–4
Golescu, Dinicu 61, 71, 75
Gombrowitcz, Witold 198
Goodman, Nelson 174
Goșu, Armand 195
Goux, Jean-Joseph 243
Gramsci, Antonio 20, 22, 171
Greenblatt, Stephen 4, 179
Greimas, Algirdas Julien 4
Grigurcu, Gheorghe 168
Groșan, Ioan 48, 227
Guattari, Felix 36
Guțu Romalo, Valeria 54
Guillory, John 27, 33

Habermas, Jürgen 60
Halbwachs, Maurice 210
Hamon, Philippe 235–237
Hasdeu, Bogdan Petriceicu 84
Hasek, Jaroslav 123, 198, 237
Hegel, Georg Wilhelm Friedrich 198–199
Heinen, Armin 111
Heliade Rădulescu, Ion 98
Hemingway, Ernest 123
Herf, Jeffrey 120
Hitchins, Keith 65, 98–99, 106
Hobbes, Thomas 5, 18–19, 25
Holban, Anton 45, 120, 126, 129
Horasangian, Bedros 48, 227–228
Horodincă, Georgeta 135
Hurezeanu, Damian 196

Iacobescu, Dumitru 142
Ibrăileanu, Garabet 38, 83, 128
Ibsen, Henrik 28
Ilis, Florina 49, 221–223
Ioanid, Ion 192, 209
Ionescu, Eugen 118
Ionescu, Nae 111–112
Iorga, Nicolae 37–39, 83–84, 86, 117, 124
Iorgulescu, Mircea 228
Iovănel, Mihai 214–215
Ivașcu, George 85

Jakobson, Roman 245–246
Jameson, Fredric 3, 13, 212
Jankélévitch, Vladimir 235–236
Jela, Doina 209
Joyce, James 2, 28, 38, 50, 123, 148

Kafka, Franz 26, 28, 52, 198, 202
Kant, Immanuel 54, 58–60, 62, 65, 95
Keith, Dowding 23, 60
Kierkegaard, Soren 136, 189
Kogălniceanu, Mihail 44, 61, 78
Kojeve, Alexandre 198
Kramarae, Cheris 247
Kristeva, Julia 243
Kuhn, Thomas 122
Kundera, Milan 50, 52–53, 109, 120, 198, 211–212
Kusniewicz, Andrzej 123

Lacan, Jacques 29, 31, 165
Lascu, Mădălina 140–142
Le Breton, David 132, 145, 149–150
Le Goff, Jaques 205
Lefter, Ion Bogdan 46, 134, 214
Lejeune, Philippe 139
Levinas, Emmanuel 21
Lovinescu, Eugen 11, 35, 37, 44–45, 82–84, 108, 112, 116–118, 123–128, 133–134, 177, 201
Luca, Gherasim 127
Lukes, Steven 12, 19, 23–25, 105, 171, 223
Lull, Janis 9
Lungu, Dan 49, 51, 200, 208, 224, 240
Lyotard, Jean François 13, 212

Macedonski, Alexandru 32
Machiavelli, Niccolo 5, 8–10, 18–19, 73, 102–103, 107, 169, 187, 194, 249
Maingueneau, Dominique 173
Maiorescu, Titu 11, 15, 31–32, 35, 37, 42–45, 75–78, 92, 109, 168, 201, 203
Malamen, Iolanda 227
Manasia, Ștefan 234
Mandelbaum, Maurice 6
Manea, Norman 49, 208, 218–219
Mann, Thomas 51, 121, 123, 133, 202, 247
Manoilescu, Mihail 117
Manolescu, Nicolae 11, 35, 43, 46–48, 50–51, 84, 86, 133, 136, 145–146, 164, 176–177, 182–183, 192, 228
Manu, Emil 179
Marger, Martin 82
Marino, Adrian 32–33
Martin, Aurel 87
Martin, Mircea 28, 34
Marx, Karl 1, 18, 28–31, 36, 47, 93, 164, 166, 170–172, 174, 179
Mateescu, Constantin 80
McLachalan, Hugh V. 19
Merleau-Ponty, Maurice 147, 152, 154, 158–159
Metzeltin, Michael 55
Michelet, Jules 205
Mihăescu, Gib 45, 142, 202
Mihăilescu, Dan C. 214–216
Milcu, Nicolae 142

Index —— 267

Milton, John 28
Mincu, Marin 31, 146
Mironescu, Doris 130–131, 139, 158
Molière (Poquelin, Jean-Baptiste) 28
Montaigne, Michel de 28
Montesquieu, Charles-Louis de Secondat, Baron de La Brède et de 60–62
Montrose, Louis 4, 18
Mugur, Florin 178, 180–181
Muller, Claude 55
Müller, Herta 49, 55, 208, 218
Murgescu, Bogdan 67–68, 109, 114–115
Mușat, Carmen 108, 121, 129–130, 222, 225
Musil, Robert 84, 123, 198, 230, 233, 243–244
Muthu, Mircea 96–97

Naum, Gellu 46, 213
Nedelciu, Mircea 48
Negoițescu, Ion 32, 39, 45, 85, 135
Negrici, Eugen 43, 174
Negruzzi, Costache 44, 84, 90, 101, 169
Nemoianu, Virgil 10–11, 17, 26–27, 31, 34, 215
Nemțeanu, Barbu 142
Neruda, Pablo 28
Nicolae, Cosana 29–30, 36
Nietzsche, Friedrich 9–10, 18, 49–50, 142, 169, 202–203, 245
Nimigean, Ovidiu 224–225
Noilles, Anna de 126
Noica, Constantin 118–119, 124, 209
Nora, Pierre 199–200, 205, 209–210, 225–226

O'Barr, Jean F. 247
O'Barr, William M. 247
Olsen, Marvin Elliot 82
Olteanu, A. Gh. 32
Oprescu, Florin 26, 58, 63, 148, 163, 199
Ornea, Zigu 111, 116–117, 119, 127
Orwell, George 20, 166, 172
Ovidiu Simonca 228

Paleologu, Alexandru 189
Pană Dindelegan, Gabriela 54–55
Pană, Sașa 147
Pann, Anton 90, 96
Pansardi, Pamela 60

Panu, George 41–42
Papadat-Bengescu, Hortensia 45, 120, 125, 129, 133–134, 158
Papahagi, Marian 230
Pareto, Vilfredo 5
Parsons, Talcott 12–13, 18–19
Pârvulescu, Ioana 110, 116, 151
Patraș, Antonio 157
Pavel, Thomas 51, 83–85, 251
Pavnotescu, Maria 32
Pecican, Ovidiu 238
Perpessicius 40, 91
Pessoa, Fernando 28, 130, 162
Petică, Ștefan 142
Petrașincu, Dan 38
Petrescu, Camil 41, 45, 51, 120, 126–127, 129, 136, 185, 202
Petrescu, Cezar 39, 111, 128
Philippide, Alexandru 127
Pillat, Dinu 135–136
Pillat, Ion 127
Plato 5, 16–17, 162, 164, 179, 248
Poamă, Andrei 165
Pop, Ioan-Aurel 69
Popescu, Bogdan 49, 221, 224
Popescu Dumitru Radu 46–47
Popovici, Vasile 180, 186
Potra, George 63, 73–74
Praz, Mario 222
Preda, Marin 46–47, 51, 57, 162, 174, 176–194, 196, 200, 204, 213, 238, 248–250
Pricop, Constantin 128
Protopopescu, Alexandru 135, 137
Proust, Marcel 2–3, 26, 28, 38–39, 51–52, 57, 123, 138, 148, 172, 202, 205

Rădulescu, Răzvan 49, 214, 221, 224
Raicevich, Ignaz Stephan 72–74
Ralea, Mihail 41, 43, 117, 128, 214
Ray, Man 153
Rebreanu, Liviu 40, 45–46, 51, 110, 123, 129, 169, 184, 213
Remarque, Erich Maria 123
Renaut, Alain 165
Resnais, Alain 153
Ricoeur, Paul 6, 207–208, 224

Risset, Jacqueline 243
Romaniuc, Bogdan 232, 239
Roth, Joseph 123
Roth, Philip 26
Rousseau, Jean-Jacques 142
Royal, Robert 10, 17, 34, 215
Rushdie, Salman 26
Russell, Bertrand 12–13

Sadoveanu, Ion Marin 87
Sadoveanu, Mihail 40, 169–172, 176, 180, 206
Sahia, Alexander 142
Said, Edward 20, 62, 78
Sainte-Beuve, Charles Augustin 2–3, 111
Salomon, Christian 50
Sârbu, Ion Dezideriu 192
Sasu, Aurel 37–39, 41
Saunders, Peter 93
Schmidt, James 58–59
Scholes, Robert 250–251
Schulz, Bruno 140
Schulz, Muriel 140, 247
Scott, Walter 106
Scurtu, Ioan 117
Sebastian, Mihail 129–133
Selejan, Ana 167–168, 174
Șeicaru, Pamfil 111
Șerban, Geo 186
Sfetcu, Nicolae 109
Shakespeare, William 2, 8–9, 14, 16, 28
Sholokhov, Mikhail 206
Simion, Eugen 86, 96, 125, 177, 184–186, 190
Simona Vărzaru 61, 63
Slavici, Ioan 15, 40, 169
Sora, Simona 214, 223
Sorescu, Marin 186
Sorohan, Elvira 235
Souriau, Étienne 4
Sperantia, Eugeniu 41
Spiridon, Monica 46
Stan, Adriana 230, 237
Stănescu, Nichita 36
Staquet, Anne 221
Ștefănescu, Alex 182–183, 214

Steinhardt, Nicolae 162, 197, 199, 209, 247–248
Stendhal (Marie-Henri Beyle) 39, 101
Stere, Constantin 83, 124
Stifter, Adalbert 211
Șipoș, Sorin 69
Șuluțiu, Octav 136
Svevo, Italo 38
Svoronos, Nikos 64

Tarde, Gabriel 44
Teodorescu, Cicerone 37
Teodorescu, Cristian 37, 48–49, 208, 218–219, 227–228
Teodorovici, Lucian Dan 209, 221, 223
Țepeneag, Dumitru 49, 200, 224
Țeposu, Radu G 139, 142, 145, 146, 226–227, 229, 230, 238, 243
Terian, Andrei 214
Thibaudet, Albert 39
Tismăneanu, Vladimir 194–195
Titel, Sorin 46
Tocqueville, Alexis de 251
Tolstoy, Leo 28
Toynbee, Arnold J. 66
Truffaut, François 153
Țurcanu, Florin 111
Turner, Jonathan H. 93

Ungheanu, Mihai 182–183
Urmuz 146
Ursu, Horia 49, 57, 93, 129, 198, 200, 208, 211, 214, 224–227, 229–234, 237–240, 243–244, 250

Valerian, Ion 39
Vartic, Mariana 37–39, 41
Vattimo, Gianni 11, 27
Veeser, Harold A. 18
Velea, Nicolae 46
Vianu, Tudor 85, 100–101, 128
Vigny, Alfred de 111
Vinea, Ion 127
Visconti, Luchino 153
Vitner, Ion 167–168
Vlad, Tudor 151

Vlahuță, Alexandru 40, 77, 117
Voronca, Ilarie 127
Vosganian, Varujan 218
Vulcănescu, Mircea 118, 128

Weber, Max 5, 12, 24–25, 82, 94
Welles, Orson 2
Wells, Herbert George 2
Whitman, Walt 28
Wittgenstein, Ludwig 245

Wolfreys, Julian 18
Wordsworth, William 28

Yourcenar, Marguerite 219

Zaciu, Mircea 191
Zalis, Henri 84
Zamfirescu, Duiliu 40
Zane, Rodica 189, 193
Zeletin, Ștefan 124

www.ingramcontent.com/pod-product-compliance
Lightning Source LLC
Chambersburg PA
CBHW031804220426
43662CB00007B/521